WITHDRAWN

Lichteim, George
Collected essays

DATE DUE

COLLECTED ESSAYS

ALSO BY GEORGE LICHTHEIM

Marxism: An Historical and Critical Study
The New Europe
Marxism in Modern France
The Concept of Ideology
The Origins of Socialism
A Short History of Socialism
George Lukács
Imperialism
Europe in the Twentieth Century

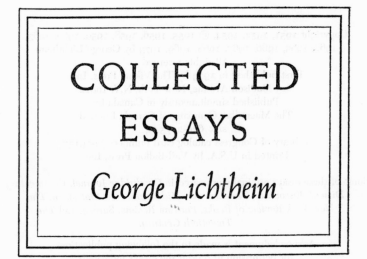

COLLECTED
ESSAYS

George Lichtheim

The Viking Press · New York

First published in 1973 by The Viking Press, Inc.
625 Madison Avenue, New York, N.Y. 10022
Published simultaneously in Canada by
The Macmillan Company of Canada Limited
SBN 670-22754-4
Library of Congress catalog card number: 72-79157
Printed in U.S.A. by Vail-Ballou Press, Inc.

Some of these essays originally appeared in *Cambridge Journal, Commentary,
Dissent, Encounter, The Listener, Midstream, New Statesman, The
New York Review of Books, Partisan Review, Survey,* and *The
Twentieth Century.*

Acknowledgment is made to the following publications
for permission to reprint the essays indicated:

Foreign Affairs: "What Is Left of Communism?"
Copyright © 1967 by the Council on Foreign Relations, Inc., New York.
History and Theory: "Sartre, Marxism, and History,"
Copyright © 1963 by Wesleyan University.
"Bridging the Gap," Copyright © 1966 by Wesleyan University.
Journal of the History of Philosophy:
Book review of Leszek Kolakowski's *Marxism and Beyond:
On Historical Understanding and Individual Responsibility.*
Copyright © 1971 by the Journal of the History of Philosophy, Inc.
Reprinted from the *Journal of the History of Philosophy,*
VII, No. 4 (October 1969), 474–77, by permission of the Editor.
The Political Quarterly: "Stalinism," October 1950.
The Times Literary Supplement:
"The Concept of Social Class," October 8, 1971

❋

To Miriam

❋

Foreword

✻✻✻

THE ESSAYS AND REVIEWS assembled in this volume were written and published over a period of two decades. It appears to me that they reflect certain underlying concerns which have not altered with the passing of time, but the judgment must be left to the reader. The book is not a critical anthology, nor is it an attempt to put a particular viewpoint across. There is heavy emphasis on political topics but no adherence to anything that could be described as a party line. There are likewise sporadic attempts to deal with literary and philosophical matters although not in the usual academic manner. On balance there is a gradual shift from political to sociological subjects, but I should state that, although I am heavily indebted to contemporary sociology, I am not a trained sociologist nor a professional historian in the conventional meaning of the term.

Some of the opinions expressed in the various essays and reviews that make up the volume may strike the reader as old-fashioned, and I am in fact more heavily indebted to the philosophy, history, and sociology of the nineteenth century than is customary among present-day writers on these topics. I have brought together material of the most varied shapes and styles, but all deal with issues that I happen to regard as central to the present time. I trust I have learned something from modern scholarship and from the literature of the past four decades, but my instinctive sympathies lie with the representative thinkers of the age that ended in 1914.

This foreword would not be complete if I did not acknowledge the work Elisabeth Sifton has done to render the material fit for publication in book form.

GEORGE LICHTHEIM

London
September 1972

Contents

❀ ❀ ❀

PARISIAN IMPRESSIONS

EUROPE IN DECLINE

FROM LENIN TO MAO TSE-TUNG

MARX AND BEYOND

THOUGHTS AMONG THE RUINS

THERE'LL ALWAYS
BE AN ENGLAND

Winston Churchill—Sketch
for a Portrait

❊❊❊

On NOVEMBER 30, 1954, a number of pressmen and photographers were assembled in Downing Street to record the celebrations attending the Prime Minister's eightieth birthday. As the flashbulbs popped, one of the journalists expressed the conventional hope that he might be present at the celebrant's hundredth anniversary. The characteristic reply he got was: "I don't see why you shouldn't, young man; you look quite healthy to me."

Winston Spencer Churchill's long and variegated life has by now impressed itself upon the world's consciousness as something midway between Homeric epic and Rabelaisian fantasy. There is not only the immense span but the cataclysmic events it has covered and the apparently boundless vitality of the protagonist. It is after all only a few years since he retired from the public scene, having entered it around 1900 under the patronage of the last surviving giants of the Victorian epoch, only to be at once hurled to the forefront in a succession of roles too numerous to be simultaneously present to the mind: not merely politician, orator, cabinet minister, military strategist (in two world wars), opposition leader, party leader, organizer of victory, architect of the Atlantic Alliance, etc.; but also cavalry lieutenant, participant in almost-forgotten colonial wars, press correspondent, escapee from Boer prison camps, young hero of imperialism, middle-aged protagonist of liberalism, diehard opponent of Lenin, Gandhi, and the British Labour Party, historian (of two wars), author, painter, bricklayer, aviator, parliamentary gladiator, and *enfant terrible* of the British governing class. Moreover, those who have read his two volumes of autobiographical sketches— *My Early Life* (1930) and *Thoughts and Adventures* (1932)— will be aware that even this long list does not exhaust the principal events of the story. It leaves out of account, for example, the important episode of his service as an infantry officer in France during World War I, after his resignation from the cabinet over the Gallipoli fiasco: from First Lord of the Admiralty to the stinking trenches and shell holes of the Western Front, and back to the cabinet, this time as Minister of Munitions, eighteen months later, to serve under Lloyd George, whom he admired—Churchill's life is full of such dramatic turns of fortune's wheel, and he gives the impression of having enjoyed them all.

Mention of Gallipoli, however, recalls an era—roughly coterminous with the interwar years—when to millions of his countrymen he stood for the most disastrous aspects of an abhorrent past. The bloody failure of the Dardanelles campaign (for which he was quite unfairly blamed and which almost wrecked his career) seemed to epitomize a sustained record of violence and vainglory. That, at any rate, was how liberals and pacifists then saw him. During those years, when a shell-shocked England tried to recover from World War I, thousands would have echoed the words that E. M. Forster put into the mouth of his dead soldier on Achi Baba hill:

> Churchill planned this expedition to Gallipoli, where I was killed. He planned the expedition to Antwerp where my brother was killed. Then he said that Labour is not fit to govern. Rolling his eyes for fresh worlds, he saw Egypt, and fearing that peace might be established there, he intervened and prevented it. . . . He is Churchill the Fortunate, ever in office, and clouds of dead heroes attend him.

The resentment which then colored the public's recollection of Churchill's role in that first great convulsion was amply fed by his monumental four-volume history of the period, *The World Crisis, 1911–1918.* Here the author displayed, to the roll of stylistic drums, a fascination with warfare that grated harshly on the

nerves of many readers. While the war was in progress he had
already impressed casual acquaintances with his absorption in the
theme of conflict. We owe a revealing pen-portrait to Siegfried
Sassoon—poet, pacifist, and infantry officer—who in 1917 visited
Churchill at the Ministry of Munitions. They talked of poetry,
pacifism, and the horrors of the war. "There came a point, however," Mr. Sassoon has recorded,

> when our proceedings developed into a monologue. Pacing the
> room, with a big cigar in the corner of his mouth, he gave me an
> emphatic vindication of militarism as an instrument of policy and
> stimulator of glorious individual achievements, not only in the
> mechanisms of warfare, but in spheres of social progress. The
> present war, he asserted, had brought about inventive discoveries
> which would ameliorate the condition of mankind. For example,
> there had been immense improvements in sanitation. Transfixed
> and submissive in my chair, I realized that what had begun as
> a persuasive confutation of my anti-war convictions was now ad-
> dressed, in pauseful and perorating prose, to no one in particular.

There are many passages in *The World Crisis*—a work published in 1923-27, when the pacifist wave was at its height—that
convey the enthusiasm which war at all times evokes in Churchill.
"There can be," he writes, "few purely mental experiences more
charged with cold excitement than to follow, almost from minute
to minute, the phases of a great naval action from the silent rooms
of the Admiralty." And he goes on to contrast "the sense of action
at its highest . . . the wrath of battle . . ." with the deadly
quiet of the control room. He was then in charge of the fleet. In
World War II, during the Battle of Britain, it was "the few" of
the RAF, guarding the island against the Luftwaffe, who fired his
imagination. Everyone recalls his speeches of the period and how
they stirred the blood. Few remember the earlier Churchill of
World War I, whose dramatic account of the ghastly slaughter
on the Western Front, the Dardanelles catastrophe, and the in-
decisive fleet action at Jutland seemed to his contemporaries to
mark him out as a public man for whom war had an altogether
unholy fascination. To Keynes (reviewing *The World Crisis*),
it seemed evident that "Mr. Churchill does not dissemble his own
delight in the intense experiences of conducting warfare on the

grand scale which those can enjoy who make the decisions," though he added "nor . . . does he conceal its awfulness for those who provide the raw material for those delights."

The qualification is in order. Churchill never hesitates to confront the other side of the picture, but he does so casually, and his rhetoric carries him along where other writers simply depict the horror. His magnificent *History of the Second World War* is written in much soberer style than the earlier book, but although the old romantic flamboyancy has given way to an Augustan calm, there is nothing in it to compare for stark realism with the diary notes on the 1940 collapse by his own Chief of Staff, Brooke, then commander of an army corps in France:

> Armentières has been very heavily bombed and we are well out of it; half the town is demolished, including the madhouse, and its inmates are now wandering around the country.
>
> These lunatics let loose . . . were the last straw. With catastrophe on all sides, bombarded by rumors of every description, flooded by refugees and a demoralised French army, bombed from a low altitude, and now on top of it all lunatics in brown corduroy suits standing at the side of the road, grinning at one with an inane smile, a flow of saliva running from the corner of their mouths, and dripping noses! Had it not been that by then one's senses were numbed with the magnitude of the catastrophe that surrounded one, the situation would have been unbearable.[1]

Such graphic passages do not occur in Churchill's writings, although he is ready enough to pay tribute to the sufferings of the fighting soldier. When he writes about war it is generally to extol the courage of the participants, or the magnitude of victory and defeat. Here is a characteristic passage from *The World Crisis* on the British army's misfortunes in the Dardanelles campaign of 1915:

> The battle was fiercely fought in burning scrub; a sudden and unusual mist hampered the attacking artillery, and although the Anzac [Australian–New Zealand] left gained and held some valuable ground, no general results were achieved. . . . The British losses

1. Arthur Bryant, ed., *The Turn of the Tide: A History of the War Years Based on the Diaries of Field-Marshal Lord Alanbrooke, Chief of the Imperial General Staff* (New York, 1957), p. 127.

. . . were heavy and fruitless. On this dark battlefield of fog and flame, Brigadier General Lord Langford . . . and other paladins fell.

"And other paladins." The writer's mind is back in the Hundred Years War, with the Black Prince, Du Guesclin, and Joan of Arc. No wonder that even his last work, the *History of the English-Speaking Peoples,* is dominated by warfare. However, to be just, it must be added that *The World Crisis* does contain some passages in which the historian rises to a somber contemplation of what war has done to modern, so-called civilized nations—and be it noted that he is talking of the 1914–18 war, before the age of death camps and atom bombs:

The Great War differed from all ancient wars in the immense power of the combatants and their fearful agencies of destruction, and from all modern wars in the utter ruthlessness with which it was fought. All the horrors of all the ages were brought together, and not only armies but whole populations were thrust into the midst of them. The mighty educated states involved conceived with reason that their very existence was at stake. Germany, having let Hell loose, kept well in the van of terror; but she was followed, step by step, by the desperate and ultimately avenging nations she had assailed. Every outrage against humanity or international law was repaid by reprisals often on a greater scale and of longer duration. No truce or parley mitigated the strife of armies. The wounded died between the lines: the dead moldered in the soil. Merchant ships and neutral ships and hospital ships were sunk on the seas, and all on board left to their fate, or killed as they swam. Every effort was made to starve whole nations into submission without regard to age or sex. Cities and monuments were smashed by artillery. Bombs from the air were cast down indiscriminately. Poison gas in many forms stifled or seared the soldiers. Liquid fire was projected upon their bodies. Men fell from the air in flames, or were smothered, often slowly, in the dark recesses of the sea. The fighting strength of armies was limited only by the manhood of their countries. Europe and large parts of Asia and Africa became one vast battlefield, on which after years of struggle not armies but nations broke and ran. When all was over, torture and cannibalism were the only two expedients that the civilized, scientific, Christian States had been able to deny themselves: and these were of doubtful utility.

Such passages could almost make one believe that their author was a pacifist—were it not for the undoubted fact that World War II aroused in him not merely an iron resolve to win but also something bordering perilously close on exhilaration.

Yet there is another side to Churchill—one of many. It is part of his charm, and indeed his greatness, that no summary can do justice to his versatility. The critic who immerses himself in the more flamboyant chapters of the story is baffled by his subject's protean ability to transform himself into his opposite. Churchill the warrior-statesman has his counterpart in Churchill the parliamentarian, to say nothing of Churchill the embattled free-trader, foe of militarism and protectionism (1904–1910), social reformer (1906–14), fighter for Irish Home Rule (he was nearly lynched on one occasion by furious Belfast Tories), friend of small nations (off and on), pro-Zionist (always), Francophile, half-American (through his mother), agnostic (discreetly but plainly), and critic of Tory narrowness. Indeed, for some twenty years—from 1904, when he crossed party lines to join the Liberals, until 1924, when he came forward once more under the Conservative banner—the average Tory loathed Churchill with an intensity for which there are few parallels in British politics. What is more, he amply repaid these feelings, though in his case it was more a matter of expressing contempt for the party to which his father had belonged and which, in the general view, had treated Lord Randolph Churchill very shabbily for his great services.

Churchill's relationship to his father is indeed the clue to his own career. There are hints in his autobiography that he is not unaware of this fact, but in his sturdy John Bullish fashion he refuses to enlarge on the subject. The story needs recapitulating only in the briefest outline. Lord Randolph and his friends were "Tory democrats" in the succession of Disraeli, whom they idolized. They did not greatly care for the other Conservative leaders, notably Salisbury, who dominated Tory politics for two decades after Disraeli's death. Nonetheless their rise was dazzlingly swift. In 1886 Lord Randolph, at the ripe age of thirty-six, was Chancellor of the Exchequer and Leader of the House of Commons, i.e., the obvious heir to the political throne. So rapid a rise might have turned any man's head; it apparently had a fatal effect on his, for in the following year he rashly challenged his colleagues and at one blow destroyed his own career forever. His subsequent mental collapse suggests an inherent instability which probably manifested itself in his precipitate resignation from office in 1887; but to his contemporaries the case looked somewhat different. In his memoirs, Winston Churchill expresses himself in guarded terms about a family tragedy which clearly had a determining effect on his own outlook:

> I can see my father now in a somewhat different light from the days when I wrote his biography. I have long passed the age at which he died. I understand only too plainly the fatal character of his act of resignation. He was the "daring pilot in extremity." That was his hour. But conditions changed with the Unionist victory of 1886. Quiet times were required and political repose. Lord Salisbury represented to the nation what it needed and desired. He settled down heavily to a long steady reign. Naturally he was glad to have the whole power in his own hands, instead of dividing it with a restless rival, entrenched in the leadership of the House of Commons and the control of the public purse. It is never possible for a man to recover his lost position. He may recover another position in the fifties or sixties, but not the one he lost in the thirties or forties. To hold the leadership of a party or nation with dignity and authority requires that the leader's quality and message shall meet not only the need but the mood of both.

It is no coincidence that these words were published at a time (1930) when Churchill was himself out of office and, what was worse, at odds with his colleagues, among whom Stanley Baldwin had begun some years earlier "to settle down heavily to a long steady reign," from which Churchill was deliberately excluded when the Conservatives returned to power in 1931. Churchill's contempt for Baldwin, however, is no index to his feelings for Salisbury, a dominating figure who awed the young cavalry officer when he was introduced to him in 1898 (on his way to Cairo to take part in Kitchener's conquest of the Sudan). Nor could he entertain anything but respect for Salisbury's nephew and heir in the leadership of Toryism: Arthur Balfour was one of the ablest men in British politics, though distinctly unfortunate as Prime Minister and destined to lead his party to a catastrophic defeat in 1906. Moreover, his principal colleague, Joseph Chamberlain, stood for everything that young W. S. Churchill then believed in—notably the enlargement of the British Empire. At any rate, when Lord Randolph's son in 1901 delivered his parliamentary maiden speech, there was no more ardent Tory imperialist in the House. Yet within three years he had "crossed the floor" and taken his seat beside Lloyd George —then regarded as a dangerous Radical, and certainly a violent critic of imperial expansion in general and the Boer War in particular.

In trying to explain this first of many metamorphoses, Churchill is markedly unconvincing. The reasons he gives are many and varied: his father had been a free-trader (in the 1880s this was still compatible with orthodox Toryism), and he himself had lately come under the influence of free-trade arguments that clashed with Chamberlain's tariff policies; he was greatly impressed by the intellectual stature of Asquith, Grey, Morley, and the other Liberal leaders; he had sympathized with the Boers, though regarding their defeat as necessary, and was repelled by the vulgar chauvinism of the Tory rank and file (indeed, he later became a close friend of Louis Botha, the Boer leader who had captured young Churchill in 1899, during the early stage of the fighting). All these explanations are plausible, but they do not quite account for so dramatic a gesture as his public repudiation of Lord Randolph Churchill's party—unless one remembers that the party had once repudiated Lord Randolph. Churchill never says so, but the student of his career cannot help feeling that in "crossing the floor" he was really getting even with the ghost of Salisbury.

At any rate he became a Liberal, and, given his combative temperament, it was inevitable that he should land on the Radical wing, in the company of Lloyd George. This is the more significant since by upbringing and conviction he was much closer to the "Liberal imperialist" group around Asquith, Haldane, and Grey than to the middle-class Radicals and the Labourites on the left wing. His new friends indeed never quite trusted him, and with good cause. They seem to have sensed that he did not really belong in their company, though for some years he did his best to sound like one of them. He certainly went out of his way to madden the Tories by representing them to the voters as the party of reaction and corruption, dispensing "patriotism by the bucketful" while extending "the open hand at the public till," and generally practicing highway robbery. Some of his more strident perorations of those years have become famous; they hardly sound like the later Churchill with whom we are familiar, except for their style. Certainly the abuse he poured on the trade-union leaders in 1926, at the time of the abortive General Strike, was equally colorful, and not altogether to the liking of Baldwin and the more moderate Conservatives; nor were his Tory colleagues pleased when in 1931 he described Gandhi as a "naked fakir," and his presence in London, to attend the Round Table Conference on India, as a disaster for the British Empire and the civilized world in general.

Was it all play-acting? And if not, where is the strain of consistency in all this extravagance? The first question can be answered firmly in the negative. Churchill always believed what he was saying, at least while he was saying it. He was a naïve young Empire worshiper in 1900, an ardent Liberal in 1910, a frenzied anti-Bolshevik in 1920, an admirer of Mussolini (but likewise of Lincoln, Smuts, and Clemenceau) in 1930, the leader of his nation against Hitler in 1940, and the de facto architect of the Atlantic Alliance in 1950—invariably with the same passion, and quite often for the same reason, or at any rate with the help of the same arguments. These arguments are essentially simple and can be reduced to a few main themes. Chief among them is patriotism, followed at a close remove by devotion to the British Empire (he never got used to the term "Commonwealth"); next comes belief in Anglo-American friendship, and lastly a conviction that Britain and America have in their joint keeping those intangible values which Churchill prizes above all—the rule of law, individual freedom, and parliamentary government (or the American equivalent thereof); to which, if he felt able to do so, he would probably add free trade, a principle to which he has clung with quixotic devotion throughout a long and stormy career (again an inheritance from his father).

If his varied and various utterances are taken as a whole, and set against the background of the countless political battles Churchill has fought for over half a century, a certain underlying consistency does in fact emerge, though at every turn a new theme is added: "Tory democracy" probably sums up one element of Churchill's political outlook where England itself is concerned. His father had been fond of saying, "I have never feared the English democracy"—in his day a notable utterance, though based on the quite reasonable certainty that the English working class was fundamentally conservative, and not at all inclined to dispense with aristocratic leadership, let alone join a revolution. Churchill is equally certain that the British people are "sound at heart" and will normally prefer conservatives to radicals. This happens to be true, though it could be phrased in less complimentary language, e.g., by saying that most British people are insular, dislike "foreigners," and do not respond readily to advanced ideas. The Labour Party has in recent years made this discovery, as the Liberals did before. (It is scarcely an accident that the catastrophe of the Liberal Party in the 1918 election coincided with the enfranchisement of masses of unskilled workers and the extension of the vote to women.) In following his father's advice to "trust the people," Churchill has therefore throughout his life placed his bet on what, from the Tory standpoint, is an extremely safe horse. The wonder is that in 1904 he thought it right to gamble on Liberalism; but then the decade before 1914 witnessed a deceptive Liberal revival, already mingled with the first stirrings of Labour as a political force. It is arguable that Churchill at that time abandoned what looked like a sinking ship; certainly the Tories thought so, and it took them long to forgive him.

Here one enters upon the second important strand in Churchill's political makeup. No matter how much he disliked the men who had rejected his father, he would not, in those days of bitter factionalism, have joined the Liberals had he not shared certain of their attitudes. Free trade has already been mentioned. "Liberal imperialism"—intellectually and morally superior to the cruder Tory brand—was another important element; the fascination of Lloyd George (and a brief interest in the Webbs and Fabianism), a third; yet all three combined only came to ripen because Churchill was already predisposed toward an attitude which, however much it stood opposed to democratic radicalism, was yet different from traditional Toryism. The secret of Churchill's political and personal career lies in the fact that he does not really belong to either of the two great streams in modern British political life. He has never been a democrat, though in present-day fashion he has often and eloquently spoken of democracy (by which he means parliamentary government); and he is only doubtfully a conservative. Even his liberalism in 1904–14 was not quite of the orthodox Gladstonian brand. The truth is simple: Winston Churchill, in one of his many aspects, is that oddest and most distinctively English of political creatures, a Whig, i.e., by modern standards a throwback to the eighteenth century; for in modern times Whiggism has dissolved into middle-class liberalism—something quite alien to Churchill even in the days when he graced a Cabinet predominantly filled with Liberals and over which there still hung the majestic presence of Gladstone.

Now Whiggism is by no means an easy phenomenon to elucidate; it is certainly far more complex and elusive than Toryism. The latter is simply defined: loyalty to Crown and Church; landed possessions; a patriarchal relationship toward one's tenants; dislike of foreigners, Dissenters, and Roman Catholics; belief in the Army and the Empire—these sentiments make up a coherent set of attitudes characteristic of that section of the old governing class which traditionally rallied under the Tory flag. (It has now been displaced by bankers and industrialists barely distinguishable from their Republican counterparts across the Atlantic, but that is another story.) Conversely, there is no difficulty about democratic radicalism, whether it takes the form of the British Labour Party with its quasi-socialist ideology, or its modern American counterparts. Gladstonian liberalism is also comprehensible, though by now distinctly old-fashioned: one has only to think of the late Senator Taft who—to the great amusement of the British—was known as a "conservative" in the United States because he stood for orthodox nineteenth-century liberalism of the straitest observance. By contrast, Whiggery is more difficult to comprehend. For one thing, it is peculiar to England: other countries have produced conservatives and radicals, reactionaries and revolutionaries, but only England has produced Whigs (though the United States once possessed a party which attached this totally unsuited label to itself). For another thing,

Whiggism has now disappeared even in England. The last of the *genuine* Whigs vanished from the scene about the time of World War I. Nonetheless it is possible, though with some reservations, to class Churchill as a modern representative of the Whig tradition, at least in one of his aspects. Such as it is, the tradition cannot possibly survive his departure, even in the attenuated form he has given it. The mold is broken and will never be recast.

What constitutes Whiggism is just what has made Churchill such a puzzle to his contemporaries: the inbred attitude of a ruling oligarchy whose loyalty was solely to parliamentary government as such, coupled with almost total indifference to the precise content of policy or legislation. An aristocracy which governed in opposition to the Tory gentry, most of the clergy, and the bulk of the country population, was bound to evolve a distinctive cast of mind. A certain contempt for the unlettered country squires who made up the backbone of Toryism went hand in hand with intellectual liberalism, agnosticism, at times even (though not in public) republicanism, or at least an ironical attitude to the monarchy. The historian of England has no difficulty in showing that the position of this privileged group alone made constitutional opposition to Crown and Church possible during the long, bleak reaction that arose out of the struggle against the French Revolution; so that aristocratic liberalism may be said to have been the real secret of England's immunity to radical revolution in the age which followed, as it was the secret of her greatness as a world power in the preceding era of conflict with monarchical France. At any rate this eighteenth-century tradition (which no other European country shared because none had a parliamentary oligarchy) has left its mark on British history. Among other things, it accounts for the fact that the leader of the Tory party in 1940, when Britain was endangered as never before, combined in his person the traditions of an ancient ruling class with an almost completely modern outlook: precisely what other European nations had failed to achieve. For though in continental Europe there have been plenty of liberals, there has never been a ruling class with a liberal outlook and a corresponding ability to understand the modern world. England is unique in having produced an aristocracy that combined political power with genuine attachment to political freedom (which, however, is not the same as democracy). And as the heir of this oligarchy, which for centuries took its unchallenged position completely for granted, Winston Churchill has been able to dazzle two generations of his countrymen—not to mention the rest of the world—with a sovereign contempt for consistency and a freedom from inhibition that only membership in a hereditary ruling class can bestow upon those lucky enough to belong to it. When in 1953, at the age of seventy-nine, he offered to take advantage of Stalin's death by going to Moscow, getting acquainted with his successors, and "drinking the Politburo under the table" by way of extracting a lasting political settlement, he was completely in character. The apparent irresponsibility which so appalled the U.S. State Department would not have seemed odd to the brilliant, self-confident, and cynical politicians who governed eighteenth-century England and conquered the first British Empire. Where John Foster Dulles was scandalized, Charles James Fox—gambling away a fortune at Brooks's in the intervals between conducting secret negotiations with the Tsar's emissaries—would have understood and approved.

It is this Whiggish Churchill—gay, sprightly, debonair, and faintly frivolous—who winks at the reader from the lively pages of his autobiography and its companion volume, *Thoughts and Adventures*. Both books were published in the early 1930s, when he was out of office, and both reflect the sunset glow of an era already past its zenith but still capable of inspiring nostalgic affection in the reader as well as the author. These writings are Edwardian in tone and to some extent in matter: *My Early Life* ends in 1908, when Churchill—a cabinet minister at thirty-four and the spoiled darling of London society—married a handsome young woman and, in his own words, "lived happily ever afterwards." *Thoughts and Adventures* is less sprightly and more thoughtful—it includes, among others, the famous essay entitled "Shall We All Commit Suicide?" (first published in 1925), which develops a Wellsian vision of ever more devastating wars, and even contains a hint of nuclear terrors to come. ("Might not a bomb no bigger than an orange be found to possess a secret power . . . to blast a township at a stroke?") Clearly the author, even in those days, was in touch with some of the scientific advisers who during World War II dominated his entourage. Yet on the whole he still gives thanks to be alive in the midst of so fascinating an age. If mankind now has the means to blast itself to bits, it has also acquired the ability to solve its most pressing problems. Science, properly employed, can bring about the golden age. What is required is the banishment of war. "Surely if a sense of self-preservation still exists among men, if the will to live resides not merely in individuals or nations but in humanity as a whole, the prevention of the supreme catastrophe ought to be the paramount object of all endeavor." The Churchill of 1925 is a convinced supporter of the League of Nations, a Wellsian progressive, almost a pacifist: all this without ceding an iota of his conviction that the British Empire must hold on to all it has. This was "Liberal imperialist" doctrine in 1910, when the rising young politician sat in the Liberal cabinet with Asquith and Grey. In 1925 Churchill has not budged an inch. He is still a Liberal imperialist, convinced that the British Empire serves the cause of peace and freedom, and that its opponents—whether Bolshevik Russians or revengeful pan-Germans—are the enemies of civilization. Thirty years later, on resigning as Prime Minister and withdrawing from public life, he still harps on the same theme, except that Germany is no longer a menace, while the defense of peace and freedom has now devolved on the broad shoulders of the Anglo-American world as a whole (to which Churchill, in virtue of his half-American background, belongs, so to speak, by right of birth).

If this is not consistency, another term must be found. The truth is that Churchill has been more acutely conscious of the dangers inherent in the twentieth century than any other states-man of his time. The gloomy prognostications of the 1925 essay are steadily echoed in his later utterances, though always quali-fied by a firm belief that, given some degree of common sense, the world's problems can be solved. What Churchill senses and tries to convey is that we are living in a transitional age, midway between the long Victorian calm and the hypothetical future world order in which the rule of law has at last been established. Yet interwoven with this central theme—representing, as it were, the Whig strand in his makeup—there runs a powerful strain of insular egotism which relates him to the conservative side of the national tradition. What has happened to the world since the end of the Victorian era is seen as happening above all to England; events and persons are refracted through the idiosyncratic prism of national loyalties. It was England who kept the long peace, England who, in Churchill's own lifetime, twice defended the civilized world against the barbarians. And all at the expense of her own greatness! Churchill never quite knows whether to marvel at the achievement, or to lament its necessity. Quite early in the first volume of *The World Crisis* he introduces this fateful theme:

> In the year 1895 I had the privilege, as a young officer, of being invited to lunch with Sir William Harcourt. In the course of a conversation in which I took, I fear, none too modest a share, I asked the question: "What will happen then?" "My dear Winston," replied the old Victorian statesman, "the experiences of a long life have convinced me that nothing ever happens." Since that moment, as it seems to me, nothing has ever ceased happening. The growth of the great antagonisms abroad was accompanied by the progressive aggravation of party strife at home. The scale on which events have shaped themselves has dwarfed the episodes of the Victorian Era. Its small wars between great nations, its earnest disputes about superficial issues, the high, keen intellectualism of its personages, the sober, frugal, narrow limitations of their action, belong to a vanished period. The smooth river with its eddies and ripples along which we then sailed seems inconceivably remote from the cataract down which we have been hurled, and the rapids in whose turbulence we are now struggling.

This was written during the interval between the two world wars, when Britain was still the greatest of the powers, though losing ground on all sides. For an inkling of the gay Edwardian optimism which preceded the catastrophe, one must go to the strictly autobiographical chapters of Churchill's reminiscences—those that come to an end before 1914. The date is important; so is the adjective "gay." The Victorians had been confident enough, but their outlook was solemn and a trifle grim. Pleasure and frivolity were not encouraged. The economist might say that the accumulation of capital was still too important and laborious for energy to be wasted on mere trifles such as the enjoyment of life. Gaiety only came in with the Edwardian era, after the turn of the century, and went out promptly in 1914. There was, so to speak, no prolonged Louis XV age of enjoyment—only a brief interlude between the gloom of the Great Monarch, and the tumbrils. The comparison is inexact—after all, 1914 was not so completely the end of an era as 1789—but it does convey something of the sentiment with which Churchill's generation watched the passing of the England they had known—*their* England.

> I gave myself over to the amusements of the London season. In those days English Society still existed in its old form. It was a brilliant and powerful body, with standards of conduct and methods of enforcing them now altogether forgotten. In a very large degree everyone knew everyone else and who they were. The few hundred great families who had governed England for so many generations and had seen her rise to the pinnacle of her glory were interrelated to an enormous extent by marriage. Everywhere one met friends and kinfolk. The leading figures of Society were in many cases the leading statesmen in Parliament, and also the leading sportsmen on the Turf. Lord Salisbury was accustomed scrupulously to avoid calling a Cabinet when there was racing at Newmarket, and the House of Commons made a practice of adjourning for the Derby. In those days the glittering parties at Landsdowne House, Devonshire House or Stafford House comprised all the elements which made a gay and splendid social circle in close relation to the business of Parliament, the hierarchies of the Army and Navy, and the policy of the State. Now Landsdowne House and Devonshire House have been turned into hotels, flats and restaurants; and Stafford House has become the ugliest and stupidest museum in the world, in whose faded saloons [sic] Socialist Governments drearily dispense the public hospitality.

The date is 1896, viewed from the vantage point of 1930. (Worse was to come, but the author, fortunately for his peace of mind, did not know this.) The world he describes is that of Henry James—a brilliant but fragile structure, uneasily poised between aristocratic past and democratic future. Already before 1914 uncontrollable forces were on the march, forces long dormant under the elegant surface of late Victorian and Edwardian society. The grandeur of Landsdowne House was to be shattered, and much else besides. What is remarkable is that the young lieutenant who drank in the splendid scene in 1896—himself by right of birth a member of the ruling oligarchy whose glory he was destined to share—should have successfully weathered the transition to the age of mass democracy, total war, and global organization.

There are, of course, those who maintain that in this achievement he was greatly helped by a certain underlying lack of fixed principles—what, for example, gave him the right, with his aristocratic background, to join Lloyd George in his campaign against the great landed fortunes? The answer perhaps is that by this time he had become a professional politician, relying for his income on writings and lecture tours, and thus in a sense living on his wits. (He had virtually no money of his own, and for years supported himself by journalism.) But the true explanation has to do with the character of British public life, which for all its archaic rules and customs left plenty of scope for new forces then emerging. The apparent rigidity of the system was social rather than political. Radicals and labor leaders were excluded from Society, but not from power. In consequence they never developed an appetite for violent revolution, or indeed an aptitude for it. Lloyd George might be ostracized by London hostesses, but he continued to sit in the cabinet and confiscate the property of their husbands. And though the solitary Labour leader who joined the Liberal cabinet in 1906 was an exceedingly tame figure, his inclusion in the magic circle suggested the shape of things to come. The governing oligarchy had never ceased to broaden its base, and it was now once more active trying to tap fresh sources of popular support.

All this was in the Whig tradition—more doubtfully also in that of "Tory democracy"—and Churchill played the traditional game with all the enthusiasm of a newcomer. He never really abandoned it. The Russian Revolution for some years dislodged him from his basic Whiggery and turned him into an aggressive opponent of Labour—he even mistook poor Ramsay MacDonald for a Bolshevik in disguise—but before long he had reverted to his old central position. When the test came in 1940, the Labour Party made it plain that no other Conservative was acceptable to them as Prime Minister, and during the war his old General

Strike opponent, Ernest Bevin, became not only a colleague but virtually an ally against the rest of the cabinet—Tories and Socialists alike.

The fact is that British public life acts as a solvent of antagonisms which elsewhere have a way of hardening into rigid enmities. Before 1914 politics was in fact a game, though it was ceasing to be one—the Irish issue in that year almost brought the parliamentary machine to a standstill. After 1918 the rise of Labour introduced a new factor, and for some years it looked as though the constitutional framework might be seriously strained. But the General Strike of 1926 fizzled out amidst nationwide church prayers for reconciliation, there was no real violence, and even the prolonged mass unemployment of the 1930s did not cause serious unrest (partly because prices were falling, and everyone but the unemployed was slightly better off). In a society whose internal cohesion had never been seriously threatened, it was possible for Parliament to remain the focus of the national life, though the standard of debate tended to decline.

Churchill himself is evidently in two minds about the impact of mass democracy upon parliamentary government. In 1930 he remarked, apropos of the election campaign of 1900 which first introduced him to the voters:

> I must explain that in those days we had a real political democracy led by a hierarchy of statesmen, and not a fluid mass distracted by newspapers. There was a structure in which statesmen, electors and the press all played their part. . . . Inside the meeting we were all surprised at Mr. [Joseph] Chamberlain's restraint. . . . He spoke for an hour: but what pleased the audience most was that, having made a mistake in some fact or figure to the prejudice of his opponents, he went back and corrected it, observing that he must not be unfair. All this was before the liquefaction of the British political system had set in.

The reference to "a real political democracy" is at least in part misleading, unless one notes the qualifying phrase "led by a hierarchy of statesmen." Churchill has always equated democracy with parliamentary government, and parliament with oligarchy, though naturally an elected oligarchy. This is Whiggism, and the antithesis of genuine democracy. Yet Churchill is right in holding that the old British system of government has disappeared. Parliamentary debates no longer decide important issues —they are settled beforehand in the cabinet and in the party caucus, where the real discussions nowadays take place. Partly in consequence, public interest in Parliament has declined, as has the intellectual level of debate. Precisely because he is not hampered by belief in democracy, Churchill has been able to say all these things, as the leaders of the Labour Party have not. The system still works, for the same reason that the monarchy remains acceptable to the British—institutions have a way of outlasting their real usefulness and acquiring a kind of symbolic meaning instead. But there is no question that the old system of government by a parliamentary oligarchy, which genuinely *debated* public issues, is dead. It has in fact gone the way of the empire which it was designed to uphold. The modern synthesis of democracy and bureaucracy which has taken its place is in many ways more efficient, and also more humane, but it is not parliamentary government in the traditional sense, and it provides no training ground for future Churchills. (Not that there is much prospect of another such personality sprouting from the soil of the welfare state.)

These considerations reinforce the sense—now widely shared among his countrymen—that Churchill is the last great figure in modern British political history. The impression is probably well-founded. Greatness does not develop independently of circumstances; it needs a wider horizon than present-day England can supply. Churchill, however, has impressed himself upon the consciousness of his age not simply as one of its great men, but as the paradoxical embodiment of traits which normally do not go together. In one of his aspects he is a political coelacanth, a prehistoric monster fished up from the depths of the past (thus he appears to British left-wingers, who are nonetheless secretly proud of him). At the same time he has managed to appear as an ultramodern organizer of the managerial age: not merely equipped with all the latest technical and scientific wheezes (he usually had some prominent scientist in his entourage), but actually in possession of a scientific cast of mind: indifferent to tradition, impatient of routine, full of Wellsian visions of progress, resolved to streamline the ancient British organism, ready to work with American politicians or Soviet commissars, and finally able to wipe the floor with Hitler. The contradiction is perhaps no more puzzling than the circumstance that this greatest of parliamentary debaters of the old school can, at the drop of a hat, transform himself into the most effective of popular orators, able to hold a mass audience spellbound for hours with a torrential flow of robust humor and picturesque abuse of political opponents.

Perhaps all this amounts to no more than the trite adage that genius is many-sided. Certainly there has never been anyone quite like Winston Spencer Churchill. It is to be feared that there never will be again. England is becoming too small a stage for actors of his caliber; or it may be that there is something about the impersonality of modern life which discourages the almost tropical growth of eccentricity so marked in the society in which Churchill had his roots. For in the end he is an intensely national figure, the most John Bullish of modern British statesmen, but John Bull in a flying suit and equipped with the latest electronic devices. Strange that one man should in the end have managed to span the transition from the Victorian age to our time, and even stranger that it should have been a descendant of the Duke of Marlborough. Now that the story is nearing its close, the originality of the protagonist stands out more strikingly perhaps than it did for his earlier contemporaries. Here at least is someone who towers above his age; a pity he has left no successors.

Finally, what of Churchill the writer, or more generally the man of ideas, the stylist, and—so far as it is possible to class him with that select fraternity—the political thinker?

It is well known that his general education was spotty. At school he was considered a dunce, and by his own account never managed to memorize a word of Greek or more than a few scraps of Latin; nor was his French ever really fluent, as his wartime radio audiences discovered. In mathematics he only managed to pass the examination barrier with the help of a crammer, and thereafter promptly forgot what he had learned. History he enjoyed, but we know from his account in *My Early Life* that he had not read either Gibbon or Macaulay until he was twenty-two and, as a cavalry officer in India, found himself with leisure hours to fill. He then, for the first time in his life, developed a zest for reading, and for two successive winters tried to close the yawning gaps in his education. Philosophy, history, science—it all came as a complete revelation to him:

> From November to May, I read for four or five hours every day history and philosophy. Plato's *Republic*—it appeared he was for all practical purposes the same as Socrates; the *Politics* of Aristotle . . . ; Schopenhauer on pessimism; Malthus on population; Darwin's *Origin of Species;* all interspersed with other books of lesser standing. It was a curious education. . . . I now began for the first time to envy those young cubs at the university who had fine scholars to tell them what was what; professors who had devoted their lives to mastering and focusing ideas in every branch of learning; who were eager to distribute the treasures they had gathered before they were overtaken by the night. But now I pity undergraduates when I see what frivolous lives many of them lead in the midst of precious fleeting opportunity. After all, a man's Life must be nailed to a cross either of Thought or Action. Without work there is no play.

On the whole he liked Gibbon and Macaulay best. They were the two authors whom he read and reread, and their abiding influence is solidly imprinted in his own style:

> All through the long glistening middle hours of the Indian day, from when we quitted stables till the evening shadows proclaimed the hour of Polo, I devoured Gibbon. I rode triumphantly through it from end to end, and enjoyed it all. I scribbled all my opinions on the margins of the pages, and very soon found myself a vehement partisan of the author against the disparagements of his pompous-pious editor. I was not even estranged by his naughty footnotes. . . . From Gibbon I went to Macaulay. . . . I accepted all Macaulay wrote as gospel, and I grieved to read his harsh judgements upon the Great Duke of Marlborough. There was no one at hand to tell me that this historian with his captivating style and devastating self-confidence was the prince of literary rogues, who always preferred the tale to the truth, and smirched or glorified great men, and garbled documents according as they affected his drama. . . . Still I must admit an immense debt.

Neither Gibbon nor Macaulay of course fits the Tory tradition, and the author's artless confession in this chapter really amounts

to telling the reader that his mind was permanently influenced
by the two leading historians of the Whig school. To these in-
fluences he later added Burke—another Whig, whose speeches
during the American War have provided countless schoolboys
with convenient epigrams for use on the liberal side of every
argument, just as his later writings on the French Revolution
gave substance to Toryism. It is significant that when Churchill
in 1904 left the Conservatives he used as an argument their failure
to conciliate the defeated Boer republics in the Burkean spirit of
magnanimity toward the vanquished—always a favorite Churchillian theme.

Meanwhile what of his general philosophical and religious
convictions? Of religion we are told that during those months
when as a young man he was busy gobbling up knowledge, "I
passed through a violent and aggressive anti-religious phase
which, had it lasted, might easily have made me a nuisance." The
phase was ended, it seems, by a tacit agreement with himself
that he would believe as much as suited him. For the rest he had
always gone to church, "and at Harrow there were three services
every Sunday, besides morning and evening prayers throughout
the week. All this was very good. I accumulated in those years so
fine a surplus in the Bank of Observance that I have been drawing confidently on it ever since. Weddings, christenings, and
funerals have brought in a steady annual income, and I have
never made too close enquiries about the state of my account.
It might well be that I should find an overdraft." Gibbon's
mockery is plainly audible in this casual passage which no genuine Tory would have penned, let alone published; so is the
characteristic Whig frivolity—a blend of skepticism and amused
disdain for the foolish multitude. Churchill is a very eighteenth-
century character.

There is a similar quality in his political thought, which is
intensely realistic and almost exclusively concerned with power—
especially British power. Yet it differs strikingly from what the
Germans used to call *Realpolitik*—by which they meant freedom
from general ideas, and concentration on material factors alone.
Churchill is never cynical when he talks about war, and he is
quite clear in his mind that Britain survived two world wars
only because she stood for certain general principles which were

in harmony with the needs of the age and the interests of other nations. His imperialism is genuinely liberal—another inheritance from the Whig era. The Whigs conducted a series of wars against the France of Louis XIV in the name of religious and political freedom, and Churchill is convinced that they were right in doing so. His monumental biography of his famous ancestor John Churchill, Duke of Marlborough, who captained the Allied armies in that struggle, is heavily weighted against the Tories— then the party of peace with France abroad and royal absolutism at home. He also makes it clear that, although Marlborough belonged to neither faction, he skillfully used both to keep himself in the saddle during the long war against Louis XIV, which of course is precisely what Churchill did when the time came for him to rally his nation against Hitler.

It may be noteworthy that Gibbon has gradually prevailed over Macaulay in Churchill's later writings—the eighteenth century asserting itself against the nineteenth. In *The World Crisis* his style is frequently flamboyant and not free from rodomontade. The massive biography of Marlborough also provided an occasion for Macaulayesque rhetoric, since here he was traveling over terrain already explored by the historian of the English Revolution, and deliberately pitting his own interpretation against that of Macaulay. The battle pieces in particular are full of purple passages:

> Sombre reflections held the mind of Fénélon's pupil, and gnawing anxiety. Here was the army of France, at whose head he had been marching a few hours before, short of ammunition and in increasing disorder, locked in deadly grapple with an enemy whose strength seemed inexhaustible, whose numbers were growing every minute, and whose confident aggression proclaimed the presence and the genius of Marlborough and Eugene. This was the battle which he, heir to the crown of France, had been sent forth to win. War, yesterday the jaunty boon-companion, now glared upon him with lineaments of fury, hate and doom. Where was Vendôme? Where was that brutal, bestial, but nonetheless tremendous warrior, who had been placed at his side to win him military glory, whose advice he could lean upon, whose decisions in the end he had been directed to obey? The Marshal was in the cauldron, fighting hand to hand, organizing and reorganizing attacks, sending messages which were incomprehensible and orders which were obsolete by

the time they arrived. The one thing the Great King had always
forbidden, and which Burgundy had above all others resolved to
avoid—namely, an infantry battle in closed and broken country—
was now burning away the grand army of France. Such is the
chastisement of those who presume to gain by easy favor and pre-
tence the glories which the gods reserve for their chosen heroes.

Compare this melodramatic and slightly absurd pathos with
the glacial calm of the opening chapter of *The Second World
War:*

> Germany only paid, or was only able to pay, the indemnities later
> extorted because the United States was profusely lending money
> to Europe, and especially to her. In fact, during the three years
> 1926 to 1929 the United States was receiving back in the form of
> debt installment indemnities from all quarters about one-fifth of
> the money which she was lending to Germany with no hope of re-
> payment. However, everybody seemed pleased and appeared to
> think this might go on forever.
>
> History will characterize all these transactions as insane. They
> helped to breed both the martial curse and the "economic blizzard"
> of which more later. Germany now borrowed in all directions,
> swallowing greedily every credit which was lavishly offered her.
> Misguided sentiment about aiding the vanquished nation, coupled
> with a profitable rate of interest on these loans, led British investors
> to participate, though on a much smaller scale than those of the
> United States. Thus Germany gained the two thousand million
> sterling in loans, as against the one thousand million of indemnities
> which she paid in one form or another by surrender of capital
> assets and *valuta* in foreign countries, or by juggling with the enor-
> mous American loans. All this is a sad story of complicated idiocy
> in the making of which much toil and virtue was consumed.

The tone of this, as of the succeeding chapters in *The Second
World War,* is consciously Augustan—dispassionate, reflective,
and only occasionally lit by flashes of scorn. Churchill has finally
reached maturity—only to discover that what suits his ripe taste
best is the marmoreal calm of his favorite eighteenth-century
authors. Intellectually, too, there is no advance beyond the tried
and tested categories of the Whig tradition. Wars are made by
"Nations," whose leaders are either sagacious or unreasonable,
and in the latter case morally wicked as well. Ideologies have
no meaning for Churchill. Bolshevism to him was a savage aber-

ration—now happily on the way out, thanks to that realist, Stalin
—while as for National Socialism, who could possibly take this
farrago of nonsense seriously, or suppose that the Germans themselves believed in it?

All of this may not seem like a very heavy mental equipment,
and indeed Churchill would at no time in his career have qualified as a systematic thinker on any subject other than British
history. He showed, however, a remarkable capacity for absorbing
both factual knowledge and general ideas, chiefly by listening
to people and gradually widening the circle of his acquaintances,
until it included such improbable figures as Lloyd George,
Mrs. Beatrice Webb, and Professor Frederick Lindemann, a well-
known physicist who during World War II became the chief of
Churchill's scientific brain trust and something like a gray eminence behind the scenes. In other directions, too, there was constant expansion of professional competence, so much so that for
some years in the middle 1920s Churchill, as Chancellor of the
Exchequer, was chiefly identified with matters like the gold
standard and the balance of trade. If his management of the nation's finances caused Keynes to deplore "the economic consequences of Mr. Churchill" as a disaster comparable only to the
Treaty of Versailles, at least it provided fresh evidence that he
literally shrank from nothing.

When one also recalls that, in the midst of all this, during the
General Strike of 1926, he amused himself by editing the official
British Gazette—all other newspapers had been shut down—in
which he poured floods of abuse upon the strikers and their
leaders, it must be admitted that there has rarely been a moment
during the half century starting from about 1900 when Winston
Churchill did not provide the British public with something to
gasp about over their morning newspapers. He himself is quite
aware of this aspect of his career, and has indicated more than
once that every moment of it—including the twenty or so election
campaigns in which he was personally involved—contributed
greatly to his own enjoyment and the entertainment of all concerned.

There is something so outsize about all this—the span of his
life, its fantastic ups and downs, the magnitude of the issues involved, the imprint upon the world of his own larger-than-life

personality—that one shrinks from a summing-up. No biographer is likely to be able to do justice to Churchill, and this despite the fact that he is basically not a complex character. It is simply that, having lived so long, enjoyed himself so enormously in so many roles, and taken so large a share in shaping events, it has become impossible to write his story without taking in huge chunks of impersonal reality as well. All the same, it is to be hoped that someone will one day try his hand at it. The result should be fascinating.

Postimperial Britain

❄ ❄ ❄

I

A stirred nation, a London sight. . . . Undistracted by empire
now, we felt intimately that we were at home, that we were seeing
our own lives. . . . There was not a trace of private rhetoric about
the funeral. The men slow-marching in the greatest occasion since
the death of the Duke of Wellington embodied a general emotion.
. . . And even to the common fear that we were seeing the end of
our own greatness with his, that meanness would now come in,
that Churchill was the last, and that to the world outside we had
become one more irrelevant folk culture. . . . There was, I suspect, an undertone of grim self-pity: we were looking at the last
flash of Victorian aplomb, we were looking at a past utterly irre-
coverable.

Thus V. S. Pritchett's eloquent account of Winston Churchill's
funeral in the *New Statesman*. Those who have the melancholy
privilege of living in the capital of what was once the British
Empire—all of us, foreign-born and naturalized as well as the
true islanders—have come to know well the feeling that greatness is gone and meanness has come in: meanness of spirit consequent upon the relentless decline of material influence and
power, for it is an illusion to suppose that nations can sublimate
themselves into moral entities impervious to the march of history. Unless, that is, they renounce their national sovereignty
altogether and retire into the protective shell of a religious community, as the Jews did when the Temple fell, and the Greeks
after the conquest of Byzantium by the Turks. But these are
extreme cases. The normal course is marked out by the familiar

Commentary, October 1966.

destinies of European nations which have survived the loss of their imperial greatness: Austria, Holland, Sweden. No sublimation here: rather a transfer of national energies from one level (politico-military) to another (socioeconomic and cultural). Or —as in the case of Spain—failure to make the transition, nostalgia for vanished glories, and an endless, lingering death-in-life.

The British (like the French) are currently poised between these alternatives, and this circumstance lends to the dreary routine of economic crises and political reshuffles a dramatic quality not immediately visible to the outsider. But there is this difference: France, whatever the continuing dispute between Gaullists and anti-Gaullists, has discovered a suitable task in the political leadership of Western Europe: a privilege which by default has fallen into her lap and which no party or faction in Paris is going to renounce, come what may. Whereas the British (as Mr. Acheson sagely observed in December 1962) have "lost an empire and not found a role." For saying this he was taken to task, with quite needless violence, by everyone in England from Harold Macmillan downward. He was, of course, quite right, and the wretched spectacle of British domestic affairs in recent years has only lent the finishing touch to what even in those days was a fairly dismal picture.

That a time would come when France would condescend to her ancient rival, and that it would come within two decades of the wartime triumvirate symbolized by the names Churchill-Roosevelt-Stalin, was something no public figure in England or in continental Europe would have thought possible even a few short years ago. The colossal humiliation of exclusion from the Common Market, in January 1963, has not been the end of the story. Worse was to follow: in July 1966 a French Premier paid a brief visit to London (shortly after his Head of State had returned from a triumphal ten-day tour of the Soviet Union) and notified his British hosts in dry language that their financial status would have to be improved before they could be considered suitable partners in an enlarged Common Market. If the incident passed without much public comment, the reason is that it was promptly swallowed up in the great financial panic of late July and early August, leading the Labour government to adopt deflationary measures (including an official wages stop) that the

Conservatives had not dared introduce. The nation was well and truly put on notice that it had been living beyond its means.

How and why did it come to this? The economists, as is their wont, have different and conflicting tales to tell, but there is at least unanimity on one point: Britain has since the war been trying to fill a world role exceeding her economic capacities. Of course the matter can also be put the other way around: the nation has not supplied its rulers with the material means required for all the various commitments into which successive British governments had entered. But this tedious quibble may be disregarded. Whichever way it is put, there is now a great and growing disproportion between what Britain as a nation is committed to externally and what Britain as a society is willing to do internally. The gap has for some years been concealed behind financial manipulations involving all the European central banks plus the U.S. Treasury, but it is now out in the open, and this is what "the crisis" is really about.

It is not about living standards: they have gone up steadily since the 1950s (which is one reason why the ordinary voter has ceased to take the newspaper talk about "crisis" seriously). Nor is it simply about the balance of trade: exports have not done as well as they might, but they have not done badly either. They have, in fact, more than doubled since 1950. On current account (leaving aside government expenditure—mostly for military purposes) the country has been paying its way; paying for its imports, that is, with ordinary commercial exports, plus "invisible" earnings from the £10,000 million (almost $30 billion) of overseas investments held by British companies.[1]

The deficit in the balance of payments (as distinct from the ordinary balance of trade) has arisen because the government has spent abroad more than the surplus earned by British exporters and investors. Most of the overseas expenditure has been for military purposes, the remainder largely for aid to "underdeveloped" countries. But for these politico-military obligations, the

1. A. R. Conan, *The Problem of Sterling* (London, 1966), p. 13. "There was a cumulative balance of over £1,000 million for the 1950's, followed by a cumulative deficit of under £500 million for the first quinquennium of the 1960's. . . . The deficit for 1960–64 is struck after debiting £1,800 million on Government account: the commercial surplus for the quinquennium was £1,300 million." Ibid. p. 99.

country would be solvent, and would even be earning a comfortable surplus, like West Germany. It is as simple as that.

These facts are recognized by government and opposition alike. The Conservative Party's official spokesman on defense, Enoch Powell (a former cabinet minister and a relentless opponent of the Labour Party and all its works, notably its vestigial belief in economic planning), puts it this way:

> The simple answer to the question whether Britain can afford to spend £500 millions a year on defense, aid and other governmental activities [2] is the same as the answer to the question whether we can afford to spend 6½ per cent of our national income on defense, or 40 per cent on purposes determined by public authorities. The answer is: "Yes, of course, if Britain wants to."
>
> It is no objection to point to Britain's persistent balance of payments difficulties and increasing indebtedness, and to draw attention to the fact that, had there been no such expenditure during the last nine years (over which period it has doubled from £253 millions to £500 millions), this country would have had a favorable overall balance of payments totalling £1,942 millions instead of a deficit totaling £1,412 millions. Figures like these bring home the fact that, contrary to vulgar supposition, the country has indeed been "paying its way" before the external expenditure of its government is taken into account. It is a calumny to accuse the British people of having consumed or invested at home, or spent or lent on private account abroad, more than they were prepared to produce and save.[3]

Since the facts are not in dispute, and since the Tory party has traditionally stood for the sort of "world role" the Labour government is trying to fill, one may reasonably wonder what the political quarrel between the two sides is about. With the exception of the Liberals—a small though influential group of politicians and intellectuals spread all over the Establishment— no sizable body of opinion has yet declared in favor of renouncing an active role in world affairs. Even Labour's left wing is split on the issue: after all, most of its leading figures are members of the government. Liberals, pacifists, and "Little England-

2. The reference is to overseas spending in foreign currency. The total defense budget is more than £2000 million ($5.6 billion).

3. J. Enoch Powell, "Britain's Overseas Spending," *The Banker* (London), August, 1966, p. 520.

ers" combined do not make a majority; and those among them
who are most insistent on cutting overseas military expenditure
are also very vocal about spending more on aid to backward
countries. Where then is the total saving to come from, and how
big is it to be? Will the £100 million ($280 million) cut in over-
seas expenditure announced by Mr. Wilson do the trick? Few
people think so, and others may wonder why economies on this
relatively small scale are necessary at all. Britain exports £5000
million ($14 billion) worth of goods annually, after all, and owns
the equivalent of $30 billion in overseas investments. What is the
matter with a country which has such assets and yet seems to
drift from one financial crisis to another?

What is the matter is quite simply that the pound sterling still
finances forty per cent of world trade, and that the burden of
acting as banker to half the world can no longer be borne by a
small country whose trade does not yield a surplus large enough
to cover military and political expenditure abroad. "The pound is
weak" because holders of sterling are afraid that it may be devalued; and they fear this because they can see the disproportion
between the colossal mass of sterling balances held by Britain's
creditors, and the smallness of the reserves held by the Bank
of England. But for having pinned this albatross around their
necks, the British would be as well off as the West Germans and
the Dutch, if not perhaps the Swedes.

But how did the country get into this position? Why must a
middle-sized European nation behave as though it were still the
center of a worldwide empire? Why cannot it relinquish the
burden and content itself with a role that does not strain its
economy, and the ingenuity of its financial and political rulers,
to the breaking point and beyond? The answers are many and
complex, and sound reasons can be advanced for the decision
to go on behaving after 1945 as though nothing had changed. It
can even be argued that in the 1950s the gamble looked like
paying off: the country went on playing a world role and had a
financial surplus nonetheless. Yet it is plain by now that this
cannot go on. Something will have to give—most likely the "world
role" so dear to Mr. Wilson, the "poor man's Churchill," as his
critics have unkindly taken to calling him. The trouble is that
Britain still carries the legacy of the real Churchill, the partner

of Roosevelt and Stalin. He was, after all, Prime Minister once more from 1951 to 1955, and during those complacent years the British fell into the fatal habit of taking themselves and the world for granted. The awakening came after he had left the scene. By now it is almost complete; but it is also very late.

II

One hears it said these days that Washington is not eager to assume the burden of world empire. Eager or not, the role has devolved upon it and must be played out to the end, for better or worse. Because Churchill knew this would happen, the record of his private thoughts during and after World War II makes fascinating reading.[4] Alongside a mass of rather painful detail, it offers an insight into the working of his mind while he was still at the height of his powers, political and mental. The decline (in both respects) dates from 1944, when Churchill was seventy and beginning to slow down. By a coincidence this was also the moment when the British Empire began to be overshadowed in the wartime counsels of the Allies by its two giant partners, the United States and the Soviet Union.

Half-American by birth (though not by education, which was conventionally British), Churchill was unique among British statesmen of his generation in treating the Anglo-American alliance as an emotional commitment and a long-term aim rather than as a simple convenience forced upon Britain by external circumstances which might be expected to change. At the same time, he remained romantically attached to the imperial vision which, for him, centered on India and the "empire on which the sun never set." The resulting tensions in his mind are faithfully portrayed in Lord Moran's dispassionate account of his private utterances during the quarter century between his "finest hour" in 1940 and his death in 1965 (though the actual record terminates five years earlier, in 1960). The conflict was never resolved. How could it have been? Churchill wanted the British Empire to remain in being, while the Americans, from Roosevelt down,

4. *Churchill: The Struggle for Survival 1940–65, Taken from the Diaries of Lord Moran* (Boston and London, 1966). Lord Moran, formerly Sir Charles Wilson, was Churchill's personal physician and medical adviser.

expected it to disappear. The Churchillian formula—a permanent union of the "two great Anglo-Saxon powers"—never obtained the genuine consent of the Americans, though they raised no objection when he brought it forward, and indeed encouraged him to believe that it expressed their own view of the future.

Perhaps they felt that in time of war it would be tactless to quarrel about it. At any rate, Churchill was loudly cheered when he addressed a special session of Congress after Pearl Harbor, but the applause faded when he spoke of opportunities missed in the past, when the U.S. and Britain, working together, might have preserved the peace of the world. Even in December 1941, with America and Britain facing the Axis powers in unison, there was no enthusiasm in Washington for Theodore Roosevelt's old theme. Another Roosevelt was in charge, but the Americans no longer saw the future of their country in terms of the Anglo-Saxon rhetoric evolved around the turn of the century by the liberal-imperialist (or Social-Darwinist) school. The coming century was to be America's alone.

On the British side, Churchill had aged but not changed. To the end, he held the faith instilled in him before 1914 by those in England who feared Pan-Germanism and Pan-Slavism, and who regarded the United States as Britain's natural ally in the coming struggle to preserve the world they believed in: a world run by the Anglo-Saxons, for the benefit of the lesser breeds no doubt, but controlled by the inheritors of Britain's "Glorious Revolution" in 1688. In the last resort it was the Whig interpretation of history, as transmitted to Churchill in his youth by the only historian he ever read seriously—Macaulay.

All this, and much besides, may be gathered from Lord Moran's account of his eminent patient seen at close quarters. No historian himself, but well versed in public affairs (and, surprisingly, a considerable stylist), he has written what may well become the politician's Boswell. Already there are signs that the publication of his diary has affected the conventional view of Churchill's last years in office (from 1951 to 1955), when Eden waited impatiently for the succession, while across the Atlantic there were still from time to time those private gatherings in the White House, with Eisenhower and Dulles listening half-convinced while Churchill poured out his urgent advocacy of peaceful

coexistence with Russia. For it is not the least remarkable revelation of this remarkable book that by 1953–54 Churchill, nearing
eighty and with failing powers, had become obsessed with the
dangers of another world war. "My thoughts are almost entirely
thermonuclear," he said on June 26, 1954, and most of his remaining energy, during these last months of his premiership, was
devoted to persuading the stubborn Dulles and the wavering
Eisenhower to seek a lasting peace with Stalin's successors. In this
he was backed up by his scientific adviser, Cherwell (Frederick
Lindemann), who tirelessly argued that the hydrogen bomb had
narrowed the choice to one between preventive war and an
understanding with Moscow. On July 3, 1954, Churchill said to
Moran:

> I am counting on the Russians wanting a better time; they want
> butter, not bombs, more food, more comfort. For forty years they
> have had a pretty rough life. They may have given up dreams of
> world conquest, and be ready for peaceful coexistence. Anyway,
> Ike has crossed the gulf which separates a mission to destroy Bol-
> shevism from living side-by-side in peace. I must admit that I my-
> self have crossed that gulf. I would like to visit Russia once more
> before I die.

Thus did the hydrogen bomb transform the old anti-Communist
crusader into a peacemonger, at any rate where the Russians
were concerned. For the Chinese ("little yellow men") he had
less use. It was Eden who reminded those around him that China
could be neither disregarded nor destroyed—Eden who throughout Lord Moran's pages appears as a secondary figure: the
eternal heir-apparent, yet indispensable to Churchill, who, for all
his towering prestige in the country, was never really taken to
heart by the true-blue Tories or by the mandarins of Whitehall.
The two men complemented each other, especially in the later
years when Churchill no longer had his former zest for detail, and
of the two it was Eden who was more "European": less inclined
to stake all on the Anglo-American connection, and readier on
occasion to cross swords with Dulles. In the end, of course, none
of this mattered. In 1956, with Churchill gone and Eisenhower
refusing to listen to Eden's desperate pleas for American backing
over Suez, the dream of an Anglo-American condominium was

shattered. It was left for Harold Macmillan to pick up the pieces and organize an orderly retreat to unprepared positions.

By now the chapter is closed. What remains of the "special relationship" has been converted into a matter of American support for sterling, pending some general reshuffle of world monetary institutions. "East of Suez" a few remnants of Britain's former empire continue to be garrisoned by troops and pilots for whom no suitable accommodation can be found at home, but that is about all. When Indian and Pakistani statesmen think it advantageous to meet on foreign soil, in order to sign a short-lived armistice, they go to Tashkent, not to London. By now, indeed, it is not merely the glory that has departed: most of the attendant illusions have gone as well. President Johnson's embarrassing praise of Harold Wilson, when that statesman visits Washington, does not impress even the dimmest voter in Britain. As for Mr. Wilson's sub-Churchillian rhetoric about his government's resolve to continue playing a "world role" (on borrowed money), it is taken—domestically and abroad—at its true value, which is close to zero. To the experts, the only question is whether Britain will manage to gatecrash its way into the Common Market before or after sterling is devalued and ceases to be a world currency. And who cares what London does with the "deterrent"? It seems an age (actually it is only a little over three years) since Macmillan went to Moscow in order to sign the treaty binding America, Russia, and Britain not to explode any more bombs in the atmosphere. It has been a short but steep decline since those days in 1914 when the British government controlled the destinies of one-quarter of the human race.

Although in his last years Churchill was conscious of the miscarriage of his great design, he seems never to have grasped that the preservation of the British Empire was incompatible with the aims for which World War II had been fought: democracy and national self-determination. Roosevelt—in many ways a shallower mind—saw this quite well and, much to the indignation of the British (or at any rate of Churchill and his entourage), hardly bothered to hide his impatience with the Empire's continued existence. On the British side, too, there were men who could see the writing on the wall. Lord Halifax (once Chamberlain's

Foreign Secretary and later sent to Washington by Churchill to serve as Ambassador) was a conventional High Tory, utterly remote from the realities of American life. Yet Moran has recorded his judgment (delivered privately in 1958) that the President and his circle during those years already thought Churchill out of date. "The Americans had never met anyone like him. He seemed to them a museum piece, a rare relic. When he told them he had not become First Minister of the Crown in order to preside over the liquidation of the British Empire, they felt that they were listening to a voice out of the eighteenth century."

As indeed they were. It was the secret of Churchill's personality that he was a throwback to the age of Marlborough—his distant ancestor. John Churchill, who became Duke of Marlborough, had led the armies of a European coalition against the France of Louis XIV. Then it was Holland that was threatened by conquest, and England that came to the rescue. Now it was England's turn, and help must come from the United States. To Winston Churchill it was still the same fight. Was not Germany a threat to the "liberties of Europe" of which England had become the traditional guardian? And was it not right that America should come into the fight? But then his consciousness of the historical filiation also told him that Holland had barely survived the war fought in her name, to become in the eighteenth century the satellite of England once peace had been signed. He never resolved the contradiction, and the thought that England was finished as a world power darkened the concluding decade of his life.

Others took a more hopeful view of the matter, adopting a nineteenth- rather than an eighteenth-century perspective. To them Churchill's resistance to Hitler recalled England's lengthy struggle against Napoleon. In 1945 the British were rather fond of this comparison (the French, for obvious reasons, thought less of it). Churchill himself admired Nelson and Wellington only a shade less than Marlborough. Trafalgar and Waterloo were splendid memories; in 1815 England had emerged for the second time as victor after a fierce contest with France, just as now she had got rid of the German menace. And the nineteenth century had brought the great age of Victorian peace and pre-eminence. Well, then, if there was trouble in the world, it might be said that the first few decades after Waterloo had been disturbed and confused too.

Sir Oliver Franks, who succeeded Halifax as Ambassador in Washington, took the long view, as befitted an eminent civil servant who had once taught moral philosophy in a Scottish university. He too by the late 1950s had come to think of World War II as Britain's last moment of greatness as a nation and an empire, but he was not discouraged. It was, he thought, chiefly a matter of adaptation to a new age. "I think the period 1945 to 1975 may be like 1815 to 1845," he told Moran. There were too many old men at the top who still thought in prewar terms. That had also been true of the post-Napoleonic period, when the aged Duke of Wellington contemplated with some bewilderment the new world of democracy and machinery. What was to be done about it? One had to wait for a new generation to come to the top. But would Britain still place its seal on the era, as it had done in the nineteenth century? In those days the industrial revolution had centered on England. Admittedly there were strains, and the Victorian compromise between monarchy and democracy (or between aristocracy and bourgeoisie) was not achieved without some trouble and even an occasional hint of violence. Still, in the end it had come about, and Britain had climbed to the pinnacle of wealth and power. While after 1945 ——Franks was too realistic to evade the critical issue: "It is possible that America may meet Russia in conference without us being at the table. After the war we acted as a Great Power, though we had not the resources. A kind of confidence trick. It came off as long as the decisions we made were acceptable to the other Powers. The trouble with these island empires has always been the same: they had too few men. America and Russia can afford a holocaust; we cannot."

In 1957, when this conversation took place, Churchill was in retirement, and his place had been taken by Harold Macmillan, whose artful practice of diplomacy prolonged for a few more years the illusion that Britain counted as a major power. By now the pretense has vanished; so, unhappily, has much of the self-confidence that went with it.

III

If Churchill represents the dynamic aspect of late Victorian England, catastrophically plunged into the maelstrom of war and revolution, Halifax stands for its quiet, passive, domesticated side.[5] Churchill (as Franks told Moran) had a "demonic" streak in him: his torrential energy and vitality, drawn from hidden springs, overwhelmed lesser men and enabled him to bounce back after the most shattering disasters. He was never happier than in 1940, when England's survival hung by a hair. Franks (a cool customer), who encountered him in those days, compared his effect upon other men to the impact produced by Luther and Calvin. It is curious that his colleagues should have included Edward Frederick Lindley Wood (1881–1959), first Baron Irwin of Kirby Underdale, third Viscount Halifax of Monk Bretton, first Earl of Halifax, Knight of the Garter, Order of Merit—a man who had been Foreign Secretary at the time of Munich and in this capacity dutifully backed Neville Chamberlain's attempt to "appease" Hitler's appetite at the expense of the hapless Beneš. No two men could have been more different, yet Halifax loyally supported Churchill after 1940, just as down to that date he had supported Chamberlain. Nor was this a matter of opportunism: Halifax was the soul of honor. He was also a wealthy and cultivated aristocrat who regarded public life as an unpleasant burden to be borne with such fortitude as one's character might permit. His true interest lay elsewhere: he was a devout Anglo-Catholic, and the only issue on which he was totally committed and unyielding concerned the doctrinal differences separating the Church of England from the Church of Rome on the one hand and from ordinary Protestantism or Evangelicalism on the other. All other matters, war and peace included, he treated as secondary and, in the last resort, unworthy of serious thought. This was the man who held the key post of Foreign Secretary in the cabinet which in September 1939 declared war on Germany. For it was Halifax who (with Chamberlain) took the responsibility for notifying Hitler that if he went

5. See the Earl of Birkenhead, *The Life of Lord Halifax* (London, 1965; Boston, 1966).

on with his assault on Poland, the British government would be compelled to stand by its treaty obligations to that country. Having delivered this momentous challenge, and committed his country to war with Germany, Halifax felt exhausted and took no further action. Honor had been satisfied. Winning the war was none of his business.

Lord Birkenhead's biography maintains the leisurely pace and subdued tone suitable to its subject. Halifax's grandfather, a member of various Whig administrations, was related by marriage to Lord Grey of the 1832 Reform Bill. His father, the second Viscount, was an eminent High Churchman and advocate of "reunion with Rome" (on terms acceptable to both parties). His mother was Lady Agnes Courtenay, daughter of Lord Devon of Powderham Castle, whose lineage was so ancient (going back to the Plantagenets) as to cause Gibbon to write, "The purple of three Emperors who have reigned at Constantinople will authorize or excuse a digression on the origins and singular fortunes of the House of Courtenay."

Does all this sound like caricature? Then the reason is that Halifax was among the last surviving members of an aristocracy that had effectively ruled England since the Wars of the Roses (in which several Courtenays lost their heads, having backed Lancaster when York was in the ascendant). What could this descendant of the Plantagenets think of Churchill, a mere upstart, whose famous ancestor, Marlborough, had climbed to fame and fortune in the "Glorious Revolution" of 1688? What, for that matter, could he make of Chamberlain: the grandson of a Birmingham businessman and himself a former mayor of that prosaic city? As for Hitler . . . Lord Birkenhead tactfully concedes that Halifax failed to understand the Führer.

Did he understand anything that was going on around him? As Viceroy of India from 1926 to 1931 he managed to stay on good terms with Gandhi, even when he felt reluctantly obliged to clap the Mahatma in jail. After all, they both shared an interest in religion. Even so, his biographer doubts whether Halifax (or Lord Irwin, as he then was) quite plumbed the depths of Gandhi's political cunning. "The Viceroy," he says tactfully, "was not a man of intellectual subtlety, and although he won Gandhi's trust and respect, it was inevitable that he should be baffled by a mind so Eastern, so unpredictable in its working, and so oddly compounded of mystical and opportunist elements." Well, perhaps, but when a few years later Halifax encountered the very un-Eastern personality of Hitler, his bafflement was no less. Nothing could have been more blatant than the Führer's cynicism and his appetite for conquest. Yet when in November 1937 Halifax was sent by Chamberlain to sound him out, he thought Hitler "very sincere." Göring, that bloated murderer and drug addict, he found "frankly attractive: like a great schoolboy, full of life and pride in what he was doing." No doubt. He could not even bring himself to dislike Goebbels, whom he met on the same occasion. "I suppose it must be some moral defect in me, but the fact remains."

It was not so much a moral defect as remoteness from ordinary life. There was of course also the important consideration that the Foreign Office had an even bigger headache than the Third Reich. As Halifax tactfully put it to Hitler on that occasion (less than a year before Munich): "Although there was much in the Nazi system that offended British opinion (treatment of the Church; to perhaps a lesser extent, the treatment of Jews; treatment of Trade Unions), I was not blind to what he had done for Germany and to the achievement, from his point of view, of keeping Communism out of his country and, as he would feel, of blocking its passage West." True, Churchill had once praised Mussolini for similar reasons, but then Germany represented a potentially mortal threat. Yet Chamberlain and Halifax were ready to gamble on Hitler's good will. So were Geoffrey Dawson of *The Times*, Lord Lothian (once Lloyd George's private secretary), and other eminent pillars of the Establishment. Weariness or despair? Probably a mixture of both. Certainly none of them had any liking or sympathy for the Führer. They simply hoped for the best—the best (in their unspoken judgment) being a war between Russia and Germany, with Britain and France acting the role of spectators. This was the logic of appeasement, yet when in 1939 matters came to the point, Chamberlain and Halifax failed to go through with it. Instead, they drifted into a war they did not want and had no hope of winning.

When Churchill (with the help of the Labour Party and much

against the inclination of a large body of Conservatives) had become Prime Minister, he got rid of Halifax by sending him to Washington as ambassador. Arrived there in January 1941, he found himself once more *in terra incognita* but made a valiant effort to come to terms with his new environment and, on the whole, did not do too badly. The Americans took to him: they liked his naïveté, so different from the traditional image of the guileful British diplomat. Halifax possessed a fund of native shrewdness (especially in money matters), but he was clearly innocent of those Machiavellian subtleties which Americans had come to associate with the British Foreign Office. Indeed, they soon discovered that even relatively simple matters, such as the system by which Congress was elected, were rather too much for him. "One funny thing about him," said his friend Walter Lippmann, "was that . . . every time an election took place he had to have the whole thing explained to him all over again." His hosts thought this rather endearing. They also sympathized with his earnest efforts to adapt himself to democracy. Though on one occasion he was publicly rebuked by Carl Sandburg for indulging in the effete sport of fox hunting while men were dying in Europe, he managed on the whole to make a good impression. His unworldliness (he had never heard of Tallulah Bankhead) was forgiven him, and his staff gradually managed to curb his lordly manner. They even persuaded him not to open his chamber-of-commerce speeches with funny stories which smacked too obviously of British caste distinctions and condescension toward social inferiors. His embassy staff (which included Isaiah Berlin) was ceaselessly active polishing his image, and on occasion their nimble wits enabled his lordship to get out of a scrape with the honors clearly in his favor. Thus, when in Detroit, on his way to call on Archbishop Mooney, he was picketed by isolationist housewives and had eggs and vegetables thrown at him (an egg exploding on his trouser bottom), he was officially reported to have said, "I am glad to see the Americans have eggs and tomatoes to throw around, when in England people are rationed and get only one egg a month." He had not thought of the remark himself (it is not recorded that he ever made a joke), but it was widely attributed to him by the American press and the incident helped to make him popular.

On more important occasions his innocence sometimes matched that of his hosts, though in their case it was more a matter of remoteness from Europe and failure to grasp what was going on there. When, for example, on arrival in Washington he met some Republican senators and congressmen, he was puzzled by their insistence that Roosevelt was "as dangerous a dictator as Hitler and Mussolini." Even Halifax knew better than that. On the other hand, he could not quite suppress a certain fellow-feeling with them. As he put it when setting down his impressions in his private diary: "My word—they do all hate F.D.R.! They regard him almost exactly as we used to regard Lloyd George at his worst; stirring up class feeling; no responsibility or knowledge of serious things; pure vote-catching, etc., etc." Lloyd George in 1909 had made an extremely abusive speech about the British landed nobility, whose representatives thereafter regarded him with deep aversion and distrust. Halifax knew exactly how those Republican senators felt about F.D.R., and while he appreciated that Roosevelt was trying to help Britain, he could not quite suppress a certain sympathy for men who were defending substantial property interests against the machinations of that man in the White House.

Withal, Halifax admired Churchill, agreed to step down from Foreign Secretary to Ambassador, served loyally through the war, and thereafter took his official duties seriously enough to help Keynes in 1945 negotiate the first postwar American loan to the newly elected British Labour government, of whose policies he certainly disapproved. Indeed, when the Conservatives, now in opposition, abstained in the House of Commons on the vote concerning the rather onerous terms negotiated by Keynes and Halifax, the Ambassador was shocked and angry. *Noblesse oblige.* Halifax had agreed to serve the Labour government, had done his best for them, and did not expect to see his old friends take a partisan view of the matter when an important agreement came up for approval. He was seriously put out, told Eden so in no uncertain terms, and took his time about letting himself be mollified. "I have never felt more humiliated by the Party to which I am supposed to belong," he wrote angrily to a friend. "His belief in

the party system, never robust, sank to its lowest ebb," we are
told by his biographer.

There is significance in the employment of the term, "the party
system," for it is an ancient term of abuse. What was "the party
system" to Bolingbroke, that ingenious heir of the Stuart tradition
of modified absolutism, inventor of the myth of the "patriot king"
above party? What was it to Halifax? The aristocracy had always
regarded Parliament as an instrument of *government:* a great
council of state assembling the learned and the wise, not a play-
thing of "factions" made up of ambitious politicians catering to
the follies of the mob. In this at least Churchill and Halifax
knew themselves to be at one, though Churchill had made his
peace with democracy and even learned to speak its language. In
the twilight of the British Empire, the last surviving representatives of the aristocracy—a class older than the state it had
founded and ruled—remained true to their guiding tradition.

IV

That tradition allowed for self-government (by landowners
and other men of property) and even for a measure of popular
participation, so long as the "popular" elements did not degenerate into democracy, i.e., the actual displacement of the ruling
oligarchy. Throughout the eighteenth century the oligarchy and
its followers prided themselves upon the "ancient liberties." They
were sincerely glad to have escaped the absolutism of continental
Europe: complete with standing armies and an irremovable executive. Parliament existed to check the king and enable the
oligarchy to conduct its debates in semi-private. Elections might
be farcical, but the principle of popular representation was observed.

It was only with the American and French revolutions that this
consensus was challenged—and then only by middle-class radicals outside the Establishment. The latter's liberal wing, led by
the Whig aristocracy, had no thought of abolishing the unwritten
Constitution which vested "the King in Parliament" with unlimited authority. All the Whigs asked for was a moderate enlargement of the franchise. When the issue was brought to the

test around 1800 by the radicals, with their demand for universal
suffrage, the Whigs promptly set up their own organization, the
"Friends of the People." Of this a modern British historian has
observed that the very title "illustrated the paternalist attitude."
These aristocratic critics of Pitt and his cabinet (most of which
consisted of former Whigs, now following the lead of Burke)
protested quite sincerely that they had no thought of appealing
to "the Rights of the People in their full extent"—meaning democracy in the French or American style. Their aim was "not to
change, but to restore: not to displace, but to reinstate the Constitution upon its true principles and original ground." [6]

This was familiar language—going back to 1688, but also recalling the original parliamentary revolt against Stuart absolutism
which had issued in civil war. Revolutionaries (at any rate in
Anglo-Saxon countries) commonly begin by appealing to ancient
rights. The difference is that the Whigs (they included Halifax's
ancestor Charles Grey) really meant it. The Constitution (by
which they meant the traditional pre-eminence of the aristocracy
within a "mixed" system) was genuinely sacred in their eyes.
Throughout the storms of the French Revolution, the Industrial
Revolution, nineteenth-century democratic radicalism, and the
crisis brought on by the American Civil War, the governing class
retained its hold upon the citadel of political power. Universal
suffrage, or something like it, was enacted in 1867, but the House
of Lords retained its functions until the eve of World War I,
and as late as 1894, Gladstone's successor as leader of the Liberal
Party was quite naturally a peer, Lord Rosebery. There was no
"bourgeois revolution"—a circumstance of which continental ob-
servers, from Tocqueville and Taine to Marx and Engels, were
well aware. Somehow or other, the *ancien régime* had survived,
and along with it "the habit of authority."

This state of affairs had lasting consequences. In the same way
that the great families who made up the Roman Senate viewed
the Republic as their property (they were the *res publica;* indeed
they antedated it), the aristocracy did not merely rule England:
it was conscious of having created the distinctive institutions of
the kingdom—all of them, including Parliament (originally a

6. A. P. Thornton, *The Habit of Authority: Paternalism in British History*
(London, 1966), p. 89.

feudal assembly and bearing the mark of its origin down to the present day). To that extent the popular tradition of the "Norman yoke" had a real kernel, though only a handful of democratic radicals followed Paine in treating seriously the notion of a golden age before the Conquest when the English were free and owned their land. It was, after all, a fact that for three centuries a French-speaking nobility had lorded it over a Saxon peasantry. The English state *was* founded upon conquest (and by alien intruders at that). In time these antagonisms had softened and a common culture had been created, but the authoritarian cast of mind was transmitted from French nobles to Tory squires who prided themselves upon being as English as the mutton they frequently resembled.

By the nineteenth century, literature had come to shed an amiable gloss over the harsh realities of conquest and subjugation. Walter Scott, as A. P. Thornton neatly puts it, "made an English hero of Richard Coeur-de-Lion, one of whose customary oaths was, do you take me for an Englishman?" But then Scott was the kind of urban partrician whose highest ambition it was to become a landed gentleman. What is remarkable is that, on the whole, this has remained the ideal of the English middle class. Those successful Victorian industrialists who backed Cobden and Bright in their struggle against the Corn Laws had no thought of displacing the aristocracy from the centers of power. Indeed, it is questionable whether they would have been capable of governing the state had they tried. The point is that they did not. It was enough for them that the monarchy and the aristocracy should adopt bourgeois habits and aims; this done, the middle class renounced the conquest of power and sent its sons to the public schools to be turned into "gentlemen." In the later years of the century a further refinement was added to this complex structure: the gentlemen-amateurs were sent overseas to rule over subject races. Thus the wheel came full circle: the descendants of the subjugated Saxons had now, so to speak, become Normans in their own right.

This transmogrification of the aristocracy into the ruling caste of an empire had as one of its side effects the spread of "imperial" attitudes through much of the home population, including the working class. Socialists too (notably the Fabians) were naïvely proud of "their empire." It was the zenith of the old order. It was also the nadir of critical thinking about Britain's position in the world. Those decades from 1880 to 1914 witnessed the onset of Britain's creeping paralysis in industrial technology, especially as compared with Germany. They were the true "locust years." (In later years, after 1940, this became the cant phrase wherein patriots reproached themselves for having wasted the interwar era of 1919–39; but the true decline had started earlier.)

Conservatives and radicals, needless to say, take different views of the enduring significance of these years, though the facts themselves are not in dispute. Mr. Thornton, an erudite and eloquent defender of the Tory tradition (an earlier work of his bore the title *The Imperial Idea and Its Enemies*), has no doubt that 1940 was "Britain's finest hour." The war, he thinks, helped to break down the barriers between the classes:

> Accordingly, that "living sense of the State" which Wells had singled out as an integral part of the national outlook, became more profound. The isolation of 1940–1, which to outsiders looked like the beginning of an inevitable end, was fashioned into a positive asset. At that time the British Empire . . . reached the zenith of its moral influence in the world; and Churchill, with his sense of drama, loved always to refer to "our island," as if geography itself was leagued with these few battalions that continued to fight for the right.

Mr. Thornton is aware that the imperial tradition was the last stand of the aristocracy, and sees no reason to regret it. Contrast his peroration with the cold blast coming from the direction of the New Left, that distinctively British amalgam of Tom Paine, Marx, and Sartre:

> The administration of an empire comprising a quarter of the planet required—notoriously—its own special skills. Imperialism automatically sets a premium on a patrician political style: as a pure system of alien domination, it always, within the limits of safety, seeks to *maximize the existential difference* between the ruling and ruled race, to create a magical and impassable gulf between two fixed essences. . . . Domestic domination can be realized with a "popular" and "egalitarian" appearance, alien domination never. There can by definition be no plebeian proconsuls. In an imperial

system, the iconography of power is necessarily aristocratic: it is a pure *presence*. The aristocrat is defined not by acts which denote skills, but by gestures which reveal quintessences: a specific training or aptitude would be a derogation of the impalpable essence of nobility, a finite qualification of the infinite. The famous *amateurism* of the English "upper class" has its direct source in this ideal. Traditionally contemptuous of exclusive application to "trade" or "culture," the businessman or the intellectual, the rulers of England were also—uniquely—neither professional politicians nor bureaucrats, nor militarists. They were at different times all of these, and so finally and magnificently none of them.[7]

V

If this long and complex story has a moral, what is it?

What for some time has vaguely come to be known as "the condition-of-England question" is fundamentally a problem of adaptation. As to that, there is no difference of opinion: Conservatives, Liberals, and Socialists (Fabians as well as New Leftists) have for years argued over the remedies to be offered the patient while agreeing substantially on the diagnosis. Each party, moreover, has claimed to be more up-to-date than its rivals. It was in the name of modernity that the Conservatives in 1962 adopted economic planning (copied—rather unsuccessfully—from France and Japan), while rejecting socialism as "old fashioned." Entry into the Common Market was urged by the Liberals (and some Conservatives) as a means of galvanizing a stagnant economy. Labour won two elections, in 1964 and 1966, under the Wilsonian banner of technological efficiency and rapid growth (no more than a sad memory today, alas). There is now indeed a new consensus, with the inherited empiricism turned to novel uses and neoliberalism, of a "managerial" or "technocratic" kind, the true doctrine of all three political parties. "Making British Capitalism Work" might be described as the real aim of the Wilson government, while Liberals pursue the goal of "Getting into Europe," and the younger Tories cast envious eyes at the Gaullist technocracy. The old imperial nexus appears to

7. Perry Anderson, "Origins of the Present Crisis," in Perry Anderson and Robin Blackburn, eds., *Towards Socialism* (Ithaca, N.Y., and London, 1966), pp. 32–33.

be dead; and over Rhodesia, both government and opposition—however hesitantly and ineffectively—have at least affirmed the *principle* of racial equality, and rejected the old settler attitudes which until the mid-1950s were still part of the inherited Tory creed.

Yet effective modernization appears to be as difficult under Labour as under the Tories. The Wilson government clings to great-power attitudes "East of Suez." There is still no real economic planning. Sterling remains sacrosanct. The Treasury and the Bank of England have once more got away with savage deflation, at the expense not merely of consumption (that would be no great loss), but of investment and growth. And the cultural fabric continues to offer effective resistance to change—even the "public schools" seem likely to endure.

The extraordinary strength of this blockage is frequently put down to national psychology: the British, it is said, simply dislike change. True or not (it is clearly no longer true of the young), this is inadequate when offered as an explanation of effective resistance to specific changes which in principle everyone seems to be clamoring for. What is it that makes people resent and resist alterations which are clearly in their interest, and which, moreover, they themselves acknowledge to be necessary? If the resistance is merely psychological, why does it not yield to the torrent of enlightening propaganda which for years has been poured out by the mass media? For the media are now overwhelmingly liberal, progressive, even iconoclastic. Why does it seem to make so little difference where it really matters—at the level of national policy?

In reality, the blockage is institutional, not simply psychological, although it certainly has its psychological aspect: above all the worship of "experience," which has now replaced "tradition" as the prizewinner. "Tradition" sounds aristocratic and conservative; "experience," by contrast, seems downright practical, positively Wilsonian. What is wrong with experience? Nothing—unless it is experience of the sort that has brought the country to its present plight. But *this* kind of experience has to be judged in the light of general ideas, even philosophical ideas, and the British are not too fond of that. Why bother about general notions when it seems to be so plain that the cure for all ills is greater efficiency, or some other technical specific?

Thus, in recent years the only marketable alternative to the exhausted Churchillian rhetoric has been the short-sighted pragmatism of the Wilson regime. Now that this too has failed to do the trick, there is considerable bafflement and a tendency to blame "the politicians" collectively for not having solved a perfectly simple problem. At a higher level—that of editorials and BBC Third Program talks—the Liberal Establishment pursues the tedious game of psychoanalyzing the national mind, in the hope of isolating the element of perversity which prevents Britain from being as modern and go-ahead as Germany, France, or others. And all the time there is a determined refusal to look at the subject historically, as though it were a matter of indifference that an ancient ruling class is played out and has lost its function.

Liberal and left-wing critics have for years made fun of the neo-Edwardianism so marked under the Macmillan regime: the semi-conscious revival of an aristocratic tradition, down to trivial details of dress and bearing. This collective re-enactment of the last great age of British hegemony, a kind of unconscious celebration of the past, was indeed the mark of the 1950s and it did considerable harm (not least to the Conservative Party, which as a result failed to modernize itself until it was too late). But the phenomenon has to be seen in historical perspective to permit an answer to the question: what is to take the place of the old ruling class? Plainly, the answer is: a new ruling class. But it is precisely this kind of realism which is eluded in the endless self-questioning over Britain's true role in the world: on the Right because it is too painful, on the Left because the Labour Party knows in its heart that it is not cut out to provide the country with a new integration of *all* its institutions—above all, its cultural institutions. British socialism has always been a sectional affair; it has not aimed at an all-inclusive view of society and the world. In some ways this empiricism has been its strength; today it constitutes a fatal weakness.

For the ancient governing class, whatever else may have been wrong with it, had a coherent view of the world, of history, and of its own role in society. Its long domination was moral as well as material. It did not merely defend interests: it instilled beliefs. And when put to the test, it was ready to fight and able to draw the whole country along behind it. The final proof was offered in 1940, when the businessmen and their associates—Baldwin, Chamberlain, Simon, and the rest—stepped down and made room for Churchill. For in 1940 Britain still had an empire and needed an imperial leader to defend it. Conversely, it was the congenital inability of the old ruling elite to make modern industrialism work which doomed the trio Churchill-Eden-Macmillan after the war. Churchill's death in 1965 did not close an epoch—the age of British paramountcy was already gone—but it set the seal on its passing. What has happened since then is quite simply this: no new elite has arisen to take the place of the old one. But these changes take time, and the postimperial age has yet to define its character.

From the Ruins of Empire

❊❊❊

I

AMONG THE PENALTIES of having pitched one's tent within the ruins of a collapsing empire, the agonizing spectacle of injured pride masquerading as stoicism must surely rank foremost for any naturalized inhabitant of the British Isles these days. Whether it be the bewilderment of British troops in Belfast and Derry hemmed in by rancorous Irish factions, or the sight of a Labour government helplessly contemplating the formal secession of Rhodesia's white-settler population, the nostalgic imperialist in 1969 does not have a great deal to sustain his flagging spirits. If anything gives him comfort, it is the thought of Mr. Nixon unable to concede defeat in Vietnam because it might cost him votes in 1972. But that is poor consolation. The British, having gone through a minor ordeal of this kind at the time of the Boer War, know all about the soul-searching imposed by a squalid colonial war. But they also know that their current troubles are of a different order. America can endure dishonor and defeat in Vietnam, if it must, because in the final analysis Vietnam is merely a discreditable episode. For Britain, the road came to an end years ago, and what is occurring now is a long and solemn post-mortem, with the entire nation assembled in the public gallery as more or less silent and orderly spectators.

There comes to hand, to assist me in my labors of composition, an intriguing piece of information from a book review by John Terraine in the London *Spectator*. Referring to a recently published official work by Major General S. Woodburn Kirby and

Commentary, December 1969.

others on the Japanese surrender in 1945, the reviewer notes, in the nonchalant manner typical of a now almost vanished breed, that the British briefly managed to win control of Vietnam before the Americans ever dreamed of getting bogged down there:

> It is by no means common knowledge that the Supreme Allied Commander, South-East Asia, found himself in control, in August 1945, of an area of one million square miles, containing 128 million people in varying stages of poverty, starvation and chaos— and that this area included not only the British territories of Burma, Malaya and Singapore, but also the independent kingdom of Siam, the Dutch East Indies (Indonesia) and that part of French Indochina which lay south of the 16th parallel (Vietnam).

The independent kingdom of Siam is also known as Thailand, and there are rumors to the effect that its independence is not quite what it seems. The British Commander-in-Chief in 1945 was Admiral Mountbatten, subsequently made Viceroy of India for the purpose of enabling the British to get out of that subcontinent, after partitioning it so that the Muslims might have a state of their own. I quote further from Mr. Terraine:

> In a previous volume of the Official History (*British Military Administration in the Far East* by F. S. V. Donnison) it has been stated: "Upon Admiral Mountbatten fell the perplexing task of conducting the early fateful contacts of the West with the upsurge of nationalism in South-East Asia which had been released, first, by the collapse of the European powers before the Japanese, and then by the defeat of the latter at the hands of the Allied Forces."

The British have always been good at this kind of reticent understatement, but modesty can be carried too far. The "early fateful contacts of the West" with nationalism in Southeast Asia go back a bit further than that. They reach back to the colonization of Indonesia by the Dutch in the seventeenth century, the establishment of British control over India in the eighteenth, and the nineteenth-century French attempt to carve out a rival empire in Laos, Cambodia, Annam, and Tonkin. The more recent American presence in the area falls into clearer perspective when it is related to these earlier enterprises. Yet there are important differences too. During those happily distant days "trade followed the flag," for the simple but sufficient reason that the flag had been planted there for trading purposes in the first place. No one is ever going to claim that the United States got involved in Vietnam because it wanted the area's markets. The motivation was plainly political and strategic. Yet similar assertions have long been made about the later stages of British rule in India. It is now indeed pretty generally accepted that while the British went there originally for trading purposes and to outwit French and Dutch competition, what kept them in India long after they should have packed up for their own good was fear of Russia (Tsarist Russia, that is) gobbling up the place. The fear may have been unfounded, but it was certainly real so far as the motivations of British statesmen went. By the same token it is arguable that what keeps the Americans in Vietnam is fear of China. If this is the case, it simply confirms what historians have long been saying: what counts in international affairs is the balance of power rather than simple profit-or-loss calculation. This does not alter the fact that imperialism also has an economic function. It just helps to place short-range goals within a framework that renders their seeming absurdity more comprehensible.

At the higher level of statesmanship, short-run and long-run considerations come together, which is just what distinguishes political strategy from ordinary tactical maneuvering. This is where "ideology" comes in: not as a mistress (perish the thought) but as a handmaiden. Of course we are all pragmatists now, especially those of us who have never encountered any other philosophy. But this does not alter the fact that even the most pragmatic statesman must have some general notion as to what he is trying to accomplish. The late John Kennedy, that prince of pragmatists, originally went into Vietnam (so it is said) in order to teach "the other side" that guerrilla warfare does not pay off. He may or may not have miscalculated the local balance of forces —there are conflicting views on this topic, notably among his erstwhile advisers—but the purpose of the exercise was clearly politico-military, that is to say strategic. It was an attempt to validate a set of principles which had been outlined, with a great flourish, by Professor W. W. Rostow in his profoundly unoriginal

and uninteresting essay *The Stages of Economic Growth,* subtitled *A Non-Communist Manifesto.*[1]

It was the subtitle that made Professor Rostow a hero to
his fellow liberals: chief among them the past, present, and
future editors of *The Economist,* that distinguished periodical
which is now almost alone in still championing the pure gospel
of liberal imperialism, vintage brand (circa 1897). What the
1960 edition of the gospel told its readers was that economic
"take-off" in backward countries could be artificially stimulated
by a judicious injection of foreign (mainly American) capital
and technology, plus local nationalism, which was there anyhow and only in need of a bit of encouragement. This was the
rationale of the Alliance for Progress, a public-relations exercise whose ludicrous failure has by now become so patent that
its propagandists have fallen silent about it. But it was also the
rationale of American involvement in Vietnam, just as it underpinned the CIA's prolonged and tender interest in that great
"socialist" Colonel Nasser, whose warlike ambitions were tactfully overlooked by his American advisers and paymasters in the
interest of global strategy (the fact that he ratted on them, just
as he is now trying to rat on his Russian backers, is irrelevant in
this context).

In all three cases the underlying assumptions had been spelled
out by Rostow & Co. before they were put into practice by the
Kennedy brothers and their courtiers. And even now, when
doubt has crept in among the Washington policy-makers, the
really consistent ideologists have not given up hope that their
aims can be validated in the long run. Thus *The Economist* on
October 11, 1969:

> The most telling argument used by those who oppose the war—
> if one leaves out the people who would actually welcome a Com-
> munist government in Saigon—is that this is just a sweaty tussle
> between two more or less equally unsatisfactory lots of Vietnamese
> politicians, and that the difference between them is not worth the
> bloodshed it has led to. Even if one accepted this argument, it
> would need to be said that by the test of the amount of personal
> liberty it allows, and probably by the test of economic efficiency

1. New York, 1960.

too, the regime in Saigon is one or two notches less unsatisfactory than the one in Hanoi. But the point is that this is not what the war has been fought for. This is not merely a quarrel about which of two presidents, or which of two cabinets, will be running South Vietnam five or ten years from now. It is a contest between two wholly different systems of government. The outcome will decide South Vietnam's prospects of developing something like a democratic system of politics, and something like a freely expanding economy, over the next half-century and more; and not only the prospects of South Vietnam, but also those of a lot of the other countries of south-east Asia behind it.

There you have it, black on white. And just so that the point shall not be missed, the argument is elevated to a higher moral level: "Between the two systems that are contending for the future of south-east Asia, the marxist one and the pluralist one, there is on present evidence little doubt which has more to offer."

Were this a seminar in political science, the author of the remark just cited would have his essay marked "C minus" and be required to read a few basic Leninist and Maoist texts before venturing to describe as "marxist" what is plainly old-fashioned populism dressed up in socialist clothing.[2] But there is no sense in getting angry with a harried editorialist who is only repeating what he learned from the pioneers of the New Frontier eight or ten years ago. Besides, for every piece of liberal nonsense about "Marxist" political systems (why not "Thomist" or "Calvinist" ones too, so long as we are going to misuse Max Weber's sociological categories?) there is a populist or Maoist equivalent. There are some distinguished American critics of the Vietnam war—for the sake of their achievements in other fields they shall be nameless—who share Rostow's preposterous ideas about the nature of the cold war, except that their own political preferences differ from his. The common factor in either case is the belief that the outcome of the Vietnamese struggle will determine the fate of Southeast Asia, and that two radically different "systems" are at grips in the fields and jungles of that tortured country.

It is odd and perhaps significant that no one in France, from

2. See Hélène Carrère d'Encausse and Stuart R. Schram, *Marxism and Asia* (London, 1969)—a scholarly and reliable selection of texts on the subject, with a very useful joint introduction by the two learned editors.

de Gaulle to the Communists, seems to share these notions, but then the French have some painfully acquired knowledge of the area. There was a time, around 1946, when they thought they could ride back to power by using the Catholics and the Buddhists to pull their chariot, but ever since the costly failure of that enterprise they have taken a suitably detached view of the region and its problems. So far as they are concerned, it matters not a whit whether Hanoi gets control of the entire country, for as they see it the real issue in Southeast Asia will always be the desire to avoid Chinese overlordship. As for Saigon being "pluralist" as against the—admittedly very real—totalitarianism of Hanoi, it takes more than a few editorials to make the French, a notoriously skeptical breed, believe in such fairy tales.

Nor, for that matter, does an intellectual Tory like Enoch Powell take much stock in liberal imperialism. He knows the imperial age is over, for Britain anyway, and has given vent to some disabused reflections on the topic which fit in with his generally pessimistic view of the world. One needs to be a liberal to get really worked up about the beauties of the "freely expanding economy" and the wonders it is going to perform for Vietnam, Indonesia, the Philippines, and the rest. Conservative pessimism, if it does nothing else, at least safeguards one from the disappointments that lie in wait for the worshiper of "economic growth." It was the liberals who got America into Vietnam. It was the conservatives—if there are any left—who will have to get her out.

II

I began by saying that there is something melancholy about the introspective character of so much British writing at the present time. The sadness is not lessened—for the authors and their public—by the reflection that the imperial burden was shed gracefully: at any rate in India, which was the centerpiece of the whole global arrangement known in its heyday as the British Empire. Enoch Powell, in the hearing of the present writer, once remarked that the consciousness of the British ruling class (those were the words he used) had been shaped for two centuries by the Anglo-Indian connection. Mr. Powell was him-

self involved with Indian affairs as a staff officer during World
War II, and if he ever finds time from more pressing engagements
he might let the rest of us know what he thinks of the 1947 settlement imposed by Lord Louis Mountbatten in his capacity as
Viceroy, acting on behalf of a Labour government which had
granted him unprecedented plenipotentiary powers—that is to
say, the right to make major decisions on the spot without referring back to Whitehall.

This elegant aristocrat, who in 1945 made a point of telling
everyone he was going to vote Socialist ("it's the kitchen staff
who are Tory—the working classes are altogether a hopeless
lot"), was admirably fitted for his proconsular role. He got on
well with those two detribalized intellectuals, Nehru and Jinnah,
who wanted to drag their respective communities into the modern age of nationalism and away from obsession with religion.
He did not get on quite so well with Gandhi, the Mahatma of
the Indian peasantry, who opposed Partition, while Jinnah insisted on it and Nehru acquiesced. In the end, the Muslims got
what they wanted (they usually do, from whatever British government happens to be in office): India and Pakistan were established as separate states, after a ghastly communal slaughter
which may have cost a million lives and which drove tens of
millions from their homes. Hindus and Muslims butchered each
other in the name of religion, as they had been doing for centuries and still do. The topic is passed over rather briefly in H. V.
Hodson's recent work on the subject, *The Great Divide: Britain-
India-Pakistan*,[3] but then Mr. Hodson is an admirer of Mountbatten. Michael Edwardes, reviewing the book in *The Times* of
September 13, 1969, struck a caustic note:

> The end of an empire almost always takes place in blood—usually
> that of the imperialists. The distinction of the British was to lose
> their empire in that of their erstwhile subjects. From the British
> point of view it was a major achievement. . . . It is easy to accept
> that Lord Mountbatten's brief was simple and straightforward—
> for heaven's sake, get us out of India with the least harm to our-
> selves. Lord Mountbatten succeeded in doing what his political
> masters required, with aplomb and the appearance of dignity. I

3. London, 1969.

do not think anyone could have done better, and most would
have done worse. . . .

Mr. Edwardes, who was in India at the time and knows the
country well, then goes on to quote from the report of the first
Governor-General of the independent Dominion (now Republic)
of India, to King George VI, dated November 25, 1948, a year
after the great massacres in the Punjab which accompanied the
setting up of two independent states on the ruins of the old
Indian Empire:

> It had been obvious to anybody that there were going to be dis-
> turbances in the Punjab on the transfer of power. But I freely
> confess that I did not anticipate the scale and extent of what was
> going to happen, nor, so far as I am aware, did anyone in author-
> ity in India, Pakistan, and the United Kingdom anticipate this.

Who wrote these lines? Why, none other than Mountbatten,
transmogrified from Viceroy into Governor-General, and still on
excellent terms with Nehru, though by now somewhat less popular with the leaders of newly independent Pakistan, who felt let
down because the Labour government was a shade less pro-
Muslim than British governments normally tend to be. In 1969
Mr. Hodson, in his quasi-authoritative account of the matter, still
takes the Establishment view that Lord Mountbatten did the
right thing when he precipitated the partition of India, in the
teeth of mounting evidence that the country would explode into
communal massacres. His sources are mostly British. Mr. Edwardes' own book on the subject, *The Last Years of British India*,[4]
was based upon the testimony of Indian and Pakistani witnesses,
"the most important of whom were dead by the time Mr. Hodson
took up his task," as he sourly notes in his review. He does not
say how many of them perished in the slaughter.

It is remarkable how stoical Europeans have usually been when
confronted with happenings of this sort—in Asia. A single British
soldier shot dead in Belfast during communal rioting between
Irish Catholics and Protestants gets banner headlines in the
papers. The great Indian disaster of 1947 has barely entered the
public consciousness. Distance, and a sense of helplessness, presumably account nowadays for this seeming indifference, just

4. London, 1963; Cleveland, 1964.

as they account for the relative calm that greets the news from Nigeria. What can one do about it, and who cares about dead African babies anyway? Certainly not the New Left: its leaders have not uttered a sound on the subject. But then there is no political mileage to be got out of a conflict which opposes Africans (with some foreign backing) to each other. As for morality, we all know by now what the *Realpolitiker* of the New Left (not to mention the Old Right) think of such sickly bourgeois sentiments.

But back to our theme. Mr. Edwardes and Mr. Hodson are joined by David Dilks in a fairly conventional biography of a fairly conventional British Viceroy: *Curzon in India* [5] deals with a bygone age of imperial splendor. It describes Curzon's septennial term, the high point of which was a squabble with Whitehall in 1901 over who was to pay for the expense of having India represented at the coronation of Edward VII in London. Curzon protested that the country had recently suffered a famine, and won his point. His other worries had to do with possible Tsarist Russian encroachments, and with the appearance on the political scene of a new kind of animal, the Bengali lawyer, decked out in European clothing and clutching a copy of J. S. Mill. His intervention made things very awkward. Curzon knew how to deal with the wild tribesmen of the Northwest ("brave as lions, wild as cats, docile as children"), but the Bengali politicians bored and irritated him. "I am an Imperialist, and Imperialism is fatal to all their hopes. I hold the scales with exasperatingly even hand, but this is the last thing they desire. . . . [It] deprives them of their most fertile source of grumbling."

Curzon was convinced that the Empire would last, if not for ever, then at least for centuries. It would do so, he thought, because the stout peasantry would always prefer the fair-minded British official to the wily Bengali. Not to mention the hill tribesmen: "magnificent Samsons, gigantic, bearded, instinct with loyalty, often stained with crime"; mostly Muslims too and thus doubly contemptuous of town-bred Hindu politicians. A reviewer in the *Times Literary Supplement* struck a suitably disillusioned note: "This sentimental polarization of noble savage and degenerate townee, subsequently to receive classic expression

5. 2 vols. London, 1969–70; New York, 1970.

from T. E. Lawrence, became one of the major weaknesses of what passed for the British ideology of imperialism, and a source of countless political mistakes."

Yes indeed, but the official ideology had two sides to it. In addition to the romantic Toryism of Kipling, Lawrence, and sundry worshipers of mounted and bedaggered tribesmen, there was the bleak utilitarianism of Joseph Chamberlain and the Webbs. Chamberlain, the chief begetter of the Boer War and a charismatic figure to many Tories, in 1903 made a resolute but tactically ill-judged attempt to transmute the Empire into a fiscal *Zollverein,* or customs union, on the Bismarckian model. At the same time, the Webbs turned the London School of Economics, which they controlled, into a nursery of the imperialist faith, preached *inter alia* by geopoliticians like Mackinder, whose wisdom was later transmitted to Britain's chief competitors by Mackinder's German pupils.

Needless to say, the British school was more civilized than the German, as anyone can discover by consulting the recently published first volume of Professor Max Beloff's definitive study on the subject: *Imperial Sunset,* subtitled *Britain's Liberal Empire 1897–1921.*[6] Himself a representative of the once-great liberal tradition, Professor Beloff writes with some nostalgia of an age when statesmen, civil servants, scholars, and journalists saw the self-governing white-settler dominions (Canada, Australia, New Zealand, South Africa) as constitutional training schools for the remainder. Unlike the romantic Tories, he has no illusions as to the evanescent nature of an imperial structure held together very largely by make-believe. Unlike the Chamberlainites, he does not think an imperial customs union could have worked. On this topic the Tory-imperialist standpoint has now been restated by Julian Amery in the concluding two volumes of a gigantic six-volume political biography of Joseph Chamberlain in progress since 1915, when it was first projected by the late J. L. Garvin.[7]

One may reasonably doubt whether Chamberlain—Beatrice

6. London, 1969; New York, 1970.
7. *The Life of Joseph Chamberlain,* vols. 5 and 6, *Joseph Chamberlain and the Tariff Reform Compaign* (London, 1968).

Potter's idol long before she married the dutiful Colonial Office clerk Sidney Webb—is really worth all this attention, but he did have a coherent view of the world: a rare thing in British politics during a century when "muddling through" was elevated into doctrine. Moreover, the imperial creed had some support from intellectuals—Carlyle, Matthew Arnold, Benjamin Jowett, and Karl Pearson among them. Not all its adherents were as repulsive as the loathsome Carlyle, whose racist tract *The Nigger Question* (1849) terminated his friendship with John Stuart Mill. The episode is not without significance. There *were* some liberal imperialists in Victorian Britain—Gladstone was merely the most celebrated—but by 1903, when Joseph Chamberlain launched his campaign, the liberal intellectuals had begun to turn away from the Empire. Its defense was left to Carlyle's spiritual heirs, Kipling among them. Even so, tariff reform gained some working-class support, and the social-imperialist creed already formulated by J. R. Seeley, the historian, had its effect on Fabians such as the Webbs and their circle. When the private discussion club they had founded split apart over the issue of protection versus free trade, Hewins—their nominee as director of the London School of Economics—resigned his post to become Chamberlain's chief propagandist. Mackinder, who succeeded him (once more thanks to the Webbs), shortly thereafter abandoned free trade, thereby complicating Beatrice Webb's intrigues with the Liberal leaders. The Liberals were loyal to the Empire, but unwilling to ditch free trade in favor of protection. Their electoral triumph in 1906 sounded the knell of tariff reform. Or rather, it delayed its acceptance until 1932, by which time World War I had wrecked the Liberal party of Asquith and Lloyd George beyond repair. The remaining liberal imperialists—including Churchill—had reluctantly joined the Tories, and in 1932–33 they hesitantly revived Joseph Chamberlain's old recipes of 1903. But by then it was too late—Japan was on the march, and so was Hitler.

Indian nationalism, too, could no longer be restrained, and its leaders had lost all interest in the preservation of the British Empire. Offered a measure of home rule by the Churchill government in 1942, when the Japanese were at the gates, Gandhi declined what he described as "a postdated check on a bank that is obviously failing." The bank did not actually fail in 1942, but went into liquidation five years later, when the Attlee government sent Mountbatten to India to wind up its affairs. Which is where we came in, for the partition of 1947 was the consequence of a war in which the Indian army, for the second time in a generation, had defended the Empire against Britain's enemies. That same army was now about to split along national and religious lines, the coming confrontation between India and Pakistan already taking shape in the massacres that spelled the end of Gandhi's vision of a peaceful and united India.

III

Is there a moral in all this? It is hard to say. During the nineteenth century the only alternative to the British Empire in India was a return to primitivism or the Russian Empire, and the Tories were not alone in holding that either would be a disaster: Marx took the same view. However abominable British rule in India might be (he told the readers of the New York *Tribune* in 1853), it was at least preferable to the continuation of Oriental despotism. The Indian liberal nationalists of the following generation reasoned along similar lines. The trouble was that even the most moderate among them failed to make an impression upon British officialdom until it was too late for anything but the hurried surgical operation of 1947. By then few even among the Tories were willing to join Winston Churchill in a last-ditch stand against liquidating the Indian Empire.

The Attlee government of 1945–51 for its part simply carried on where the Liberals had left off. It did not repudiate imperialism as such. Rather it proclaimed that India had become ripe for self-government. This was the Gladstonian or liberal-imperialist faith in a nutshell. It had nothing whatever to do with socialism, popular notions to the contrary notwithstanding. Like the Fabian tradition in general, it was rooted in Bentham and Mill. But at least Mill was preferable to Carlyle with his savage contempt for colored races. Liberalism in this sense made possible a transition that did *not* commit the British to a disastrous attempt to hold down Indian nationalism by force: the sort of thing Germany and Japan committed themselves to in the 1930s. There are different imperialisms, even if they all suffer from the same basic taint.

The historical background is sketched in, with admirable clarity and precision, by that wittiest of contemporary British historians, V. G. Kiernan. *The Lords of Human Kind: European Attitudes Towards the Outside World in the Imperial Age* [8] is full of shrewd observations on the British Empire and its passing. It also has the merit of being composed in a graceful style and bearing its load of learning with an appearance of effortless ease:

> During the first millennium B.C. three new civilizations were taking shape, which among them came to rule or influence most of Asia, and which through many changes have lived on to our own day— the Persian, Indian and Chinese. They borrowed from the older ones; they differed from them first of all in their far greater size and comparative remoteness from each other, which allowed each to feel itself, like every human being, the hub and center of all things. Greece, the first "Europe," was also appearing, scattered in small units from Asia Minor to the western Mediterranean— a distance about as great as from India's north to south tip. It floated on the sea, the others belonged to dry land. The permanence of these four, with least continuity in Europe and most in China, has been as striking as the failure since then of any radically new civilization to grow up, except in Central and South America and, by synthesis of older and new elements, in the Islamic world.

Anyone capable of carrying on in this fashion for over three hundred pages deserves public commendation. Mr. Kiernan conceals a mass of solid erudition behind a style modeled on Lytton Strachey. For good measure he is an undoctrinaire socialist. The combination of such rare gifts presumably accounts for his failure to climb the higher rungs of the academic establishment. The British have shed much of their Victorian solemnity, but it is still not considered quite proper for a scholar to display stylistic grace. Consider the following passage:

> Schopenhauer refuted pantheism by pointing out the absurdity of any God transforming himself into a world where on an average day six million slaves received sixty million blows. In the history of Negro slavery the extraordinary thing is the ability of the race to

8. London and Boston, 1969.

survive, though myriads of individuals perished; it lacked the faculty which Chinese exiles owed to a more complex social evolution of mastering a new environment and rising in it. It was the endurance of the African, where other enslaved races sank under the white man's burden, that made him so profitable; while his weakness in collective organization in his own land made him an easy prey. It warped his masters, Arab or Turk, Spaniard or Englishman, as much as it degraded him; it conditioned Western Europe to think of all "native" peoples as destined bondsmen.

I suspect promotion will be slow to come Mr. Kiernan's way. He knows too much, he writes too well, and he treads on too many toes. The dullards and the embattled political fanatics (of all colors) will see to it that he is kept out. Meantime the public should read his books. He writes as well as A. J. P. Taylor and is more trustworthy as a source of information.

This question of tone is not to be dismissed lightly. In the heyday of British imperialism, between 1870 and 1914, its spokesmen affected a grave and learned manner, to the point of misquoting Hegel and other German philosophers. Their opponents frequently did the same. When in 1915 the first German bombs fell on London (from a Zeppelin—there were as yet no rockets), Professor L. T. Hobhouse judged the time ripe to rend the Hegelians. Bosanquet's *Philosophical Theory of the State,* he told his hearers, had helped to spread pernicious Germanic notions, and the bombs now falling on their heads were but "the visible and tangible outcome of a false and wicked doctrine . . . the Hegelian theory of the God-state." Thirty years later Professor Karl Popper (with less excuse, since he was in New Zealand at the time, and no bombs were dropping on him) revived this piece of nonsense. But where did Hobhouse proclaim his message to the world? Why, at the London School of Economics, where imperialism (Conservative, Liberal, or Fabian) never lacked defenders! It is true that the Webbs and their circle were Benthamites, not Hegelians. It is no less true that they supplied the Establishment with an authoritarian doctrine suitably adapted to the age of imperialism.

With more old-fashioned Tories, who had mostly been brought up on Anglicanism, the Empire in some cases represented a transference of religious emotions to a secular object of worship. Imperial proconsuls occasionally felt in need of a Higher Power to sustain them in their labors. Lower down the social scale a kind of cynicism crept in after 1919 which foreshadowed the subsequent collapse into fascist nihilism. The classic case of course is T. E. Lawrence: "Lawrence of Arabia" to his admirers, "Lawrence the impostor" to readers of Richard Aldington's deadly biography, first published in 1955. Impostor or not, Lawrence already possessed some elements of a political outlook which became fairly common in the age of Stalin, Hitler, and Mussolini. This can be seen from the latest and most long-winded of the many books about him, *The Secret Lives of Lawrence of Arabia* by Phillip Knightley and Colin Simpson.[9] While most reviewers, like the authors, fastened on his sexual aberrations, this one was struck by a passage in Lawrence's correspondence which casts light on the imperialist mentality in its pre-fascist, but already distinctly smelly stage. He was outlining his plans in September 1919, at a time when he was busy intriguing simultaneously with the Arab nationalists and the Zionists to push the French out of Syria, and this is what he had to say in a confidential note to a close collaborator:

> The French will be on their best behaviour for months, and give Feisal his money unconditionally. Then they will try to turn the screw. He'll say he doesn't want their money, because by then the Zionists will have a centre in Jerusalem, and for concessions they will finance him (this is all in writing, and fixed, but don't put it in the Press for God's sake and the French). Zionists are not a Government, and not British, and their action does not infringe the Sykes-Picot agreement. They are also Semites and Palestinian, and the Arab Government is not afraid of them (can cut all their throats, or better, pull all their teeth out, when it wishes). They will finance the whole East, I hope, Syria and Mesopotamia alike. High Jews are unwilling to put much cash into Palestine only, since that country offers nothing but a sentimental return. They want 6 per cent.

The vulgarity of the style matches the contents of a mind seemingly destined for a career among Mosley's Blackshirts had Lawrence not been killed in a road accident in 1935. His latest

9. London, 1969; New York, 1970.

biographers are duly shocked because it turns out that he never had any use for the Arabs either: all he wanted was to turn the Middle East into another British protectorate. But who, except for his foolish admirers, ever doubted this? Of course Lawrence was a fraud. What else could a man be whose professional life was spent in betraying people to each other, intriguing behind the scenes, and posturing as the hero of a "desert rebellion" which never occurred anywhere but in the fevered imagination of some newspaper readers? It may be said with certainty that neither the Arabs nor the Jews were taken in by him: he was too clearly a poseur. But there is a not wholly trivial point to be made about Lawrence's language. That business about the Jews having "all their teeth pulled out" (even better than having their throats slit)—where did he get it from? I was puzzled for an answer until I came upon a passage in John Gross's recently published *The Rise and Fall of the Man of Letters* [10] recording Carlyle's opinion of the Jews:

> One of the less attractive medieval customs recorded, with a grim satisfaction, in *Past and Present* was the habit of extorting money from Jews by pulling out their teeth; and a vivid passage in Froude's biography describes Carlyle standing on the edge of Hyde Park, gazing at the Rothschild mansion and miming the same operation with an imaginary pair of pincers.

From *Past and Present* (1843) to *The Nigger Question* (1849) was no great jump for Carlyle. It would have been no great jump for Lawrence either. When all is said and done, the rise and fall of the imperialist ideology has a certain consistency about it.

10. London and New York, 1969.

Shaw, the Webbs, and the Labour Party

❊ ❊ ❊

I

Lloyd George announces his intention of going to Russia in the recess and will come back as a qualified admirer of the Soviet Republic. Austen Chamberlain, to whose lifeless voice and pompous intonation we listened over the wireless the other night, is booming Mussolini as the saviour of Italy and the originator of a "great and successful experiment" in social reorganization. We regard Soviet Russia and Fascist Italy as belonging to one and the same species of Government; the creed-autocracy insisting on the supremacy of one social philosophy bringing unity to the people over all conflicting creeds and sectional interests. Russian Communism and Italian Fascism are both alike a reaction from caste or syndicalist anarchy.

Beatrice Webb's *Diaries* [1] for 1924–32 would be worth reading if they illuminated nothing but their author's sudden conversion to one particular brand of totalitarian "creed-autocracy." The book is, of course, far more than a record of personal disillusionment with the Labour Party and with "gradualism." It is a huge quarry that historians will continue to mine for years to come. Mrs. Cole has pruned the manuscript text, but enough is left to furnish the raw material for some pretty searching studies of what happened to the British labor movement in the years of MacDonald's two minority governments, the General Strike of 1926 (here represented as a ludicrous fiasco), and the great economic slump. And

The Twentieth Century, June 1956.
1. Edited and with an introduction by Margaret Cole (London, 1956).

when those studies are written they will show that Labor's growth to political maturity, whose slowness so exasperated Mrs. Webb, followed a curious rhythm of alternate upward and downward swings, as though every advance had to be paid for by some colossal blunder and the consequent discrediting of another batch of leaders—until the diarist could stand it no longer and at the age of seventy-three departed for a voyage of discovery to Russia. But although the reader of this fascinating volume is taken behind the scenes, they are not precisely the scenes of the working-class movement; here, one feels, is one section of the London political world reacting to processes beyond its control. When Mrs. Webb comments on the General Strike, she is detached, aloof, almost an outsider: "If it had not been for a few ambitious spirits like Bevin, egged on by middle-class theorists, there would never have been a General Council endowed with power to call out the whole movement." There is a pleasant period flavor about an account of the 1926 conflict in which Ernest Bevin figures as a dangerous radical and Winston Churchill as a determined enemy of the working class. The General Council of the Trades Union Congress, alas, was inefficient—and that, in Mrs. Webb's eyes, was really the worst aspect of the whole silly business. Failure she could forgive, ineffectiveness never.

> The Government has gained immense prestige in the world, and the British Labour Movement has made itself ridiculous. A strike which opens with a football match between the police and the strikers, and ends in unconditional surrender after nine days, with densely packed reconciliation services at all the chapels and churches of Great Britain attended by the strikers and their families, will make the continental Socialists blaspheme.

True, this bloodless outcome showed that the country, unlike much of Europe, was eminently sane. But

> We are all just good-natured stupid folk. The worst of it is that the governing class are just as good natured and stupid as the Labour Movement! Are we decadent or is this growing alarm over the future only a reflection of my old age? I have lost my daydreams, I have only the nightmare left—the same sort of nightmare I had during the Great War—that European civilization is in the

course of dissolution. Sidney scoffs at my fears, "And even if Europe fails," says he, "there is always the USA—a selfconfident and overwhelmingly prosperous race. The USA may not be to one's liking, but it is clear she is not going to develop *our* social disease —her will to wealth and power is not going to be paralysed by social conflict and social disorder!

A surprising solution for a very Fabian set of worries; but in the end the U.S.S.R. proved more attractive.

II

For an understanding of what Fabianism has meant one must, however, go back to Mrs. Webb's earlier writings. And here the point to bear in mind is that it took her a long time to abandon "permeation" of the ruling class in favor of Labour politics. On the whole, Labour's development has borne out the Fabian expectation that the movement would gradually acquire a socialist character by the simple process of trying to find its way in the political world. Yet at the start this outcome appeared far from probable to the majority of its own leaders. Confidence in the inherently socialist nature of the new party was certainly not widespread; it was emphatically not shared by the Webbs, as their biographer has recently recalled with some emphasis:

> Permeation of the older political parties together had in fact failed as a policy by the end of 1905. Unless the new Liberal Government could be diverted into Socialism, which in view of its thumping majority and the inclusion in its ranks of politicians like Asquith and Winston Churchill was highly unlikely, the only future for the Socialists lay in the little new Labour Party with its membership of 30, mostly elected by agreement with the Liberals. But in 1906–14 the Labour Party was not Socialist—though it included Socialists—had no defined policy and no individual membership. It did not look at all capable of becoming the government of the country within measurable time, and though the Fabian Society had taken part in its foundation and was officially part of it, the leaders believed it to be of barely marginal usefulness, and some of the rank-and-file, particularly ardent Socialists who joined the Society during the Radical boom, came, under syndicalist influences, to regard it as an actual drag on working-class progress.[2]

2. Margaret Cole, *Beatrice and Sidney Webb* (London, 1955).

It seems noteworthy that during this early period the Webbs saw the main obstacle to the adoption of socialist measures by a Liberal government in parliamentary factors and in the personal attitude of Asquith and Churchill—surely a remarkable tribute to their faith in permeation. But then permeation had, of course, gone pretty far during the preceding decade, although we learn from Mrs. Cole that it had also run into obstacles. Generally speaking,

> the Fabian idea was if possible to convert future Ministers and persons in key positions to Fabianism, or, as that would not be possible in most cases, to station Fabian advisers at their elbows, and to persuade parties, groups, committees, councils or what not, to endorse pieces of a Socialist programme as it were unawares. For these purposes it did not matter in theory whether the persons or groups to be "permeated" were Tories, Liberals (or Anarchists!); the Fabians were ready to try their hand on anyone, and in fact the nineteenth century history of British social development gave some colour to the view that, for bringing about separate pieces of social change, one major Party was about as hopeful as another.[3]

Still, the principal efforts were for some time concentrated on the Liberal Party, if only because the politically conscious workers generally supported it. But by the 1890s Liberalism had proved a broken reed. "Its zeal for reform seemed to have waned or vanished." Chamberlain had deserted to the Tories, and Liberals like Rosebery were toying with imperialism. "Though the Fabians and the Radicals had by clever tactics forced upon the Party's 1891 conference a policy of advanced social reform . . . they did not believe that the existing leadership would carry it out." Neither, it may be added, did Keir Hardie and the other leaders of the International Labour Party (to say nothing of the Social Democrats under the "Marxist" Hyndman), who were then beginning to make an impression upon the Liberals' working-class following. It is evident in retrospect that the 1890s were a turning point, in that they marked the moment when the Socialist sects for the first time made genuine contact with those lower-echelon trade-union organizers who had hitherto been active on the Radical wing of the Liberal movement. It was then that the decline of Liberalism began, although the Liberal Party was still able to

3. Ibid., p. 19.

win elections. The whole process was subterranean and took time
to work itself out. Since even now many of its aspects are
shrouded in obscurity, it is not surprising that the contemporaries
hardly noticed what was happening. The Webbs were indeed
aware that the Liberal Party had lost its impetus, but their immediate reaction was to look for recruits among the Tories! Mrs.
Cole is illuminating on this point:

> It seemed to some of the Fabians that there was much to be gained
> by bringing together in discussion Liberals of their way of thought
> and intelligent Tories who could be awakened to the inevitability
> of *some* social change, particularly if there could be added to the
> discussion civil servants and administrators already inoculated
> with Fabian ideas.
>
> In this way was "permeation" born; on the Liberal side its
> chief participants were Haldane and Edward Grey—and to a less
> extent Asquith; among the Tories the chief prize was Arthur Bal-
> four, Prime Minister from 1902 to 1905, a philosopher-politician
> who always had great charm for Beatrice; and a good deal of the
> discussion took place at dinner parties in 41 Grosvenor Road—so
> convenient for the House of Commons. Beatrice was still not then
> a politician in her own right; she was a politician's lady running a
> *salon*. But her personality was beginning to take on more and more
> importance in the political world; Grosvenor Road was beginning
> to be a place which counted; and her *Diaries* show how much
> she enjoyed those evenings and lunches of discussion and high-
> principled semi-intrigue over the future of the London County
> Council, the London School of Economics, the party system, the
> Balfour Education Bill, and so forth—enjoyed them all the more, as
> she candidly pointed out, because the standard of living, of dress,
> and of general conversation was more like "what she was brought
> up to" than that of Trade Unionists and their wives at Co-operative
> teas.

With the Condorcets and Turgots of Britain's future bloodless
revolution thus on the threshold of power, the ruling oligarchy—
if not the provincial middle class, which for some time still preserved its faith in the established order of things—concurrently
offered a more appreciative audience for writers like Shaw. If
in a general way it can be said that the oligarchical character of
British political life before 1914 was the secret of Fabian "permeation" (in what other country could those dinner parties at

41 Grosvenor Road have taken on genuine political importance?),
there is a special sense in which the Shavian influence belongs
to the picture of a society where power radiated outward from a
small and highly concentrated circle in the metropolis. The frequently heard comparison with the *ancien régime* is not altogether devoid of sense, especially if one bears in mind that
down to 1914 effective control—for all the Lords' loss of power in
1911—was still vested in the very topmost layer of the old ruling
class. This made for an ambience quite different from the ferocious intolerance characteristic of a ruling class recently arrived
in power. The society which the Webbs were busy evangelizing
was one in which the governing elite was beginning to feel uneasy (hence the Grosvenor Road dinners), but it was also one in
which a group of reformers like the Fabians could exercise influence by becoming the intermediaries between the new social
forces and the more intelligent representatives of the old order.
Aristocratic liberalism was the counterpart of Fabian socialism;
a situation not altogether dissimilar from that which enabled the
physiocrats to play their part in the general decomposition of the
old regime in France. Of course, as we all know, there has
been a happy ending instead of a catastrophe; but this important
difference belongs to the pathology of the body politic. In principle the role of the Fabians before 1914 was not so very different
from that of the physiocrats and their allies. It is true that no
attempt was made to provide anything like an encyclopedia of
the new *Weltanschauung*, although the London School of Economics did for a while become the source of a distinctive manner
of dealing with social problems. Indeed, sociology itself may be
said to have been in part an outcome of the silent revolution:
if the Fabians did not exactly invent it, they were at any rate
among the first to perceive its relevance to subjects which had
hitherto been treated in a hit-or-miss fashion; and it was this
that gave them access to the higher ranks of the civil service,
long before they had converted a single political leader of standing.

It is relevant to note that no major deception was practiced
by the Fabians upon those whom they sought to convert, for it
was part of their creed that socialization is a slow process which
tends to transform the attitudes of *all* classes of society. On this

point they differed, if not from Marx, at any rate from his doctrinaire British followers, and they certainly made the most of their tactical differences with Hyndman. But their interlocutors were never left in doubt that behind their detailed reform proposals there lurked a more comprehensive scheme for reorganizing the body politic. It was precisely their achievement before 1914 that the gradual and piecemeal assimilation of socialist, or at any rate, post-liberal, thought came to be regarded by the leaders of the traditional parties as a means of avoiding wholesale socialization on the threatened continental model. In this respect a Tory like Balfour was if anything a step ahead of a Gladstonian like Asquith or a Radical like Lloyd George. There was of course a limit to all this, and it is obvious that the Webbs were slow to recognize it. But it is at least arguable that before 1914 they had no choice; Labour was neither strong enough nor socialist enough to present itself as an alternative to "permeation." That at any rate was their belief, although it was plainly not shared by some of their younger followers.

<h3 style="text-align:center">III</h3>

In a society so delicately poised between oligarchy and democracy, a writer like Shaw could manage to keep a foothold in the fashionable world, without ceasing to be an active Socialist. He has often been called the Voltaire of the bloodless revolution; in some ways he was perhaps closer to being its Beaumarchais. Certainly he lacked Voltaire's hardheadedness. There is a streak of absurdity in Shaw's political pronouncements which becomes overwhelming as time goes on, but is already noticeable in his earliest writings. Although remarkably well-read in economics, he was never hampered by an exact understanding of how things work in the political world, or indeed by an urgent desire to find out. That was the job of dull fellows like Sidney Webb. His own carefree flings at the established order have just that quality of irresponsibility which one does *not* encounter in Voltaire, who for all his egotism possessed a good deal of shrewd political sense. One cannot read Shaw without becoming aware how much it meant to him that he never had to face anything more perilous than an unfavorable review. Things were not as easy as that in

eighteenth-century France, not even for a privileged critic like
Voltaire—who after all lived in the shadow of the Bastille long
enough to turn himself into a voluntary exile. If an expression of
personal preference is permitted, I would say that Shaw seems to
me to be the greater writer: his best dramatic work (including
Heartbreak House rather than the overpraised *Saint Joan*) will
surely outlive his and our epoch, whereas Voltaire's plays were
unreadable and unactable even when they were being penned.
Shaw's pamphleteering is another matter. It has been praised by
countless critics, and even an orthodox Communist like Maurice
Dobb, who deplores his attachment to Jevonian economics, has
a good word to say for his brilliance as a controversialist. Personally I am more impressed by his gift for ridicule than by his
analytical powers. To say, e.g., that "the interest on railway stock
is paid mostly to people who could not invent a wheelbarrow,
much less a locomotive" may be an adequate way of dealing with
a writer like Mallock, but it does not tell us how public property
is to be organized. Again, Mallock may have "confused the pro-
prietary classes with the productive classes, the holders of ability
with the holders of land and capital, the man about town with
the man of affairs." Did not Shaw confuse epigram with analysis?
Who or what are "the productive classes"? Is everyone except the
idle rich to be made welcome in the socialist commonwealth? In
that case what becomes of the claim that socialism will give the
"associated producers" control over the means of production? If
Shaw foresaw some of the difficulties inherent in the latter concept, he did not bother about them, unless one chooses to regard
his subsequent penchant for totalitarian regimes as a belated
recognition that the new society would have to embody a new
governing hierarchy to take the place of the old one.

The characteristic flavor of Shavian political thinking is already evident in so early a product as Tract No. 2, *A Manifesto:*

> The Fabians are associated for spreading the following opinions
> held by them and discussing their practical consequences:
>   That under existing conditions wealth cannot be enjoyed with-
> out dishonour or foregone without misery. . . .
>   That a life interest in the Land and Capital of the nation is the
> birthright of every individual born within its confines. . . .
>   That the established government has no more right to call itself

the state than the smoke of London has to call itself the weather. . . .

That we had rather face a civil war than such another century of suffering as the present one has been.

The last line is pure bravado, probably meant to show that the Fabians were just as revolutionary as their Marxist and Anarchist competitors in the 1880s (this was before the era of the Grosvenor Road dinners). The joke about the government and the smoke of London is Shavian all right—that is to say, it is an entertaining but misleading way of stating an important proposition. Examined coldly, its literal meaning evaporates faster than chimney smoke. The government of the day, after all, was in complete control of all the powers vested in the executive, and thus by the usual criteria had every right "to call itself the state." It would have been more to the point to argue that the state defended interests at variance with the needs of society. As for the problem of enjoying "wealth without dishonour," it was clearly not one that the average citizen could be expected to appreciate. But then Shaw was not addressing himself to the average citizen but to Nietzschean intellectuals like himself, the vanguard of the new social order. *They* were to be rendered immune to the vulgar influence of bourgeois liberalism, with its catchpenny creed and its asinine optimism about the future. Shaw always disliked the Liberals more than the Tories, and his socialism had a Nietzschean ring even before continental Europe began to sprout dictatorial movements. "The Perfect Wagnerite" was both a romantic and an authoritarian before his time.

By the 1930s he was ready for the new fashion:

At the same time Signor Mussolini, banking on his belief that the people, out of all patience with the delays, obstructions, evasions and hypocrisies of endlessly talking *fainéant* Parliaments, wanted not liberty (which he described boldly as a putrefying corpse) but hard work, hard discipline, and positive and rapid State activity: in short, real government, threw Constitutionalism to the winds and became at once an acknowledged and irresistible dictator. Similar *coups d'état* followed in Spain, in Yugoslovia, in Poland and Hungary, all proving that the old Liberal parliamentary systems, which had grown up in opposition to monarchical autocracy and had brought to perfection the art of paralysing State enterprise

under cover of preserving popular liberties, were falling into disillusioned contempt, and could be suspended or abolished without
finding a single effective defender.[4]

The note of exultation is unmistakable; so is the family resemblance with the earlier outburst about the smoke of London
having no business to call itself the weather. Shaw never cared
greatly about the mechanics of political change, provided it did
away with the obstacles that stood in the path of his vision. He
was miles removed from Arthur Henderson's naïve conviction that
all would be well once the House of Commons had become a
"house of the common people." And the elite concept was fused
in his mind with the idea of a dictatorial short cut that would
usher in the new age at one stroke. At first sight this romantic
notion looks out of place against the humdrum background of
Fabian research work and committee-mongering; and, needless to
say, it was not seriously entertained by the genuine theorists of
the Society, for all that Wells imputed to them in *The New
Machiavelli*. But there was just enough of the oligarchical about
pre-1914 Fabianism as practiced by the Webbs for Shaw to be
able to combine his romantic nostrums with his socialist pamphleteering and his genuine critique of existing institutions. It
took World War I and the attendant political upheaval to bring
about a fusion of Fabianism with the new democracy of the
Labour movement, and in this process Shaw understandably took
no interest and played no part.

IV

But the Webbs did. They are indeed generally held to have
rendered their most striking service to the Labour movement during and immediately after the war, when they helped the new
party to find its feet politically and to adopt a socialist platform.
The story of how this was done is both complex and fascinating;
much of it is recorded in Beatrice Webb's *Diaries* for the years
1912–24.[5] "The Webbs did much to make Britain as we know it
today. It is of absorbing interest to learn how they did this, almost wholly without official position or power," says Lord Bev-

4. Preface to the 1931 edition of *Fabian Essays*.
5. Margaret Cole, ed. (London, 1952).

eridge in the introduction to the volume. Their secret was that they were the chief intermediaries between the trade unions and the government (hence a revival of those semisecret confabulations at 41 Grosvenor Road in which the Prime Minister of the day came increasingly to figure): "Lloyd George naturally makes many appearances, often at lunch or dinner, as with Haldane in March 1918 to discuss with the Webbs the machinery of Government, or in February 1919 to discuss the constitution of the proposed Commission on Coal Mines." [6] Haldane subsequently joined the Labour Party and served in the short-lived MacDonald government of 1924. Among the other visitors, Arthur Henderson turned out to be the most important. When he joined Lloyd George's new government in December 1916, the Webbs were far from enthusiastic. Beatrice's diary entries indeed evince considerable disgust with all those Labour leaders who tended to accept Lloyd George's offer of minor jobs in the coalition government:

> It is very difficult to analyse the state of mind of these men. The prospect of six offices with an aggregate income of £16,000 a year, to be distributed among eighteen persons, is a big temptation. . . . But I don't believe that this pecuniary motive was dominant in the minds of the eighteen who voted for accepting office . . . their main motive . . . is the illusion that the mere presence of Labour men in the Government . . . is in itself a sign of democratic progress. . . . Neither as individuals nor as a class do Labour men realize that they are mere office-mongers when they serve with men of trained intelligence or even with experienced middle-class administrators. It was this illusion that brought Clynes round; he argued that Labour must have some say in the terms of peace. Poor Labour men, they will not get much say in the terms of industrial peace at home, let alone those of the peace of the world! (December 8th).

> The Lloyd George government, announced to-day, is a brilliant improvisation—reactionary in composition and undemocratic in form . . . for the first time we behold Labour leaders in open alliance with Tory chieftains. . . . (December 12th).

What upset the applecart, and gave the Webbs their chance, was the February 1917 revolution in Russia, followed as it was

6. Beveridge, Introduction, ibid., pp. x–xi.

by an outburst of pacifist sentiment that caused Henderson to fall in with the popular demand for the Labour Party to be represented at the International Socialist Conference in Stockholm, in the summer of that year. When Lloyd George went back on his promise to issue passports for British Labour delegates to the conference, and climaxed this reversal by forcing Henderson to resign from the war cabinet, he drove the strongest Labour leader of the period into the Socialist camp. The folly of this action became plain after the war, when the Labour Party turned its guns on the Liberals. In August 1917 it seemed to be merely a question of Henderson's vanity having been hurt, but more was at stake, as Beatrice noted in a footnote added in May 1918:

> We none of us realized the enormous importance of Henderson's ejection from the Cabinet. We gathered aferwards that it was not so sudden as it appeared. He had apparently become aware, for some time, that he was a mere hostage for the good behaviour of Labour, and that he had no say in policy. At Petrograd he took himself seriously—at Stockholm he came under the influence of Branting and Huysmans and was converted to International Socialism as a way of ending the war. Hence he expected his colleagues, on his return to London, to treat his opinions with respect: instead of which they kept him "on the doormat" while . . . they discussed his conduct. . . . He came out of the Cabinet with a veritable hatred of Lloyd George, who insulted him at their last interview. . . .

Henderson was the Bevin of that generation, and it was his readiness to associate with the Webbs that enabled Sidney in 1918 to provide the party with its first detailed program—a Socialist one. For all his personal dullness he is a more important figure than MacDonald, who made a reputation in 1914 by resigning from the chairmanship of the Parliamentary Labour Committee and taking up a pacifist position in regard to the war. (When challenged at stormy wartime meetings, he customarily fell back on Wordsworth:

> Were half the power that fills the world with terror
> Were half the wealth bestowed on camps and courts,
> Given to redeem the human mind from error,
> There were no need for arsenals or forts.)

The Webbs' ability to draw Henderson into the Socialist camp after his quarrel with Lloyd George must be seen in the context of those continuing dinner parties with the Prime Minister, which went on right throughout the period. It was the secret of their amazing influence that they had one foot in each camp, and this role in turn was made possible for them by the fact that oligarchic government gave way in 1914–18 to something more complex and less easy to define. It was not "Parliamentary democracy," for Parliament was far from being democratic, but Westminster was gradually filling up with democratic elements, and the Webbs were there to guide them. In a sense this is still the role of Fabianism, although the society's influence has declined as the movement has become more mature and less dependent on its advice.

For the spirit of the Webbs lingers on. During and after World War II Sir Stafford Cripps continued the tradition. Today his mantle (and Beatrice's) has fallen on Hugh Gaitskell, who for precisely this reason has such an irritating effect on Mr. Bevan. Yet each needs the other. If party history were written by sociologists (R. T. McKenzie has recently taken a considerable step towards this goal) it would be easier to trace the line of development from the pioneers to their descendants; easier also to account for those internal struggles that go back to the original fusion of the Socialist sects and the Labour movement. The Fabians came to be of importance because they bridged the gap between oligarchy and democracy, and because they did so at a time when the trade unions were beginning to lose faith in the ability of British capitalism to guarantee a rapid rate of development. That was all, and it was quite sufficient to "socialize" the British labor movement, and—after World War II—British society as a whole. There were two important turning points in the story: the first came during the 1890s, when the more active labor organizers in the constituencies began to turn away from the Liberals; and the second in 1917, when an important Labour leader was converted to Socialism. On both occasions the significance of what was happening was largely missed by all concerned. Today when the story is pretty nearly finished—for one does not see how another chapter can be added—it is worth studying the record for what it discloses about the seemingly haphazard way in which unconscious social processes and highly articulate intellectual speculations can, under favorable circumstances, combine to produce something new and unexpected. For the Fabians in their way were as successful as the Marxists in launching a major political movement. Like the Marxists, too, they have in the end come up against barriers to further advance along the route originally chosen: the welfare state has become the biggest obstacle to progress in the direction of Socialism. But that is another story.

Prometheus Unbound

※ ※ ※

MANY READERS of *New Fabian Essays* [1] must have been struck by
the eloquent passage in which R. H. S. Crossman contrasts two
alternative modes of human behavior in time of stress. Comment-
ing on the current retreat from optimism and belief in progress,
he suggests that this emergence of a more sober attitude need not
weaken our determination to make the world a better place:

> The recognition that progress does not necessarily bring freedom
> has led a considerable number of socialist intellectuals to accept
> defeat and to withdraw from politics into mysticism and quietism.
> But this is not the only conclusion which can be drawn. Facing
> the century of totalitarianism, we can choose between two philoso-
> phies, symbolized by the figures of Buddha and Prometheus. Bud-
> dha represents the withdrawal from the struggle for freedom. For
> the Oriental Buddhist, or for the Western defeatist, intellectual
> humility is the greatest virtue; the good man is not involved but
> detached; he accepts the world as a vale of woe and seeks realiza-
> tion in a transcendental eternity. The other philosophy, that of the
> sceptical humanist, is symbolized by Prometheus, chained to his
> Caucasian peak, with the eagle pecking out his liver. Prometheus
> stole fire from the gods in order to help his fellow-men. He did not
> believe that any law of nature or divine purpose would automatic-
> ally give freedom and happiness to his fellow-men. Neither God
> nor history was on his side. It was his duty to steal fire, in defiance
> of law and order, and to prefer eternal agony to the denial of truth.

Various reflections are suggested by this remarkable passage,
the first and most obvious being that Mr. Crossman has misread
the legend of Prometheus. It is misleading to speak of the Titan

The Twentieth Century, July 1952.
1. R. H. S. Crossman, ed. (London and New York, 1952).

having tried to benefit "his fellow-men." They were not his fellow creatures, but beings of a lower order, and the revolt he staged was largely for the purpose of demonstrating his contempt for Zeus and the other Olympians. Prometheus, *pace* Mr. Crossman, did not steal the fire because he considered it his duty—such Kantian or Stoic notions were foreign to him—but because he saw no reason why the hated Olympians should monopolize it. For one thing he wanted to play with it. (Mr. Crossman ought to read Freud or Jung on this fascinating topic.) For another thing he wanted to make himself independent of Zeus. Although idealized in later poetry, he remains primarily a rebel whose archetypal significance is plain to modern psychology. The *puer robustus sed malitiosus*, to adapt Hobbes's description of the unruly plebs which worships such image-breakers, is still discernible behind the tragic mask of the Aeschylean hero. Even if one takes the myth at its face value, Prometheus chained to his peak appears as an antinomian figure. His refusal to surrender was motivated (if we can trust Aeschylus, who is after all our principal authority) by hatred of Zeus, contempt for the Olympians generally, and faith in his own final victory. There are some famous lines in English poetry which breathe a kindred spirit:

> What though the field be lost?
> All is not lost; th' unconquerable will,
> And study of revenge, immortal hate
> And courage never to submit or yield,
> And what is else not to be overcome . . .

Milton's Lucifer is a straight descendant of Prometheus (this is not an original discovery). And what of the Arch-Milton sitting at Chalfont and brooding over the defeat of his party? One has only to glance at *Samson Agonistes,* notably the close ("Fully revenged—hath left them years of mourning . . . Soaked in his enemies' blood," etc.), which breathes the true Classical-Biblical spirit. Again in more modern times, Prometheus (or Aeschylus) has inspired a succession of kindred spirits, not the least important being Marx, whose doctoral dissertation opens with a hymn of praise to the Titan: "Prometheus is the foremost saint and martyr in the philosophic calendar." This then is the historical background of Mr. Crossman's declaration of faith. One sees at once that he moves in select company, but it is likewise evident that he has introduced a new and discordant element into the traditional story: his Prometheus has, as it were, read the Stoics and acquired a conscience, and a notion of duty, which strike one as modern, not to say existentialist. He sounds a little like Jean-Paul Sartre.

The next question is whether the transition from myth to reality in the passage from Mr. Crossman I have quoted is not perhaps a shade too abrupt. We are to "choose" between Buddha and Prometheus. This seems a loose and confusing way of stating the issue. Buddha, when all is said and done, is a real, though remote, historical figure, whose disciples, like himself, existed in the flesh, shared his thoughts, and after his death founded a religion. Prometheus, for all his incontestable merits as a symbol, lacks reality. We cannot choose between them, any more than we can choose between, say, Bertrand Russell and Dostoevsky's Grand Inquisitor. If someone at the back of the class objects that the historical Buddha is a shadowy figure, I merely observe that the distinction between reality and myth is not affected by length of time. If the argument is that Prometheus has full metaphysical status as a timeless embodiment of suffering and struggling humanity (the sufferings and struggles being real enough), I can only say that I prefer a flesh-and-blood hero to one who owes his existence to the poets and myth-makers. Human beings require symbols, and it is undeniable that the humanists have made Prometheus their standard-bearer; but it makes a difference whether people attach themselves to an authentic saint or a mythical one. Prometheus chained to his peak, with the eagle devouring his entrails, is a tremendous and terrifying figure. I vastly prefer him to Buddha. But I cannot get round the fact that in sober truth he did not exist.

The trouble with these poetic images is that they lend themselves to unconscious manipulation. One can never be certain that the symbol will over a stretch of time continue to have the same meaning for different people. Having sprung fully clothed from the poet's head, it remains dependent upon our human vagaries in a way in which the authentic saint or hero, however misunderstood and travestied by disciples and clerical corporations, does not. An example of this process is unwittingly provided by Mr. Crossman when, having evoked the Titan on his lonely crag, he goes on to draw a brief sketch of the archetypal Fabian:

> If freedom is to survive, it is essential that neither the USA nor the Soviet Union should win, and that ideological passion should subside. What the Western socialist needs today is not a crusading creed, but a critical attitude to both ideologies; and the role of the British Labour Movement is to furnish an example of this critical humanism in action. Sceptical, but not cynical; detached, but not neutral; rational, but not dogmatically rationalist. The Promethean social conscience, which I have described on an earlier page, is the only force which can prevent the modern state from degenerating into a managerial society, or the East-West conflict into World War III.

I hesitate to guess what this passage may suggest to other readers. To me it suggests, not Prometheus on his rock, but the Editor of *The New Statesman* at his desk, weighing the pros and cons. "Sceptical, but not cynical; detached, but not neutral; rational, but not dogmatically rationalist." If not exactly a Promethean image, it is certainly a civilized and pleasing one. It calls to mind a succession of eminent humanists to whom our world owes what little urbanity it possesses: Montaigne, Hume, Goethe, or—going further back—Epicurus. A Chinese might find a surprising resemblance to Confucius and reflect that Mr. Crossman has after all merely restated the ancient contrast between the practical Confucian and the mystical Taoist attitude. What cannot, I think, be seriously maintained is that we have here an adequate picture of the Titan who refused to bow the neck to Zeus, though tortured beyond endurance. It may be that Mr. Crossman is too civilized to see Prometheus in these Aeschylean terms. What seems clear is that the archetypal rebel does not fit very well into the Fabian pantheon: "Haughty thy speech and swollen with pride, as becomes a servant of the gods. Ye are but young in tyranny, and think to inhabit a citadel unassaulted of grief; yet have I not seen two tyrants fall therefrom? And third I shall behold this present lord cast down in utter ruin." Speaks thus the voice of skeptical humanism, of Fabian moderation? No, it won't do. If things are brought down to that level one thinks rather of Trotsky in exile, shortly before the assassin-executioner got him. But the whole pretentious effort to convert metaphysical and poetical imagery into the small change of politics is misconceived. Mr. Crossman has fallen victim to the disastrous fashion started by Professor Toynbee.

The ravages of this cult are visible on every page of his essay: "Judging by the facts, there is far more to be said for the Christian doctrine of Original Sin than for Rousseau's fantasy of the noble savage, or Marx' vision of the classless society." This sounds impressive, until one remembers that the doctrine of original sin says nothing about institutional arrangements. What it does is to affirm a certain view of human nature which remains true (or the reverse) whatever the historical destiny of mankind. The correct Christian deduction is not that the classless society is impossible, but that its coming would not alter man's fundamental predicament. The misuse of such doctrines for purposes of polemical phrase-making is not intrinsically superior to the banal sentimentalism which depicts the founder of Christianity as a social reformer. It is a pity to find Mr. Crossman sinking to what might be termed the Sayers level. It also shakes one's faith in his consistency, for what is the value of his Promethean affirmations if the entire humanist position is thus evacuated without a shot? His Prometheus began by sounding like Jean-Paul Sartre, went on to display the benign skepticism of Anatole France, and now reveals himself as a colleague of C. S. Lewis. Again, what are "the facts" in the light of which Mr. Crossman judges the doctrine of original sin to be true after all? The facts of yesterday's political situation? Theology requires a firmer basis. If there is "something to be said for" the Christian doctrine, we ought not to have to depend upon the latest news about concentration camps. In fact we don't. It is a characteristic error on Mr. Crossman's part to suppose that what matters to politicians must also be important to philosophers and theologians. Karl Barth's *Römerbrief* was published at the height of the post-1918 Wilsonian euphoria, when all good liberals hailed the flimsy League of Nations as the guarantee of perpetual peace. Conversely, the liberal-humanist belief in perfectibility and human goodness, as we all know, arose originally as a reaction against the furies unleashed by the Wars of Religion. If you make your appeal to history you must be prepared for such dialectical surprises. "Judging by the facts," as they appeared to thinking people in Europe after the devastation of the Thirty Years' War, those who believed most fervently in original sin were also most fervent in holding that heretics should be denied toleration, from which it seemed to follow that to be orthodox was to advocate massacre. Anyone can demonstrate in two minutes that this argument is unfair and irrelevant, but the historical evidence then appeared conclusive, and some of us persist in regarding the subsequent reaction as salutary. If Mr. Crossman wants to reinstate the orthodox view he must take his stand on firmer ground.

But what chiefly prejudices one against his judgment in matters of history is his evident lack of discrimination in awarding certificates of merit or demerit to writers whose works have come to his notice. It is not merely that he is irritatingly brash but that he seems unaware of the existence of different levels of significance. For Mr. Crossman one writer or thinker is as good as another. It is all one to him whether a remark was made by Rousseau, by Lenin, or, allegedly, by Buddha. The universe in which he moves is peopled by authors of interesting works of fiction, sociology, and metaphysics, and all without distinction are in turn called upon to present their credentials. His essay teems with casual allusions to Rousseau, Marx, Wells, Buddha, Professor Toynbee, Arthur Koestler, Prometheus, and Aldous Huxley, and while he is more severe on some than on others, there is no suggestion that he recognizes intrinsic distinctions among them. He hails them all as colleagues and subjects them to the same brisk, slapdash treatment:

> Most of us would now agree that Toynbee's sense of direction was better than that of the early Wells. . . .
> Here is one point where Toynbee's picture is more acceptable than that of Wells or Marx. . . .
> By rejecting the automatism of Wells and Marx, and the defeatism of Koestler and Aldous Huxley . . .
> After 1918 Western man lost his faith in the White Man's Burden. . . .

And so on. The comparison between Buddha and Prometheus, the portrait of the "Promethean" skeptic, and the learned excursion into original sin have already been quoted. Frankly, one cannot feel that Mr. Crossman is at his best in thus imitating Shaw. The effect is one of pastiche, and even of unconscious parody. Mr. Crossman has not learned to distinguish between thinkers and litterateurs. Can this be the reason why his own contribution to *New Fabian Essays* falls so flat?

When he descends from these unaccustomed heights into the political grassland he becomes at once more interesting and less irritating. He has some sensible things to say of the intelligentsia's role in backward countries, and of the harm done by modernizing primitive economies without altering the political regime. But in the concluding paragraph he is off again: "We must first accept the Cold War as the central fact of twentieth century politics (just as class war was the central fact of nineteenth century politics) and then disprove the prophets who prove that it must end in World War III." One sees his meaning, but wishes nonetheless that he had expressed it differently. Professor Toynbee has much to answer for.

Hobsbawm's Choice

❊ ❊ ❊

A USEFUL WAY OF DEALING with an important and difficult book is to announce beforehand that one is not going to bother with most of the contents but come straight to the main theme. I propose to follow this line in approaching what I take to be the central argument of Eric Hobsbawm's essay collection *Labouring Men*,[1] much of which has to do with highly specialized subjects, such as the controversy over the impact of the industrial revolution on nineteenth-century society. These matters are important, notably in their bearing upon the perennial debate between liberals and socialists over working-class conditions in Victorian Britain. But they involve a number of technical issues that only economic historians are really able to judge, and Mr. Hobsbawm is much more than an economic historian, though he can hold his own in any argument among experts in this field. As readers of his *Age of Revolution* have already discovered, he is both a specialist and a "generalist," and it is this unusual combination that makes him a challenge to the profession.

Labouring Men is a collection of studies ranging from a brief sketch of Tom Paine, via some detailed investigations into trade unionism, to a reconsideration of the Marxian and Fabian traditions in the British Socialist movement. Having decided to ignore the more technical aspects, I am under a moral obligation at least to say very briefly that in his capacity as an economic historian the author restates the socialist argument and does so in what seems a very convincing fashion: notably in dealing

Encounter, XXIV, No. 3 (March 1965).

1. *Labouring Men: Studies in the History of Labour* (London, 1964; New York, 1965).

with some latter-day attempts by academic liberals to suggest that (*a*) there never was an industrial revolution, and (*b*) insofar as there was one it was uniformly beneficial in raising working-class standards of living. Some of the more tendentious arguments in this field are demolished by Mr. Hobsbawm, and with a wealth of technical reference which should satisfy the experts. He is particularly good in defending Marx and Engels against the charge of having exaggerated the horrors of early capitalism. My only complaint here is that he does not go far enough. More could have been said about the contrast between social conditions in Britain and on the Continent, and about the extra price paid by the British working class during a lengthy period when society was wholly unprepared to cope with the catastrophic effects of sudden industrialization. On the Continent the upheaval came later, and generally took less disastrous forms. Even today Milan, Lyons, and Düsseldorf compare favorably with Manchester. At a time when everyone demands to know what is wrong with British industry (and with the unions), this topic would have merited some additional consideration.

Having chosen to treat the subject in isolation from general European conditions, Mr. Hobsbawm concentrates on what happened before and after the free-trade boom of 1850–75 led to a rise in real wages and a corresponding improvement in living conditions. In this way we get the familiar picture of British labor (notably its skilled "aristocracy") coming to share the benefits of Britain's dominant position on the world market and—a little later—of the "imperial" enterprise. This is the point where Mr. Hobsbawm injects his Marxian approach into the socialist tradition he shares with other writers. Socialism and Marxism are of course difficult to disentangle—notably in relation to Britain, since much of Marx's argument was constructed around the British case. This tends to be overlooked, and he does well to recall it. Whether it entitles him to take the further step toward a Leninist interpretation of imperialism is another matter. The reader had better know that Mr. Hobsbawm is not just a Marxist, but a Marxist-Leninist, though a very sophisticated specimen of the breed. If one happens to believe that Leninism is irrelevant to *any* of the problems that arise in connection with West European economic and political history over the past century, one

will tend to take his more topical reflections with a large helping
of salt. In case some of his readers be put off by a suspicion that
he is trying to make a political case, let it be said that this is
quite unwarranted. Mr. Hobsbawm really does know an enormous amount about his subject and has a first-rate critical mind,
as well as a truly remarkable intellectual range. It is just that his
residual loyalties occasionally get in the way of his perception.

The point can be illustrated by a consideration of his treatment of what to every Marxist must clearly be the most puzzling
feature of British labor history in this century: the strength of
the "reformist" tradition. For a start Mr. Hobsbawm very effectively disposes of a pseudo problem by demolishing the tedious
nonsense about the labor movement having always been "more
Methodist than Marxist." As against Elie Halévy's well-known
thesis that Methodism saved Britain from revolution during and
after the Napoleonic age, he makes the perfectly sound point that
there never was a revolutionary situation during those years, so
that no savior was needed. He also reminds the reader that not
all the Nonconformists were as conservative as the Wesleyans—
some in fact were (by British standards) pretty radical. Next, he
traces the ancestry of the London labor movement (from which
the Social Democratic Federation arose in the 1880s) to the anticlerical radicalism and rationalism of Paine. He also defends the
SDF against the imputation of having always been an unimportant sect: it was in fact the training ground of an entire generation of important labor leaders (including Ernest Bevin, who
joined this "Marxist" organization as a young man because it was
more militant than the evangelical ILP). He even has a good
word for the eccentric H. M. Hyndman, who dominated the SDF
from its founding in 1881 to the outbreak of war in 1914. And,
needless to say, he takes due note of the fact that most (though
not all) of these prewar Social Democrats in 1920 joined the
Communist Party.

He then asks the inevitable question why Marxism has, on the
whole, failed to capture the British labor movement, and gives
the sensible reply that the country lacked a revolutionary tradition. As he puts it, "On the Continent mass movements could
develop on the basis of a political attitude which in Britain

merely isolated a militant minority." The reference here is not to Communism but to the pre-1914 Social Democratic parties in France and Germany. These movements had no counterparts in Britain (except for the tiny SDF) because—as he very convincingly shows—the outlook of the working class was overwhelmingly liberal-radical rather than revolutionary. *No one* in Britain thought in terms of conquering political power; and this in turn was due to the fact that the country had missed the formative experience of the French Revolution.

To me this explanation seems wholly convincing; but it knocks a rather large hole into the Leninist approach to which Mr. Hobsbawm is attached for other reasons. If the determining factor in the orientation of the British labor movement was ideological (in the widest sense of the term,) we do not need to be told quite so much about the economics of imperialism. The simple fact appears to be that British labor has traditionally shared the conservative outlook of the British middle class, just as French labor has inherited the Jacobin tradition of French bourgeois republicanism. The decisive factor, in other words, was a difference in the historical inheritance. This translated itself, *inter alia*, into the absence of that very French (and Russian) phenomenon: the revolutionary intelligentsia. There was no such stratum in Britain, and consequently the labor movement never became acquainted with Marxism, except in the tedious, sectarian, and irrelevant version dished out by Hyndman (and, though Mr. Hobsbawm disputes this, by the Communists after 1917).

The obverse of this picture is presented by the success of Fabianism: a topic Mr. Hobsbawm finds distasteful, as well he might. Matters of taste aside (he is not alone in thinking the Fabians provincial and boring), there remains the question why they succeeded where the Marxians failed. The nearest Mr. Hobsbawm comes to clarifying this topic is in a passage where he observes that the Marxist tradition in Britain

> was first and foremost a proletarian one. . . . The SDF neither attracted nor held home-grown middle-class intellectuals in any quantity. . . . The junction between the intellectuals and the labour movement was not made until the period of, say, 1910–20, for before then even the Fabians, who did attract them, kept aloof

from the labour movement. Hence incidentally the abnormal weakness of British socialist theory, including Marxism, in this, the golden age of international Marxist thinking. The British counterpart of Luxemburg and Hilferding was not a socialist, but a liberal, J. A. Hobson.

I read this passage as a reluctant admission that a viable socialist movement requires "the junction between the intellectuals and the labour movement." Presumably Mr. Hobsbawm has been assisted toward this discovery by his Leninist background, but the same conclusion can also be reached by different ways: the Fabian road among them.

Mr. Hobsbawm dislikes the Fabians, though partly on grounds not shared by all their critics. (I should say it is possible to dislike them for better reasons than the ones he advances.) At the same time he is too acute not to see that their strength lay precisely in the feature which so irritated Engels: their social composition. The Fabians were a body of professional men and women drawn from the middle class; they were thus able to reformulate socialist doctrine in terms which appealed to the rising managerial stratum and to the educated class in general. Moreover, their ideology was anti-Liberal as well as anti-Marxist. It thus made contact with the authoritarian temper prevalent among civil servants and others disgusted with laissez-faire and vaguely sympathetic to "planning." (It also caused the Webbs and Shaw to flirt simultaneously with Stalinism and Fascism in the 1930s, though Mr. Hobsbawm tactfully forbears from making the point.) The Fabians, in short, could turn themselves into the nucleus of a new governing elite, while their Marxist rivals could not (at any rate in Britain). In our present technological age this is a considerable advantage. Mr. Hobsbawm grudgingly concedes the point and then falls back on sociology: the Webbs represented a "new social stratum." Well, so they did, and what is wrong with that? After all, planned economies have to be administered by economists and other bureaucrats, and it is just as well if the bureaucrats have had some sort of socialist background. However boring Fabianism may be, it is less irrelevant to the problems of a socialist economy than Leninism. Messrs. Brezhnev and Kosygin would be better off if they had a small Fabian planning staff, though of course under Soviet conditions there is no need to persuade the unions to accept a wage stop: wages are centrally fixed, and that is that. One feels that Mr. Hobsbawm has not quite thought his analysis through to the end. *Of course* Fabianism did not reflect working-class sentiment: who ever said it did? This does not make it less a socialist doctrine.

"Among the many failures of the Fabians, the failure to analyse the nature and historical basis of their model of the socialist élite is not the least striking." Well, perhaps, only it has to be added that they were pretty successful in taking over the administration of the new society. Whether they can make a success of running it, now that they are in charge, is of course another matter. If they fail, who is there to replace them on the Left? Not, I should imagine, the heirs of Lenin. The fact seems to be that Marxism has twice missed the boat so far as the British labor movement is concerned. In the 1880s it was introduced by Hyndman—a disaster from which it never recovered, despite all that Mr. Hobsbawm has to say about the man. Then after 1920 Marxism was taken over, and thoroughly wrecked, by the British Communist Party: another working-class sect (though somewhat larger than the SDF) which failed to make contact with the intellectuals, a few shining exceptions apart. The simple truth is that a Marxist movement (or any other) can establish its hold over society only if it begins by winning over the intellectual elite. This—as Mr. Hobsbawm well knows—has been the secret of Italian Communism. Inversely it explains why the British CP has always been such a hopeless failure. Laboring men by themselves cannot make a revolution. Lenin knew this; so did the Fabians. Mr. Hobsbawm does too. Why does he not say so?

A Settled Habit of Behavior

✱ ✱ ✱

NEOCONSERVATISM is not so influential in the present decade as it was in the 1950s, when the postwar reaction against all forms of radicalism was in full swing. A defensive tone has once more crept into it, replacing the former self-confident assertiveness. Its spokesmen still maintain an attitude of considerable hauteur toward their opponents, but they seem less sure that the argument has been finally decided in their favor by the wave of disillusionment which originally sparked it off. These swings of the intellectual pendulum clearly owe something to external pressures, but they also reflect the intrinsic character of a debate which by its nature cannot come to a permanent stop. Conservatives and radicals will go on arguing as long as there is something to argue about. Currently it may also be that we are witnessing the emergence of a middle group that borrows from the two opposing sides with the aim of promoting a synthesis. In our postrevolutionary climate this would correspond to the spread of liberalism in the 1830s, after Jacobins and anti-Jacobins had done their worst and exhausted their vocabulary. Perhaps a modern, streamlined version of nontotalitarian socialism is due to fill the gap.

Any such perspective, however unwelcome to "true believers" in the gospel according to Lenin, is equally unpalatable to the school of thought represented by Professor Michael Oakeshott, Harold Laski's successor to the chair of political science at the London School of Economics.[1] By now the surprise occasioned by

Commentary, February 1963.

1. See his *Rationalism in Politics, and Other Essays* (London and New York, 1962).

this appointment and by the new incumbent's inaugural lecture in 1951 has had time to wear off. The news has even got around that in choosing a Conservative to succeed Laski, the Governors of the LSE simply reverted to tradition. Laski's tenure was a fluke, and his evanescent influence a by-product of the stormy 1930s: the Popular Front era. By 1945, when the Labour government came in, he had already passed his peak. When Oakeshott succeeded him in 1951—at the height of Labour's unpopularity with a middle class which had come to associate socialism with rationing, petty bureaucratic meddling, shabby clothes, "mousetrap" cheese, and a pervasive atmosphere of seediness and discomfort—it was time for the pendulum to swing back.

It did so in the now famous inaugural lecture on "Political Education," which proclaimed as the foremost principle of statesmanship the duty not to rock the boat. The case had been put before—notably by Burke, the *fons et origo* of British conservatism —but rarely with such an air of intellectual superiority. Professor Oakeshott's elegant style (distinctly Whiggish, but then Burke was himself a renegade Whig: the real home-grown Tories, if the truth be told, are not very good at thinking or writing) fitted the mood of the moment. The public, including a sizable slab of the intelligentsia, was tired of wartime austerity, fed up with democracy, disappointed with socialism, and nostalgic for the charms of a stabler and more cultivated age. It voted Winston Churchill back into office, and cheered Oakeshott when he proclaimed the great Whig-Tory doctrine that the purpose of sound politics is to keep things as they are, with the minimum of concessions to such change as can be shown to be absolutely necessary. The counterrevolution—a very British, very genteel, very well-mannered counterrevolution—had triumphed.

It didn't last, of course: nothing ever does. While it lasted, which was for about ten years, things were a bit dull, but not markedly uncomfortable even for radicals. There was no purge: Britain produced no McCarthy; instead it got Macmillan, the very epitome of conservative respectability and aristocratic elegance (though his grandfather was a Scottish crofter). The country turned even more insular as its global power dwindled; its intellectuals tended to become parochial (while urging their continental neighbors to be "outward-looking"); and its academics retreated further into their cloisters. They now had solid philosophic reasons for concerning themselves with trifles. These were the years when the late Sir Lewis Namier's pedantic reconsideration of British politics in 1760 was solemnly hailed as a major intellectual revolution. Historians went back to the eighteenth century, and then further back, to the Tudors (they still do—it is their favorite epoch). The emphasis once more was on research. General ideas were at a discount: they had been shown up as untrustworthy, only fit for foreigners. This mood still persists, as any reader of Professor Oakeshott's essays can see for himself, but it is less complacent now than it was a decade ago. For one thing, foreigners—Americans, Russians, Europeans— went on making history, while the BBC duly reported the doings of the Royal Family and the latest score in the England-Australia cricket match; for another thing, Conservative muddling-through turned out to be uneconomic in the plain sense of the word: it didn't pay. After a while even quite ordinary people began to notice this and to fret about it. By now the laissez-faire doctrine expounded by Professor Oakeshott as the "political economy of freedom" is under fire. There are heretical mutterings in the least expected quarters, and *The Times* itself has been heard to question whether doing nothing is necessarily the best policy under all imaginable circumstances. In short, the swing back has begun.

It will not be halted by Professor Oakeshott's essays, though its intellectual expression will be affected by the need to take account of them. No reaction is ever completely lost, any more than a revolution can be erased. The two movements complement each other: with luck, the next turn of the screw is an upward one which conserves the lessons of the past. Burke taught the radicals of his day something they had overlooked in their enthusiasm over what was happening in Paris. Professor Oakeshott is no Burke, but his elegantly phrased diatribes against radicalism and rationalism have their value in the context of a debate which must go on as long as people ask themselves serious questions about society. There are great names on both sides: Hegel, Acton, Tocqueville, Burckhardt, all had their share in deflating the wilder hopes and illusions born in 1789. In continuing their work, contemporary Whigs and Tories place their opponents under an obligation to examine their own beliefs, and where necessary restate them. In short, they fulfill the essential function of seeing to it that the unending dialectic of these conceptual tournaments stays as close as possible to the political facts.

This said, the conservative argument in itself need not be treated with excessive gravity. It never alters, though from time to time its formulation does. The essential theme is always the same: history is continuous, and even revolutions take place within a traditional continuum (Professor Oakeshott affirms this explicitly of the Russian Revolution); statesmanship is the art of the possible; its true function is to lessen discord and enable men to live together without violence; utopian aims defeat themselves in practice; abstract liberty, equality, and fraternity are illusions —noble perhaps, but empty; private property, on the other hand, is no illusion but the basis of society and the precondition of the good life; all genuine change is slow and imperceptible; when it becomes rapid and turbulent, this is to be regarded as a pathological phenomenon and a sign that doctrinaire rationalists have temporarily seized power, for the greater glory of their own silly selves and to the detriment of their unfortunate fellow citizens; general principles take the place of unspoken beliefs and habits when the cake of custom has been broken—the greatest disaster that can befall any society; all revolutions are hostile to individual liberty, whatever the aims professed by their leaders; freedom is preserved by not allowing anyone to do too much or to accumulate too much power; it is safest in a society of small property owners; doctrinaire reformers are to be distrusted; sound politics are about ordinary matters; that government is best which governs least.

It will be evident that this is not the authentic Tory doctrine, for it is silent on social hierarchy, traditional morality, and the divine right of kings. Professor Oakeshott indeed, like a true Whig, is indifferent to monarchy (save insofar as it keeps things stable) and vaguely critical of Christian morality. His observations on this latter subject (in the essay entitled "The Tower of Babel") make awkward reading for idealist philosophers and theologians in search of allies, for by his own rigorous standards even religious idealism, however attenuated in practice, suffers from the fault of being concerned with abstract principles. It has for many centuries been "dominated by the pursuit of moral ideals" instead of contenting itself with being simply a way of life.

> In so far as this is an unhappy form of morality, prone to obsession and at war with itself, it is a misfortune to be deplored; in so far as it cannot now readily be avoided, it is a misfortune to be made the best of. . . .
>
> The predicament of Western morals, as I read it, is first that our moral life has come to be dominated by the pursuit of ideals, a dominance ruinous to a settled habit of behavior; and secondly, that we have come to think of this dominance as a benefit for which we should be grateful or an achievement of which we should be proud.

Whereas if we had more sense we would recognize that *all* ideals are ruinous.

This is the doctrine of Hume, another conservative skeptic with a great respect for "a settled habit of behavior." It is Whiggish (Hume's affected Toryism has never deceived anyone) and eighteenth century: English Whiggery descends from Hume and Gibbon even more than from Burke. The true focus of its sentiment is individualism, i.e., a particular tradition, not tradition as such. There are indeed many Burkean passages to be found in Oakeshott, e.g.: "With eyes focused upon distant horizons and minds clouded with foreign clap-trap, the impatient and sophisticated generation now in the saddle has dissolved its partnership with its past and is careful of everything except its liberty." But then this particular essay ("The Political Economy of Freedom") deals with the socialist critique of private property, and even the most languid Whig becomes a bit impassioned when this subject is raised. In any event, "liberty" embodies enough of tradition to satisfy most Tories.

> To be brief, collectivism and freedom are real alternatives—if we choose one we cannot have the other. And collectivism can be imposed upon a society educated in a love of freedom with an appearance of not destroying *continuity* [author's italics] only if men forget their love of liberty. This . . . is how the matter appeared to . . . Tocqueville, Burckhardt and Acton, when the character of modern collectivism was in process of being revealed.

It is important that this issue should be *felt*, not argued. In an earlier essay Professor Oakeshott showed himself suspicious of F. A. Hayek, a liberal in the Whig tradition, because his cast of mind is rationalist. "A plan to resist all planning may be better than its opposite, but it belongs to the same style of politics." What is required is not a particular doctrine but an absence of doctrine and an attachment to the status quo. Now this mode of reasoning is available to conservative liberals only at the cost of some unpopularity. It is not, for example, compatible with modern welfare-state liberalism, which by its nature tends dangerously toward "collectivism"—if only to keep a step ahead of the socialist competition. In practice this reduces the political appeal of the doctrine, a circumstance which to a philosopher perhaps matters less than it does to ordinary political thinkers, except that Oakeshott's main criterion has to do with consensus and custom in his native Britain, a country spared the worst ravages of continental thinking. It must be a disappointment to him that faith in traditional ways of life has not quite managed to keep these troublesome innovations out.

From the viewpoint of his transatlantic admirers there is the further difficulty that while his economics are acceptable, his politics are not: clearly it is not possible for Americans to join him in treating the Declaration of Independence (together with its French counterpart) as a prime source of the "rationalist" fallacy from which all our present evils have sprung. Yet from the introductory essay in this collection the reader will learn that "the early history of the United States of America is an instructive chapter in the history of the politics of Rationalism." He will learn that rationalism, after giving birth to the American and French Revolutions, culminated in socialism. This is arguable, though it overlooks the antirationalist influence of Hegel, who had absorbed Burke's critique, and was in turn absorbed by Marx. But true or not, it is not a doctrine that can be of the slightest use to *Time* magazine or Senator Goldwater. It can be employed only by people who are willing to go the whole hog in treating the Declaration of Independence as

a characteristic product of the *saeculum rationalisticum*. It represents the politics of the felt need interpreted with the aid of an ideology. And it is not surprising that it should have become one

of the sacred documents of the politics of Rationalism, and, together with the similar documents of the French Revolution, the
inspiration and pattern of many later adventures in the rationalist
reconstruction of society.

No doubt this is what some American conservatives suspect in
the privacy of their thoughts, but it is not something to be affirmed in public. Toryism, even of the modified Burkean kind,
simply will not take root anywhere save in English soil.

It may be said that this is irrelevant: what counts is whether a
statement is true, not whether it is popular. But on Burkean principles what is "true" of England need not be true of all other
countries, notably if one applies Oakeshott's criterion for judging
the usefulness of a mode of thought, which is broadly whether or
not it conforms to "a traditional manner of behavior." For may
not rationalism itself be in tune with tradition and the cake of
custom? In fact we are told: "Long before the Revolution . . .
the disposition of mind of the American colonists, the prevailing
intellectual character and habit of politics, were rationalistic."
This was unfortunate, for "Rationalist politics . . . are the politics of the felt need, the felt need not qualified by a genuine concrete knowledge of the permanent interests and direction of
movement of a society, but inspired by 'reason' and satisfied according to the technique of an ideology: they are the politics of
the book." Still, if the American colonists were addicted to this
deplorable mode of reasoning, it is difficult to see how on traditionalist grounds they can be blamed for acting upon what had
become *their* tradition.

Then again, consider the filiation of ideas from the English
Revolution (good) to the American Revolution (bad).

For the inspiration of Jefferson and the other founders of American
independence was the ideology which Locke had distilled from the
English political tradition. They were disposed to believe, and
they believed more fully than was possible for an inhabitant of
the Old World, that the proper organization of a society and the
conduct of its affairs were based upon abstract principles, and not
upon a tradition which, as Hamilton said, had "to be rummaged
for among old parchments and musty records." These principles
were not the product of civilization; they were natural, "written
in the whole volume of human nature."

So much for Locke's American pupils. True, a few years later Burke, in his alarm over what was happening in France, also appealed to natural law, but then *his* deductions were conservative and therefore acceptable, whereas the conclusions drawn by the American and French radicals were subversive of the existing order, and thus reprehensible. This doctrine was a great comfort to supporters of the *ancien régime* (and subsequently to slave-owners threatened by the emancipation of their human cattle), but its theoretical standing has always looked questionable to people not impressed by conservative rhetoric. Incidentally one learns from Professor Oakeshott's analysis of property that the "right to enjoy the ownership of his personal capacities *and of anything else obtained by the methods of acquisition recognized in the society*" (my italics) is self-limiting: "for example, it proscribes slavery, not arbitrarily, but because the right to own another man could never be a right enjoyed equally by every member of a society." This suggests that what is wrong with slavery is that it cannot be made universal. In fact, of course, it was pretty nearly universal in antiquity, given the tacit understanding (part of the "traditional manner of behavior") that only free citizens counted as members of society. This may help to explain why conservative writers are so fond of Plato, or if they are slightly Whiggish, of Aristotle. It may also explain why their own thinking has not advanced significantly beyond the categories worked out by their classical ancestors.

The Birth of a Philosopher

✳✳✳

BERTRAND RUSSELL HAD THIS to say about the Whig aristocrat who
headed the Russell clan during most of the Victorian era:

> My grandfather, whom I remember vividly, was born on the 18th
> of August 1792, a fortnight after the poet Shelley. . . . The
> French Revolution was just getting under way, and it was in the
> month of his birth that the monarchy fell. . . . His first (unpub-
> lished) work contained an ironical dedication to Pitt, then still
> Prime Minister. . . . He visited Napoleon in Elba, and had his ear
> pulled by the Great Man, as was usual. When Napoleon returned
> from Elba, my grandfather, who had been for two years a mem-
> ber of Parliament, made a speech urging that he should not be
> opposed. The Government, however, being in the hands of the
> Tories, decided otherwise, and the Battle of Waterloo was the
> result.

The statesman in question, Lord John Russell, died in 1878,
when the future philosopher was six years old. There are unlikely
to have been many conversations between them, about Waterloo
or anything else. Still, it is nice to have this vignette stamped
upon the record, as a reminder that there is more to Russell's
Voltaireanism than the conscious acquisition of a style proper to
the man. The *philosophe* who lurks in the empiricist—successor of Locke and Hume: both great favorites with the French
writers who collectively produced the Enlightenment—is not ac-
cidentally the grandson of a Whig who in 1815 counseled restraint and tolerance for Napoleon. The Russells were on the
side of liberalism, hence of France, whereas the Tories preferred
Germany (they still do, though less noisily). If one likes, one

may also attribute some significance to the fact that Lord John's advice was not taken. In 1830, though, he had the satisfaction of becoming a member of Lord Grey's Whig administration, the July Revolution in Paris having scared the Crown and the oligarchy into abandoning the Tories for a while. His grandson has had to content himself with triumphs of a different order.

Bertrand Russell's heredity is too much part of the story to figure merely as background. In his autobiography [1] he fills out some of the blanks in the earlier record. His parents, Lord and Lady Amberley, were on the radical side of the Victorian intellectual cleavage. They were friends of John Stuart Mill, championed unpopular causes such as birth control and votes for women, and held unconventional views about marriage. Unluckily for the boy, they died before he had reached his fourth year, and he was left in the care of stern maiden aunts and old Lady Russell, an authoritarian who combined Whig principles with relentless moralizing. He claims to have been a happy child, which seems doubtful, and a lonely adolescent, which is hardly surprising. The gloom was somewhat lightened by his early discovery of the beauty of mathematics—a realm of formal purity and absolute certainty which made up for some of the earthly disappointments. Philosophers are born, not made (at any rate those who possess reasoning powers beyond the normal), but his Spartan upbringing must have helped to launch Russell upon the career that made him famous.

As an autobiographer Russell combines formal restraint with intellectual candor to a degree uncommon in this age, when a Rousseauist addiction to verbal extravagance and romantic self-deception is the quality most highly prized in biographies and memoirs. But then he stems from a tradition of aristocratic liberalism not easily merged with the sentimentality of the middle class. Here and there (e.g., in the passages where he relates his amorous affairs) it is even possible to discern a trace of frivolity. He had to work hard to effect this liberation from a puritanical background. Certainly he got little help from his relatives. When in 1893, at the age of twenty-one, he married Alys Pearsall Smith —five years his senior and an American Quaker girl, hence un-

1. *The Autobiography of Bertrand Russell, 1872–1914* (London and Boston, 1967).

suitable—they did all they could to wreck the engagement. As usual he had his way in the end, but early scars remained. He is a trifle reticent as to what exactly caused the marriage to collapse a decade later, but it is plain enough that there was a clash between his upbringing and the natural vigor of his sensuality. The strains were violent enough to bring on recurrent moods of suicidal depression. And all this while he was in the throes of writing his first great work!

Here one enters what for a layman is dangerous ground, mathematics not being everyone's hobby. Fortunately, Russell dwells more upon the manner in which he arrived at his discoveries than upon their precise significance. An interesting point emerges, namely the crucial (to Russell) importance of being suddenly confronted with a blinding new light. He describes two such mental revolutions, one relating to logic, the other to ethics. The first occurred in the summer of 1900 when he had gone to Paris to attend an international congress of philosophy, made the acquaintance of Peano and his mathematical logic, was overwhelmed by a sudden revelation, and there upon underwent a period of great intellectual excitement lasting for about a month and culminating in important logical discoveries. This was followed early in 1901 by an acute depression probably brought on by the impending breakdown of his marriage, and it was then that he had his second conversion: this time to a new conception of the moral life. The incident that touched off the crisis was a painful heart attack suffered by Mrs. Whitehead, with whom the Russells were staying. The distress this caused the visitor brought on a quasi-religious experience which Russell describes as follows:

> Suddenly the ground seemed to give way beneath me, and I found myself in quite another region. Within five minutes I went through some such reflections as the following: the loneliness of the human soul is unendurable; nothing can penetrate it except the highest intensity of the sort of love that religious teachers have preached; whatever does not spring from this motive is harmful, or at best useless; it follows that war is wrong, that a public school education is abominable, that the use of force is to be deprecated, and that in human relations one should penetrate to the core of loneliness in each person and speak to that.

The passage is of great interest for judging Russell as a person and for an understanding of his views. "At the end of those five minutes," he writes, "I had become a completely different person. For a time a sort of mystic illumination possessed me." Some doubt as to the permanent effect of this experience arises from his account of his life in the years following, which does not disclose any very marked concern for others. One episode at least exhibits him in a thoroughly discreditable light. Nonetheless it does seem evident that he had undergone something of a conversion, if not to a different mode of feeling, at any rate to a different set of principles. To a reader (though not to the author, who has a blind spot on the subject) it seems plain that the sight of a helpless woman in distress activated the long-dormant anxiety felt by the boy many years earlier at the loss of his mother. The fashionable absurdity today consists in supposing that these derivations exhaust the meaning of a spiritual crisis. What Russell experienced was clearly more than an uprush of self-pity, since his outlook changed and he acquired the ability to feel for and with others. His emotional capacity, to put it crudely, had been blocked, and some of the barriers had now come down, though the mystical exaltation did not last.

What did last was the queer set of more or less Tolstoyan principles he acquired at that moment: war was wrong and public schools were wrong (he had not attended one, but the army crammer to whom he was sent by his benighted relatives before escaping to Cambridge was no great joy either). Russell tells us quite solemnly in the same passage:

> Having been an Imperialist, I became during those five minutes a pro-Boer and a Pacifist. Having for years cared only for exactness and analysis, I found myself filled with semi-mystical feelings about beauty, with an intense interest in children, and with a desire almost as profound as that of the Buddha to find some philosophy which should make human life endurable.

The world was to be saved by love. It was the time of the Boer war, hence Russell—having until that moment followed the lead of Bernard Shaw and the Webbs in taking the imperialist side—instantly became a pro-Boer. That the Boers were not particularly pleasant people, notably in their treatment of Africans, did not have to concern him: they were a small nation trampled upon by a brutal Empire. But how were they to be aided? Not by force, for Russell had become a pacifist (he had to go back on the absoluteness of this creed in 1940, when Britain was the last holdout of anti-Hitler resistance and pacifism had become morally impossible). The way to help the Boers—and all other oppressed on later occasions—was to denounce the oppressors, for politics had now been revealed as a moral issue: the weak suffering the violence of the strong. Ought the weak to resist? Probably, though Russell as a pacifist would take no responsibility for that. His duty was simple: it was to proclaim that war and oppression were abominable. This, more or less, is what he has been doing ever since, though with occasional backslidings into bellicism, e.g., in 1948 when he so far forgot himself as to advocate the use of the nuclear bomb against Stalin: another brutal oppressor, probably identified in his mind with whatever caused Mrs. Whitehead to suffer such atrocious pains in 1901.

But the psychological derivation is not very relevant. All sorts of people have come to all sorts of conclusions by way of unconscious identification with parents or friends. What matters is that Russell seems never to have grasped the difference between discovering a new principle in mathematics and acquiring a new set of convictions in ethics. To him one illumination was as real and compelling as the other. Just as in September 1900 he had suddenly "seen" the new mathematical logic, so in the following year he "saw" with equal clarity the need for a new ethic (or an old one that had not been taken seriously). And it was a matter of endless surprise to him that otherwise sane and wellmeaning people—his friend Alfred Whitehead among them—were unable to share his vision.

Whitehead, indeed, was destined to be a puzzle to Russell, once their joint labors on *Principia Mathematica* (1911) had come to an end. Personal eccentricities apart—Russell's account of their relationship hints at a streak of barely controlled irrationality in the older man—there was Whitehead's Platonism, his general fondness for metaphysics, and his indifference to Russell's political concerns, which were those of an ardent pre-

1914 liberal. To an outsider, Whitehead seems the more interesting thinker of the two, brooding in his cloudy fashion over problems that never troubled Russell. If Collingwood's account can be trusted, Whitehead rediscovered Hegel without having read him. What is certain is that Russell, who *had* read Hegel, failed to understand him. This may be the reason why to someone brought up on German philosophy Russell has always seemed to lack an entire dimension: the historical.

For proof one may consult his writings on political and social matters. Setting aside the nonsense he has uttered on a great many topics of which clearly he had no knowledge, there is at the core of Russell's thinking about politics an unresolved dilemma already inherent in the conversion experience described in the autobiography: of certain practical choices it is asserted that they are required by morality, but the ultimate source of moral authority is never clarified. It cannot be religious, since Russell has no use for religion. It cannot be simply utilitarian, for there are occasional references to absolutes—love, beauty, "the good life"—which seem to reflect a hierarchy of values not reducible to subjective estimation. Yet the principle governing his moral assumptions is never stated. Is it then purely arbitrary?

In his *History of Western Philosophy*, Russell comes close to suggesting that the ultimate choice in morals and politics is not reducible to rational argument. In a passing reference to the incompatibility of democratic and Nietzschean doctrines he observes: "I do not myself believe that this disagreement can be dealt with by theoretical arguments such as might be used in a scientific question. Obviously those who are excluded from the Nietzschean aristocracy will object, and thus the issue becomes political rather than theoretical." He might have added that the only way to deal with people who are serious about exterminating others is to kill them first, but perhaps such a suggestion would have been thought shocking in a philosopher.

The problem is a real one, and Russell is not to be blamed for not having solved it. Those critics—whether Christians or Communists—who have rebuked him for failing to rise above the unsolved dilemmas of late Victorian rationalism are themselves weighed down by theoretical and practical failures on a scale to match the evident dissolution of liberal individualism. The fact remains that Russell, by pushing to an extreme the doctrines he imbibed as a young man, has unwittingly laid bare their inadequacy. Rational principles of conduct supposedly abstracted from a fixed and unchanging human nature whose dispassionate study will yield a science of morals and politics—are there many people left who *believe* this sort of thing? It is to Russell's honor that he has kept the flag flying for over half a century, but the attempt to reconcile the rationalist myth with historical reality must surely by now be reckoned a failure.

The Illusionist

❊❊❊

Having in the past miraculously breathed some life into the dry bones of Bonar Law, Britain's dullest and least significant Prime Minister, Robert Blake, the Oxford historian, has now turned to the very different figure of Benjamin Disraeli.[1] From his patient labors in the archives there has emerged a splendid portrait of the enigmatic character who presided for almost four decades over the Tory half of Victorian politics and letters. In the process he has destroyed a few legends and unearthed a good deal of circumstantial detail not recorded by Disraeli's official biographers, the worthy if long-winded pair of Monypenny and Buckle. Yet the reviewers who predictably pounced on the scandalous side of the record—Disraeli's bizarre journalistic exploits in the 1830s, his debts, his quarrels, his weird entanglement with Henrietta Sykes, his invention of an aristocratic background for his own highly respectable bourgeois family—have cantered off in the wrong direction. Mr. Blake is no Lytton Strachey and not interested in scandal. Not only is he a professional historian and careful scholar: his assessment of Disraeli's baffling character is based on a profound understanding of the environment which made him possible. The central fact about Disraeli—missed by earlier biographers and firmly established by Mr. Blake—is that he was an adherent of the Romantic movement which climaxed in the 1830s and collapsed two decades later. His early fame as a novelist, an amateur parliamentarian with a few brilliant speeches to his credit, and the central figure of the "Young England" group of aristocratic

Partisan Review, Winter 1967.

1. *Disraeli* (London, 1966; New York, 1967).

Toryism was won in the 1840s, when it was still possible for an aspiring politician to imitate Byron. To this period belong his amorous adventures, which gave offense to the respectable, and his financial speculations, which left him permanently debt-ridden. Then, by an extraordinary stroke of luck aided by some rapid maneuvering, he made the transition from Byronic adventurism to Victorian solemnity at the very last moment before the train pulled out of the station. The great economic gearshift of the 1850s had enthroned the middle class and wrecked the kind of aristocratic Toryism in which Disraeli believed. He survived the transition, as he survived all subsequent ones, by exploiting to the full his intellectual ascendancy over the bewildered cohorts who sat behind him after having been abandoned by Peel and Gladstone. More than that: he made himself their leader by taking up what had become a lost cause. Peel's "betrayal" in 1846 (his abandonment of the Corn Laws on which the predominance of the landowners rested) opened the way for Disraeli. His meteoric rise from the back benches was effected by a single speech: a three-hour oration, improvised on the spur of the moment, which more than a century later still casts a spell upon the reader. In the hour of defeat Toryism had found a new champion.

It was an amazing achievement, and only an adventurer with a touch of genius could have brought it off. That genius Disraeli possessed, and for the sake of it generations of Conservatives have forgiven him everything, from his shady tactics to his novel-writing. At the time, though, what they chiefly felt was bewilderment. Their leaders had abandoned them. Their ancient cause lay in ruins. Instinctively they clung to the orator who put into words their dull resentment and their secret conviction that they alone could govern England. They were a defeated party and Disraeli restored their self-confidence. In return they gave him, not their trust (that he never received), but the backing he needed to reach the top.

It was a bargain, and Disraeli soon made his supporters feel that they had not lost by it. In an age of accomplished parliamentary debaters he outshone all his rivals. Moreover, the record makes it clear that from a languid amateur he gradually turned himself into a hard-working professional. Skill in debate and maneuver was matched by organizing ability and a genuine gift for public administration. But at the heart of the phenomenon there lay something more elusive—something Disraeli allowed to emerge only in his novels and in the more outrageous of his letters. Mr. Blake has caught the Luciferian tone which runs through the performance. A latter-day Byronist, and for good measure a Jewish convert of the generation which on the Continent produced Heine and Lassalle, Disraeli from an early age had fixed a sardonic gaze, half amused, half contemptuous, upon the society he was determined to conquer. His fantastic novels light up an interior landscape remote from the familiar iconography of Victorian politics. The heir of the Regency wits, with his carefully cultivated Mephistophelian appearance, is seen to drag a metaphorical clubfoot across the stage. His family background (Spanish according to him, Italian in reality), his highly personal and altogether unorthodox Judaeo-Christianity, his saturnine looks and mordant turn of speech repelled and fascinated. All in all, Disraeli appealed to the submerged romanticism of the English. The faint whiff of brimstone that clung to him alarmed the pious Gladstone. It did not bother Victoria, and it enchanted the audience of the great illusionist.

For it is as a master of political trompe l'oeil that Disraeli has gone down in the annals of statesmanship. All his triumphs were illusory, and so were the methods whereby he secured them. He split the Tories in the name of principle, and then kept them in the wilderness for a generation, but did not lead them to the promised land. For all his impassioned faith in the permanence of the "aristocratic settlement," he did not save the cause of the landowning nobility. He did not even secure their economic interests: farm prices collapsed during his administration, thus bringing about the ruin of agriculture he had predicted for thirty years. He did not reconcile the alienated working class to the Establishment—that was done independently by the rise of reformism. The "two nations" of *Sybil* (the novel that won the hearts of Young England) remained apart. The social reforms enacted while he was in office were useful but marginal, and in the end their chief beneficiaries were the trade unions. He carried on a rearguard action against democracy, and then took credit for surrendering to it. The most dazzling of his tactical triumphs, the Reform Bill of 1867 which gave the franchise to the urban working class, was a personal tour de force at the expense of conservatism, and the new electors thanked him by voting for Gladstone. Nor did he accomplish anything permanent abroad. The elevation of the Queen to the dignity of Empress of India flattered British pride but did not stem the rise of Indian nationalism. The showdown with Russia in 1878 and its sequel, the Berlin Congress in the same year, was another empty stage triumph, and its only practical result, the temporary prolongation of Turkish rule in the Balkans, was thoroughly undesirable. Disraeli's imperialism, like all the rest of his career in office, was nothing more than a brilliantly conducted rearguard action.

Why then did the Tories follow him wherever he led? Certainly not because they trusted him. Salisbury, the ablest of them and eventually his stoutest supporter, as late as 1868 (when Disraeli was over sixty and had just become Prime Minister) thought him "an adventurer and . . . in an age of singularly reckless statesmen . . . beyond question the one who is least restrained by fear or scruple." The truth is that they had no choice. Disraeli possessed the genius they lacked, and his willingness to spend himself in the service of what he and they knew to be a lost cause made it inevitable that he should lead them. They needed a faith and Disraeli gave them one—imperialism, the vision of England as the center of a worldwide empire held together by loyalty to the Crown. Illusory or not, it refloated the aristocracy and revived its morale for a couple of generations. It also made Disraeli popular, so that in the end he became a national hero also. His opponents, Gladstone above all, denounced him as an immoralist and the enemy of responsible statesmanship. These were Victorian judgments passed upon a man who in his youth had taken Byron for his model and, like his hero, resolved to live dangerously and for glory alone: the only immortality in which he believed. It was his good fortune that circumstances permitted him to play a role which in a different age would have led to disaster. As it was, he infused that streak of romantic recklessness into the Tory personality which at a later day enabled Churchill to bring the curtain down upon the scene with a final gesture of defiance.

AMERICA SEEN
FROM A DISTANCE

The Politics of 1970

❊❊❊

THE TITLE CHOSEN for this essay accords in at least one respect with a forecast frequently made by official and private study groups: it assumes that by 1970 the technological revolution under way since 1945 will have brought about a drastic rearrangement of the military and political institutions inherited from the preceding era. This is the burden of a report recently published on behalf of the National Planning Association under the suggestive title *1970 Without Arms Control.* From this document one may learn, for example, that during the coming decade the world will gradually traverse the somewhat indeterminate stage of military technology with which statesmen and scientists are presently struggling; we shall then have attained a higher level, with rockets taking the place of aircraft, and at most fifteen minutes' warning of impending attack by enemy missiles. Note that by then the major powers are expected to have developed automatic retaliation systems capable of going into action even if there is no one alive to press the button, or indeed to benefit from its use. In the words of the report, "It is a disturbing fact that while weapons grow increasingly effective, they also tend to outgrow previous control possibilities. . . . Plans for a control that works in one stage of technology will be rendered useless by later developments." As for the chances of voluntary assent to effective international control on the part of the powers, the report does not rate them very highly.

Notwithstanding the gloomy tone of these and similar predictions, the general public continues to manifest a marked degree of stoicism. This is probably due as much to indifference as to

Partisan Review, July 1958.

helplessness in the face of increasingly alarming statements now uttered with growing frequency by reputable scientists and others in authority. The element of simple common sense embedded in this widespread skepticism should not be underestimated—the common man is not merely understandably reluctant to contemplate the possible dissolution of his familiar world; he is also sufficiently tough-minded to discount some of the more extravagant fears of his guilt-ridden intellectual betters. It is nonetheless apparent that we are nearing the close of the transitional period between World War II and the attainment of a new technological level unperceived in 1939 or even in 1945. Whether new wars can and will be fought on this level, before mankind achieves an adequate degree of control over the new means of destruction, is a question so much debated now that it becomes difficult to think of anything new to say. When heads of government take to writing letters to the press in an effort to persuade the uncommitted that they stand for disarmament (unlike the opposing side, which presumably favors all-round suicide), the political scientist is driven back upon higher ground. If he cannot find a fresh vantage point, his occupation vanishes, as does confidence in his ability to discern those elements in the situation that are hidden from statesmen and diplomatists. The question, in short, is whether in all this welter of public and private comment on the world situation there is still room for what used to be known as theoretical thinking.

Fortunately the answer is yes. This is not to say that such thinking will necessarily yield results not available to common sense. What is intended here is not a refutation of commonsensical reflection, but a grounding of such reflection in something more systematic and less subject to constant revision under pressure of events. Such revision is prompted by failure to relate political events to structural conditions. One such failure, to take an instance out of many, occurred in 1956–57 in connection with certain misjudgments of the situation in China after Mao Tsetung had delighted the unwary with his "Hundred Flowers" speech. It could then have been foreseen—and was in fact foreseen by the Yugoslav Communists—that despite such superficial symptoms of liberalization, China would turn out to be the last great bulwark of unreconstructed Stalinism: a circumstance which today hardly needs emphasis. Yet in 1956 and 1957 there were those who, on the strength of what they saw in the newspapers, were ready to cast theoretical thinking to the winds and take their stand (as they supposed) on the plain evidence of their senses and the concurrent judgment of the well-informed.

At the moment such excessive reliance on political expertise, and the related indifference to the kind of thinking that concerns itself with long-term processes, is more in evidence where Europe is concerned. We have become so used to discussing European affairs in terms of military disengagement, German unification, and so forth, that there is a tendency to overlook the less dramatic but ultimately more important structural changes which have been going on since 1945, on both sides of the Iron Curtain. One discerns a certain reluctance to concede that Eastern Europe may have to remain part of what is called "the camp of socialism," even if the Russian occupation armies are withdrawn. There is hope—based, it seems, on little except wishful thinking—that the Poland of Gomulka will eventually follow the example of Tito's Yugoslavia. A similar lag in official thinking inclines the policy-makers to discuss European affairs as though countries like Britain, France, or West Germany still mattered in the way they did before 1939. At the same time their basic stability tends to be underrated. The fact is that despite some superficial evidence to the contrary, West European politics tend increasingly to be of the municipal kind. By 1970, when unification may be expected to have reached its goal, the various national legislatures are unlikely to be able to harm the interests of their respective countries in any domain that really matters, though they will doubtless continue to reflect popular passions on the subject, for example, of financial support for church schools. In brief, the European nation-states tend to lose ground politically as they become more democratic and at the same time less sovereign. This process does not necessarily enhance the safety of the whole area—in a major war waged with nuclear weapons all Europeans will simply have to rely on their luck; but it does suggest that such a world disaster is unlikely to be triggered by purely European events.

This way of looking at the situation naturally goes counter to much excited talk about present and future upheavals. Like

Spain and Italy, though in a lesser degree, France is liable to suffer political upheavals of the classical type which in a fully integrated and democratized Western Europe are unlikely to recur. In this respect, too, the present phase is transitional. One need only compare the French situation with that in politically stable northwestern Europe on the one hand, and with the perennially troubled Iberian peninsula on the other, to grasp the importance of those social changes which are gradually transforming the whole of Western Europe in such a manner as to preclude revolutions of the classical type. The process is not uniform, but despite occasional violent interruptions it is both effective and irreversible. Post-Hitler Germany offers the clearest possible evidence of what happens to a country when it has finally become a bourgeois democracy. The smaller democratic countries of northern Europe—Scandinavia, Holland, Switzerland—have long been in the van of this secular movement. Britain, Germany, and France—until yesterday great powers—are about to follow suit, though not without difficulty and internal stresses, in the case of France rising to a sudden dramatic pitch. It was never very likely that medium-sized, on the whole democratically governed countries would retain their former outlook in an age in which even the superpowers are having difficulty with the growth of their arms budgets. Nuclear arsenals are for those who can afford them. The countries of Western (and Eastern) Europe are not among that number, though one or the other may now and then let off a Hiroshima-type bomb for prestige purposes. In this respect, too, the politics of 1970 are clearly going to be a very different type from those of 1939, not to mention 1914, when the terms "great power" and "European power" were very nearly synonymous.

If one looks beyond Western Europe to the regions that were once the chosen field of European expansion, the conclusion is similar. European expansion, political and economic, is now very much a thing of the past. Here and there a rearguard action is still being fought, but, in general, West European society may now be said to have effected the great withdrawal and turned in upon itself. The expulsion of the European powers from Asia is well-nigh complete; the Middle East and North Africa have pretty nearly achieved the corresponding objective; and Africa south of the Sahara is not far behind. What this is going to mean in terms of economic development remains for the moment an open question, but one thing is already certain: the bulk of foreign investment will not in the future be European, though Britain and France still invest heavily in Africa, and some profits are being plowed back into Middle Eastern oil. No major West European country is likely in the foreseeable future to stake an economic claim comparable to the pre-1939 foreign holdings of Britain, France, or Holland. The old certainties are gone, political risks have mounted, and democratic pressures in the industrial countries work in the direction of letting both investment and charity commence at home. Socialist economics favor the domestic consumer, and most West European countries are now semi-socialist and likely to go further in that direction. Moreover, the global economic pull reinforces these trends. To quote from an author who has made a professional study of the subject:

> Western Europe has failed since 1945 to attain more than a precarious satisfaction of the economic demands of its own people. This failure is the more striking since output has risen much faster than in the United States. Europe nevertheless preserved a net dependence on dollar aid and could not provide capital of its own for the risky venture of investment in the poorest countries—or where it could, as in Germany, there was more profit in investing at home. It is a fact of the first importance that the United States has no real Western European partner in the economic development of the poorest countries. What Communism may in the future be able to extract from its subjects without asking for their consent, the richer Western European peoples could not provide with democratic goodwill.[1]

The basic challenge comes from societies in the transitional stage between agrarian stagnation and industrial progress. This is now almost a commonplace. What is not so well understood is the political mechanism whereby these societies effect the transition. Here one still comes across evidence of the old uncritical worship of mere progress and the ideologies instrumental thereto. The underlying assumptions tend to be on the optimistic side. Where motives are imputed they are generally of the nobler

1. Oscar Gass, "The United States and the Poorest Peoples," *Commentary*, February 1958.

sort. Thus in an otherwise hardheaded and professional discussion of the topic there occurs the following characteristic passage:

> Both historically and at present the building of modern economies and centralized modern governments has been driven along less by the profit motive than by the aspirations for increased national and human dignity. Merchants and the profit motive played their part in the modernization efforts of Bismarck's Germany, Meiji Japan, Witte's Russia and Ataturk's Turkey; but soldiers, civil servants and nationalism were the most powerful agents. And so it is today in Asia, the Middle East and Africa.[2]

A reflection that comes to mind upon reading this instructive passage is that the authors seem to have imbibed something of the mercantilist ideology characteristic of the countries in question at the moment when they made the transition to the modern world: at any rate the distinction between sordid commercialism and patriotic idealism is in the best nineteenth-century Prussian or Japanese tradition. Oddly enough it was this very emphasis on the superiority of their respective national ideologies over the Western bourgeois mentality which subsequently led the rulers of these societies astray, with results fatal to their plans. What after all has become of Bismarck's Germany and Meiji Japan, not to mention the Russia which Count Witte tried so industriously (and ineffectively) to modernize without touching its central political institutions? And if the future of the Turkish Republic looks somewhat more promising, may this not be due to the fact that it owes its origin to a revolution? In principle, Mr. Millikan and Mr. Rostow would not of course deny this, but a certain facile optimism keeps breaking through; witness the following passage:

> If the local political leader concentrates merely on consolidating his central power or on rallying his people around an external objective, he may well achieve short-run success; but he will not meet the demand for economic and social progress pressing up steadily from the grass roots. He runs the longer-run risk of creating a centralized state without a viable political basis; or of exhausting his popular mandate in efforts to assert the sovereignty and power of the new

2. M. F. Millikan and W. W. Rostow, "Foreign Aid: Next Phase," *Foreign Affairs*, April 1958.

nation against the external world, efforts which fail to satisfy his people's rising expectations for material advance. To be successful, a politician in a transitional society must, in the end, link nationalist fervor and the new centralized state to programs of economic and social substance.[3]

I submit with all due deference that this is at once too general and too optimistic. There lurks behind it what Marx called the liberal illusion—the illusion that all interests are ultimately in harmony. The fact is that all interests are *not* in harmony. What is called the national interest may be partly or wholly at variance with other important interests, including the interest of world peace. I take the passage I have just quoted to constitute a polite hint in the direction of Colonel Nasser, but to be realistic it would have to be more outspoken. Is it really in the interest of the world that so important an international shipping lane as the Suez Canal should be at the mercy of an uncontrolled military dictatorship? Or that a strategically located country should be governed by adventurers without a mandate other than their own highly dubious interpretation of what is called the general will? These things happen, and it is useless to deplore them, but one should at least be clear about the consequences. And why introduce the term "grass-roots," which inevitably conjures up a quite misleading picture of the relationship between government and the governed in societies with an unbroken tradition of despotism, reaching back in some cases three thousand years or more? There is very little grass in Egypt, and no political roots to speak of, and the same is true of most other Asian and African countries.

Again, how does such a terminology enable one to draw meaningful distinctions between the Turkey of Kemal, the Egypt of Nasser, the Yugoslavia of Tito, and the Poland of Gomulka, not to mention the Italy of Mussolini or the Spain of Franco? These regimes evidently have, or had, something in common, and that something is presumably related to an underlying socioeconomic constellation, to which the term "backwardness" is more or less appropriate. But if one goes further to inquire what precisely constitutes the distinguishing mark of Kemalism, Nasserism, Titoism, and Fascism, one begins to see that there are structural fac-

3. Ibid.

tors at work which favor one solution rather than the other. Mussolini's rise would not have been possible without the evolution of Italian nationalism, and this evolution in turn was promoted by the decline of European liberalism after World War I, to say nothing of Hitler and the impact of that catastrophe on the political destinies of half the world.

At this point it becomes even less possible to stay out of controversy. Nowadays we are often told that nationalism is the principal agent of modernization in backward countries, but there is no indication as to what kind of nationalism is likely to become predominant in them. The issue is customarily presented in a somewhat simplified manner, the opposing parties being labeled "Nationalist" and "Communist," as though it went without saying that these are mutually exclusive terms, whereas the Chinese experience should have taught us that this is not so. There is indeed a growing awareness that the failure of what should perhaps be called "classical" nationalism may open the way to a second, Communist-led wave of the revolution, and the authors just quoted show some grasp of this fact when they remark, "There is little doubt that Moscow and Peking regard Nasser, Nehru, Sukarno, and the other non-Communist leaders of the new nations as the Chiang Kai-sheks of the future." But it is not made sufficiently clear that the Communists expect to win this struggle under the nationalist banner and not as representatives of a "proletarian internationalism" that went out of fashion a long time ago. At most it is conceded that they may try to deceive people into regarding them as authentic patriots; but where is the deception? Mao Tse-tung is a more authentic representative of Chinese nationalism than Chiang Kai-shek. It is time to dispense with slogans that bear no relation to any observable reality. There is no such thing as "international Communism," or at any rate it is no more international than the rival ideology of Western liberalism. There are two global camps or parties; for convenience's sake they might be designated "the American party" and "the Russian party," just as in the Napoleonic age people in Europe quite naturally referred to "the English party" and "the French party," meaning the two contesting camps which were then at grips all over the world. Most countries now group themselves under the somewhat tattered banners of liber-

alism and communism, and in so doing they automatically qualify
for membership in either of the two "camps" now contending
for mastery of the globe.

The chief intellectual fault in this respect lies in the failure to
perceive that nationalism can take many forms. There is no such
thing as "pure" nationalism. The nationalism of the *Risorgimento*
was liberal, because liberalism happened to be in the ascendant
in mid-nineteenth-century Europe; half a century later many of
the descendants of these liberal nationalists turned fascist and
followed Mussolini. Germany in the twentieth century supplies
evidence of the same process in a more disastrous form. The
nationalism of France is profoundly marked by the Jacobin tradition of the Revolution. Modern Russian or Chinese nationalism
represents a synthesis of patriotism and Leninism. No one can
say with any certainty what the future holds in store for the Indian subcontinent and the Islamic world. There is at least a possibility that these ancient civilizations will turn away from the
threshold of modernity and retain their conservative outlook: in
other words, abandon the attempt to modernize and remain content with the role of onlookers. But this choice is not likely, and
in any case it is not one that the West can afford to promote. If
we were to adopt the attitude that the problem presented by
these countries is probably hopeless, and in any case none of
our business, it is only too clear what the result would be.

It is undoubtedly tempting to decree that the economic problem facing the countries in question is too big to be solved in
this generation. Specifically, that no government—or at any rate
no popularly controlled government—can cope with the task of
simultaneously raising output and holding down the birthrate.
Recent figures show that since about the time of World War I,
in contrast to earlier periods, the industrial countries have been
exhibiting a slower rate of population growth than the undeveloped areas as a whole. In absolute figures, China is the biggest bloc, with an official count of over 600 million and every
prospect of reaching the billion mark before the end of the century. By the same date, according to some recent computations,
the total population of the Western hemisphere, north and south,
will grow to some 900 million. Taking a somewhat earlier and
less speculative date, the Population Branch of the United Na-

tions estimates that between 1960 and 1975 the population of North America will rise from 197 million to 240 million, that of Latin America from 206 million to 304 million, Europe (outside Russia) merely from 424 million to 476 million, and Asia by contrast from 1620 million to 2210 million. It is the latter figure, plus that for Latin America, which now holds the attention of political scientists. There is little doubt that Europe and North America will maintain their secular march toward a steadily mounting level of well-being, though within eastern and southern Europe there are regions where progress may be slow. Latin America presents a less hopeful picture, and when one comes to Asia and Africa it is difficult to avoid the conclusion that what is now happening in those regions is largely the inevitable, though long delayed, consequence of steadily rising population pressure upon inadequate resources. Some Asian countries, notably Japan, have managed the transition to industrialism so as to expand their resources just in time to catch up with population growth and even surpass it; others have not been so lucky. In particular, China, India, and Egypt have been caught by the "population explosion" at a very awkward stage in their development, and it is undeniable that they have not been helped by the kind of political and economic regime that went with foreign domination. In all backward countries the great question is not how to raise consumption standards but how to make the initial investment that will spark the process of self-sustaining advance across the threshold of stagnation and growing misery. And the overriding political problem is whether this can be done democratically; as to which a certain degree of skepticism is legitimate. Can peasant electorates be expected to support policies which boil down to financing the growth of industry, while the income of all other groups of society is either artificially held down or at any rate not substantially increased? And if the electorates fail to sanction such policies, can some form of dictatorship be avoided? And given the choice between the various brands of authoritarianism, are not the Communists remarkably well placed to win this particular race? There is no definite answer to such questions, but it is in these terms, more or less, that the issue presents itself to the political and intellectual elites in the backward countries, which is another way of saying that the politics of 1970 are going to be significantly different from those of the liberal era. The uncommitted countries have to choose between two alternative ways of solving their basic problem. It may be as well to recognize that the Communist alternative is a genuine one, in the sense that it offers a political and economic model which is attractive to the governing elites of undeveloped countries. It may also be helpful to realize that the United States is a conservative power at grips with revolutionary rivals; there is nothing to be gained by trying to mask this fact. Talk of "permanent revolution" sounds silly coming from apologists of an institutional setup which even by Western democratic standards is fairly conservative. The West does not in this age stand for a radical reconstruction of society. Democratic socialists cannot offer sweeping solutions or drastic rearrangements that take no account of individual liberties, and people or nations who want to make a *tabula rasa* of all existing institutions should be frankly advised to take their troubles to the rival firm—though with a caution that they will be fortunate if they emerge from the experience with a whole skin: not perhaps a very inspiring or heroic stance, but one that is in accordance with the realities of the situation in which we find ourselves.

The Private Philosophy

✳ ✳ ✳

THE TRANSATLANTIC DIALOGUE TODAY consists for the most part of
European exhortations to America to brace up, get busy, and resume the march of progress and of American admonitions to Europe to sit still, reflect on the past, and consider the merits
of tradition. Each side plays devil's advocate to the other. For
every European admiringly envious of America's success in mastering technology there are two Americans anxiously fretting
over their countrymen's reluctance to build Gothic cathedrals
and read Papal encyclicals. Propagandists are busy crossing
the ocean in both directions, urging socialized medicine on
Americans or Thomist education on Europeans as the case may
be. With so much intellectual cross-fertilization going on, it
would seem at first sight that the publicist's task ought to be getting easier; in fact it is becoming more difficult. Each side has
not merely its favorite nostrums but its own way of misunderstanding the other. Europeans see a potential Hitler in Senator
McCarthy, while Americans mistake the parliamentary system
for a version of their own democracy. Americans, too, are either
for or against something called liberalism which has no counterpart in Europe; as European conservatism is quite different from
the American brand.

Intellectuals are among the chief agents in this multiplication
of problems. Politicians know from experience that almost any
doctrine can be pressed into the service of a workable cause,
and that once a course of action has been decided it will not
be long before it acquires some theoretical sanction. Most writers, by contrast, are strong for the opposing view: that policy

is determined by preconceived notions about the nature of the universe. Walter Lippmann, for example, argues in *The Public Philosophy* that the growing debility of modern democracy is due to loss of faith in natural law. Let there be a revival of such faith and society will recover its vigor. Political health and sickness are traced to intellectual currents. Philosophers are not perhaps all-powerful, but "the decline, which is already far advanced, cannot be arrested if the prevailing philosophers oppose this restoration and revival." [1] This is orthodox Platonism. It became the fashion in Greece, if we remember rightly, after democracy had broken down, and it proved unable to arrest the further disintegration of society.

The special mark of this philosophy is authoritarianism—the belief that certain truths can and must be inculcated from above *because* they are in opposition to the common sense of the majority. This is something quite different from conservative traditionalism. The genuine conservative appeals to tradition as the sanction of the prevailing community beliefs and customs. The authoritarian school makes its appearance after the "cake of custom" has been broken, and in opposition to the democratic appeal for the establishment of a new, rational consensus. Not that rationality is ignored—for is not natural law itself revealed to right reason? But the historical incorporation of reason is located in an educated minority, which is also the ruling minority. "In the literal sense, the principles of the good society must be unpopular until they have prevailed sufficiently to alter the popular impulses. For the popular impulses are opposed to public principles." [2] It is not made clear whether this was always so or whether the present state of affairs goes back to the time when the majority of people entered the political stage, i.e., when Western society became democratic. But there is a suggestion that the U.S. Constitution owes its rationality to the fact that in 1787 only about five per cent of the people cared to exercise the vote. Now this circumstance had been noted before by writers who drew different conclusions from it. It is a commonplace that democracy arrived by stages and that its beginnings did not look very hopeful. For that matter, it is arguable that democracy

1. *The Public Philosophy* (Boston, 1955), p. 178.
2. Ibid., p. 179.

is currently in danger of breaking down. But it does not follow that this threat can be averted by the adoption of an undemocratic philosophy.

It should be obvious that this is not a conservative doctrine but one that registers the disappearance of traditional sanctions. Genuine "divine right" conservatism is of course no longer with us, certainly not in Britain—reputedly a conservative country. We have to make do with substitutes, of which the most popular at the moment is Whiggism in the style of Burke and Tocqueville. This, since it is itself rationalist, leaves room for such contrivances as a reformed educational system to inculcate sound principles. In a different form such ideas occur during revolutions, when attempts are made to reform the public mind by direction from above. The "public philosophy" certainly was very much in the thoughts of the leading Jacobins; Robespierre, by refusing to sanction armed resistance to a hostile Convention, even paid it the compliment of sacrificing his life to it. The Jacobins were indeed uncommonly doctrinaire in trying to make their countrymen swallow the whole system of republican morality at one gulp, and in the process they not only came to grief themselves but very nearly succeeded in discrediting the democratic cause in France. Still, on grounds of principle there is a certain bond between them and other moralists, and one would therefore expect some sympathy for them from writers who hold that political institutions are grounded in natural law, and that the majority must be compelled to be virtuous. But Jacobinism has a bad press at the moment, largely for reasons connected with the cold war, and Mr. Lippmann is severe on it. He seems to have been unduly impressed by Dr. Jacob Talmon's work on French revolutionary origins. It is becoming the fashion to discern two conflicting trends in French eighteenth-century "thought": one liberal and tolerant, the other totalitarian and leading to Lenin. This kind of game can be played endlessly, but when all possible variations have been exhausted there remains the problem of accounting for Clemenceau, and, through Clemenceau—in many ways the archetypal French democrat— for the fact that the Jacobin tradition has repeatedly proved to be the mainspring of whatever public spirit there is in France; much as the demand for a stronger executive, which runs through

Mr. Lippmann's book and causes him to be described as a "conservative" in America, is in France put forward by Gaullist and neo-Jacobin heirs of the revolutionary tradition. The best way to escape from these seeming contradictions is to admit that the "public philosophy" is not the sole property of disillusioned liberals.

That there is ground for concern over the present state of democratic institutions no one would wish to deny. George Kennan, who is anything but doctrinaire, in *Realities of American Foreign Policy* [3] adduces some very good additional reasons for doubting whether democratic legislatures are really competent to formulate policy, especially "foreign" policy, although his sharpest criticism is reserved for the practice of passing high-sounding but meaningless resolutions at the intergovernmental level. Perhaps the two problems are connected. It is certainly the case that the British and other Europeans were constantly baffled during World War II by the American demand for generalized slogans of the "Four Freedoms" type. But since the British were likewise fighting for democracy, and the House of Commons maintained fairly close control over wartime policy, it is arguable that this tendency is traceable not to the growing pressure of public opinion upon the executive—Mr. Lippmann's chief worry—but to factors peculiar to the American political climate. In any case, the "Four Freedoms" did not interfere with Yalta, though they apparently caused Roosevelt to demand some kind of face-saving formula with regard to Poland—something to show the voters, in fact. With the exception of this slightly discreditable episode it is difficult to think of any major instance where the Western governments during the war paid much attention to what their publics might want.

Mr. Kennan is dealing, of course, with a more specific problem—the influence of Congress upon American policy-making. On this topic the non-American can only say that it seems to represent an unsolved problem, but not an insoluble one. The more general issue of making sovereign legislatures renounce some of their authority in favor of supranational organizations entails practical problems of the most hair-raising kind, but none that can be dignified by terms appropriate to political

3. Princeton, N.J., 1955.

philosophy. There would seem to be no principle which forbids democrats to recognize the limitation of democracy, just as patriots may be brought to admit that the nation-state must surrender some of its sovereignty to a world organization. Anyone can point to legislatures—the French Assembly is only the most notorious example—which clearly would be much happier if left to debate such topics as the school-leaving age, with more important issues turned over to an elected, but relatively pressureproof, supranational body. Since the whole trend of affairs in the Western world is in this direction, one may assume that discussion of the principles involved will become increasingly vigorous. One must hope that it will not become entangled with arguments from the sphere of metaphysics, for people who differ altogether on the substance of natural law—or even on whether there is such a thing—may yet be brought to agree on the steps necessary to make democracy work under modern conditions.

On the general attitude appropriate to a pluralist society Mr. Kennan is sounder than Mr. Lippmann:

> Let us, by all means, conduct ourselves at all times in such a way as to satisfy our own ideas of morality. . . . But let us not assume that our moral values, based as they are on the specifics of our national tradition and the various religious outlooks represented in our country, necessarily have validity for people everywhere.

Now it is arguable that values are inherently objective and consequently universal; but there is something pedantic about this contention, for in practice each particular culture can only "realize" some specific values at the expense of others, which may be equally important to different people. Mr. Lippmann would like the Western world to believe in a natural law grounded in God; but if such a belief once became general it would certainly acquire exclusive and dogmatic features and would probably need a universal church to uphold it. This conclusion need not frighten a Thomist, but it is not one that liberals can afford to toy with. For better or worse, the society we live in is distinguished by its ability to dispense with unifying faiths of this kind. One may even hold that this is its most attractive feature. And if one believes that a new integration is needed to replace the fading confidence in liberal humanism, one may still think

it likely that the new attitude will emerge spontaneously before crystallizing in a system of thought; its protagonists probably will for a long time look like dangerous radicals to the
defenders of what a scholar has called the "inherited conglomer-
ate" of community beliefs. The fact is that restorations are
rarely successful. The best hope for a wider acceptance of the
"public philosophy" lies not in the forcible imposition of private
systems of belief, however respectable, but in the removal of
obstacles to human solidarity.

The New Science: "Is There a Sociologist in the House?"

✻ ✻ ✻

AMONG THE TOPICS that strike a European visitor to the United States, not the least remarkable is the obsession of articulate Americans with the subject of class. There can hardly be an extended conversation that does not branch out into the theme, usually with a side glance at the rising flood of literature devoted to the complexities of social status in an allegedly classless society. Both the literature and the talk betray something beyond ordinary practical concern—a kind of horrified fascination, rather reminiscent of the manner in which sex used to be discussed in the days when it was still considered good form to pretend that there really was no such thing. Indeed, the American attitude to class and the Puritan attitude to sex seem to have a lot in common. Both phenomena evidently evoke guilty feelings and a desire for some kind of rationalization. To the European, coming from an environment where class distinctions, like sex distinctions, are as much taken for granted as the weather, there is something odd about this almost panicky reaction, though of course it does not take long to discover that many Americans privately share the European attitude.

It also does not take long to realize that the official taboo is related to a circumstance of which many Americans are well aware: the fact that the United States is unique in the Western world in having a genuine proletariat—meaning a sizable stratum of people who are not only propertyless but socially dispossessed and excluded from the ordinary life of the commun-

ity: people who form the great bulk of the more or less permanently unemployed, and who in addition suffer from various
racial and social stigmata of a kind practically unknown in
other Western countries. These people, as any visitor can perceive with the naked eye, not merely are slum dwellers—to find
the equivalent of the Negro slums in some of the less affluent
parts of the U.S.A. one has to go to North Africa: there is
nothing like it in Europe, not even in Spain—but exist at the
lowest rung of a social pyramid whose slopes they cannot possibly hope to climb. When this state of affairs is considered in
the light of the democratic ethos, it is scarcely surprising that
some Americans should display signs of uneasiness, and that a
good deal of recent literature should be devoted to an agonizing
reappraisal of the familiar assertion that all, or nearly all, inhabitants of the United States belong to the "middle class."

It must be said, however, that this aspect of the matter is not
foremost in four recently published works I wish to consider
here.[1] Although their authors, like most of their countrymen, are
fascinated by the subject of class—indeed hardly able to talk
about anything else—they do not, for the most part, approach it
in a straightforward manner; nor are they primarily concerned
with the two-thirds of their fellow citizens who belong to the
industrial working class, let alone the sizable stratum at the bottom of the social heap; their existence is more or less taken for
granted. What really interests these writers is the stratification
to be found within the remaining one-third. This is doubtless
natural: sociologists, like other scholars, are themselves members of the middle class, and the problems of this group inevitably loom large in their eyes. But it does lead to a marked emphasis on "status questions," which are not, strictly speaking,
germane to the issue of class in the wider sociopolitical sense.
This is recognized by Leonard Reissman, whose *Class in American Society* is altogether distinguished by a certain cautious willingness to look facts in the eye. The currently fashionable concern with social classification is due, he thinks, to "the shift from

1. Leonard Reissman, *Class in American Society* (Glencoe, Ill., 1961);
Seymour Martin Lipset, *Political Man* (New York, 1969); William Kornhauser, *The Politics of Mass Society* (Glencoe, Ill., 1960); Pitirim Sorokin
and Walter Lunden, *Power and Morality* (New York, 1960).

the Marxian emphasis upon *class* to the current American emphasis upon *status*. . . . A 'status' orientation and vocabulary can
easily avoid the unwanted innuendoes . . . that Marx attached
so firmly to the idea of 'class.' " Indeed it can, and Mr. Reissman
consequently is at some pains to demonstrate that it is possible to
speak about "class" without being subversive. This clearly is not
easy in an environment where such talk has acquired alarming
connotations. It seems that the only respectable class is the
middle class, at least to the organizers of opinion polls. On the
other hand, though everyone (or almost everyone) belongs to
this divinely favored group, there are really no classes at all!
Mr. Reissman gives an amusing example of how such surprising
statistical results are achieved by those whose business it is to
instruct the public about the facts of life:

> The immediate reaction as late as the 1940's was that "there were
> no social classes in the United States." When pressed, however,
> as they were in a Gallup poll in 1939, 88 percent of those asked:
> "To what social class do you belong?" answered "middle class"; the
> remaining 12 percent divided equally between "upper" and "lower"
> class. There is really not much contradiction between the initial re-
> action of "no classes exist" and the answer of "middle class" given
> by most Americans. Both responses are part of the same configura-
> tion of a belief in social equality. The psychological emphasis is
> upon the word "middle" and not upon the word "class."

But the pollsters also had something to do with it. This came
out when a somewhat differently worded questionnaire was
framed ten years later:

> In 1949 Centers asked a national sample of adults to what class
> they belonged, and found that 52 percent said that they were
> "working class," 36 per cent said "middle class" and the rest signi-
> fied "lower" or "upper class." Part of the differences in identifica-
> tion shown between this poll and the one by Gallup ten years
> earlier . . . was due to the fact that Centers had included the cate-
> gory of "working class" to overcome the negative connotations of
> "lower class," with which few persons could identify.[2]

So the earlier result was obtained by not mentioning the term
"working class"! If only all social problems could be as easily
solved.

2. Reissman, op. cit., pp. 12–13.

Behind this kind of intellectual muddle there lurks what Reissman calls "the belief in social equality" or, to put it differently, the notion that "class" signifies "caste." This is an old story, and by no means confined to America. It has been an important factor in the rise of democratic movements all over the Old World. Even today one can hear British public men *of all parties* declaim about "the abolition of class distinctions," i.e., the discarding of outworn and superfluous status symbols. "A classless society" in *this* sense is simply another name for democracy. The odd thing is that England, having no significant racial minorities, probably stands a better chance of reaching this goal within measurable time than does the United States. However, this is another story. Let us get back to our four authors.

In view of what has just been said it is not surprising to find that they are all haunted by the ghost of Marx. This is true even of Professor Sorokin, the well-known inventor of a rival system, who might be expected to look with some disdain upon a mere nineteenth-century theorist, and who does in fact take a rather lofty view of the matter. His colleagues, being closer to the ground, are correspondingly more worried. Mr. Reissman is the most worried of them all, clearly because he knows most about the subject. Marx crops up in practically every one of his chapters, invariably to the detriment of the argument, since whenever the fatal topic rears its head, he takes refuge in obscurity. Even so he manages to insinuate a good many conclusions that smell distinctly of subversion, though wrapped in several layers of academese and decked out with copious references to Max Weber, Talcott Parsons, and other authorities of unimpeachable respectability. There is, for instance, Weber's notion that "the class relations of the economic order belong at the level of the national society. Relations at the community level, as a separate analytical dimension, involve the 'status' order." This was also one of the themes of *The Power Elite*, and all through *Class in American Society* one can feel the shadow of C. Wright Mills dogging Mr. Reissman's uneasy footsteps. Whenever this kind of subject comes up, he assumes the embarrassed mien of a church elder caught playing dominoes, but underneath his opaque style there is a firm, though cautious, commitment to the notion that there must be *some* structure in the social order and that possibly Weber had the clue to it. This kills two birds with one stone, for Weber had a theory of society in which social status is almost as important as economics. To quote from his own formulation (as cited by Reissman): "With some simplification, one might say that 'classes' are stratified according to their relations to the production and acquisition of goods; whereas 'status groups' are stratified according to the principles of *consumption* of goods, as represented by special 'styles of life.'"

"As has been intimated throughout," Reissman observes, "Weber's analytical distinctions offer the most meaningful framework for interpreting and understanding stratification in a modern industrial society. The theory is broad, ranges far, and includes a variety of different manifestations of stratification under one explanatory roof." It is also incompatible with some cherished academic foibles, among which Reissman lists the custom of conducting empirical "research" on the assumption that "class" means "occupation group." His own nomenclature displays some uncertainty over whether any and every considerable "status group" may be described as a "class"; and so we get the familiar game of trying to establish how many "classes" there are in "Hometown," Reissman's ideal-typical small town. "The number of classes that is recognized varies, depending on the number of social differences that Hometowners can detect and agree upon," he says gravely, as though such differences were not, in principle, numberless.[3] (In practice it turns out that there are just three classes: those at the top, those at the bottom—the manual workers—and, in between, the socially active and church-going middle class, which sets the tone and in particular informs all comers that "We don't have classes in our town.")

Notwithstanding his academic caution and a tendency to describe a spade as an agricultural implement, Reissman is basically disposed to admit that things are not invariably what they seem. He even commits the alarming heresy of stating that "the economic institution provides the major dimension for stratification in American society . . . it is the economic base that is generic and all others are derivative." Translated back into ordinary language this comes pretty close to saying that ownership

3. Ibid., pp. 69, 161, 182.

is what distinguishes one class from another. If this is not actual heresy, it is the nearest thing to it, and since Reissman also notes that class lines show a tendency to harden, the picture one gets from him is not so different from that painted by Mills. It is true that, by way of light relief, he also provides a certain quantum of standard sociological textbook absurdities, e.g., "Hyman has reported the results of an NORC survey, in which it was found that not only the class of the individual but also the class of his parents was important in explaining his aspirations." [4] But I take this kind of solemn nonsense to be a ceremonial bow to the reigning academic fashion. Presumably if one wants to hold one's own in the fraternity, one has to include a minimum amount of this kind of thing, on pain of not being taken seriously. On the whole Reissman is on the side of the angels. His work is much superior to that of his near-namesake, and hence unlikely to win him fame and promotion. It may even give him a reputation for being dangerously inclined to question some of the established idols of the marketplace.

No such fate threatens Seymour Lipset, whose essay collection *Political Man* brings together a number of previously published studies and some new material ranging from strictly professional writings to semipopular reflections on a variety of current issues. Even a cursory reading of this closely printed and densely argued work shows the author to be well in tune with the prevailing consensus of opinion upon almost every imaginable topic. At first sight the reader who has just absorbed a heavy diet of Reissman is agreeably impressed by Lipset's fluent style; but the comparison does not altogether work out in his favor. Reissman's pontifical manner—like that of his masters, Weber and Parsons— is the penalty exacted from a writer who has something important to say and is careful to guard against misunderstanding by a triple layer of impenetrable academic prose. This does not make for lively reading, and one turns with some relief to Mr. Lipset's commonsensible discussion of German history, French politics, English social life, the genesis of McCarthyism, and other topical matters of concern to the intelligent citizen. It is

4. Ibid., pp. 205, 297 ff., 340 ff., 365.

only as one delves deeper into these brisk, chatty, well-informed essays that one discovers the flaw in the performance.

It is not that Mr. Lipset does not know his subjects well enough—on the contrary, he has read practically everything and in addition drawn on the combined services of research institutes in a dozen countries, not to mention a staggering list of people who have given him the benefit of their individual and collective help and advice. The trouble is that all this frantic cerebration has been sieved through a conceptual apparatus which is not really attuned to the serious business of generalizing about politics. Not, at any rate, European politics. It may be that Mr. Lipset is sound on the history and the institutions of his native country: it is not for a foreigner to say, though I experienced a slight twinge of disbelief on being informed that the late Senator McCarthy drew his principal support from people classified as "nineteenth century liberals" (quaintly defined by the author as "those who were opposed to trade unions and to the large corporations"). [5] Perhaps he did; and then again, perhaps not. It is at any rate an arguable proposition (though one would have thought that on ordinary methodological grounds it was dangerous to draw such far-reaching conclusions from an opinion survey limited to "respondents from a small New England city"). What cannot be argued—what indeed stands out like the proverbial sore thumb—is that when he comes to areas outside the United States, Mr. Lipset does not know what he is talking about.

Of this lamentable circumstance many examples could be given, but only a few can be mentioned in this space. In connection with the passage just quoted, the author—after a parade of opinion-poll figures that give a spurious air of profundity and scientific rigor to the proceedings—advances to a general historical summation, and what is it that he tells his readers? "Like Poujadism, McCarthyism and nineteenth century liberalism are primarily the reactions of the small businessmen." Now I submit that this statement—taken alone and without any corroborating evidence—is sufficient to demonstrate that Mr. Lipset has no real hold upon the historical categories he employs, or rather brandishes, with such an air of authority. It is possible—although one doubts it—that there were as many shopkeepers among Sen-

5. Lipset, op. cit., p. 169.

ator McCarthy's followers as there were among those of M. Poujade; it is likewise arguable that keeping shop has the effect of predisposing a man against trade unions as well as against taxes; at a pinch it could also be argued that there were sizable numbers of shopkeepers and small manufacturers among those who in the nineteenth century voted for liberal parties. But even if all these assertions are allowed to pass, the statement remains what it was before: a self-evident absurdity. For the whole point about "nineteenth century liberalism" is that it was in total and unbridgeable opposition to everything that Poujadism, McCarthyism, or any other form of reactionary Populism, stands for. In short, the examples cited by Mr. Lipset are radically incomparable, or at least they have in common no more than a single feature which, taken by itself, explains nothing. Rebellious shopkeepers or even small farmers (another group greatly favored by him as potential carriers of fascism) do not by themselves add up to a political movement, or determine the character thereof, though they may provide its mass support. It depends entirely on the situation what sort of movement—democratic or antidemocratic—they attach themselves to, and the "situation" is invariably a *historical* one; that is to say, it is determined by an irreversible constellation of unique circumstances. Thus the fact that Poujadism was a ludicrous failure, even as a protest movement, was determined by the discredit thrown upon this particular type of reactionary rebellion by the antecedent failure of the Vichy regime. Or again, that Hitler was able to impose himself upon Germany clearly had a great deal to do with German nationalist reaction to the loss of World War I. In short, what counts is the exact moment on the time curve, and the historical situation of which such moments are part.

Now it is improbable that Mr. Lipset would dispute this. On the contrary, it is more than likely that if the point were put to him he would fervently agree, and then cite half a dozen farfetched examples to illustrate it. For the trouble is that he seems genuinely incapable of seeing the difference between historical and sociological thinking, and hence is perfectly willing to substitute some slapdash historical generalization for his standard reliance upon statistics, or "analysis of public opinion surveys." It is all one to him whether a "fact" belongs to the distant past or the immediate present, whether it illustrates a historical trend or a current fad, and what sort of situation it forms part of. Anything that can be reduced to measurable dimensions is grist to his mill. Hence his analysis of fascism in general, and Hitlerism in particular, though weighed down with learning and brimming over with factual information, never comes to grips with the subject. It is typical of his color blindness that in relation neither to Italy nor to Germany does he so much as mention the crucial role played in the political life of these countries by the belated emergence of nationalism. Instead the reader is presented with statistical breakdowns of election figures and other sociological trivia: not as an incidental help to the understanding of what took place—as such the information would be quite useful and legitimate—but as the centerpiece of a theoretical argument purporting to explain why and how these movements rose to power. Neither does he grasp the fact that, notwithstanding competition for votes between Conservative and Fascist parties, there was an effective alliance between the two wings of the reactionary, antidemocratic, movement: failing which neither Mussolini nor Hitler could have captured the state apparatus. In short, anything not reducible to quantitative measurements, or psychological twaddle about "insecurity" and "extremism," is beyond his purview.

The kind of psychology that is employed to fill the holes in such constructions is well illustrated by Mr. Lipset's attempted analysis of Communist totalitarianism. This, of course, is a "mass movement," hence presumably subject to the general rules applicable to "mass society." One of these rules specifies that, under modern conditions, there are large numbers of people whose social life is badly integrated and that most of these people are located at the bottom of the social pyramid. In a chapter headed "Working-Class Authoritarianism," these not very illuminating concepts are employed to explain—what? Lenin's concept of the party as a centralized vanguard! The argument proceeds as follows:

> The lower-class individual is likely to have been exposed to punishment, lack of love, and a general atmosphere of tension and aggression since early childhood—all experiences which tend to produce deep-rooted hostilities expressed by ethnic prejudice, po-

litical authoritarianism, and chiliastic transvaluational religion. . . . All of these characteristics produce a tendency to view politics and personal relationships in black-and-white terms, a desire for immediate action, an impatience with talk and discussion. . . . It is interesting that Lenin saw the character of the lower classes, and the tasks of those who would lead them, in somewhat these terms. He specified as the chief task of the Communist parties the leadership of the broad masses, who are "slumbering, apathetic, hidebound, inert and dormant." These masses, said Lenin, must be aligned for the "final and decisive battle" . . . by the party which alone can present an uncompromising and unified view of the world and an immediate program for drastic change.[6]

And so on, following earlier observations on the readiness of the masses "to follow leaders who offer a demonological interpretation of the evil forces (either religious or political) which are conspiring against him" (*sic*). To this Mr. Lipset adds the following priceless footnote: "Most of these characteristics have been mentioned by child psychologists as typical of adolescent attitudes and perspectives. Werner Cohn, in an article on Jehovah's Witnesses, considers youth movements as a prototype of all such 'proletarian' movements." Why "proletarian"? the reader of either Mr. Lipset or Mr. Cohn may well ask. Apparently because this adjective is intended to denote "an aura of social estrangement." That the Bolshevik party had about as much in common with Jehovah's Witnesses as chalk with cheese; that its core was made up of "professional revolutionaries" stemming from the intelligentsia, who also staffed its chief rival, the Populist movement (SR); that the ideology of Leninism is to be understood in terms of the Russian intelligentsia's traditional radicalism—these and other decisive historical circumstances find no place in such attempts at system-building. (Incidentally, Hitler's concentration camps were full of Jehovah's Witnesses who apparently did not regard him as a suitable leader to follow, despite his "demonological interpretation of the evil forces (either religious or political)" conspiring against him.)

If these lapses stood by themselves, they might be regarded as a passing aberration. But they appear to reflect a mental climate characteristic of the school to which Mr. Lipset adheres. In

6. Pp. 120 ff.

quieter and less pretentious, more baldly factual, and for this very reason even more alarming and brain-curdling form, they also occur in the writings of Professor William Kornhauser.

The Politics of Mass Society, like Mr. Lipset's essay collection, has for its theme the analysis of what happens to democracy when it has to operate in a postbourgeois environment. (Not that either Mr. Lipset or Mr. Kornhauser would agree to this statement: they favor a more involved nomenclature.) In such a society there are "masses," i.e., people who own no property. (This point too is not much stressed, since it conflicts with the dogma that we live in the best of all possible worlds.) Such people are not well integrated, and their behavior, as Mr. Kornhauser notes with concern, "tends to be highly unstable," reflecting "social alienations," and leading to "resentment against the social order." This mental condition is the seedbed of "mass movements," which in turn may (but need not) acquire a totalitarian character. "Mass movements are miniature mass societies; totalitarian movements are miniature totalitarian societies." Such movements "appeal to the most extreme dispositions of individuals and their readiness to go to any extreme in the pursuit of their objectives." This makes them dangerous to democracy. "Mass society is characterized by an abundance of mass movements. Other types of society are characterized by different kinds of social movements." [7] How does such a state of affairs come about?

> The major set of circumstances associated with the emergence and development of mass movements must include those factors that weaken social arrangements intermediate between the individual and the state. . . . Such factors are those associated with *major discontinuities in social process* as measured by the rate, scope and mode of social change. . . . Where the pre-established community consists of small, homogeneous units, rapid urbanization and industrialization are highly favorable to extremist mass movements.[8]

And—one might add—where there is *no* significant urbanization and industrialization (for example in the Middle East), "extremist mass movements" have been a prominent feature of social life,

7. Kornhauser, op. cit., pp. 46–50 passim.
8. Ibid., p. 125. Author's italics.

not only in recent times but at *all* times. But never mind. Let us not worry either about Kornhauser's queer definition of "extremism," which could easily be stretched to include every shade of patriotic activity, notably that of national resistance movements. Let us rather turn to his political conclusions:

> In summary, where the introduction of democratic rule is based on a pluralist society, especially a balance of classes and religious groups, it will tend to be strong and viable; but where its introduction is not accompanied by multiple independent groups capable of fighting for the sustenance of individual rights, and at the same time ready to support a basic framework of authority, democracy may readily lose out to new forms of autocracy.[9]

This is probably meant to suggest a reason why democracy works fairly well in the United States and in England, but it leaves unexplained why it failed to work in the Weimar Republic—than which no more pluralist balance of classes, churches, and even territorial units ever existed. Of course the answer is that the "balance" was not a harmonious one, but how were the framers of the Weimar Constitution to know? On paper they had created the perfect pluralist balance. If it came unstuck, the explanation once more has to do with history—a closed book to Messrs. Lipset and Kornhauser.

Now for a sample of the new sociology when applied with minute care and extreme statistical precision to a single problem:

> Data showing that extreme personal deviance and extreme political behavior do not vary together . . . indicate that different social conditions may give rise to each. Thus, if the proportion of the electorate which supports the Communist party may be taken as an indicator of the extent of extremist political behavior in a society, and if the proportion of the population recorded as suicides, manslayers, and alcoholics may be used as indicators of the extent of personal deviance in society, then it may be shown that countries characterized by relatively strong Communist movements are not generally characterized by relatively high rates of personal deviance. . . . More precisely, if Australia, Canada, Denmark, Finland, France, Italy, Norway, Sweden, Switzerland, the United Kingdom and the United States, are ranked by size of the Communist vote in the first election after 1949, and if they are ranked by propor-

9. Ibid., p. 141.

tion of suicides in 1949, *the rank order correlation between suicide rate and Communist vote is* −.26. If the same countries are ranked according to rate of homicides rather than suicides, *the rank order correlation between proportion of manslayers and of Communist voters is* −.08. If these countries are ranked by proportion of alcoholics and of Communist voters, the correlation is −.38. We may conclude that there is *no evidence here for a positive relation between conditions that favor mass deviance and those that favor personal deviance.*[10]

We may also conclude that a sense of reality (not to mention a sense of humor) is not among the prerequisites of this kind of "research." Otherwise it might have occurred to Mr. Kornhauser that there is something seriously wrong with a method that enforces such absurdities as trying to compare suicide rates and voting behavior. What would he say if it were suggested to him that to the average citizen in the industrial belt around Paris, voting Communist seems a perfectly ordinary thing to do, rather like going to the corner bistro for a drink, and not in the least comparable with cutting one's throat or swallowing arsenic? Would he brush such objections aside or would he mentally tag the critic as a potential subversive? Probably both.

We pass from one brand of academic daydreaming to another, slightly less respectable. Our target so far has been the correlation—to use professional language—of sociological research-mongering with accelerated decontrol over ordinary reality. With our final specimen, *Power and Morality*, by Pitirim Sorokin and Walter Lunden, we take leave of sense altogether and enter a realm where the mind ranges freely over subjects as remote from each other, and from any conceivable relation to the ostensible theme of discussion, as the philosophy of Yang Choo and the suicide of Ivar Kreuger. Here, for what they are worth, are a few extracts, chosen from among literally dozens of a similar kind, and by no means madder than the others:

> These ideologies [sc. of Machiavellism] have been more fully developed by many thinkers of ancient, medieval and modern times, like the "Indian Machiavelli" Kautalya (in his *Arthasastra*), Yang Choo in China, Thrasymachus, Thucydides, Callicles, Carneades,

10. Ibid., pp. 91–92. Author's italics.

Sextus Empiricus, and Lucian, in the [sic] ancient Greece and Rome; by Pierre du Bois, Marsilio of Padua, Machiavelli, Vico, Bodin, Hobbes, Croce, Sorel, Pareto, Lenin, Stalin, Hitler, Mussolini, and other defenders of rulers' freedom from moral restrictions, of the autonomy of politics from ethics, of the justification of a morally reprehensible but successful policy by its very success. . . .

A moral and mental schizophrenia seems to characterize all forms of government which govern mainly by murderous, "diplomatic," and other compulsory means. . . . Similar split personality was shown by Stalin, Hitler, Napoleon, Peter the Great, Cromwell, Charles V and Philip II of Spain, Louis XIV, Henry VIII, Elizabeth I, Nero, Diocletian, Constantine the Great, Asoka, and by most monarchs, dictators, commanders, inquisitors, etc. In a milder form this moral schizophrenia also marks the high ranks of democratic government personnel. . . . P. Jacoby, F. A. Woods, P. A. Sorokin, and other investigators of the mental and moral properties of monarchs, unanimously [sic] agree that *the percentage of geniuses as well of the feebleminded and insane is much greater among the royal families than among the general population.* Also, the frequency distribution among monarchs in the categories of: above average, average, and below average, differs quite markedly from the frequency distribution of scholastic grades among the students of our colleges. . . . Of the 354 monarchs studied by F. A. Woods, 143 were above average. . . .

Despite the lack of precise and systematic statistics, the existing data do not allow any doubt that *the powerful, and/or autocratic rulers of the states display in general a much higher rate of patricides, matricides, fratricides, uxoricides, and murders of their relatives, than does their ruled population.* . . . Depending upon the period, country, occupation, sex, age, race, etc., the murder rates for the ruled population fluctuate between 0.0008 and 0.2 per 100 persons of the total.[11]

After this it comes as something of a relief to learn that in democracies the trouble consists mostly of "crime against property, sex, good mores, and in lighter crimes against person" (*sic*); though the authors note with concern that if one compares the record of 20,000 average American citizens with that of 20,000 outstanding citizens (including "all the Presidents and Vice-Presidents of the United States and members of their Cabinets"),

11. Sorokin and Lunden, op. cit., pp. 19, 50–52, 58–61.

the crime rate for the latter group is markedly higher.[12] Still, by comparison with such people as Thucydides, Nero, and Machiavelli, the United States comes out fairly well.

While criminality among rulers appears to be a constant phenomenon, a special problem characteristic of our epoch arises from the alarming circumstances that "the Sensate form of culture which has been dominant in the Western World during the last five centuries is disintegrating," in consequence of which "Ideologies of John Locke, Rousseau, Marx, and other varieties of democratic, liberal, progressive, conservative, socialist, syndicalist, communist, anarchist ideologies; those of equality, freedom, free enterprise, planned economy, welfare society—all these ideologies which previously inspired are at present about dead."[13] Exactly what my Aunt Ida always said. Does someone object that Professor Sorokin is not a real, honest-to-goodness sociologist, but a Toynbeean prophet in sheep's clothing? Then let him consider the almost endless list of his publications, and his apparent success in getting both the public and the academic world to take him seriously. Another possible explanation might be that the author of the passages quoted above is quite simply dotty. This I believe to be the case, but the fact remains that his colleagues have not so far mustered up sufficient courage to make a public announcement to this effect. Could it be that they fear the resulting discredit to their profession, were it officially admitted that one of its most widely known representatives is, to put it plainly, not quite in his right mind?

Whatever the answer to these and similar questions may in the end turn out to be, it must, I think, be admitted that sociology offers the layman more entertainment and a wider range of bizarre contrasts in tone and substance than any other intellectual discipline, not excluding psychoanalysis. Perhaps this state of affairs should not be taken tragically. After all, every new branch of learning has had to go through a phase of wild growth. Medicine sprouted from primitive witch-doctoring; chemistry is supposed to have had its roots in alchemy. There must at one time have been numbers of otherwise sane and respectable people—doctors, pharmacists, and the like—who in their spare time

12. Ibid., p. 75.
13. Ibid., p. 117.

dabbled in magic. How long was it before they reluctantly abandoned their search for the philosophers' stone, or gave up trying to make gold in their back kitchens? Bearing in mind the time it took to shed these aberrations, one should not perhaps worry too much about the Sorokins of this world. The real trouble lies elsewhere. It has to do with the uncritical veneration of quantitative measurement, and the resulting superstitious belief that meaningful conclusions can be extracted from the juxtaposing of heterogeneous evidence—if I may for a moment be permitted to lapse into jargon. This belief, alas, is not confined to the more eccentric members of the profession; it has its stalwarts among people who, by the usual criteria, must be classed as sane. Until they are cured of their delusion, it is to be feared that the public will continue to treat even the most serious and reputable productions of the school with a skepticism doubtless wounding to their authors but not wholly unmerited and in any case less harmful than the mutual praise and encouragement practiced within the walls.

The Triumph of the Fact

✿✿✿

SOCIOLOGY, one foot firmly planted on the grave of metaphysics, the other tentatively poised on the elevator leading to the summit of political power, is the master discipline of our time. Other ages may have done more for philosophy, literature, or art. Even the nineteenth century, if truth be told, was rather better at the business of intellectual synthesis. But none can dispute our preeminence when it comes to the social sciences. There is nothing in the past to match the devoted labors of those trained researchers who have taught us how to quantify, tabulate, and analyze our social environment: the people inhabiting it, the customs inspiring them, and the assumptions by which they live. It is true that the foundations were laid in an earlier and darker age: Comte, Marx, Durkheim, Pareto, and Weber toiled and wrought with simpler tools. But now that the scaffolding has been removed, the structure that shines forth is unmistakably a skyscraper. Moreover, its spare lines bear witness that its architects are the peers of those builders in steel and glass who have created our modern cities. If the effect strikes a certain chill, it is undeniably impressive. Its beauty is of the hygienic sort, but it is beauty nonetheless.

The work of David Riesman [1] takes its place within this collective composition as a bridge or corridor, perhaps, guiding the student toward the inner recesses of pure theorizing. The reader's path is eased by the skill with which the author's style dissembles his learning, though there are footnotes on almost every page

Partisan Review, Autumn 1964.

1. See in particular *Abundance for What? And Other Essays* (New York, 1964).

to remind one that mastery of complex subjects is not attained without hard work. Does the question concern the mental stress involved in migration from country to town? "Some Observations on Interviewing in a State Mental Hospital" will indicate the source material which has served as the basis for more far-reaching conclusions. Are shopping habits to be considered? A signpost to a learned paper (not the author's) on "Contributions to the Theory of Reference-Group Behavior" will refresh the mind, followed perhaps by a dip into "The Career of the Funeral Director" (Ph.D. dissertation, University of Chicago, 1954). Is the theme under discussion connected with the career plans of Harvard students? A glance at "The Validation of Expressed Interests As Compared with Inventory Interests" (*Journal of Applied Psychology*, XXXIX, 1955, 184–89) will supply the desired information. Or is the researcher anxious to discover why some people prefer to live in one place rather than another? He will be directed to "Amenities as a Factor in Region Growth" (*Geographic Review*, XLIV, 1954, 119). The wealth and precision of these footnote references is such that practically every generalization may be said to carry its burden of proof. "Three Centuries of Women's Dress Fashions: A Quantitative Analysis," by Jane Richardson and A. L. Kroeber (*Anthropological Record*, V, 1940, 112–50) is merely one out of literally hundreds of such casual allusions to source material.

To the envious reviewer, gently stewing in what Zelda Fitzgerald once called "the boiling oil of sour grapes" (this quotation is not from Riesman, I discovered it elsewhere), such a profusion of learning inevitably acts as a challenge. Thirty collected essays, six hundred pages of rigorously scientific, yet colloquially presented information on very nearly every subject under the sun—who can blame the poor critic if he starts looking for flaws? Alas, wherever he turns he is met with the same firm, yet gentle and persuasive guidance to the ultimate authority: that of the fact. Whether the subject is international relations, social tensions, suburban life, or the motor car (there is an extremely learned discussion of Detroit's production and styling problems), the reader is discreetly steered through the maze of controversy to conclusions imposed by dispassionate reasoning and backed by mastery of the relevant literature. The conclusions may be unexciting, but they are never hasty; the mode of reasoning may derive from too uncritical an acceptance of the current empiricist orthodoxy, but all possible counterarguments are considered in advance; the whole may give the impression of a tremendous accumulation of data devoted to the end of buttressing an evanescent faith in the mores of an enlightened middle class: but *this* criticism (like every other, from whatever point of the compass) is anticipated by the author and built into the structure of his argument. Marx, Freud, Weber, Veblen, the critics of "alienation," even the anarchists—they all get their due, and are duly consigned to rest beneath the tombstone of a learned apparatus which yet, surprisingly, does not interfere with the flow of an easy, sprightly, almost conversational, style. Who said sociology is dull? Riesman almost manages to make it entertaining.

In an ideal world, a writer who combines this breadth of information with an intelligent grasp of Keynesian economics, Freudian psychology, and the complexities of the arms race would carry the kind of authority which is actually reserved for specialists in these various disciplines. Much of Riesman's work is in fact concerned with the need to establish connections between separated fields of study: specifically between behaviorist psychology, empirical sociology, and contemporary politics. He even ventures into Sovietology, at the risk of irritating the incumbents. I must confess there are times when I am uncertain what he is getting at. Consider a passage such as the following:

> More generally, I have long thought that we need to reevaluate the role of corruption in a society, with less emphasis on its obviously malign features, and more on its power as an antidote to fanaticism. Barrington Moore in *Soviet Politics*, and Margaret Mead in *Soviet Attitudes Toward Authority*, present materials documenting the Soviet campaign against the corrupting tendencies introduced into the system by friendship and family feeling—some of Mead's quotations could have come from Bishop Baxter or other Puritan divines, and others from American civil service reformers. While Kravchenko shows how one must at once betray friends in the Soviet regime when they fall under State suspicion—and here too the Soviets are more tyrannous than the Nazis who expected friends to intercede with the Gestapo—it would appear that such

human ties have never been completely fragmented, whether by Puritanism, industrialism, or their savagely sudden combination in Bolshevism.[2]

I am able to follow the general drift of the argument, but it does not seem to me to lead to any conclusion more sensational than the statement that human nature is pretty constant. Assuming this to be so (though in fact I don't believe it), how does it help one to understand what has been happening in the U.S.S.R.? Riesman to the contrary, I remain obstinately convinced that the proper way to understand Bolshevism is to study Russian history; the way to understand Nazism is to study German history; the way to understand industrialism is to study economic history. There may be a common factor, but if there is, it escapes me. I suspect it also escapes Riesman, although he devotes a good deal of effort to the business of isolating it and fixing the label "totalitarianism" upon it. This seems to me a waste of time. The Puritans, incidentally, were not totalitarian, for the good and sufficient reason that their ideology did not compel them to undertake a thorough reshaping of the social order: they contented themselves with the imposition of a new set of manners (or rather with the generalization of manners and customs already prevalent among their followers). It is also worth remembering that Puritanism—or for that matter any other ideology—is a historical product. To say that Bolshevism "combines" "Puritanism" and "industrialism" is to abstract from the specific historical occurrence of all three. It is no doubt true that there was a puritanical streak in the character of the early Bolsheviks, and it is arguable that every industrial revolution is accompanied by an emphasis on hard work and sacrifice. But if we label this emphasis "puritanical," and then argue back from modern industrialism to seventeenth-century Calvinism, we are moving in a circle. The fact is that no one knows why the industrial revolution succeeded in some places and failed in others, though the fate of the Protestant Reformation in various European countries supplies a clue to the answer. Lastly, it is just as well to bear in mind that prior to 1917 Russian industry was already expanding at a rate it has rarely exceeded since, and this without the benefit of a puritanical ideology, or any other.

2. Ibid., p. 84.

The whole subject is full of puzzling complexities. The French Revolution, by promoting social equality, clearly hampered France's economic growth in so far as it slowed down capital accumulation; yet it also laid the base of a subsequent advance at a later stage, after the shock had worn off. This, incidentally, renders questionable the notion that the modernization of backward countries is best promoted by introducing egalitarian social reforms. A strong case can be made for the proposition that poor countries have to choose between equality and progress. If this is so, it is tantamount to saying that in such areas liberal democracy is unworkable. This conclusion can be grasped in the absence of further information about particular circumstances, the moral standards prevalent in the society, or any other feature of interest to cultural anthropologists. It is simply a consequence of the social setup. Similarly, corruption "as an antidote to fanaticism" has existed since time immemorial. What renders its role important today is the part it plays in preventing backward countries from modernizing themselves. Corruption, by the way, can take numerous forms, some of them outwardly legitimate. Bloated urban economies flourishing at the expense of an impoverished and neglected countryside, for example, tend to "corrupt" their trade unions by paying them high wages. Meanwhile the hinterland is left to rot until there is an explosion. Such symbiotic relationships are quite common in "underdeveloped" countries; as long as money does not change hands in ways that are stigmatized as illegal, the system looks stable and respectable. One is not sure how Riesman would categorize such a situation. I should call it "prerevolutionary," on the assumption that eventually an armed minority is going to rebel. But this supposition is reasonable only because contemporary politics are what they are. In past ages, these people would have gone on passively enduring their lot, human nature notwithstanding. Human nature appears to be very largely what we make it.

I have perhaps devoted too much space to a subject that happens to be of topical concern. *Abundance for What?* is not really about the Cold War or the problem of "underdevelopment." As the title indicates, it is for the most part about what Professor Galbraith some years ago described as the problem of "affluence." No doubt this matter is very real to some people. It must be, seeing that there is such a vast literature around it. Personally I don't find the problems of suburbanites and the worries of consumers very fascinating, but there are millions of them, and they are clearly entitled to the best professional attention they can get.

The more technical papers have been crammed into the second half of the volume. They include a thoughtful appraisal of Veblen, and the inevitable reconsideration of Tocqueville. One sometimes wonders how many of his readers are aware that *Democracy in America* is much inferior to Tocqueville's later work. Riesman takes him perhaps a shade more seriously than he deserves. The remaining essays include one on the technique of interviewing: a practice that has clearly been brought to a fine art, since it has now become possible to make it the subject of theoretical considerations. (The title of this paper is "The Sociology of the Interview.") It had not previously occurred to me that the political views and voting habits of middle-class women can be analyzed with the same degree of precision as the incomes of their men, but apparently it can be done.[3] If a general impression emerges from these papers dealing with the worries of the educated middle class, it is that their author is in close rapport with the state of mind manifested by those interviewees who profess themselves faintly puzzled by the current state of the world, though willing to keep an open mind about it. Both sides to the dialogue seem to embody the same uncertainties, combined with a resolve to go on searching for an answer. This is apparently to be done by accumulating yet more data on the voting preferences of middle-aged housewives, the "scale of tolerance" manifested by college-educated (as distinct from non-college-educated) respondents, and the extent to which people are "worried more or less now than they used to be, and what about." Here at any rate is something Tocqueville had not thought of, but then serious research has come of age only with the invention of the questionnaire.

3. See James G. March, "Husband-Wife Interaction over Political Issues," *Public Opinion Quarterly*, XVII, No. 4 (Winter 1953–54), 461–70.

Bridging the Gap

❋ ❋ ❋

THE ORIGINS of the symposium *Sociology and History* [1] go back to an annual meeting of the American Sociological Society in 1954, and more specifically to an exchange of views between Werner Cahnman and a number of colleagues on the topic of forming a Committee for the Sociological Study of Historical Documents. Formal sessions on "Sociology and History" were organized at annual meetings from 1956 onward, about eighty sociologists having previously associated themselves with the committee, and these rather elaborate proceedings resulted in the compilation of the present volume. As is natural in the circumstances, most of the contributors are sociologists, though they also include a few historians, one anthropologist, a professor of Romance languages, and the Professor Emeritus of Spanish at Princeton, Señor Américo Castro. The best known of the historians, Marc Bloch, is represented posthumously by an extract from his standard work, *La société féodale*. The two editors contribute five individual papers, a joint introductory essay, the preface, and a concluding summary, in addition to jointly prepared linkage texts to Parts One ("Evaluation of Theories") and Two ("Recent Research"). Their concluding chapter is intended, *inter alia*, to take the place of a formal bibliography, and thus assumes the form of an editorial survey of significant literature, both classical (i.e., nineteenth-century) and contemporary.

Given this arrangement, two questions present themselves: have the essays been selected with a view to overcoming the differences between historians and sociologists? and have the edi-

History and Theory, V, No. 3 (1966).
    1. Werner J. Cahnman and Alvin Boskoff, eds. (Glencoe, Ill., 1964).

tors succeeded in evolving a new methodological approach? To neither question is an unequivocal answer possible. Certain essays represent a successful fusion of generalized and particular thought about the processes of social change in history. Others pursue the aim without contributing much of value. Still others appear to be addressed solely to specialists in one or the other field. Moreover, there is considerable unevenness in intellectual and scholarly quality. Some of the contributions, though competent enough, are evidently intended for the intelligent student in need of a general introduction to his particular topic. Others appear to have been written for the author's colleagues—and only a small handful of these. When it comes to methodology, the gap is very wide between writers who are equally at home in the sociological and in the historiographical approach and those who flounder helplessly in the no man's land between the two disciplines. By a coincidence which is perhaps not altogether fortuitous, the most original contributions—e.g., Robert A. Nisbet's fascinating discussion of kinship groups in Roman society— are distinguished by their successful bridging of the interdisciplinary gap. At the other extreme, one encounters Alvin Boskoff's paper on "Social Indecision in Two Classical Societies," which might be taken for an involuntary parody of what is sometimes supposed to be the sociological approach. This essay manages in less than ten pages to present most of the fallacies that have prejudiced historians against sociology. Its weakness is underlined by the surprising exclusion from this volume of any work by M. I. Finley, whose reflections on the topic of Graeco-Roman history would have been eminently worth having.

In general there appears to have been some capriciousness in the choice of contributors. Marc Bloch's posthumous fame hardly accounts for the inclusion of an extract from his great work under the general heading of "Recent Research." On the other hand, Robert Marsh's paper on bureaucratic promotion in prerevolutionary China constitutes "recent research" all right, but it has no apparent relation to history or to the stated aim of the editors. It is an exercise in Weberian analysis of bureaucratic patterns, though conducted with an analytical rigor foreign to the master. Tung-tsu Ch'u refers airily to "Chinese class structure" and "Chou feudalism," as though it went without saying that these concepts are applicable to traditional Chinese society, but at least he is concerned with the history of social change. H. A. R. Gibb and Harold Bowen, moving with lightning speed through several centuries of history, attempt in less than seven pages to deal with the social structure of the Arab provinces in the Ottoman Empire. Some of the themes of their joint essay, notably the social function of Islam, recur in Cahnman's paper "Religion and Nationality," which *inter alia* seeks to contrast Oriental and European attitudes on religious affiliation. This is an important theme, but can it really be maintained that "in Western Christianity, the idea of the Kingdom of God is interpreted as referring to a purely spiritual realm with no political connection," whereas "oriental Christianity and traditional Judaism, as well as Islam, do not dissociate religion from social life"? Does Roman Catholicism "dissociate religion from social life"? For that matter, did Protestantism during its formative period? Norman Birnbaum's excellent paper on the Zwinglian Reformation in Zurich would seem to bear out the contention that the Reformation was as much a social as a religious phenomenon, and that whatever dissociation took place must have occurred at a later stage.

No useful purpose would be served in attempting to classify some of the other papers in this section. Their inclusion testifies to a laudable desire to encourage specialized research, without for that reason adding much to the general theme. William Miller's essay, "The Business Elite in Business Bureaucracies: Careers of Top Executives in the Early Twentieth Century," comes closer to the theme of the collection, but his uncritical employment of terms such as "business leaders" and "bureaucrats"—the latter apparently a synonym for senior officials in any large organization—reflects an undue reliance upon the vocabulary current in the social milieu which forms the ostensible subject of his analysis.

The methodological discussions are for the most part grouped together in Part One ("Evaluation of Theories"). The editors lead off with some reflections on the subject of generalizing and particularizing modes of thought. The statement that "types are meant to be conceptual images, not descriptions of the events

themselves" introduces an important theme which recurs in Mr.
Cahnman's lengthy and thoughtful paper on Max Weber. This
is by far the most substantial contribution to the debate. Most
of the other essays are in the nature of introductory surveys.
This applies in particular to Joseph Maier's discussion of "Cyclical Theories"—a discursive recital of exploded notions. Some
skepticism must attach to the judgment of an author who casually alludes to "the modern cyclical theories of Hegel, Pareto,
Brooks Adams, Spengler, Toynbee and Sorokin," especially when
this catalogue is succeeded by a reference to Lorenz von Stein
and Karl Marx as thinkers of approximately equal importance.
Surely Nietzsche would have made a better companion of Spengler and the other cyclists than Hegel? And if Pareto "stresses
sameness exclusively," how can he take rank with a philosopher
who "portrayed history as a dialectical process moving toward
the realization of freedom"?

With Cahnman we are on firmer ground. Wisely he limits himself to Weber and the *Methodenstreit*. What he has to say on this
subject, though highly compressed, is of great interest, notably in
bringing out the dependence of the German "historical school"
upon the romantic movement of the early nineteenth century.
This is indeed the crux of the matter, for the "collectivist" bias
of the "historical school" went back to the romantic revolt against
individualism—a revolt that did not exclude the "cult of the individual," provided the latter could be seen as the executor of
the popular mind or some other "organic" force. The school's
emphasis on "organic growth" proceeded from Burke's critique of
the French Revolution, but in the German setting it inevitably
took on a different coloration, with the emphasis on the *Volks-
geist* and the cultural community of the nation—the latter concept not differentiated from the tribal unity of the "folk." All
this belongs to the pathology of German nationalism rather than
to the general inheritance of English and European conservatism, but that is just what renders the topic important. If these
national peculiarities are set aside, Weber's intervention in the
famous *Methodenstreit* of the 1890s takes its place within an
intellectual tournament from which the new discipline of sociology emerged, as a compromise between the rationalist insistence
on general laws and the romantic emphasis upon the unique

and specific: in different terms, as a bridge between (Ricardian) economics and (Rankean) historiography. Across the Rhine a similar compromise was achieved in the later nineteenth century by Durkheim, of whom Cahnman notes that one cannot understand his position "if one overlooks his indebtedness to De Bonald, to Maistre, to Boeckh, to Fustel de Coulanges." The problem in both cases was the same, with the significant difference that Comtean positivism was vastly more influential in France than in Germany, where the positivist attitude was substantially confined to the Marxian school (a point neglected by Cahnman). Quite naturally, the *Methodenstreit* arose within the framework of what was then called "political economy" (though the Germans preferred to talk of *Volkswirtschaft*—an innocuous term connoting the kind of patriarchal domesticity to which they were still accustomed). Institutional economics and historical sociology were elaborated as a critical response to Anglo-French rationalism and positivism. What rendered British classical economics in particular suspect to the Germans was not merely its insistence on invariable "laws" but also—as Cahnman puts it— the "underlying nominalistic assumption . . . that the social world was an aggregate of individual wills": precisely what the romantics had always denied.

All of this is of the highest importance, and it is to be regretted that Cahnman is almost alone among the contributors in having grasped the philosophical implications of the debate, as well as the peculiar relevance of Max Weber as a mediator between the "individualist" and the "organic" approach. What he has to say about the tension between the generalizing and nominalistic procedure inevitable in economics, and the "collectivistic tendencies and artistic aspirations which are of the essence in history writing" goes straight to the heart of the whole debate. It is useful to be reminded that Weber "argued as a latter-day disciple of the historical school" in directing his criticism against theorists like Menger, who seemed to him to mistake "theoretical concepts for segments of reality." His own commitment to the notion of the "ideal type" was an attempt to escape from the dilemma by forging a conceptual tool which was *not* meant to describe the essential features of a particular historical reality, but to set up a "model" against which they could be measured.

That this purpose was misunderstood, even by sympathetic critics, is indicated by Serge Hughes's suggestive discussion of Croce's views. "Preoccupied with other matters and loyal to Hegel, it was enough for him to realize that Weber's sociology rested principally on Rickert, Windelband and Dilthey to lose interest." He may indeed have exaggerated the extent of Weber's indebtedness to the neo-Kantian school, which was always counterbalanced by his own empiricism. However this may be, it is indisputable that Croce developed his philosophy of history in conscious opposition not only to Marx (whom he scarcely understood) but also to Weber. The equation of history with liberty was indeed incompatible with the notion of a "value-free" descriptive science paradoxically dependent, in the last resort, upon values not reducible to first principles. It is possible to feel that, on the philosophical essentials, Croce's instinct was sound when he refused to bother with this tired neo-Kantianism. But by virtually ignoring both Marx and Weber, he effectively cut himself off from sociology itself.

It must be a matter of regret that the editors have not chosen to organize the volume systematically around a discussion of these themes. An opportunity has been lost to acquaint the public with the full dimensions of the conflict out of which the new discipline of sociology arose. Even in its present imperfect shape, *Sociology and History* has some admirable features. In principle at least, a step has been taken toward that historical sociology the absence of which is so much felt at the present day. Some of the contributions—Wallerstein's essay on West African nationalism in particular—can be regarded as pointers toward the kind of fusion from which both historians and political scientists (not to mention the policy-makers themselves) may benefit some day. And in his concluding chapter, entitled "The Rise of Civilization as a Paradigm of Social Change," Cahnman once more raises the discussion to a level of generality at which the philosopher, too, may feel at home. I cannot resist a quotation from this essay, which appears to me to mark a successful synthesis of the descriptive and the normative approach:

> In comparison with the cities of antiquity and the European cities of the middle ages, African cities are distinguished by the fact that no sacred fire is kindled, no common allegiance generated. The

pluralism of family groups and ethnic units is not transcended; the citizen's city is conspicuous by its absence. The reason is that urbanization in Africa, instead of being an independent process, is coincidental with industrialization and the formation of nation-states. This is what is indicated by the term "combined development."

Once sociology comes to be associated with writing of this kind, rather than with the fanciful speculations of Sorokin or the trivial accumulation of pointless data, philosophers and historians will cease to cavil at it.

The Romance of Max Eastman

❋ ❋ ❋

AMERICAN RADICALISM is a standing puzzle to Europeans. It is at once more violent and more innocent than its Old World counterpart, more flamboyant in its rhetoric of denunciation, yet at the same time so optimistic as almost to resemble a hymn of praise for life as it is lived. Moreover, it seems from the start to have been infused with a paradoxical certainty that while mankind's past history has been a mess, the future is certain to be agreeable. The best is yet to come—especially in the United States. Goethe thought the Americans were fortunate in not being weighed down with memories, and monuments, of past failures. Others have been irritated by their habit of taking it for granted that Europe's past was but an antechamber to America's present. There have even been subversive hints to the effect that this is an illusion they share with the Russians.

Certainly the Russian Revolution has meant different things to Americans and Europeans. In Europe it was seen as the fulfillment of gloomy forebodings which had haunted the ruling classes since at least the abortive uprisings of 1848, if not since 1789. It was close at hand and dangerous; it was also easy to understand, though even socialists for the most part disliked the form it took. There was nothing totally strange about it, though much that was repellent. To Americans it came as a surprise for which their experience had not prepared them. The fall of Tsarism was indeed welcomed; all the rest—Lenin, Bolshevism, and the talk of world revolution—seemed mere fantasy: a spectacle remote and vaguely terrifying, but not dangerous, since the United States was happily immune to such infections. Even the

The New York Review of Books, January 14, 1965.

handful of American Communists did not really believe they could pull off a revolution: most of them were too busy learning English and integrating into American society to entertain such illusions. At most they thought the distant volcanic eruption might lend some significance to their own burrowings. For the rest, the Bolsheviks and their doings made a splendid subject of conversation. This no doubt explains why Communism at one time was fashionable in Hollywood and in café society generally. It involved no commitment beyond the voicing of advanced opinions of Lenin (a learned bore), and no danger of the Red Army marching in. It was an age of innocence, and the memoirs of Max Eastman [1] are a monument to its vanished glories.

For gone they are. Today one can no longer talk of Communism without having actually read Lenin; just as one cannot in good conscience discuss current topics without some understanding of Russian history, Soviet politics, even—dreariest subject of all—Soviet economics. Happy the age that has no need of such pedantry! Around 1920 one could "take a stand" on the Revolution in total ignorance of what was involved. A great many people did, and the bleached skeletons of their former selves are all around us, in the shape of lengthy confessions of error and elaborate explanations of how it all happened and what it was that misled them.

As a chronicler of his personal journey through this distant age, Mr. Eastman falls somewhere between Frank Harris and Whittaker Chambers. By this I do not mean that he is untruthful: merely that he has been fortunate in being able to combine the Stendhalian temper of the one with the ideological fervor of the other. Radicals—at least in Europe—usually tend to be gloomy and ascetic. Mr. Eastman was born into an ascetic environment (both his parents were Congregational ministers) and has been running away from it ever since. He seems to have dropped Puritanism—what was left of it, i.e., the conviction that pleasure was sinful—at an early age and embarked upon Enjoyment from the moment he could afford it. This happened, notoriously, in Greenwich Village, where he was introduced simultaneously to Love, Poetry, and Socialism. The penultimate chapter of the memoirs

1. *Love and Revolution: My Journey Through an Epoch* (New York, 1965).

chronicles his disillusionment with Socialism, and his graduation
to an editorship on the *Reader's Digest,* but there is no suggestion that he has ever been untrue to either Poetry or Love. There
is something reassuring about this. After all, there are millions
of socialists, but only a handful of poets, and—if one can believe
the psychologists—not too many accomplished lovers. If a choice
has to be made, I for one am willing to trade a carload of political prose for a single solitary glimpse of either love or poetry.
In this sense it appears to me that Mr. Eastman—for all the staggering banality of his mature political and philosophical views
and the insipidity of his poetic tastes—has chosen wisely.

I am bound to report, however, that this is not quite how he
sees himself. Not that he is reticent on the subject of Love. On
the contrary, he relates his experiences with the greatest of candor and in somewhat perturbing detail. For my hypocritical English taste there is a trifle too much stress on the theme of
physical enjoyment, understandable perhaps in a refugee from
the ministry, but slightly alarming nonetheless: much as Frank
Harris's rather similar celebration of his gargantuan sexual appetite had the effect of making his readers a bit uneasy about
both the subject and the author. With the best will one cannot
help feeling a little skeptical (as well as envious) when confronted with such an unflagging record of erotic conquest. It is
not this aspect of Mr. Eastman's memoirs, however, which really
troubles me, but rather his naïve conviction that the story of his
political and philosophical disillusionment with Communism is
really worth telling once again (for, after all, we have heard it
before) in detail. One can see of course that the two topics go
together, inasmuch as the Greenwich Village Revolution of 1910
led straight (for its participants) to the October Revolution of
1917. Nonetheless the fact remains that in truth the two events
had nothing to do with each other.

It is here that the comparison with Harris imposes itself. There
is, I suppose, a sense in which the Social Revolution and the
Sexual Revolution can be regarded as two aspects of a global
upheaval in progress since World War I. But this kind of detach-
ment is possible only for Americans. It cannot be shared by
Europeans, who have had to endure the catastrophes of two wars
and the horrors of totalitarianism. Mr. Eastman's Stendhalian

voyage of discovery through our epoch was marked, inevitably and through no fault of his, by the irresponsibility of the uncommitted outsider. In the end he was a tourist: there was a place to which he could always return. It might be Hollywood or the *Reader's Digest*, love affairs or literary friendships, courtroom speeches or fisticuffs with Hemingway: the life he led was not that of a "professional revolutionary" (not even of an unprofessional conspirator like Chambers) but that of a literary man who could (and did) at any moment disengage himself from politics to pursue his private affairs. That indeed is how civilized people *should* live. But in our wretched world such a style of life is the mark of the dilettante—even if he happens to be a dilettante who has been to Russia and made the acquaintance of Trotsky. Mr. Eastman is an ex-radical, but not an ex-professional. He was an inspired amateur from the moment a girl friend explained Marx to him in three easy lessons. (There is no evidence, despite his professions to the contrary and an enthusiastic endorsement from Edmund Wilson, that he ever went deeper into the subject.)

All this may sound a little patronizing. It is perhaps a mistake to take poets seriously when they stop writing about Love and get on to History. But Mr. Eastman insists on being taken seriously, not only as a Great Lover, but also as a Deep Thinker, and this is where I am obliged to part company with him. I do not grudge Mr. Eastman his mature conviction that the political commonplaces of his boyhood, which he rejected around 1912, are solid truth after all. I merely observe that he might have reached this conclusion by a shorter and less wearisome route. His present reflections on Marx, Lenin, Communism, and so forth, are not merely trite: they are trite in a peculiarly amateurish sort of way. It is regrettably evident that in all the years when he preached the doctrine he later came to renounce, he really had no notion of what he was talking about.

It also has to be recorded that Mr. Eastman shares with other romantic egotists a naïve self-worship whose dimensions must have been the awe of his contemporaries, as its manifestations are plainly the pride of its possessor. Here too a national element appears to enter. In hypocritical Europe we are trained to conceal the extent of our narcissim. However much we may be secretly convinced of our superiority, we try to put on a suitably modest air in public. Americans do not seem to suffer from these inhibitions quite to the same degree, and Mr. Eastman certainly is one of the least inhibited specimens of the breed ever to make an appearance between hard covers. It comes as the most natural thing in the world for him to say of one of his writings that it "would have changed the history of the world if the authorities in Washington had read and believed it." I doubt whether this is so, and in any case it seems a little odd (if I may for a moment indulge in understatement) to make such claims on one's own behalf. But it is part of Mr. Eastman's charm that he does not think it in the least odd, and indeed his book is full of such quaint displays of self-admiration. This facet of his character, along with his strikingly handsome appearance, must have been a great help to him in the pursuit of Love, but I cannot help feeling that it has hampered him in the more prosaic business of clearing his mind of political cant. The cant after all had got there in the first place because he was so carried away by the Revolution and by his acquaintance with Trotsky. Its ultimate replacement by a different, and even sillier, sort of cant does not seem to have resulted from an increased capacity for taking thought: merely from middle-aged disillusionment and a very natural desire to find an emotional haven among the half-forgotten certitudes of one's childhood.

In the nature of the case, the more interesting chapters are those dealing with the author's stay in Russia in the early 1920s and his impressions of the Bolshevik leaders. But before he reaches this point, the conscientious reader has to work his way through a fairly lengthy account of how Mr. Eastman in 1917 almost singlehandedly tried to stop the United States from getting into World War I. He still thinks this was worth doing, and devotes a good deal of space to the resultant court cases involving *The Masses* and *The Liberator* magazines, of which he was editor. His courtroom triumphs are described at considerable length and with somewhat humorless insistence upon the pathos of the occasion, the brilliance of counsel for the defense, and the impact produced by the chief accused himself, who on at least one occasion managed the not inconsiderable feat of appearing in the dual role of pacifist and indignant patriot. There

was some legal fencing, which *inter alia* involved Judge Learned
Hand and other luminaries, and Mr. Eastman seems on all occasions to have been treated with perfect courtesy. This of course
is a credit to the American system, but it rather detracts from
the notion that he was carrying on a heroic battle against a
brutal tyranny. My own impression is that he was having a
splendid time and getting a lot of free publicity. He also managed to offer some unsolicited advice to President Wilson, and
in return received a very polite letter acknowledging that civil
liberties had been a little strained, and that it was difficult in
wartime to draw a line between legitimate restraint and improper
censorship. In a subsequent account of the 1920 "red scare," the
author notes that he and his friends were left alone. "Why our
Liberator office was not raided we never could guess, unless it
was that Wilson failed so miserably in his two previous efforts to
put us in jail," he says severely. This seems questionable. Is it
not more likely that Mr. Eastman was not really regarded by
those in authority as such an important person?

The Bolsheviks were a different breed of men altogether. They
had no compunction about jailing their opponents without trial,
or indeed shooting them out of hand. But then they were running a victorious revolution and moreover had been involved in a
savage civil war. Mr. Eastman, without becoming one of them,
was prepared to make allowances. He was profoundly impressed
by Lenin and struck up an intimate acquaintance with Trotsky,
not to mention Krylenko (then in charge of Justice, i.e., repression), whose sister he married. His feeling about the Bolsheviks
on the whole was that, given the situation they were in, they
really had no choice, and that the Terror was inevitable. This was
perhaps a reasonable view to take, but it led to some curious
ideological entanglements, since it put him in the position of having to apologize for Bolshevism without being a Marxist. That
was a familiar phenomenon at the time, but not all fellow-trav-
elers were as prominent as Mr. Eastman, nor were they all as
muddled as he about the philosophy of the whole thing. For it
has to be said that he was very muddled indeed. While nursing
an obscure grudge against Marx, on account of his literary manners (which were actually no worse than those of other nineteenth-century polemicists), Mr. Eastman was quite willing—for

some years at least—to put up with the political behavior of
Lenin and Trotsky. He was of course strictly an indoor Marxman
—not required to shoot anyone or even to denounce people for
failing to be wholehearted about the Revolution. Yet the whole
business somehow leaves the impression that, as on previous
occasions, Mr. Eastman was wholly carried away by a Great
Idea he had failed to understand.

The author's progressive disillusionment with the Revolution
forms the subject of the concluding chapters. As usually happens
with literary men, it all began with a quarrel over authorship.
Trotsky, after Lenin's death in 1924, had dropped some indiscreet
remarks to Mr. Eastman, and in the following year there occurred
a celebrated literary row, in the course of which Trotsky dis-
claimed all responsibility for some statements attributed to him
by Mr. Eastman in a book which alluded to Lenin's famous unpublished "testament." Trotsky of course knew better; in plain
terms, he was lying. Mr. Eastman was and is indignant about
this. I must confess that my sympathies in the matter are wholly
with Trotsky. He was fighting for his political life and could not
afford to have Mr. Eastman buzzing around, adding to his troubles. But literary men are notoriously touchy about such matters,
and Mr. Eastman took the incident in bad part. It shook his faith
in Trotsky's integrity, and even implanted the seed of doubt
about Lenin. Later he published another book (called *Marx,
Lenin and the Science of Revolution*) which completed his dis-
grace in Moscow. Among other things it contained some reflections on Hegel—a remarkable feat considering his ignorance of
the subject. "My criticism of Marx's Hegelian philosophy was, I
think, cogent and scholarly," he says modestly. "But my proposal
that, following the line of Lenin's instinctive heresies, we convert
the whole thing into an applied science of social transformation,
had the serious defect I have mentioned: it ignored the question
who is to be the scientist and whence comes his authority." One
could name a few other defects, but there is no need to be
pedantic. Indeed, if Mr. Eastman did not take himself so seriously
as a thinker, there would be no point in mentioning the subject
at all.

I hope I have not given the impression that Mr. Eastman's
memoirs are not worth reading. They are full of splendid anec-

dotes, many of them doubtless true, and there are some excellent character sketches of John Reed, H. G. Wells, and other literary figures. Moreover, Mr. Eastman is an engaging writer éven at his silliest, and when he forgets about Hegel and comes down to matters within the range of his mental comprehension, he is both lively and informative. He has an eye for personalities, though unfortunately no head for abstractions. He cannot grasp the simplest philosophical notion, but he can paint a scene and bring to life the passions aroused in a country such as Russia by the turmoil of civil war. His vanity does no harm to his descriptive and biographical passages; it becomes tiresome only when he tries to sound grave and important. Besides, he was an ardent traveler, always off to some new destination, and his later chapters afford glimpses of Spain and the Middle East. Only toward the end, when the final break with Trotsky has to be chronicled, does he once more become solemn and tedious. His warrant this time is a letter Trotsky addressed to his American followers warning them against Mr. Eastman's philosophical heresies. Trotsky by then was in exile, and, while grateful to Mr. Eastman for having translated his *History of the Russian Revolution,* he felt obliged to caution his American disciples against what he called Mr. Eastman's attempt "to translate Marxian dialectics into the language of vulgar empiricism."

He need not have worried. Mr. Eastman's empiricism is not of the kind that has a seductive effect upon the followers of rival philosophies—but that is beside the point. The point for Mr. Eastman was that, just as Wilson in 1917 had refused to take his advice about the war, so now Trotsky had failed to accept his views on the revolution. It was the end, in every sense. A few years later he had the satisfaction of being denounced in the *Daily Worker* as a "British agent," having been named as such in the Moscow "trials." By then most of his wife's Russian relatives had been swept away in the Purge, and Mr. Eastman himself, though resident in New York, was a trifle worried about his own safety—unnecessarily. It was a grim finale to a great infatuation, though I am not sure I understand the logic of his "convalescing from socialism," as he calls it in his penultimate chapter. Where does socialism come in? (Or Marxism for that matter?) But logic was never Mr. Eastman's strong point, and now that he is in his anecdotage (as the *Reader's Digest* would say), it would be pointless to split hairs.

As the record of a personal journey through a turbulent epoch, this self-portrayal, though often vulgar and silly, has a permanent value. Moreover, the book itself is splendidly produced and the period charm it exudes is well sustained by the photographs. Thus when all is said and done the reader need not feel cheated. I have indeed heard it said that "it is all the fault of people like Max Eastman that there is no Socialist movement in America." But though constitutionally skeptical of literary men, I find this difficult to take. How can it be the fault of a poet if in prosaic fact there was nothing for him to do but to go abroad and fall in love with a woman, and a revolution, in a strange land where people were killing each other for the sake of an idea they had misunderstood? Let us not grudge Mr. Eastman his tranquil old age, his *Reader's Digest* philosophy, or his conviction that he has disproved Marx and Hegel. He has earned his repose, and I for one am able to enjoy even his absurdities.

PARISIAN IMPRESSIONS

De Gaulle—A Summing Up

✻✻✻

I

THE EIGHT MILLION INHABITANTS of Paris are currently about to go on their annual vacation in a fairly relaxed mood. Most of them are entitled to four weeks' statutory paid holiday, a piece of legislation not yet enacted in some countries which fancy themselves more advanced. The others seem to be making their own arrangements for going abroad or staying with country cousins, the net result being an atmosphere curiously remote from last year's near-revolutionary ferment. In part this is plainly due to exhaustion. No volcano erupts twice in a year, and even the French must pause before they can resume the national pastime of unmaking governments.

This, then, is a season for stocktaking. Most students are pleased to have got rid of an elderly ruler who had overstayed his welcome. The middle-aged think back to the 1939 military parade on July 14—the last before the outbreak of war; also the last occasion on which cavalry served a more than purely ornamental purpose (though as a matter of fact the French army in 1940 had more tanks than the Germans: it just did not know how to use them, having failed to listen to the warnings uttered a few years earlier by a then widely unknown staff officer named Charles de Gaulle).

This officer was not universally liked by colleagues and superiors. Students of his writings cannot fail to discern at least one good reason why this should have been so: he never hesitated to say and do unpopular things. His early reflections on military leadership—published in 1932 under the promising title *Le Fil de l'épée* (*The Edge of the Sword*)—ran clean counter to the then prevailing rhetoric, which was both pacifist and democratic. Their author put forward what might fairly have been called an elitist view of politics, clothed in the sort of intellectual arrogance that comes natural to Frenchmen of all political parties: casual allusions to Tolstoy, Bergson, and Flaubert; sweeping historical judgments; and an undercurrent of late Roman stoicism, unusual, to say the least, in a practicing Catholic. "Evangelical perfection does not lead to empire." "The man of action is not conceivable without a good dose of egoism, pride, hardness, and cunning." No hypocrisy here. A modern-minded technocrat, too, who had read his Spengler:

> Nowadays individualism is in retreat. . . . Everywhere there appears the need for association. . . . It is for the Army to take a share in this evolution. . . . Instruction, training, and uniform are in no way contrary to the century of trade unions, highway codes, Taylorism, and great department stores.

How very true. But not exactly what democratic politicians like to be told. And what were the pious to make of this?: "For after all, can one comprehend Greece without Salamis, Rome without the legions, Christianity without the sword, Islam without the scimitar, the Revolution without [the battle of] Valmy, the League of Nations without the victory of France?" Two years later the work that made him famous, *Vers l'armée de métier* (mistranslated *The Army of the Future*), terminated with a flourish: "For the sword is the axis of the world, and greatness cannot be shared."

Oh dear, oh dear, oh dear, this will never do. Let us go and hide under the bed. Let us join the Peace Pledge Union. Let us preach "collective security" without rearmament. Let us applaud the Munich surrender. Let us, in short, be good American liberals or British Labourites: spiritual heirs of John Locke, who spent a lifetime trying to make people forget what that dreadful man Hobbes had been saying: "And covenants, without the sword, are but words, and of no strength to secure a man at all." How *could* anyone say such a thing! John Locke never did. John Locke was a stockholder in the slave-trading Royal Africa Company, but he never in so many words defended the actual practice of the trade: he simply averted his embarrassed gaze from it. He also provided the Whig aristocrats, whose servant and pensioner he was, with a political doctrine suitable to their aims *after* they had seized power (illegally) in 1688. John Locke had many descendants, including Jeremy Bentham, James Mill, and John Stuart Mill. And Mill begat the Fabians, but he also begat Neville Chamberlain, that earnest Unitarian and municipal reformer of whom Lloyd George said contemptuously in 1917: "He would make a good mayor of Birmingham in a lean year." But he made a very bad Prime Minister in 1937.

Not that the French were any better off. Their leaders (Clemenceau having died in 1929) were Daladier, Bonnet, Blum, and Reynaud. Unlike Chamberlain they were intelligent and had few illusions. But they were helpless too. Daladier—War Minister from 1936 to 1940—was the most helpless of the lot. Popularly known as "the bull of Vaucluse" on account of his frequent but futile rages, he was the man responsible for letting the amiable but feeble Gamelin ruin the French army. The other military leaders were either senile defeatists like Pétain or stoical pessimists like de Gaulle. When, in March 1940, two months before the collapse, a group of British parliamentarians called on Brigadier de Gaulle at the headquarters of his armored division, he greeted them with the words "Gentlemen, you will be seeing an army that is going to be defeated."

What could one do with a man of this sort? Especially when he insisted on going on with the war after his military and civilian superiors had surrendered, thereby at one stroke becoming a hero and making all the others look foolish? Ever since those days when de Gaulle wrenched himself loose from the military caste into which he had been born, its senior members have hated him with a deep hatred. He had had the effrontery to be right about the use of armor before 1940, and now he had put himself at the head of a motley volunteer army largely composed—as he once remarked in a cynical aside—of "Jews, Negroes, and Communists." In addition to this, he publicly identified himself with France, even allowing it to be understood that a distant ancestor had fought and bled under Jeanne d'Arc's banner. Churchill, a Tory romantic, half understood him and on occasion made a feeble attempt to shield him from Roosevelt's petty spite and the solemn idiocy of Cordell Hull, but for the most part de Gaulle had to rely on bluff. Only in 1943, when the underground resistance movement in France went over to him, did the American and British governments reluctantly renounce their fatuous plans for putting the bovine Giraud in his place.

Ever since those stirring days *les Anglo-Saxons* have been in the General's bad books, but there was more to it than resentment. De Gaulle's idiosyncratic personality hid a popular undercurrent—vaguely describable as Bonapartism—with which the French are familiar but which they find difficult to explain to foreigners. The syndrome is made up of nationalism, Catholicism, a certain amount of Jacobin republicanism (the *Marseillaise,* the Tricolor), military romanticism, contempt for parliamentarians ("a lot of windbags"), faith in popular sovereignty (*la nation*), belief in an abstraction called "France," and lofty disdain for fifty million actually existing Frenchmen. Dislike of foreigners comes into it, too, but no particular resentment against the Germans. Anyway the Reich was gone, and the Bonn government was all for working with France. When de Gaulle returned to power in 1958 he could have it both ways: be friends with Adenauer, and still run the continental show. He could also preach disengagement in Central Europe and an end to the cold war, until the Russians marched their battalions into Prague and thus brought to nought his plans for circumventing the NATO alliance.

For the economic infrastructure of the European movement—the Common Market of the Six—de Gaulle was in no way responsible. On the contrary, he had been against it, and on taking office once more in 1958 he accepted it reluctantly as part of a package deal with the Socialists and Christian Democrats. Their leaders had come running to Colombey when the army in Algeria threatened to get out of hand, and in due course President Coty invited "the most illustrious of Frenchmen" (as he termed him in an address to the National Assembly) to form a new government.

But although de Gaulle towered above his ministers, the party system was then still intact, and the majority had staked its all on the Common Market, on Franco-German amity, and on keeping the British out of continental affairs until they were ready to be "good Europeans." De Gaulle inherited this orientation and, for all the differences in style, did not really introduce any basic change, except that he gradually became friendlier to the Russians and less friendly to the Americans. He was quite willing to make the most of the Paris-Bonn axis, but he rarely troubled to hide his belief that Germany would and should stay divided. And he publicly went out of his way to proclaim that France recognized the Oder-Neisse line as the new frontier between Germany and Poland. This was something the parliamentarians of the Fourth Republic had never dared to do, just as they had never dared to cut the Gordian knot in Algeria by giving the country its independence. To that extent the Fifth Republic did represent something new. It had become a Presidential regime. The President since 1965 was elected by the people, and once installed he could do more or less what he liked.

Across the Rhine the political landscape had altered too. When the Allies in 1945 abolished Prussia as a political entity, turned its eastern regions over to Russia and Poland, and allowed the remainder, plus Saxony, to become a Soviet satellite, they created a new balance of forces within West German society. The ancient love-hate relationship with France went on in the breast of each individual German, but the pro-French tendency within the political elite now had the upper hand. In the days of the Weimar Republic it had always been in a minority. Only the Social Democrats and the left wing of the Catholic Center party genuinely favored reconciliation, and they lacked real power. The Communists had their new spiritual homeland in Russia; the Right dreamed of a war of revenge, and the Right controlled the army. Conservative opinion in Prussia for over a century had seen France as the hereditary enemy, the *Erbfeind,* and the traditional Conservatives, by way of the Lutheran Church, possessed a secure hold over masses of people in town and country whom the liberal intellectuals (mostly Jews anyway) could not reach. All this changed after 1945. The Bonn government now had a predominantly Roman Catholic base, and even a conservative Bavarian like Franz Josef Strauss preferred France to other potential allies—Britain included.

When in 1966 the Christian Democrats felt obliged to take the

SPD into partnership, the pro-French orientation was reinforced, even though the Social Democrats did not have much use for de Gaulle. The extreme Right, such as it was, kept quiet. Its leaders grudgingly conceded that there was no alternative to the French alliance. Some of them developed a discreet admiration for the General. The others thought it best to await his departure. They did not care for his pro-Soviet orientation, and they were bitter when he formally recognized Polish sovereignty over the lost provinces, but in public at least they said nothing. In the old days they would have raged and foamed. This was not just a matter of political prudence. Something had changed in the depths of the national psyche.

Viewed from Whitehall this Francophilia was a trifle alarming. Churchill had favored it. His successors were less happy about it, especially when in the 1960s Britain's international standing was slowly eroded. Europeanism was all very well, but a Europe run jointly by the French and the Germans might become too powerful for comfort. If these Continentals could no longer be manipulated, the Foreign Office's chief occupation was gone. The Common Market had come into being despite persistent British obstruction. When the Macmillan government, urged on by the Kennedy administration, finally sought entry in 1961–62, de Gaulle slammed the door and the Germans did nothing to help. Nor was the Wilson government any more fortunate with its application. In any case Britain's financial troubles made it doubtful whether membership in the EEC might not prove the kind of "cure" that kills the patient.

The Tories meanwhile had begun to turn away from their ancient concern with an Empire that had become a Commonwealth of unruly—and mostly colored—republics. The anonymous London wit who remarked, "Once the Union Jack has been hauled down, I don't care if the natives start eating each other," spoke for many. Europeanism began to make converts. So did crypto-Gaullism. The most nationalist Tory of them all, Enoch Powell, was also the brainiest, and his public pronouncements were distinctly modeled on Gaullism. He had no use for the Empire, or for the Americans and their war in Vietnam. He wanted the troops brought back from Singapore and sent to the Rhine. He did not want colored immigrants—in fact he wanted Britain to be both independent and European; and he was reputedly willing to share nuclear secrets with France. It was all very disconcerting: the Foreign Office could no longer control the Tory party. It could not even control *The Times*, which under its new Roman Catholic editor had become pro-Europe and pro-Biafra, and on both grounds critical of the Whitehall mandarinate. The weekly *Spectator*, long the organ of Conservative intellectualism, had gone Gaullist too. It raged against the arming of Nigeria, sneered at the Foreign Office for mismanaging relations with France, and snarled at the Treasury for wrecking the country's finances. The mandarins were no longer sacred! It was as though the *Osservatore Romano* had told the College of Cardinals to go jump in the Tiber.

The General's abrupt return to Colombey superimposed itself upon this situation and brought the latent crisis to the boil. Strauss came to London and invited the British to join a federal Europe, whereupon Whitehall promptly discovered that it did not really like political union: all it wanted was entry into the Common Market. But the European federalists were now once more in the saddle, and Strauss added to the embarrassment by blandly urging the British to pool their nuclear armaments with the French. As for himself, he wanted no part of any nuclear arsenal (he said). Here was a new sort of Gaullism, this time coming from the Germans. It signified that Bonn expected the Tories to return to office and to cut loose from their American protectors.

There was trouble on the home front too. Various eminent public figures (including a former newspaper tycoon with Liberal-Labour sympathies) announced that the country was not being effectively governed. They even hinted that Mr. Wilson might be something of a joke. *The Times* urged him to resign. *The Economist* protested that it was undignified for Britain to be so deeply in hock as to incur supervision from the International Monetary Fund. There was, one newspaper declared editorially, "a smell of Weimar in the air."

There was no smell of Weimar when I passed through West Germany in May on my way to Paris. Nor is there any such smell in the Paris air, rumors to the contrary notwithstanding. It is true that France currently gives the impression of having reverted a short distance back to Fourth Republic politics, but this is a pause the country can afford. It has recently accomplished two-thirds of a social mutation and can permit itself the luxury of looking a bit trite after years of grandeur. Why and how this has happened is our next subject.

II

At the peak of the 1968 general strike, with ten million workers in occupation of the factories, an exhausted police force on the point of nervous collapse, and a governmental machine in full disarray, there was a moment when de Gaulle toyed with the idea of resigning. Had he done so, the electoral battle would in all probability have been won by the parties of the Left, and their candidate would have been installed in the Elysée. On one condition: the Communists would have had to back a moderate Socialist for the presidency of the Republic. They were in fact committed (on paper) to voting for Mitterand, who had polled 45 per cent of the popular vote against de Gaulle in 1965. But there was a snag: Mitterand had announced his intention to make Mendès France Premier, and the CP did not want Mendès France. Hence it ended the general strike, thus enabling de Gaulle to stay in power for another year. In the process it destroyed its credibility with the revolutionary minority among the workers and students, but that was a small price to pay.

For the benefit of domestic and foreign critics, the Communists employed a more respectable argument: there was (they said solemnly) a danger of civil war which the working class could not hope to win. The threadbareness of this excuse became evident when it transpired that the army never had the slightest intention of using force against the workers, though it was ready enough to crush an armed insurrection (which no one had proposed). The whole point about the general strike was that it made possible a peaceful takeover by the democratic Left. This was precisely what the Communists were determined to prevent. If they could not seize power—and they knew it was impossible—then it was best to let the strike fizzle out. Otherwise

they might have ended up supporting a government committed
to democratic socialism, and that would never do.

Twelve months later the problem returned to plague them. De
Gaulle having bowed out after his defeat in the April referendum,
the Left might have closed ranks behind someone whom the
ordinary voter could trust. Mitterand was no longer in the running. Doubly discredited by his unconstitutional behavior in
May 1968 and by his refusal to break with the Communists after
the Russian invasion of Czechoslovakia, he stood revealed as the
unprincipled demagogue he had always been. The Socialists having nominated the eminently respectable but rather dull Defferre,
the CP put forward its own candidate: Jacques Duclos, a jovial
veteran of seventy-two, famed for his gargantuan appetite and his
unflinching loyalty to the party line. There was no question
(Georges Marchais, on behalf of the Politburo, declared over
the airwaves on May 7) of the Communists backing Mendès
France for the presidency: "In the name of what party, what
political force? Are we to have Mendès France presented to us
all over again as a miracle man who can solve all problems?"
They were confident that Duclos would pull out the entire Communist vote (over 20 per cent of the total), thus coming third in
the race, as indeed on June 1 he did.

On May 13 Mendès France broke a long silence by coming
out for Defferre, thereby disappointing his few remaining admirers. Both men knew well enough that they stood no chance,
but they felt that the time had come to put the CP in its place.
As Mendès France explained in a long interview the following
week, it was a matter of bringing democratic socialism back to
life. There was a potential mass following for a candidate of the
democratic Left, on the next occasion anyway, but the bulk of
this electoral army would not support a coalition dominated by
the Communists.

It is an established fact, confirmed by opinion polls taken before de Gaulle's departure, that whereas 60 per cent of the voters
vaguely favor some kind of "socialism," only 5 per cent want
"Soviet socialism." Even three-quarters of the Communist electorate don't want it! The CP, for all its solid organization and
its millions of voters, is a colossus with clay feet. It has long
ceased to be a revolutionary force in the traditional sense and it

lacks credibility as a reformist one. Its leadership is mired in stale Muscovite slogans and loyalties. It has been outflanked on its Left by the dissident Parti Socialiste Unifié, and since the invasion of Prague it has once more come to look pestiferous to ordinary democrats who in 1965–67 had hesitantly moved toward a Popular Front. It is losing some of the younger workers to Trotskyist and Maoist splinter groups which, for all their sectarian rigidity, have inherited the ancient syndicalist "direct action" tradition. Its intellectuals are fed up with the East European police state which has for so long been presented to them as the incarnation of socialism. Why then waste time on aged stoneheads like Waldeck Rochet and Duclos? Why go into partnership with a lot of crapulous Stalinists whom the ordinary voter does not trust, whom the New Left denounces as traitors to the revolution, and whom the Old Right regards as traitors to the nation? The Socialists have to think of the future, and the young technocrats of the Parti Socialiste Unifié are even less inclined to take the Communists seriously. They are looking to a day when socialism will no longer be identified with Moscow. When that time comes, it will be the end for the CP, as well as for its Trotskyist and Maoist offshoots: all of them mouthing a language that is fifty years out of date.

It will also be the end for that section of the Right which for decades has kept going by casting itself in the role of the Archangel Michael battling the demons of hell. De Gaulle, who never took the Communists seriously, for years made a habit of warning his television audiences of the awful fate in store for them if Satan's legions were to invade the heavenly citadel. He knew as well as anyone that few Frenchmen were intent on being governed by a bunch of Stalinist liars and murderers, but it suited him to pretend otherwise. Gaullism defined itself in nationalist terms, and Malraux never tired of proclaiming that Frenchmen must choose between the nation and its enemies. When the General stepped down, men like Debré stood ready to repeat the same tune (while privately telling the Russians not to worry: French foreign policy would remain unchanged). But something unexpected happened: the Right having lost its Man of Destiny and the Left having committed hara-kiri, the voters plumped for Pompidou.

The French people put up with de Gaulle for a decade because they were tired of the parliamentary circus and because
the General appealed to the romantic streak in them. They knew
him too well to think of him as a dictator, and they greatly enjoyed his rudeness to foreigners. Unlike the more imaginative
foreign correspondents stationed in Paris, they did not see him
as a threat to their liberties. The boredom of state-controlled
television apart (and one could always tune in to foreign sta-
tions), the Fifth Republic was not particularly oppressive. The
gendarmerie behaved no worse than it had done under the
Fourth. Every conceivable party and sect went on flourishing,
and the entire press—including Trotskyist and Anarchist journals
—drew concealed state subsidies in the form of lowered cable
and telephone rates. The universities were full of old Marxists,
and the film studios overrun by young Anarchists. When a few
left-wing organizations were "dissolved" (on paper) after the
general strike, they moved next door and gave themselves a
new name. Wages were low, but they finally went up after the
strike. The only real sufferers were the mainstay of Gaullism—
the country folk in general and the smallholders in particular.

For these were the years when France at last became a modern
country, and the Gaullist technocracy had no use for the peasant.
It wanted him to leave his village for the nearest town, and it
did its level best to speed his departure. Millions did leave,
thereby worsening an already grave housing shortage and swelling the number of opposition voters. The regime in fact sawed
off the branch on which it was sitting. Its electoral clientele was
overwhelmingly made up of peasants, shopkeepers, housewives,
pensioners, and elderly veterans of two world wars. It systematically discriminated against them in favor of industry, large-
scale mechanized farming, supermarkets, motor cars, and nuclear
arms designed to replace the traditional infantry. The trick
worked for a decade because the country was enamored of
Charles de Gaulle. While he held the stage it was possible to
overlook the fact that his ministers were bankers or planners
who had no use for the old traditional France of the peasant
farm and the corner grocery.

The general strike in May 1968 briefly terrified the peasantry
and the lower middle class into voting for the Gaullists, but by

April of the following year the General's magic had begun to
pall. The referendum campaign was lost because a section of the
conservative electorate stayed home on polling day. Peasants and
shopkeepers had been angered by a further tightening of the
tax screw, and their faith in the General was on the wane. "They
know they're condemned by the modern world and they're at
their wits' end," a senatorial conservative remarked with engaging candor after the referendum results were announced. "All
they ask for is a little understanding—just enough to give them
time to adapt themselves to the situation." It was this section of
Old France which briefly looked to Poher. He seemed sympathetic to their needs—the other candidates less so.

Gaullism had always meant two different things: the General
and his party. The former drew 80 per cent of the popular vote
in his first referendum of October 1958, when a new Constitution
was adopted after the parliamentary regime had collapsed. He
held the loyalty of 60 to 80 per cent of the voters during the
years of the Algerian drama, when the country was poised on the
edge of civil war. He got his new Constitution amended by over
60 per cent in 1962, with the presidency for the first time thrown
open to popular vote. Three years later he was forced into a
run-off under the very electoral law he had driven through. Yet
all the time his party never approached a majority. It polled no
more than 20 per cent of the vote against his own 80 in 1958,
and barely 47 per cent ten years later, after the failure of the
general strike. This same 47 per cent turned out once more in the
April referendum. It was not enough. The magic had begun to
wear off. Too many angry shopkeepers stayed at home. Too many
workers, politicized by the general strike, followed the lead of
their unions and voted "no." Too many young people, for whom
talk of 1940 and the Resistance meant nothing, demonstrated
against what they called a "police state" (they had never seen a
real one). Too many pro-Americans, pro-Europeans, or pro-
Israelis concluded that it was time for the Old Man to go. He
had traded on their fear of chaos, but that fear was diminishing.
In June 1968 the French had discovered Pompidou. In April
1969 some of them discovered a hitherto unknown senator called
Poher. If it was a matter of exchanging Don Quixote for Sancho
Panza these voters knew where to turn.

III

The General knew it too. His departure was in character. The man who had reproached Napoleon for having "muffed his exit" was determined to choose his own manner of going. There was to be no Waterloo, rather a dignified retreat from an untenable position. If the nation rejected him, he would retire to his country estate like a true Roman. But why gamble on the outcome of yet another popular referendum, when the proposed reform legislation could have been rammed through the National Assembly by the compact Gaullist majority? Quite possibly he thought he could win. The terrain had been carefully chosen. Decentralization of government was popular and under normal circumstances would have swung the small-town conservative vote. The reform of the Senate was copied—down to details—from Mendès France's very similar proposals in his book *La République moderne* (1962). There was nothing wrong with the broad strategy of the appeal. The tactical mistake lay in underrating the resentment of a provincial middle class which had been paying for the country's modernization. These people traditionally took their lead from the local *notables:* the half-million town councilors and other worthies who administer France's 38,000 urban and rural communes. In the past they had underpinned the parliamentary Republic. Then for a decade most of them had supported or tolerated de Gaulle from fear of revolution. In May–June 1968 they discovered to their amazement that the Communist party was a paper tiger. Thereafter they began to think in terms of *"après de Gaulle."*

Class analysis led to similar results. The *grande bourgeoisie* of bankers and industrialists was mostly for Pompidou: a great organizer and a man to be trusted. The managerial stratum was split: a section of it favored Mendès France. Younger technicians, professional men, and white-collar workers looked into the mirror and what they saw bore some resemblance to Michel Rocard of the PSU: a Socialist but a youthful technocrat too, no friend of revolution and other lost causes that might appeal to students besotted by the bearded image of Che Guevara. Christian Democrats and most Social Democrats would eventually vote for Poher, thus swelling his popular following. Was that enough to elect him? And, if elected, would he take the country back to parliamentary rule? In any case he represented those elements of Old France who urged that the tempo of modernization be slowed down.

The rest was standard stuff, including the poisonous remark about "Jewish gold," attributed to France's official delegate at the United Nations, and promptly denied in Paris when the inevitable protests rolled in. Mudslinging is part of the game, and the French have traditionally excelled in it. Old-timers in Paris can recall the days when elections were lost or won by accusing one's opponents of being in the pay of foreigners. "This is going to be the dirtiest campaign ever," some of these veterans said with relish in early May. It wasn't—television saw to that. The medium does not lend itself to the sort of character assassination that is promoted by underhand whispering campaigns impugning a candidate's personal honor. A certain amount of filth was duly put into circulation, but it was tedious stuff, hardly worth the bother. Mme. Pompidou was said to have attended Parisian orgies also frequented by other fashionable people vaguely involved in the squalid Marcovic murder case. Mme. Poher was said to have gone mad and to have been shipped off to South America by her husband; this came as a surprise to the neighbors who saw her shopping as usual. By the standards of the Fourth Republic—not to mention the Third—it was a poor performance, and a lot of it boomeranged on the organizers. The France of 1969 had outgrown *Clochemerle*. It had at long last become a modern country, and as such it chose Pompidou.

The real issues had been blurred by the General's idiosyncratic style, his personal charisma, and the ceremonial aspect of Gaullism as a system of government. Both Poher and Pompidou were obliged to repudiate this part of the heritage, and Poher at least managed to sound like a Fourth Republic politician. The small-town electorate liked his modesty. The professional stratum was less enthusiastic. A section of it had been seduced by the technocratic aspect of Gaullism while the others hankered after socialism. With Poher one would have republican democracy, but was that enough?

The General did nothing to make things easier for the faithful.

His departure for County Kerry looked like a gesture of disdain, but it could also be interpreted as a silent disavowal of his heir apparent. Had de Gaulle lost faith in Pompidou? At any rate he did not help him much by vacating the scene in this manner. It was one thing to return to Colombey. It was another matter to leave the country without a word of encouragement for his former Premier, now battling for his political life. In May 1968 de Gaulle had looked like Canute trying to hold back the tide. A year later he seemed intent on playing Lear or Timon. It suited his temper to signify that the French were unworthy of him, but it did not help Gaullism as a movement capable of surviving its founder. Nor did it advance the cause of "participation" (for practical purposes meaning profit sharing in industry). This had been an ancient hobbyhorse of socially minded Catholics. The employers did not care for it, and neither did the unions. But if "participation" went down the drain, what was left of Gaullism? And if Gaullism was a lost cause, then the choice narrowed down to Pompidou's technocratic "pragmatism" (blessed word), and the small-town respectability of Poher, "the French Harry Truman."

How genuine was the choice anyway? Pompidou—born in the mountain village of Montboudif in the Auvergne (a source of endless hilarity to his countrymen)—was the son of a Socialist schoolteacher and the grandson of a peasant. Himself a professor of Greek before becoming a civil servant, then a banker, finally de Gaulle's Premier, he could be said to represent both the old France and the new. Win or lose, his cause would go marching on. And what was that cause if not the transformation of France into a modern industrial country? And Europe? But the Europe of Poher and his friends was not easy to distinguish from that of Pompidou. The Gaullists indeed had always opposed federalism: the creation of a supranational European government. But if the Christian Democrats were closer to Bonn on this issue, the Gaullists might discover a certain fondness for the Britain of Toryism and Enoch Powell: a politician who seemed marked out for the cause of Anglo-French reconciliation in the 1970s. Such a reconciliation would mean the sharing of Britain's nuclear arsenal with that of France, but once the Big Two had come to terms, there would be no difficulty about that. If Washington and Moscow were willing to cooperate, then why should Europe not concentrate on its own affairs? And if Europe were to include Britain, then why should a British government not pool its nuclear forces with those of the Continent? *Pour quoi faire? Mais mon Dieu, pour ne rien faire!* A federalized Europe would be a neutral Europe. Does anyone suppose that West Europeans will volunteer to serve in a war against China? They have not even sent a battalion to Vietnam!

Every age has its own cant. Ours is that of "pragmatism," a phrase designed to conceal the fact that the old conservative-liberal ideologies are dying and nothing else has yet taken their place. Technocracy? But how can one glamorize it? Call it "socialism" or what you will, but don't go about proclaiming that henceforth the world is going to be run by astronauts and suchlike characters, not to mention nuclear physicists or prophets like Herman Kahn. Technocracy is a state of affairs, and pragmatism is a state of mind. Neither represents a system of beliefs, and people have to believe in something: France, Europe, America, the Soviet Union, the Cultural Revolution, Black Power, or what-you-will. Technocracy fills the vacuum left by the disappearance of liberal democracy in its nineteenth-century form, but it is not something that anyone is going to shed blood for. This was the hard core of sense in de Gaulle's sneers about the "stateless bureaucrats" in charge of the Common Market. Europe? A splendid ideal, but not at the expense of France if you please. France has been there for a thousand years and men have died for it. This is how nations are born. It is still true. If Nigeria ever becomes a nation, it will have been at the cost of blood. Not to mention Israel . . . ("Of course they are admirable people," the General blandly remarked to protesting Gaullists the day after he had imposed the arms embargo). Are the Europeans ready to die for Europe? One doubts it.

At Colombey the old soldier now has time to complete his memoirs, while his successors divide his heritage. For the rest one may be sure he will carry on as usual: thinking of France and despising the French. "They will return to their vomit," he said contemptuously some years ago when asked what would happen to the country after his departure. They have in fact decided to go forward so as to become part of the modern world, and while the process is not quite complete, it is far enough advanced to make it improbable that anyone can reverse it. Now that the archaic armature of Gaullism has been removed, the lineaments of a new society are becoming discernible. Strange to relate, it is a society not greatly different from the new Germany across the Rhine. When the historians get down to writing this chapter, they are likely to conclude that Charles de Gaulle presided over a transformation that spelled the death of everything he believed in.

Leninism à la Française

❊ ❊ ❊

THE ANNIVERSARY SEASON is upon us once more. Three years ago it was the outbreak of war in 1914 that furnished historians and essayists with a theme for reflections upon the course of the preceding half-century. Now it is the Russian Revolution in 1917, or rather its opening phase, for the civil war went on until 1921 and there were further upheavals to come. During those years of turmoil something of importance happened to European civilization, but what? Was it merely given a new shape, or did the life go out of it? Everyone is pretty well agreed that the nineteenth century terminated in World War I, for what came to an end then was not merely the familiar balance of power but something more important: a particular culture generally associated with bourgeois liberalism, parliamentary government, national patriotism, and European pre-eminence in world affairs. Socialism was transformed too—the Second International split, and Bolshevism arose to confront Social Democracy. Yet Eastern and Western Europe were affected in quite different ways. It is even possible to hold that in some respects Western Europe turned out to have more in common with North America than with the eastern half of the European continent.

Robert Wohl's long and learned study *French Communism in the Making, 1914–1924* [1] makes a significant contribution to this theme, though only if one is willing to follow him to the end. This demands patience, for Mr. Wohl belongs to a school of historians (more numerous, and certainly better equipped, in the

The New York Review of Books, April 6, 1967.
    1. Stanford, Calif., 1966.

United States than elsewhere) who are reluctant to leave anything out. Having climbed to the top of a mountain of source material, he still craves for more. There can never, it seems, be enough evidence for him to digest. After describing at length the founding of the Parti Communiste Français in December 1920 and giving the names of all its leaders, he asks:

> Who were their troops? We would like to know in detail the social origins, occupations, and state of mind of the 110,000 Socialists who followed the party into the Third International in the first six months of 1921. This information is lacking, and it may never be assembled.[2]

It is indeed lacking and for good reason: no one can possibly know what 110,000 people were all doing and thinking in 1921. However, we do know something about them, and Mr. Wohl deserves much praise for having sorted it out. He has had help from other historians—notably Annie Kriegel, whose great work on the founding of the PCF (published in 1964) is even bulkier than his own—but it is clear that he has done an impressive amount of spade work. Moreover, unlike Mme. Kriegel, who stops in 1921, he goes on to 1924 and even a short distance beyond. Thus his readers can discover how the dissensions in Moscow after Lenin's death affected the International, and how the Comintern emissaries operated behind the scenes to install leaders loyally obedient to Moscow.

All this is relevant, if not precisely exhilarating, but the real interest of the book lies elsewhere: in explaining how Communism arose in the decade 1914–24 and what it signified. The French Communist Party was formally constituted in December 1920, when a majority of the Socialist delegates at Tours decided to join the newly founded Third International. But the split had a long and complicated prehistory, going back to the pre-1914 disputes between parliamentary Socialists and revolutionary Syndicalists, and ultimately involving all the old doctrinal quarrels symbolized by the brief and tragic Paris Commune of 1871. Mr. Wohl's introductory chapter on the pre–1914 movement has the considerable merit of making it clear that the real issue in those days lay between Socialism and Syndicalism, not (as

2. Ibid., p. 217.

in Germany) between "Marxists" and "revisionists." In the first place, there were few Marxists in France; secondly, they had by 1914 been converted to parliamentary democracy; and, lastly, the non-Marxists (e.g., Jean Jaurès) were far more combative and radical than all but a tiny handful of German Socialists. Again, the real radicals, the Anarcho-Syndicalists, who before 1914 virtually controlled the French unions, had no counterpart in Central Europe, for they not only talked about "the social revolution," they actually thought it was imminent. Moreover (unlike Lenin) they believed it would be a *proletarian* revolution. No infallible Central Committee for *them*! Their faith was staked on the revolutionary spontaneity of the masses! As for parliamentary government in general, and parliamentary socialism in particular, they were convinced that both were on the way out.

In retrospect it is clear enough that these were illusions. There was indeed a spirit of revolt in some quarters, but not (as the radicals believed) because of the overripeness of capitalism in France but because of its weakness. France—like Italy and Spain —was not yet properly a modern industrial country. Economic growth was slow; social life was stagnant; and the industrial working class was firmly excluded from the official culture. Its revolutionary vanguard reacted by seceding from society and repudiating its symbols, notably patriotism and democracy. But the Socialist Party (including its Marxist wing) was committed to both. More important, the bulk of the working class and peasantry was solidly republican and patriotic. The outbreak of war in 1914 brought down the entire house of cards. The Socialists joined the government, and the Syndicalists were unable to mobilize even a handful of workers for the revolutionary general strike they had planned for so long.

The Russian Revolution in 1917 superimposed itself upon this debacle. It came just when the country had begun to weary of the endless bloodletting at the front, and by 1919 the Bolsheviks had succeeded in splitting the Socialist International. By the end of 1920 the issue was formalized: should French Socialists adhere to Moscow, and with what sort of perspective? Adhere many of them did, but not all of them believed it was possible to follow the Bolshevik example. The Syndicalists, moreover, while all for revolution and workers' councils, had to swallow their old distaste for state socialism and party dictatorship. For a while the personal prestige of Lenin and Trotsky helped to bridge the gap, but by 1924, when Lenin was dead and Trotsky in eclipse, Communists in France had to ask themselves what they believed in. The answer they found was basically simple, though overlaid with a great deal of verbiage. In essentials it came down to this: the Bolsheviks were the model to be followed, if and when the opportunity arose, but pending this event, the Communist Party should provide the workers (and if possible the peasants) with an all-embracing organization: a closed universe shut off from the rest of society and indifferent to its symbols. In short, the PCF was to repeat, on a larger scale and with far ampler means, the Syndicalist experiment of organizing a proletarian secession from the body politic.

"Communism" in France thus came to mean, not the revolutionary conquest of power (for this turned out to be impossible), but the creation of a "subculture" which was also a permanent opposition against the established order. The unintended result was to reinforce the conservatism of bourgeois society, for with all the revolutionary energies drained off into the Communist ghetto, the conservatives (including the governing "Radical" Party) had an easy time. In this paradoxical manner, the PCF helped to perpetuate not only the rigid class alignment, and the *ouvrieriste* pathos, of its Syndicalist ancestors but the preindustrial stagnation of a large sector of French society. This interplay between Right and Left underlay the peculiar immobility of the Third Republic in its declining phase, a social torpor from which France was awakened (at great cost) by the defeat of 1940 and the wartime Resistance movement.

The political and ideological disputes in the course of which the PCF arose on the wreckage of the old pre-1914 revolutionary movement are analyzed in remorseless detail by Mr. Wohl. His patience must have been put to a stern test, but he comes through intact, never flagging from the task of tracking down the personal and factional splits, quarrels, and maneuvers from which in due course the centralized apparatus of the Thorezian bureaucracy emerged: a bureaucracy remarkably like that of a great modern corporation, down to the care devoted to the training of loyal office staff and the relentless weeding-out of nonconformists. None of the old pre-1914 revolutionary labor leaders and intellectuals survived the endless purges, once loyalty to the Kremlin had become the test of orthodoxy. In fairness to the Russians, and to the Comintern, it has to be said (and Mr. Wohl is right to make the point) that Moscow acted mainly as a catalyst. At the bottom, the French Communists knew what they wanted: a party that would give them control over the working class, and a home-away-from-home for men and women deeply alienated from their fellow citizens. And what were they going to do with this splendid organization when they had it? Nothing at all— just live inside it, and try to capture as many municipalities as possible. In short, become another Social Democratic party in all but name. Fifty years after the Bolsheviks seized power, that is what they have become, though they will never admit it.

For in France it will not do to admit that "total" revolution is no longer on the agenda. The moment of truth may be drawing near, though, for the country has now at last become fully industrialized, and correspondingly the working class is no longer as alienated as before from the remainder of the nation. The dreadful secret is almost out: socialism and communism have proved effective in helping to integrate the proletariat into the new industrial society. Indeed the PCF, with its irremovable bureaucracy and its control over a greatly enlarged union movement, has shown itself far better at this task than the old pre-1914 Socialist and Syndicalist groups, which never reached the masses. Ideology still stands in the way, but it is being subtly transformed. As the Sino-Soviet split deepens, loyalty to Moscow becomes an unconscious means of reviving some elements of the pre-1914 Social Democratic tradition which (a circumstance often forgotten) was also a Marxist one. We can already look forward to a situation in 1972 when something like Communist participation in a government responsible to a democratic parliament may become possible. It remains to be seen whether the French Communist Party can shed its vestigial Stalinism fast enough to become respectable by the time a left-wing majority has been obtained.

In a country like France where the socialist movement arose directly from the aftermath of the great upheaval of 1789, problems of this sort are familiar and indeed inescapable. After all, the Bolsheviks had modeled themselves on the Jacobins. Blanqui, the father of all believers in "proletarian dictatorship," was a Jacobin before he became an early Communist, and so were his Russian pupils, Peter Tkachev and the rest, from whom Lenin inherited the tradition. That archetypal Jacobin Georges Clemenceau, who in 1919 launched the first anti-Soviet crusade, had begun his political career as an adherent of Blanqui, *l'enfermé*—the man who spent thirty-six of forty-eight working years in prison—and most of his surviving followers went over to Marx after the defeat of the 1871 Commune; while Clemenceau moved in the other direction, to found the Radical Party. Who then has been betraying whom? Does this kind of language even make sense?

Mr. Wohl, though perhaps more concerned with politics than with history, has enough historical sense to let the reader feel the continuity underlying the surface froth. Roy Pierce, another political scientist by trade, deals lucidly with the analysis of ideas. His *Contemporary French Political Thought* ³ has an interesting theme: political thought in France as reflected in the work of six representative writers: Jean-Paul Sartre, Emmanuel Mounier, Simone Weil, Albert Camus, Bertrand de Jouvenel, and Raymond Aron. There are also some observations on Maurras and on Alain, the philosopher (if that is the word) of the Radical Party.

This is a useful introduction to the subject, and a model of organization. Professor Pierce has worked his way through a vast amount of literature, gives concise account of the topics he has selected for analysis, and provides a large enough scholarly apparatus to keep both students and examiners happy. Moreover, and for this he deserves special praise, he has integrated his critical studies with enough biographical material to bring out the interrelation between what his writers thought and what was happening in the larger world around them. If his style is a trifle pedestrian, he makes up for it by being always clear and sensible. He is indeed so levelheaded that his readers may be

3. London and New York, 1966.

in danger of failing to grasp the mental and moral chaos reflected
in the writings of his protagonists. French history in this century has been tragic, and Professor Pierce shares the Anglo-
American distaste for extremes, though he manfully tries to overcome it. At times this results in an uneasy compromise. Thus he
makes Camus sound reasonable and well balanced. He even
defines him as a "liberal moralist," which seems an odd choice of
language. Camus was many things in his life, including a near-
Communist and a near-Anarchist. The one thing he always
managed to steer away from was liberalism, at least in the conventional significance of that familiar term. But then the only
authentic liberal in Mr. Pierce's collection is Raymond Aron, and
even he writes for a conservative paper (*Le Figaro*), because
there is no liberal daily in Paris. (That great journal *Le Monde*
is democratic and Christian Socialist, which is a different matter.)

Another possible criticism of Mr. Pierce's work is that his
historical sense works sideways, but not backward or forward.
His topography takes in the Resistance period and its aftermath,
e.g., Camus's dispute with Sartre and his unhappy silence about
Algeria during the last phase of his life, but he seems reluctant
to pursue historical roots beyond the cutoff date of 1914. He is
vague about Marxism, conventional about Maurras, and silent
on some of the minor, but important, political strands, e.g., that
highly original fusion of popular Catholicism and Jacobin republicanism which has been a factor in French life since the great
Revolution (and but for which there would have been no Resistance movement, no Christian Democratic movement, and much
less in the way of Gaullism). Again, a writer like Mounier is
difficult to understand if one does not relate him to a Christian-
Socialist tradition going back to the Saint-Simonism of the 1830s;
his ancestors include that fervent Catholic and early socialist
Philippe Buchez, who launched the cooperative movement in
the 1840s and in the stormy year 1848 rose to become chairman
of the National Assembly. It is not irrelevant that Buchez was a
lifelong admirer of Robespierre. French political history is not
just a matter of *le rouge et le noir,* or at least these colors have
often tended to get mixed. And how is one to translate into English a phrase found in (of all places) *Le Monde* in 1961, at the
time of the last despairing resistance of the Algerian *ultras* to

the coming of independence: *"L'OAS, c'est la Commune de la Droite."* Try to make sense of French politics (or Camus) without grasping the full import of these words, so shocking to ordinary democratic sentiment! No wonder the "Anglo-Saxons" fail to understand the General—a former Maurrassian who admires Clemenceau and is secretly admired by the extreme Left. It is perhaps a trifle unfair if one regrets that these convolutions remain beneath the surface of Professor Pierce's eminently sound and sensible discussion of the topic.

Catching Up with History

✳ ✳ ✳

AMERICAN AND BRITISH WRITERS rarely perceive what is most striking about France: the commitment of so many Frenchmen of all political hues to a kind of doctrinal rigidity foreign to the Anglo-American mentality. There is not, in this respect, much of a choice between General de Gaulle and his critics, with the possible exception of a few determinedly "Atlantic" and pro-American liberals such as Raymond Aron or Jean-François Revel; and even they tend to sound more doctrinaire than their British or American colleagues.

The roots of this situation can be traced back all the way to the failure of the Reformation (but wasn't Calvin a great deal more doctrinaire than Luther, if it comes to that?) or even to the impact of the Latin tradition. Whatever the remote causes, France has usually been a battleground of conflicting parties locked in mortal combat, while the task of "synthesizing" their incompatible aims in some sort of illogical but workable makeshift arrangement fell to others: notably the British. Fundamentally, compromise is anathema to the French mind: an affront to the intellectual and ethical rigorism on which the great French moralists have prided themselves. This state of affairs antedated the Revolution and has survived it. George Sand, writing at the close of the Romantic era in the 1840s, was in the national tradition when she proclaimed that the class struggle between bourgeoisie and proletariat was a life-and-death matter for the antagonists: "Le combat ou la mort; la lutte sanguinaire ou le néant. C'est ainsi que la question est invinciblement posée." It is no accident (as they saw in Moscow) that Marx composed the *Mani-*

festo after he had been through this kind of schooling in Paris. Anyone familiar with contemporary French affairs knows that this state of mind is not a party matter. It runs through the entire spectrum from left to right, and even the democratic Center pays reluctant lip service to it. Not long ago, during a parliamentary debate on the *force de frappe,* when a Socialist spokesman cast doubt on the readiness of any putative head of state to "press the nuclear button," the Minister of Defense replied, "We must hope he will," while a prominent Gaullist deputy famed as a war hero in 1939–45 shouted furiously, "La patrie ou la mort!" Clemenceau would have approved.

It is the great merit of H. Stuart Hughes' new book *The Obstructed Path* [1] that he has caught something of the spirit that informs French public life, as distinct from the scholasticism that infuses the endless theorizing about it. The Tragic Muse, traditionally the presiding deity of French history, must be at the back of an author's mind if he is to do justice to what representative Frenchmen and Frenchwomen have said and done in this century. One of the troubles with Roy Pierce's otherwise very scholarly study *Contemporary French Political Thought* was a tendency to underplay this aspect of the situation. Professor Hughes is properly aware of it, as may be seen from his opening chapter. There he briefly reviews the consequences of the 1914–1918 blood bath, the false euphoria of the 1920s, and the collapse into despair during the decade following. He might perhaps have started off with Verdun, where the pre-1914 generation went to its grave (or, like Captain de Gaulle, discovered the twentieth century in the act of standing up to the German artillery barrage at Fort Douaumont). His treatment of this crucial episode is located—somewhat idiosyncratically—at the close of Chapter Four ("The Quest for Heroism") and preceded by a lengthy discussion of the work of four writers who do not, to my mind, have a great deal in common: Roger Martin du Gard, Georges Bernanos, Antoine de Saint-Exupéry, and (inevitably) André Malraux. The latter's *Antimémoires* having recently become available,

1. *The Obstructed Path: French Social Thought in the Years of Desperation, 1930–1960* (New York, 1968).

any historian who meanwhile has incorporated a chapter on Malraux in a study of modern France is naturally "caught short," but Mr. Hughes escapes substantially undamaged. I doubt if in future editions he will find it necessary to revise much of his present text, although in the light of Malraux's memoirs (or the fraction currently available) he may feel inclined to say less about their author's rather spurious Marxism and more about his very genuine Romanticism. For the record, I hereby align myself with Jean-François Revel, who in a review of the *Antimémoires* quite accurately described their author as "fundamentally a disciple of Nietzsche and Spengler." It is indeed difficult to see how Malraux could ever have imagined himself a Marxist. What happened to him in the 1920s was that he found Communism more attractive than Fascism because his stay in Indochina had filled him with loathing for the colonial administration. Since the Communists were the only effective nationalists in China and Indochina (they still are), he adopted Communism in order to be on the side of the only authentic revolutionaries he could find in those parts. The same, more or less, applies to his role as an active combatant during the Spanish Civil War. Then in 1939 Stalin made his pact with Hitler, and Malraux decided he had had enough. As he puts it in his autobiographical sketch, his commitment had been to the anti-Fascist cause, not to Russia. This was also the attitude of the majority of his Resistance comrades, who in 1945 followed his lead in refusing to back the Party's bid for dictatorial power.

The *Antimémoires* have come too late for Mr. Hughes, which is a pity, since they clarify some of the topics he has selected for discussion. In other respects he has been well served by his sense of timing: notably in regard to the Vatican Council and the modernization of Catholic doctrine. His chapter on this subject will doubtless be read with approval by liberal Catholics. It should give particular satisfaction to French readers, since he duly emphasizes the pioneering role the French laity and clergy played after 1945 in preparing the ground for the reforms of the past few years. It is no great exaggeration to say that the Conciliar movement would have been stillborn but for the tenacity of the French in pressing for a purification of doctrine and practice: another aspect of that peculiar French moral rigorism which the Vatican—a very Italian institution—has always found so tiresome. More could perhaps have been said about the Gallican element in this situation. It was, after all, not the first time that French Catholics had cause to feel concern about the sort of moral and intellectual guidance they were getting from Rome. (French Communists are now in somewhat the same dilemma vis-à-vis the seat of *their* Church.) What does one do if one's spiritual mentors turn out to be inadequate? Mr. Hughes is perhaps a trifle too anxious not to cause hurt. He duly notes that World War II had a regenerative effect upon the French Church, but omits to stress that it was only the *lower* clergy who entered the Resistance: their superiors, to a man, backed the Vichy regime. It is certainly a noteworthy fact (though not one to which Mr. Hughes gives much prominence) that Gaullism and Gallicanism went together around the time in 1945 when the Papal Nuncio in Paris felt obliged to resist the General's demand for a wholesale purge of the French Episcopate—most of them last-ditch Pétainists and far from sharing the democratic sentiments of the intellectuals. As for the Vatican's role, it did not need subsequent revelations to disabuse the more intelligent French Catholics of any illusions they might have entertained on this perennially painful topic.

Admirably judicious and fair-minded though he shows himself to be in dealing with these contentious matters, Mr. Hughes would not claim to be uncommitted. He has his preferences like the rest of us, and makes no secret of them. The democratic current within French Catholicism happens to suit him—though clearly for political rather than for philosophical reasons. His sympathies in consequence go out to Jacques Maritain and Gabriel Marcel alike. Yet he is constrained to note that Maritain's neo-Thomism and Marcel's Existentialism represent incompatible positions. Moreover, the two men have always entertained a healthy dislike for each other qua philosophers even when they were following more or less the same line politically. This presents Mr. Hughes with something of a problem, since he admires both of them. He gets out of it as best he can by stressing their common "distaste for both idealism and positivism in their familiar late-nineteenth-century forms. Both were equally opposed to the tradition of Descartes." Moreover, both were, as he puts it, "philosophers who were Catholics" rather than "Catholic philosophers." This makes them look reassuring to a liberal, which Mr. Hughes happens to be. I am not certain that all or most Catholics would regard it as a recommendation. Be that as it may, we can all agree that France is one of the three European countries (Germany and Holland being the two others) where the Catholic Church has conserved its hold upon a section of the intellectual elite. Mr. Hughes notes in passing that in Italy this elite is wholly outside the Church, but does not suggest an explanation for this curious circumstance. Could the role of the Vatican have something to do with it?

France being the sort of country it is, the existence of a Communist mass movement—side by side with a rejuvenated popular Catholicism—was bound to encourage an unending intellectual tournament between the adherents of these rival orthodoxies. An eminent French sociologist (who for obvious reasons must remain nameless) once said to me, "There are only two parties in France—the Catholics and the Communists. What is called liberalism is represented by a couple of Jews: Mendès France and myself." He was joking, of course. There are plenty of liberals in France, some of them in key positions, e.g., the present Premier, M. Pompidou, and his chief parliamentary gadfly, Valéry Giscard d'Estaing.

So the battle (from a liberal standpoint) is far from lost. It is, however, a remarkable fact that liberalism has since 1945 been on the defensive intellectually. Mr. Hughes does what he can with Raymond Aron's *Opium of the Intellectuals,* but it is somehow significant that all the intellectual heavyweights in his survey turn out to be either Catholics or Gaullists or Marxists of some kind. Try as he may, he cannot unearth a liberal philosopher, for the simple reason that there are none. Instead, he devotes an entire chapter to those two distinguished historians Lucien Febvre and Marc Bloch. But Febvre was an old-fashioned romantic patriot in the tradition of Michelet, while Bloch was a positivist whose work as a historian clearly reflected the influence of Marx. Both men were republicans and democrats in the French tradition, which is to say the Jacobin tradition, and Bloch was duly murdered by the Nazis. But somehow neither of them quite fits the "liberal" label.

French Marxism is fairly idiosyncratic too, though getting less so now that the French have assimilated German philosophy, and at the same time have emancipated themselves from their semiliterate Russian tutors. Mr. Hughes has a section on "The Marriage of Phenomenology and Marxism," in which justice is rendered to Husserl, if not to Hegel. He brings out the importance of Maurice Merleau-Ponty. It was one of the oddities of Mr. Pierce's book that he barely mentioned him, while devoting a whole chapter to Camus. Yet Merleau-Ponty's *Humanisme et terreur* (1947) represented the only consistent defense of Stalinist terrorism ever undertaken by a Westerner. It had a profound effect on Sartre (unlike its author's subsequent rejection of Russian Communism, following the revelations about Stalinism as a system of economics resting upon forced labor). Merleau-Ponty, far more than Sartre, was the key figure in these debates during the late 1940s and early 1950s, just as he, more than anyone else, was instrumental in awakening the French intelligentsia to the importance of German philosophy for the understanding of Marxism as a system of thought. In addition to righting this imbalance, Mr. Hughes deals at some length with Sartre. Having had a shot at this target myself, I admire the patience with which he pursues his elusive quarry. Sartre is difficult to pin down—just when you think you have finally done it, he turns around and confronts you with a new and unsuspected aspect of his many-sided personality: as in *Les Mots* (1964), where he suddenly allowed his Cartesianism to peep through the borrowed Marxist clothes. Still, he remains a major intellectual figure. This cannot, I am afraid, be asserted of Camus, although Mr. Hughes does his best. Nor am I convinced that Teilhard de Chardin is as significant as Mr. Hughes would like us to believe. As to Lévi-Strauss I freely confess my incompetence.

It should by now be clear that Mr. Hughes has provided the student with an admirably lucid and well-balanced introduction to the French intellectual scene, and there we must leave it. If a general conclusion emerges, it is that the France of the 1960s, unlike the confused and distrait country of the 1930s, has at last caught up with history and with itself.

The Nouvelle Frontier

❈❈❈

WHEN JEAN-JACQUES SERVAN-SCHREIBER's *Le Défi Américain* was published last year, it was immediately a best seller all over Western Europe. One can see why. The subject it dealt with—America's threatening technological hegemony—was important. The author was chief editor of an influential liberal weekly, *L'Express.* There was a ready-made audience in the shape of all those modern-minded youngish businessmen and managerial types who a decade earlier had briefly hearkened to the voice of Mendès France. Moreover, M. Servan-Schreiber, while decidedly no Gaullist, could not be written off as a simple-minded anti-Gaullist either: he stood, and stands, for a greater degree of European independence from the United States.

This is not to say that he is a political force in his own right. Arthur Schlesinger, who has contributed a brief and enthusiastic preface to the American edition,[1] seems a trifle short on reliable information about public opinion in France; otherwise he would not have suggested that *The American Challenge* may do for European unity what Thomas Paine's *Common Sense* did for American independence. He is right in saying that the book has made an impact upon businessmen and civil servants hitherto unaware of the technological gap between the Old World and the New. It may also have helped the federal gospel, according to which Western Europe can raise itself by its economic bootstraps only if it has the sense to federate politically. Unlike the General, M. Servan-Schreiber makes no fetish of the nation-state. This indeed is his chief quarrel with the Gaullists, as

The New York Review of Books, June 20, 1968.

1. *The American Challenge* (New York and London, 1968).

readers of his frequent editorials in *L'Express* must be aware. On the other topics—e.g., the election of the President by popular vote, and the consequent dethronement of Parliament—he has reluctantly come around to the Gaullist viewpoint. So, by the way, has M. Mitterand.

What then is *The American Challenge* principally about? Perhaps the easiest way to answer the question is to quote a somewhat lengthy passage which occurs at the close of the American edition (the French original also has some appendices—including a comment by Herman Kahn—which for some reason have not been translated):

> The American expeditionary corps will leave Vietnam, where there is nothing more to gain and everything to lose. But American industry will not leave Europe, where it has made new conquests and increased its formidable power. Even if we were not faced with such a challenge by the Americans, we ought to find in ourselves the power and the desire to build a more intelligent and bountiful post-industrial society. . . . The American challenge really adds only an external pressure to what is an internal necessity. . . .
>
> The training, development, and exploitation of human intelligence—these are the real resources, and there are no others. The American challenge is not ruthless, like so many Europe has known in her history, but it may be more dramatic, for it embraces everything. Its weapons are the use and systematic perfection of all the instruments of reason. . . .
>
> We can no longer sit back and wait for the renaissance. But it is not going to be evoked by patriotic rhetoric or clarion calls left over from the age of military battles. It can come only from subtle analysis, rigorous thought, and precise reasoning. It calls for a special breed of politicians, businessmen, and labor leaders.

The concluding paragraph should help to explain why orthodox Gaullists regularly go purple in the face at the mention of M. Servan-Schreiber's name. But it also explains why he has been howled down by left-wing students, not only in Paris but also—believe it or not—in Madrid, where his appearance some months ago caused a near-riot—not because he was too far to the Left, but because the student radicals (they have them in Spain, too, and they are beginning to speak up) thought him too conservative! Too friendly to the Americans in fact. For M. Servan-

Schreiber is that new phenomenon, a modern-minded liberal who believes in Keynes and Galbraith, styles himself on the late John F. Kennedy, likes and admires the United States, and yet wants Europe to be more independent.

But how much more? There's the rub. The Communists (and the Gaullists too) suspect that all he wants for Europe is a more influential voice within an Atlantic Free Trade Area, which in their eyes would simply be a decorous camouflage for the American Empire. Hence the unmitigated hostility with which he and his paper are treated by those left-wing Gaullists who are close to the Communists on foreign policy. Hence, too, the difficulty he has had in maintaining his links with those socialists who follow the lead of Mendès France within the somewhat amorphous Federation of the Left nominally headed by M. Mitterand. Consider a passage such as this, with which the volume concludes:

> If criticism of an oppressive capitalism led these "founding fathers" of socialism to challenge the explicit liberties capitalism dispensed to a few thousand of the privileged, it is equally true that they wanted, on the whole, a society of individual initiative. These objectives are completely contemporary. Their vision of an open society where men are *mobile* and continually *regenerated* by continuing education is magnificently confirmed today.

Is it indeed? A lot of French students don't seem to think so, but M. Servan-Schreiber has a ready reply to that: the French educational system is out of date and must be modernized. By now everyone in France, from the General and M. Pompidou downward, is in agreement on this theme. But once again the awkward question arises: what exactly is all this modernization to be for? The answer, so far as one can gather from the enthusiastic rhetoric of *The American Challenge,* amounts to this: France and Europe must pull their socks up and march resolutely into the electronic future mapped out by Herman Kahn and his colleagues. If they don't, they will have only themselves to blame if Europe becomes a mere annex of America. Now this may well be true—it probably *is* true—but it eludes the problem of social organization. After all, there are different ways of conceiving the kind of society which can make optimal use of the human and natural resources placed at its disposal by modern technology. Suppose someone were to suggest that "a society of individual initiative" is not what is wanted. Then where would M. Servan-Schreiber be? Why, exactly where he belongs—among those modern-minded representatives of "the Left" who want the new technocratic setup to be as liberal and humane as possible so long as they themselves go on controlling it.

Now this must not be misunderstood. Those Parisian students who during the recent upheaval brushed Mitterand and his friends off as caretakers of a future "bourgeois" government were talking nonsense. "Bourgeois society" is not a serious issue in France. Everyone, or nearly everyone, is against it (for the sound reason that it is dead and can no longer defend itself). Even Valéry Giscard d'Estaing, whose "independent Republicans" are officially to the right of the orthodox Gaullists, would protest loudly and energetically were anyone to describe him as "bourgeois." As for M. Mitterand and M. Servan-Schreiber, they are of course socialists. I say "of course" because ever since Henri de Saint-Simon invented the idea, if not the term (which made its appearance somewhat later), it has been the fashion on the French Left to describe oneself as a socialist.

For practical purposes this usually meant being in favor of centralized economic planning. By now this is not only technically possible, but politically popular, indeed necessary if the economy is to stagger on. There has to be some sort of planning, because things have moved beyond the primitive stage where the market could be relied upon to allocate economic resources more or less rationally without causing vast dislocations and mass unemployment. The socialists were first with this notion, and thanks to them the Left eventually grasped it before the Right did (although the intelligent section of the Right has now caught up). All the same, M. Servan-Schreiber is being a trifle disingenuous when he writes, "It is the Left that brought rational decision-making to the economy, and thanks to the Left that the idea of the Plan came to France." The "idea of the Plan" was brought to France in the 1930s by Henri de Man, whose pupils went over to Fascism when "the Left" idiotically turned him down. And when by 1945 the Resistance movement had made planning respectable, the Gaullists profited most from it, while the section of the Old Left from which M. Servan-Schreiber stems (the Radical Party) virtually went out of existence.

Yet it remains true that so long as a Frenchman sticks to the Saint-Simonian vocabulary, he cannot be faulted for inconsistency if he chooses to call himself a socialist. Some of the more prominent Saint-Simonians in the past century ended up as bankers and railroad directors (they also built the Suez Canal). M. Servan-Schreiber is in an old and (in France) respectable tradition: that of industrial modernization in the name of socialism. After all, people have to believe in something, and few people these days believe in capitalism. Did they ever? As Schumpeter used to say, "The Stock Exchange is no substitute for the Holy Grail." I doubt if anyone other than Senator Goldwater ever "believed in" an abstraction called "capitalism." People generally tend to believe in solid entities such as "the home," "the family," or "private property." These institutions made up what Schumpeter called "the civilization of capitalism," that is to say, bourgeois civilization. This particular social milieu having disintegrated—even in France—it is no longer possible to run the country in the name of private entrepreneurship. Hence the cult of planning, now baptized socialism.

There is nothing wrong with all this. In fact, France needs a lot more of it, and will get it as soon as M. Mendès France succeeds M. Debré at the Treasury: that is to say, when the General is gone and M. Pompidou (who, by the way, is a political heavyweight compared to his present assailants) has vacated the field. And of course it is all going to be called socialism. What else should it be called? But that is just where the trouble is going to start: especially for the Communists, who by then will be in the government and will have to explain to their followers that democracy in the workshop can only go so far.

These considerations may seem more relevant to the present political outlook in France than to M. Servan-Schreiber's book (which, after all, came out before the workers and students had started their wave of sit-down strikes). But anyone who reads the book—and it deserves to be widely read—will soon discover that the author's technological enthusiasm has distinct political implications. European federalism is only one of them, although the most notorious and the best advertised. Nationalization is another, though not much talked about at the moment. What do you do if your computer industry is being taken over by the Americans? M. Servan-Schreiber's reply is: found a European computer industry. But suppose the leading European firms are so closely tied to their American partners that they find it convenient to sink back into the role of satellites? Or suppose the various European governments cannot make up their collective minds about concerted countermeasures? Then—if you have ruled out nationalism as antiquated—what have you got to fall back upon if you want to meet the challenge? The present technological imbalance, to which M. Servan-Schreiber devotes the bulk of his work, has social consequences, which in turn reflect themselves in the political sphere. Let us hear his own statement of the problem:

> During the next few years American investment in Europe will continue to grow far more rapidly than European investment. Its profits are already half again as large as ours. It is taking over the major role in strategic areas of development. This is not happening through ordinary investments, but through actual take-overs of European firms that the Americans then transform into rich and powerful corporations. And they do this with European money that our own businessmen do not know how to use.

Sounds rather Gaullist, doesn't it? In Britain, that eccentric Tory Enoch Powell is beginning to make similar noises, and no one could be more remote from socialism (or even from central planning) than *he* is. Patriotism does strange things to people. If Scotland secedes from England, or if Mr. Powell sweeps his bumbling rivals aside and becomes England's next Tory leader (two distinct possibilities), it won't be in the name of socialism but of nationalism: an old-fashioned creed, but still a potent one. If M. Servan-Schreiber's highly sophisticated analysis of the current European malaise has an intellectual flaw, it is his tendency to underrate the force of national sentiment. In all other respects he is as up-to-date and well informed as one could wish. And he is *not* anti-American. That must be emphasized, for the benefit of readers who may have been misled by the passages I have quoted (there are a lot more, some of them couched in rather alarmist terms). He is simply voicing a very common sentiment among Europe's intellectual elites, and doing it in the classical French manner: clear-headed, self-assured, and secure in the faith that Reason has the power to set all things right— even the student unrest in his own country. But there he may come up against imponderables fed by a subterranean source as ancient as his own: that of Rousseau.

When the Light Failed

·❊ ❊ ❊

IN JUNE 1942 Gestapo representatives in Paris, acting on urgent instructions from Eichmann in Berlin, put pressure upon the French authorities to facilitate the deportation of all Jews resident in France, foreigners and French nationals alike. Since there were only three thousand Gestapo men in the whole of Occupied France, the active cooperation of the French police was essential to this undertaking, notably in Paris, a city of about three million people harboring perhaps as many as 150,000 Jews, many of them stateless refugees in hiding. Laval, then in charge of the Vichy government presided over by the senile Pétain, compromised to the extent of agreeing to hand over all Jews who were not French citizens. Being a generous fellow, he threw in the children of stateless Jews, for whom the Germans had forgotten to ask. All told, about 120,000 were rounded up and deported, half of them to the extermination camps. At his trial in 1945 Laval defended himself on the grounds that he had at any rate saved the lives of French nationals. "I did all I could, considering that my first duty was to my fellow countrymen of Jewish origin, whose interests I could not sacrifice."

Abominable though it was, Laval's conduct disclosed a naïve conviction that there was an essential difference between Jews of French nationality (whom in some fashion he regarded as fellow citizens) and others who were foreigners and thus might be shipped off. To the Germans this distinction was meaningless, and, had the Occupation continued, all the 300,000 Jews in France would have suffered the fate of the deportees. But the distinction had no meaning, either, for most French Catholics (though many of them risked their lives to help the persecuted). It went back to the Revolution: specifically to the new laws enacted by the Constituent Assembly in 1790 and 1791. This legislation, for which the philosophical basis had been provided by the literature of the Enlightenment, did away with religious discrimination and placed all French citizens on an equal footing. It is noteworthy that in regard to the Jews (though not in regard to the far more numerous and influential Protestants, who were emancipated at the same time) this new concept of citizenship was opposed by the representatives from Alsace—some future Jacobins among them—on the grounds that Jews would never make decent citizens. Doubtless these skeptics had their reasons for voicing the general antipathy then felt for the Alsatian Jews by the natives of that province. There was no bother about enfranchising the smaller and more respectable Jewish communities in the South, mostly descendants of Portuguese crypto-Jews—the Marranos—who had long been settled in and around Bordeaux and become thoroughly assimilated. In any event the great majority of the Constituent Assembly went ahead with the emancipation decrees, and later French governments (including that of Napoleon) confirmed them, at any rate in principle. The new secular concept of nationality thus introduced into legislation was unprecedented. There is reason to believe that Rousseau would have approved of it. The case of Voltaire is less clear. On balance it is arguable that the influence of his writings, while clearly favoring Protestant emancipation, predisposed the legislators against the Jews rather than in their favor. Voltaire had always stood out against religious persecution. What mattered was that he was prepared to concede only toleration to the Jews—no more.

The bulk of Arthur Hertzberg's scholarly study on the social and intellectual background of the legislation enacted after 1789, *The French Enlightenment and the Jews*,[1] is devoted to a meticulous analysis of Jewish communal existence in France since the sixteenth century, with special reference to the Jews' role in overseas trade and economic life generally. This turns out to have been marginal, though on balance beneficial from the mercantilist standpoint: which is why the more clearheaded adminis-

1. New York, 1968.

trators, from Colbert in the seventeenth century to Turgot in the
eighteenth, tended to favor them—at any rate to the extent of
granting them a degree of toleration. This of course had nothing
to do with citizenship. It was simply a matter of allowing a few
privileges to an unpopular but economically useful group of religious heretics. The Revolution, by turning them into French
citizens with equal rights, introduced a totally new principle.
On this subject Dr. Hertzberg is in a quandary. On the one
hand, he naturally approves of the emancipation acts passed after 1789. On the other hand, he deplores the fact that the philo-
Semites generally expected the Jews to give up their separate
communal existence, not to mention the commercial practices
to which they had been reduced by centuries of oppression.
Moreover, he is constrained to note that the French Enlightenment had its roots in Spinoza's critique of the Bible, a circumstance which to a believing Jew (Dr. Hertzberg is a rabbi as
well as an historian) presents a certain embarrassment. Spinoza,
he suggests, induced enlightened Frenchmen of his age to think
ill of the Old Testament. Possibly, but he also presented the
hitherto unknown spectacle of a Jew who was a distinguished
philosopher. It is by no means as certain as Dr. Hertzberg appears to believe that this was a misfortune. It is even arguable
that Spinoza's prestige with the writers of the Enlightenment
outweighed their dislike for the Jews they came across.

That most of them detested both the Jews and their religion is
evident enough. There were exceptions, but in general even
those who advocated emancipation added a rider to the effect
that Judaism as a faith was undesirable, if only because it had
given birth to Christianity. Voltaire was notably eloquent on
this topic, and the Encyclopedists took their tone from him. Voltaire, needless to say, disapproved of persecution in general and
the Inquisition in particular, but he also disapproved of the
Bible. Since he could not well employ the standard theological
arguments against the Jews, he fell back upon the pre-Christian
anti-Judaism of classical antiquity. Dr. Hertzberg documents this
at some length, but the real point of his thesis is that anti-Semitism, having predated Christianity, might also postdate it. That
is indisputable but does not bear out his contention that "the
defeat of the emancipation of the Jews of Europe existed in

embryo even before that process began." The emancipation was reversed not in France, which had accomplished its revolution at the peak of the Enlightenment, but in Germany, where the national movement got going under the banner of Romanticism, beloved of theological and political conservatives. Dr. Hertzberg is, however, in two minds about the French Revolution. It was, he thinks, a very ambiguous affair from the start. "The idea of freedom for all sort of ideas was the major intellectual force for liberating the Jews at the end of the eighteenth century. The idea of remaking men to fit properly into the new society was the seed-bed of totalitarianism." We already have it on Professor J. L. Talmon's authority that Rousseau was the prophet of "totalitarian democracy." If Dr. Hertzberg is to be believed, Diderot and Voltaire were totalitarian liberals because they had no use for religion. At this rate the concept of totalitarianism is shortly going to be emptied of all meaning.

Dr. Hertzberg has dug up some interesting material on the debates preceding the emancipation decrees of 1789 to 1791. For the most part this legislation was the work of men who took their ideas from Montesquieu and their political lead from Mirabeau: notably liberal aristocrats like Clermont-Tonnerre who held the stage during the early phase of the Revolution. But there was also a radical wing which pressed for equal citizenship: the commune of Paris, the Jacobins (except for their Alsatian deputies), and some heretical Catholic radicals: above all the Abbé Grégoire, who for years had advocated Jewish emancipation on quasi-mystical grounds derived from a millenarian tradition descended from the persecuted Jansenists. It is an agreeable thought that Port Royal may have contributed to the legislation of 1789–91, though Pascal would hardly have approved of it: he took the conventional view that the Jews were deicides who richly merited their fate. This did not interfere with his veneration for the Old Testament as divinely inspired. Grégoire combined Jansenism with millenarianism, and thus arrived at a standpoint which has become that of present-day Christian democrats in France. Dr. Hertzberg clearly prefers him to Voltaire, and it may well be that his intervention was the decisive factor in reconciling his fellow Catholics to the laws then passed.

But in the main the battle was fought out on the terrain of a new concept of man and the world. Morality was the common possession of all. Religion, on the other hand, was a subjective affair, and all faiths must be tolerated. This was to become the liberal standpoint. It is plain enough that the emancipation of Protestants and Jews in 1789–91 was secured because the intellectual elite (although not as yet the masses) had been won over to the philosophy of the Enlightenment. For the Protestants, who then gained their freedom, the battle was over. For the Jews it had only begun. "What has not been noticed," writes Dr. Hertzberg, "is that an anti-Jewish left-wing intelligentsia arose at the same time." It has not been noticed for the sound reason that no such phenomenon occurred. Dr. Hertzberg confuses anti-Semitism with dislike of religion. Setting aside his doctrinaire thesis, he has written a useful book which deserves to be read for the information it contains but will probably be cited for all the wrong reasons.

A French View of Israel

❋ ❋ ❋

THE PUBLICATION IN FRANCE IN 1966 of Georges Friedmann's
The End of the Jewish People?, almost coinciding as it did both
with a special issue of *Les Temps Modernes* on the Arab-Israeli
conflict and with the latest round in that seemingly unending
struggle for possession of the Promised Land, seems to have had
a calming effect on at least some of the Parisian literary bystanders. The reason is easily discoverable from the preface to the
very welcome English translation (by Eric Mosbacher) which
has now made its appearance.[1]

Professor Friedmann, a distinguished French sociologist, is
also a veteran of the wartime Resistance movement, into which
(as he candidly explains) he was precipitated by the anti-Jewish
decrees issued in October 1940 by the Vichy regime: a regime,
by the way, which enjoyed the enthusiastic support of almost
the entire French Catholic hierarchy (though not of the lower
clergy, many of whom joined the Resistance and did all they
could to help Jewish victims of persecution). Himself an intellectual of the Left, Professor Friedmann recovered his shaken
humanist faith in the company of the men and women whom he
encountered in the underground movement. Nonetheless he had
suffered a shock, though, as he puts it, "the French resistance
demonstrated the soundness of my motto *civic gallicus sum.*"
It was thus in a mood of critical expectancy, not unmixed with
hope, that he visited Israel in 1963 and 1964, to see what its
citizens had made of their unique opportunity.

The result is a book that is unlikely to satisfy anyone save the

The Listener, August 10, 1967.
    1. London and New York, 1967.

minority of noncombatants who share the author's own sympathetic and discerning assessments of Israel and its inhabitants.
Coming at the present time, it is liable to be read primarily for
what light it throws on the Arab-Israeli imbroglio; but these passages, through no fault of the author's, are precisely those that
have been rendered out of date. It is no longer relevant to argue
the pros and cons of Israel taking back the Arab refugees who,
for one reason or another, fled in 1948. Most of them are now
located in territory administered by the Israeli authorities, and
the real issue is whether Israel can become what some of its
founders, and most left-wing socialists, intended it to be: a binational state rather than a purely Jewish one. It is a tribute to
the author's perspicacity that, writing in 1965–66, he deals with
this thorny subject. Indeed he has very definite views about it:
views which will not make him popular either with the Arab nationalists, who still dream of destroying the state, or with the
bulk of Zionist opinion.

Broadly speaking, he favors a solution that will enable Israel to
integrate itself into the Middle East and by the same token cease
to emphasize the Jewish connection. This of course is heresy to
the older generation, brought up on the Zionist myth of "ingath-
ering," or on some variant of the religious faith. It may, however,
for reasons which he sets out at some length, shortly become
acceptable to the young. For the fundamental fact about Israel—
a fact rarely stated with the candor Professor Friedmann brings
to the topic—is the radical incompatibility of its daily life with
the aspirations of the Zionist movement from which it was born.
Like communism in Russia, Zionism in Israel has become a hollow shell, the ideological remnant of a buried East European
past. The author puts it with commendable clarity:

> There is no Jewish nation. There is an Israeli nation. The state
> that came into existence as a result of Herzl's prophecies is not a
> "Jewish state." The Israeli state is creating an imperious national
> community that is conscious of itself, but does not include in that
> consciousness belonging to a "Jewish people." There seems to be
> a widening gap (among the extremist zealots it is an impassable
> abyss) between that part of the population that sees itself as essen-
> tially Israeli and that other part, consisting of the orthodox, that
> regards itself as essentially Jewish.

He has a good deal to say on the subject of the "Jewish person-ality," both in its historical aspect and in relation to contempo-rary Western culture, which will displease the more ardent Zion-ists, and yet he does not dispute that there was once an entity (albeit not a biological one) which could be described as "the Jewish people." He merely happens to believe that it is about to vanish from the stage of history, and that the establishment of Israel, so far from perpetuating it and ensuring its survival, will speed its disappearance. As he puts it, in a challenging statement the truth of which must be apparent to every observer who keeps his eyes and ears open when visiting that fascinating country: "In the land of Palestine, in a sum-total of geographic, climatic, social, cultural, political conditions profoundly differ-ent from those that formed it, the Jewish personality is disinte-grating. The 'Jewish people' is disappearing and giving place to the Israeli nation."

This being the last thing in the world that the old generation of Zionists wants to hear, one may expect their criticism to take the form of an airy dismissal of Professor Friedmann's work on the grounds that he is a shallow liberal with no sense of re-ligious or national values. But in fact he is invulnerable on this score, for he accepts both the reality of Israeli nationhood and the enduring strength of Jewish religious consciousness. He merely holds that they are incompatible. Israel is going to be-come a secular state (and probably a binational one) as a matter of survival and because the majority of the young are bored with religion. As for the orthodox minority, it will increasingly, he thinks, retreat into a mystical realm of its own.

If I have a reservation about this learned and stimulating book, it is that the author seems unduly impressed with Sartre's perverse definition of the Jew as someone whom "the Others" regard as a Jew. The matter is not quite so simple, and anyhow Professor Friedmann undercuts this bizarre notion by dwelling at length on the record of medieval Christianity in fashioning "the Jew" in its own image. He also has some polite but implacable remarks on "the silences of Pius XII": remarks which will, one hopes, give acute pain to the Vatican's apologists. Altogether a splendid book: readable, authoritative, and totally unbeholden to any organized body of opinion.

EUROPE IN DECLINE

European Civilization

❀❀❀

EUROPE, we are often reminded these days, is more ancient than the nations composing it. Or, if that sounds paradoxical, the idea of Europe antedates the rise of the sovereign nation-state. There was a common European civilization, albeit confined to a thin stratum of rulers and thinkers, before the various nations struck out on their own. In those days, Frenchmen, Germans, Netherlanders, even the insular English, thought of themselves as members of the same spiritual family. Or did they? No one knows for certain what ordinary people felt, but it seems safe to say that their lords temporal and spiritual held some such assumption.

The Carolingian Empire, and the Roman Church which sanctified it, had instituted the habit of identifying Western Christianity with an entity known as "Europe," even though the term "Christendom" was preferred. Europe, or Western Christianity, was conceived as the heir of the Roman Empire, or at any rate of its western half. It comprised that portion of the known world which was neither Islamic nor subject to Byzantium. It therefore excluded the Greek Orthodox schismatics and Muslim Spain (until the *Reconquista*). Poland was part of it but Russia was not, even though the Tsarist domains counted as a heretical part of Christendom. Fundamentally this is still the Roman Catholic view. It conditions a good part of European historiography, and even the politics of the ruling Christian Democratic parties.

The central issue here is the dialectic of Europeanism and nationalism. The gradual emergence of the various nations, and the concomitant stress laid on national sovereignty, disrupted medieval civilization: "the first Europe," as Delisle Burns called it in his interesting study of medieval origins.[1] Roman Catholic writers—Christopher Dawson comes to mind—naturally tend to emphasize the medieval roots of contemporary Europe, while their Protestant or secularist colleagues are more concerned to stress the national peculiarities. French historians are in the happy position of being able to do both: they can claim Joan of Arc as well as Charlemagne when enlarging on the topic of *gesta Dei per Francos*. The eldest daughter of the Church was also the first to set up as an independent nation-state under the rule of a sovereign king no longer subject to the post-Carolingian Empire.

The Germans, in this as in other respects, are less well placed, for the dissolution of the medieval Empire terminated their hour of national greatness. German hegemony during the Middle Ages was tied to the pre-eminence of the Holy Roman Empire, supposedly the heir of Rome and the rival of Byzantium. When the Empire fell on evil days, the Germans lost their claim to special status. An exception was provided by the Habsburg domains, which remained the seat of the medieval *Reichsmystik*, originally worked out in the early Middle Ages to buttress the claims of the Emperor in his struggle with the Papacy. Austrian Catholicism conserved this peculiar heritage, and from the nineteenth century onward, sentiments of this kind fused with Romanticism to give birth to the poetry of Rilke and Stefan George, the metaphysics of Heidegger, and the politics of Count Stauffenberg: Hitler's would-be assassin, albeit down to 1940 a fervent admirer of the Führer. The "Third Reich," to adherents of this school, signified the advent of a European order in which Germany would once again shine forth as the paramount power because invested with a sacred mission. Their chief complaint against Hitler rested upon the belated perception that he was too vulgar to understand what they were talking about.

Friedrich Heer's learned work *The Intellectual History of Europe*,[2] published in Germany in 1953, stems from this ancient tradition of Baroque Catholicism, although its author belongs to the postwar generation of Austrian scholars and in some measure represents a reaction against the conservatism of his elders. His *Aufgang Europas* (1949), though critical of the Imperial *Reichs-*

1. C. Delisle Burns, *The First Europe* (London, 1947; New York, 1948).
2. London and Cleveland, 1966.

mystik, could still have been described as Papalist in spirit: it was the Church, not the medieval Empire, which had made it possible for Europe to find its early unity on the basis of a common civilization. By now the Church, too, or at any rate the specifically Roman tradition embodied in the Vatican bureaucracy, has come to incur his displeasure. For Professor Heer, though launched on his path as a historian before the second Vatican Council, is very much a liberal Catholic and impatient of the hierarchy. In the dozen or so years since his work was composed there have been some stirrings, and today he no longer sounds quite as heretical as he must have done to his fellow Austrians in 1953. By other standards his liberalism seems even now a trifle wobbly. However, there is no denying that he has let some air into the stuffy atmosphere of German Catholicism, and for this feat even a non-Christian may be duly grateful.

The standpoint chosen by Professor Heer for his survey of European intellectual history since Augustine is perhaps best described as a modified form of Erasmianism. His particular heroes are the Renaissance scholars who combined fidelity to the Church with a cautious humanism, and his chief regret is that Erasmus himself was unable to inspire the peaceful reform which a handful of conciliar statesmen and scholars had initiated until they were blown off course by the storm Luther had unleashed. In this form the argument has a respectable ancestry, but is clearly too academic to appeal to anyone save a handful of likeminded souls. The author, though, has chosen to address himself to the educated laity. The result is a hybrid: a massive work which somehow manages to read like a propaganda tract rather than a dispassionate study of intellectual history. Fortunately the translation has eliminated the irritating stylistic peculiarities of the original, so that the general reader can follow the argument without puzzling his head too much over theological hairsplitting.

If his patience lasts to the end, he may even discover how the author's politics are made to rhyme with his somewhat idiosyncratic view of traditional European culture as the creation and possession of a thin aristocratic elite. Professor Heer, though something of a liberal, is by no means a democrat and has small use for ordinary folk, or even for their folk culture. As a reac-

tion against the frenzied demagogy of the Third Reich this distaste for popular passion is welcome. And certainly no liberal
will dissent from the author's strictures on such earlier outbursts
of controlled ferocity as the Counter Reformation's savage treatment of the Spanish followers of Erasmus. It is all very civilized,
if a trifle remote from the crude realities actually experienced by
the contemporaries of these distant events. One would hardly
gather from his account that the Inquisition was primarily a
means of ridding Spain of its Muslim and Jewish minorities (and
confiscating their property for the benefit of the Crown and the
Church). The notion that Erasmian humanism could somehow
have become the vehicle of a peaceful reformation strikes an
agreeably fantastic note: rather like those touching tributes to
the superior wisdom of Mme. de Stael and her friends which still
figure in all the standard liberal diatribes against the Jacobin
regime.

Professor Heer's own relationship to the political doctrine of
his German-Austrian coreligionists is somewhat ambiguous. He
has of course no use for the Third Reich and its spiritual precursors, among whom he includes most of the Romantics. On the
other hand, his own cast of mind is decidedly conservative and
Little European. On balance he is well able to do without the
Protestant North. As for England, it appears as "the counterweight to Europe."

> England does not belong to Europe. Since the eighth century En-
> gland has considered itself another world, *alter orbis,* circling the
> Continent like the comet on the Bayeux tapestry which was re-
> garded as an omen of the Norman conquest in 1066. It was the
> same comet that Newton's friend Halley calculated in 1692. Ac-
> cording to popular belief, comets appear in times of crisis. Thus
> England has always intervened in the history of Europe when a
> religious, spiritual or political balance was disturbed.

This, by the way, is a fair sample of the author's style, which
leans heavily on evocative metaphor and on occasion manages
to dispense with ordinary logical sequence. The meaning, though,
is clear enough: British keep out! They should find this all the
easier since, according to Professor Heer, the entire spiritual
history of England, since the Pelagian heresy in the fifth century, has been one of rebellion against the Roman inheritance.

"In a sense England's nationalism has been religious from the beginning. The Roman Church was never very strong in England." This was the legacy of Pelagius, but there was also, it seems, a Manichaean inheritance,

> a cruel naked splitting of the cosmos into a kingdom of grace and faith, and an earthly kingdom of strife, of natural necessity, of human knowledge. From Wyclif on, the three movements against Rome and Europe ran parallel: the political action of the kings and their bishops, the scientific movement of the theologians and professors, and the political movement of the people of the lower class and their priests.

All told, the British appear to have been a subversive lot. At a later stage their condition was unfavorably affected by "the filthy and abominable factories of the Calvinist 17th and 18th centuries" when "the poor and the propertyless deservedly atoned for their damned existence. To this very day, in the Calvinist countries of Switzerland, Holland, England and America (as in the Dutch language), sin is primarily linked with the loss or the squandering of money."

Given this regrettable inheritance, it is surprising that "England could affirm itself as a conservative country because its political and spiritual superstructure was constantly nourished through a thousand channels from below." There is even a suggestion to the effect that the islanders profited from their geographical isolation, which left them free to cultivate the virtues of tolerance and moderation. A conventional bouquet is also thrown to their adventurousness as pioneers in distant lands. On the whole, though, one is left with the impression that Europe, as seen from Vienna, can get on without the British.

A learned controversialist writing about history rather than a historian, Professor Heer is at his best in dealing with general ideas (especially theological ideas), at his worst in elucidating simple matters of fact. It is no use going to him for information about anything that actually happened, whether it be the Thirty Years' War or the French Revolution. On the other hand, he has interesting sidelights on medieval German mystics, or on Renaissance figures such as Paracelsus. He also deals some quite shrewd blows at "a certain Catholic conformism. The conformists are prone to admire Rilke's 'Franciscan' soul, Heidegger's Catholic ontology, and Hitler's *Reich*. These sort of thinkers can confuse European thinking."

That is putting it mildly.

Taylor's Germany

※ ※ ※

ALL THROUGH 1964 historians and publicists were busy with 1914. A. J. P. Taylor's latest essay collection, *Politics in Wartime*,[1] swims with the tide of reminiscence. Its bulk is devoted to the men who came to the fore in 1914–18, and to the events which preceded and followed the war. A few minor pieces range further back, but although Cromwell and Metternich are dragged in, the author's heart is not in it. He rounds off his collection with brief sketches of George VI, Neville Chamberlain, and Mussolini.

It is generally held that occasional pieces are Mr. Taylor's forte. Personally I prefer him in the role of serious historian. His 1959 lecture "Politics in the First World War" reads just as well as it did when it first appeared. It puts Namier's technique to the test and comes out triumphant. The 1961 lecture on Lloyd George is almost equally dazzling, though less closely reasoned. These are the two star performances: they provide an excuse for charging the reader a guinea for the volume. The other pieces are less impressive, and one or two are downright silly. Mercifully, there is very little about Hitler and 1939, but what there is reaffirms Mr. Taylor's well-known perversities on the subject.

These contrasts illustrate the difficulty of writing about subjects remote from one's experience. When he describes the personality of Lloyd George or the events preceding Asquith's fall, Mr. Taylor is on his home ground and almost impossible to fault —at any rate by someone who is not himself a professional. When he turns to other countries, the note of authority vanishes,

1. London, 1964; New York, 1965.

and what we get is mere assertion: confident, cocksure, misleading. Even the nonspecialist can see that he is wrong in treating Mussolini as a silly clown without roots in the life of his country. He does not grasp that Fascism was an outgrowth of the Nationalist movement which had driven Italy into war in 1915, or that Mussolini himself attempted a fusion of syndicalism and nationalism. He knows there was a radical tradition in Britain; he does not realize there was a nationalist one in Italy. For him the Italians are comic foreigners, Mussolini the most comical of all.

When it comes to Germany, the misconceptions get bigger and more alarming. Most Radicals in 1914 held that war with Germany was not only undesirable but unnecessary: caused by a sequence of stupid accidents. All the Germans wanted was a free hand against Russia and a few concessions in Africa. Mr. Taylor treats the catastrophe as due to a series of blunders. He stops short of suggesting that Grey was the chief culprit, but hints that peace might have been preserved if he had exerted himself a bit more. Peace in general, or peace between Britain and Germany? Mr. Taylor eludes the difficulty, then suggests that the Germans in 1914 did not even want a continental war against Russia and France. This is nonsense, and he ought to know it.[2]

If Germany was not responsible for the outbreak of war in 1914, then no one was responsible. This is in fact Mr. Taylor's thesis. Yet the evidence shows that the Reich government launched what it regarded as a preventive war against Russia and France, and did not shrink from the risk of involving Britain as well. The decision was taken with the full consent of Bethmann Hollweg, Imperial Chancellor from 1909 to 1917. The facts have been established, and for good measure we now have the diary of Bethmann Hollweg's private secretary, Riezler, which shows conclusively that the Chancellor—as much as William II and the General Staff—had by July 1914 opted for a European war: largely because he felt that time was working against Germany and that it was a case of now or never. Mr. Taylor could not have known about Riezler—the diary has only

2. The matter was adequately cleared up in 1961 by Professor Fritz Fischer of Hamburg in his monumental *Griff nach der Weltmacht*, a work Mr. Taylor is unlikely to have overlooked since it roused a storm in Germany. He does not mention it, and gives the impression of not being concerned with its argument.

recently begun to appear in print—but he cannot have failed to read Professor Fischer. This does not prevent him from serving up the old legends concocted by German historians and their apologists. William and Bethmann, we are told, were merely rattling the saber a bit, as was their silly habit.

It is odd that Mr. Taylor fails to understand Bethmann, for there is really no mystery about him. Unlike Hitler a generation later, the Imperial Chancellor was neither an upstart nor a fanatic—any more than were the Japanese statesmen who took the plunge in 1941. Unlike Bismarck, whom of course he greatly admired, he was no genius. Mr. Taylor has written brilliant non-sense about Bismarck and tedious nonsense about Hitler. He might have been expected to write sense about Bethmann, who was commonplace enough, even though he did want to annex half of Europe before the Marne sobered him (thereafter he only wanted Belgium and Poland). But to see the German government as it was in 1914—determined to make war while Austria still hung together, and before Russia had rearmed—means giving up the Liberal legend. This lays it down that World War I was a fiasco which might have been avoided if Asquith and Grey had not been asleep on the job: in short, that one could have both imperialism and business-as-usual. The Tories realized that this was impossible; so, in their different way, did the more radical socialists and pacifists. The only people who still believe it are the heirs of the Liberal backbenchers in 1914. A few years from now they will probably have persuaded themselves that World War II might have been avoided too. After all, Mr. Taylor has already argued that Hitler stumbled into it through inadvertence.

The technical part of *Politics in Wartime* hinges on the so-called Schlieffen Plan: the German march through Belgium which brought Britain into the war. Mr. Taylor thinks it was foolish of the Germans to stake all on such a gamble. In retrospect it clearly was, but the gamble *was* taken, and the men who took it had their eyes wide open. They thought they could knock France out quickly, and were quite willing to take Britain and Russia on as well. Their underlying attitude was fully shared by the civilian bureaucracy headed by the Chancellor; by big business and the German middle class; by intellectuals like Sombart and Max Weber; by all the Conservatives, most of the Liberals, and not a few Social Democrats. (Bethmann's wartime supporters included some prominent SPD leaders.) There is no excuse —now that Professor Fischer has blown the gaff on the official apologetics—for going on with the old nonsense about Germany having "drifted into war" in 1914. There is also no need for it. The whole thing no longer matters. We are all citizens of diminished Europe, and our quarrels belong to the history books. The only thing that now remains is getting the facts straight.

Mr. Taylor quotes a memorandum drawn up in 1913 by Moltke (the Chief of Staff) which says as plainly as anything that the march through Belgium must not be renounced even for a promise of British neutrality, for "we should give up the only chance of a quick and decisive victory which we need." In other words, British hostility must be risked. Mr. Taylor gets out of the difficulty by suggesting elsewhere that "the German government" (which he seems to regard as an entity remote from the General Staff) had not foreseen that its own army would march through Belgium in the event of war with France! "Though Bethmann had been told vaguely of it years before, he had not taken it in and made no diplomatic preparations," he writes. But even under William II things were not quite so chaotic as that. What happened was that the Germans gambled on the Anglo-Russian antagonism, and when that gamble failed, they marched through Belgium anyhow. They were encouraged by memories of how Frederick of Prussia had got away with something very similar at the start of the Seven Years' War. Frederick had been a hero to the British public, which cheered his blitzkrieg and raised no objection to the subsidies paid him by the British government. William and Bethmann could not hope for similar treatment, but they did not quite foresee the indignation their treatment of Belgium aroused even among pro-German Liberals. It was a miscalculation due to their upbringing, and it was shared by German historians like Meinecke to whom the Prussian tradition was sacred.

Today all these controversies are dead. They are here recalled only because readers of Mr. Taylor's volume will search in vain for mention of the historic Anglo-Prussian alliance which foundered in 1914. It had lasted for 150 years, and the Germans were duly resentful when it collapsed. Of course no alliance lasts forever—especially when one partner begins to build a navy for use against the other. Nowadays the competition is over trade with third countries, and Anglo-German wrangles have to do with export credits and others subjects unlikely to raise anyone's blood pressure. The only people who still keep up some of the old animosity are historians—chiefly on the German side. But then Germany lost, and losers must be allowed some extra time to get over their resentments.

On the Rim of the Volcano

❋ ❋ ❋

THE EXHAUSTION of a national tradition does not make an ideal
subject for an essay ostensibly devoted to the theme of
Western Germany's intellectual standing. On the face of it there
is no lack of energy and enterprise. Controversies abound. The
traditional themes are steadily pursued, and in addition the postwar surge of self-criticism has made for a healthy readiness to
welcome foreign imports. To all appearances the Federal Republic is as cosmopolitan as Weimar ever was, though the cultural
melting pot of Berlin has shrunk to the dimension of an enclave
in hostile territory. Modernism has finally triumphed in the arts
(though not in the lowbrow domain of film, where mediocrity
reigns supreme). The 1920s have been canonized. Bertolt Brecht
plays to full houses. Arnold Schönberg and Franz Kafka have
become classics. Philosophy is dominated by the various existentialist schools, sociology by the current fashionable concern
over mass production and the alienation of the individual. So
far as the availability of modish intellectual products goes, the
cultural consumer in the *Bundesrepublik* is no worse off than his
opposite number in Paris, London, or Manhattan.

It is when one views the scene in the light of the country's
past that all this effervescence appears insubstantial, an attempt
to conjure up the mood of an age when the volcano was still
active, and when Germany itself was more than the Clapham
Junction of the West. The intellectual revolution which ran its
course between 1910 and 1930 coincided with the closing phase
of Germany's political hegemony in continental Europe. There
was already something fraudulent about certain manifestations

Encounter, XXII, No. 4 (April 1964).

of German intellectualism during the Weimar period—one need only consider the vogue of Oswald Spengler—but even the frauds and the false prophets had their importance in the context of a situation which was soon to give birth to the monstrous apparition of the Third Reich. Today no one expects the Federal Republic—or even a unified Germany, should it ever come about—to set the tone for the remainder of Europe. There is indeed no lack of talent, but most of it relates to specifically domestic issues. The international resonance is gone. Where it persists—as with Jaspers in philosophy, or with Bultmann and his school in theology—it rests on the work of writers who had already made their mark before the war. In psychology, general medicine, and the natural sciences—at one time a steady source of Nobel Prize laureates—the contrast with the prewar situation is alarming enough to have induced pessimistic forecasts about the coming need to import scientists, as well as workers, from abroad. The kind of fundamental research in which German scholars used to excel is quite simply not being done in sufficient quantity to keep pace with the needs. No amount of industrial prosperity can conceal the fact that the country is no longer intellectually self-supporting.

Whether this change should be lamented or treated as an aspect of West Germany's integration into a wider European whole must in part depend on the value one attaches to the old Central European culture of which Germany was the dominant factor. It is worth remembering that this culture included the former Habsburg territories. The German-Jewish-Hungarian-Slav synthesis, which *inter alia* produced Kafka (and Lukács), had already passed its peak in 1918, but the afterglow lasted until Hitler's occupation of Vienna in 1938, and in some respects it was brought to an end only by the Communist take-over in Prague a decade later. These two events completed the destruction of a fabric whose peculiar character was bound up with its supranationalism.

The absence today of a common language—in both the narrow and the wider sense—between Vienna, Prague, and Budapest (not to mention Warsaw) is a factor in the situation of which thinking Germans are very conscious. The intellectual nullity

of East Germany and the sterility of the official culture sponsored there by the most philistine of all satellite regimes aggra-
vate what is anyhow a novel situation so far as Central Europe is
concerned. In this particular context the erection of the Berlin
Wall in 1961 was significant in that it coincided with the decision
of Professor Ernst Bloch, doyen of East German Marxists, not to
return to Leipzig—where he had in any case been deprived of
his chair—but to remain in West Germany. (He is now teaching
at Tübingen, where Hegel once spent five formative years as a
student in company with Schelling and Hölderlin.)

Mention of Ernst Bloch at this point is indeed inescapable.
Sympathetic critics of his work have pointed out that his
thinking is related to the pantheism of the early German Romantic movement.[1] The fact that his intellectual roots are embedded
in this particular soil does not perhaps seem very startling to
Germans, by now quite used to the spectacle of a Marxist who
claims Goethe, Schelling, and Kant among his spiritual ancestors. Was not Goethe's pantheism—itself in part derived from
Spinoza—the seedbed of Feuerbach's humanism? This intellectual climate accounts both for Bloch's current vogue and for the
virtual impossibility of translating him. In the latter respect he resembles Martin Heidegger, whose thinking finds an echo in his
own recent utterances. The two men are contemporaries. Bloch
was born in 1888, a year before the author of Sein und Zeit, and
his first published work, a study of Thomas Münzer (1921), already displayed some characteristics of his later writings: notably
the conjunction of a romanticized Marxism with a style made
familiar by the expressionist manifestos of the 1920s.

The comparison with Heidegger may seem unfair to both men;
that it is not wholly unreasonable must be apparent to the reader
of Heidegger's recent study of Nietzsche. Bloch would presumably acknowledge as his own particular weakness a certain incapacity for sustained logical construction. In other respects the
distance between Freiburg and Tübingen may appear less con-

1. Bloch's major work, a two-volume treatise entitled *Das Prinzip Hoff-
nung*, is available in a West German edition (Frankfurt, 1959). His *Natur-
recht und menschliche Würde* (1961), a bulky essay on the philosophical
implications of Natural Law doctrine, is also available, as is the first install-
ment of his *Philosophische Grundfragen* (1961). The latter bears the characteristically untranslatable subtitle, *Zur Ontologie des Noch-Nicht-Seins*.

siderable to outsiders than to Germans involved in the intellectual and political upheavals of the past three decades. Heidegger's notorious rectoral address in 1933 welcoming the onset of the Third Reich had its counterpart in some of Bloch's less fortunate utterances during the Stalin era. It would be wrong to conclude that German philosophers are inherently prone to such aberrations: most of them got through those turbulent decades without saying anything at all. Those who rushed in where lesser men feared to tread were animated by a genuinely romantic belief in the duty of philosophers to give voice to those inchoate stirrings in the souls of their contemporaries which had found a temporary echo in their own minds. It was Heidegger's misfortune that his pronouncements in 1933—clearly intended as a continuation and a counterpart of Fichte's patriotic speeches against Napoleon in 1813—served a cause to which in the end no sane person could subscribe. Bloch's gradual disillusionment with Stalinism has run a similar course, and its roots are likewise to be found in a kind of naïveté about history's way of disclosing its inner purpose. The fact that both men have consistently found it possible, in their published utterances, to dispense with the kind of commonsensible reasoning about public affairs that is elsewhere thought compatible with profundity may be an index to their failure as political prophets.[2]

Put thus baldly, the record appears more damaging to foreigners than to Germans aware of the complexity of their history. The basic fact about Germany since the eighteenth century has been the failure of the Enlightenment to strike root, and the subsequent Romantic revolt against what little rationalist thinking had penetrated into the country from the West. Germans critical of their country's past are conscious of this but find it difficult to explain the matter to foreigners, the more so since self-criticism may give rise to grotesque misunderstandings abroad. If even Kant—not to mention Hegel—can be seen by outsiders as a

2. For Heidegger's checkered career under Hitler, and in particular for his attempt to adapt Nietzsche to contemporary use, see Karl Löwith, *Heidegger: Denker in dürftiger Zeit* (Göttingen, 1960). A rather journalistic essay by the late Paul Hühnerfeld (*In Sachen Heidegger*, Hamburg, 1959) has the merit of being candid about Heidegger's role in promoting the mental climate which made the capitulation of the German academic world in 1933 such a wholesale and wholehearted affair.

purveyor of Teutonic mysticism (there have in recent years been some notorious examples of such an approach), it becomes tempting to treat the whole matter *en famille*. Paradoxically, Marx now benefits from this new mood of domestic self-examination. Since it is felt that foreigners are incapable of understanding him, educated Germans increasingly tend to include him in the national pantheon. This has its dangers, but it has also been beneficial in promoting a good deal of scholarly writing about the Hegelian roots of Marxism. Bloch's own works have their place here, even though his rhapsodical manner is not conducive to clear thinking about the peculiar fate of Marxism in its own homeland. *His* Marx, needless to say, is the author of those pre-1848 writings which have lately swept three continents and even provoked comparisons with Zen Buddhism: the contemporary of Schelling whose name recurs throughout the 1600 pages of Bloch's *opus magnum*. If one bears in mind that Schelling's divinization of Nature accords with Goethe, and that Nietzsche (like Feuerbach before him) drew on the same source, one obtains an inkling of what all this means to Germans in whom the Romantic tradition is still alive. I express a purely personal view when I say that Bloch seems to have succeeded—quite contrary to his intention—in retransmuting this tradition into speculative mysticism. It is in this curious guise, as a latter-day reincarnation of the seventeenth-century mystic Jakob Böhme, that this learned exegete of Hegel and Marx has made a niche for himself in the soberly bourgeois *Bundesrepublik*.

The case of Heidegger is not so dissimilar as it may appear to his followers, accustomed as they are to take him at his own valuation. For Heidegger too has a Master, and moreover one whose influence was closely related to the German catastrophe. In recent years it has grown increasingly evident that Nietzsche has come to occupy in Heidegger's mind the place reserved for Hegel and Marx in the thinking of Bloch. The external sign of this is the massive study already mentioned. Though published only in 1961, most of it was composed between 1936 and 1941, that is to say during a period when Nietzsche—in the words of Karl Jaspers—had been proclaimed the official philosopher of the

Third Reich.[3] No one familiar with Heidegger's public utterances in those years will think it strange that Nietzsche should have provided the theme of his wartime lectures in Freiburg. Their publication in 1961 was described by the author as an attempt to clarify "the mental road I have traversed from 1930 to the *Letter on Humanism* (1947)." For the benefit of the noninitiated this cryptic statement requires an explanatory note.

In 1929 Heidegger had published a study of Kant which, for all its eccentric treatment of Kant's categories, was still in the tradition of academic philosophy in that it made an attempt to elucidate the meaning of various logical and epistemological concepts. This, however, proved a turning point. From about 1930 Heidegger seems to have felt that the whole enterprise was a waste of time. In his lectures on Nietzsche, traditional philosophy, and in particular the analysis of experience—i.e., the Kantian problem—is treated with a disdain not inferior to that which Nietzsche himself displayed when obliged to comment on the scholastic labors of his mental inferiors, who were actually foolish enough to suppose that there was something to be gained by following in the footsteps of pedants like Descartes and Kant. Heidegger has inherited Nietzsche's conviction that the history of philosophy is at an end, and that we are at the beginning of a new aeon: which is something rather different from Jaspers' cautious acceptance of Nietzsche's vitalism as a necessary complement to the Kantian analysis of logical concepts.

The difference is one between rationalism and irrationalism, for the latter implies a commitment that goes far beyond the recognition of a supersensible dimension closed to ordinary discursive thinking. It is also the difference between the acceptance of poetry as a legitimate function of the human mind, and the attempt to build a world view upon the kind of vaticination

3. Preface to the second (1946) edition of Jaspers' own *Nietzsche,* the first edition of which appeared in 1936 (and was subsequently banned). A discussion of Jaspers' role as the principal representative of the "internal emigration" of philosophy during the Hitler period cannot be undertaken here. His postwar commitment to a rather traditional and conservative liberalism is perhaps most clearly defined in lectures published in 1950 under the title *Vernunft und Widervernunft in unserer Zeit:* in the main a critique of Marxism and psychoanalysis along lines already familiar from his prewar writings.

Nietzsche undertook in his *Zarathustra*, and which Heidegger, in his learned commentary on his predecessor, treats with the same deadly seriousness that he has elsewhere bestowed upon the visions of Hegel's and Schelling's unfortunate poet friend Hölderlin. One can scarcely ignore the—surely not fortuitous—circumstance that Jaspers (like Thomas Mann, whose attitude to Nietzsche closely resembled his own) was appalled by the Third Reich, whereas Heidegger welcomed it as the fulfillment of Germany's national destiny (which indeed in an unintended sense it proved to be). The famous rectoral address with which Heidegger in 1933 assumed the "leadership" of Freiburg University would not be the important document it is, were it not so patent an application of the "existential" thinking worked out in *Sein und Zeit*. The terms of this eminently political discourse—existence and resolution, acceptance of one's fate, willingness to serve one's people, "total revolution of Germany's existence" (*eine völlige Umwälzung des deutschen Daseins*)—were derived from the categories of Heidegger's previous "existential analysis." They did not just "happen to fit" the current political jargon: they *were* this jargon!

It may seem purposeless to harp on this painful theme, but the point needs to be made for the sake of clearing up the confusion which still surrounds the mention of Nietzsche outside Germany. It *is* possible to take a critical and nonobscurantist view of Nietzsche, as has been shown by Jaspers (and by Nietzsche's most recent editor, Karl Schlechta, thanks to whom there now exists an edition of the *Works* purged of the deliberate falsifications introduced by Nietzsche's sister). It is likewise possible to follow in Nietzsche's footsteps, so far as this can be done by someone who is not himself a seer. This is what Heidegger has been doing, and while it would be foolish to treat this theme as an occasion for moral censure, it is just as well to be clear about the fact that the most influential German philosopher of our time —Heidegger is unique in the fascination he exercises upon the wider public, as witness even minor details such as his ability to fill the largest lecture hall—is wholly committed to the tradition of radical irrationalism.

However, the joke here is on Heidegger. Readers of *Sein und Zeit* in 1927 had their attention drawn to a hitherto neglected author, Count Paul Yorck von Wartenburg, whose correspondence with Wilhelm Dilthey was posthumously published in 1923. In paying tribute to Yorck (*et pour cause,* for this learned amateur turned out to be a far more original thinker than his celebrated friend), Heidegger obliquely put Dilthey in his place; and since the latter had dominated the study of *Geistesgeschichte* for many years, this was a way of depreciating the academic world in general. In 1927 this amounted to a minor sensation within the larger excitement stirred by Heidegger's assault on traditional post-Kantian philosophy.

By now the wheel has come full circle: Heidegger has long been the great panjandrum of German academic philosophy, but now it is he whose throne is insecure. In 1956 Yorck's literary remains appeared in print [4] and it became possible to gain a clearer picture of this profound though unsystematic writer who in his own fashion had thought his way through to a new understanding of the Greeks. The least one can say is that the comparison does not flatter Heidegger. The fragment published from a manuscript completed before 1897 displays an intellectual power which Heidegger has not approached since *Sein und Zeit* and which, to judge from his *Nietzsche,* has been absent from his thinking since the mid-1930s. In the end it may turn out that what he has lacked all these years is simply a new mental stimulus comparable to the one he received when in 1923 he chanced upon the Dilthey-Yorck correspondence. On the evidence of the ponderous and extremely repetitive volumes he has devoted to Nietzsche, no fresh source of inspiration has taken the place of the earlier one: perhaps not surprising when one considers that by the 1920s Spengler had already served up a form of Nietzscheanism for the middlebrow public. Heidegger's disdain for Spengler as a kind of poor man's Nietzsche is unmistakable; that he has himself for years been busy pumping up water from the same well would perhaps be denied only by the most fervent of his admirers.

The point is relevant for an understanding of Heidegger's place in modern German philosophy: a subject to which it is necessary to recur, for all the distaste which his followers predictably evince when their attention is drawn to his obsessive

4. *Bewusstseinsstellung und Geschichte,* Iring Fetscher, ed. (Tübingen, 1956).

brooding over the unique significance of the historical moment. Heidegger's celebrated political misadventure in 1933 would be a mere curiosity had it not been related to his cast of thought. In fact it sprang from his concern with the contemporary European situation, which he interpreted in a quasi-Spenglerian manner. At the same time he activated a principle of historical interpretation already made manifest in Hegel's thinking and increasingly influential throughout the nineteenth century among German writers brought up in the Hegelian tradition.

> The immediate starting point of Heidegger's anticipatory and retrospective thinking is . . . the experience of the present moment. It is the decadent character of our epoch which orients his essentially historical thinking toward the future and at the same time motivates it as a process of regression and retreat from the pinnacle of European metaphysics [attained] in Hegel.
>
> In principle, however, Hegel's constructive progressive ascent and Heidegger's destructive regressive descent are not dissimilar. Both have their being within the same modern aberration of an intellectual and ontological historicism, whereby the absolute of the Spirit, or of Being, is made historical.
>
> The contemporary of Napoleon conceived his completion of European philosophy as the fulfillment of a primary undeveloped origin; the contemporary of Hitler conceives the identical history of the European spirit as the gradual epiphany of nihilism.[5]

The unflattering implication that Heidegger stands in approximately the same relation to Hegel in which Hitler stood to Napoleon is naturally resented by Heidegger's followers, the more so since it suggests disquieting thoughts about Germany's past and present role in Europe.

Reflective Germans are now very ready to concede that nationalism has had its day, and that the defeat of 1945 sounded the death knell of ambitions which antedated the Third Reich. Beyond this point the mental picture becomes a little blurred. It is temptingly easy to dwell on France's rather similar discomfiture in 1815. The point stressed by Löwith is that Heidegger is a figure of the European decadence, whereas Hegel represented the summit of Europe's intellectual achievement. The turning point—for Löwith and those who share his fundamentally con-

5. Löwith, op. cit.

servative interpretation—is marked by the 1840s, when Marx and
Kierkegaard, proceeding from different standpoints, reacted almost simultaneously against Hegel, and against what Löwith
rather quaintly describes as the "bourgeois-Christian world," i.e.,
the culture of the European middle class which in the following
generation found its last expression in the work of Jakob Burckhardt. Readers of Löwith's *Von Hegel zu Nietzsche* (1941) and
of the writings he has published since returning from New York
to Heidelberg in 1952 may on occasion be tempted to wonder
whether this learned critic of "historicism" has not been infected
by the spiritual malady he diagnoses in others. However that may
be, his trenchant critique of Heidegger places him on the "left"
within the current German spectrum, even though his own politics are hardly more radical than those of an old-fashioned liberal
like Jaspers. What is implied for educated Germans who are *not*
professional philosophers by the thought that the 1945 catastrophe terminated both Germany's national history and the culture
associated with the names of Goethe and Hegel, may be gauged
from that eminently philosophical novel Thomas Mann's *Doctor
Faustus*. Mann, like Jaspers, grew up in a culture that hailed
Nietzsche as a liberator from bourgeois stuffiness. Unlike Jaspers,
he came round in the end to a firm, though reluctant, awareness
that the roots of the German disaster are traceable to attitudes
which a more lighthearted age had judged in merely aesthetic
terms. That the "Faustian age" has come to a terrible end (at any
rate for the Germans) is a conviction shared by all these writers.

For genuine radicalism—which in West Germany today means
"revisionist" Marxism—one has only to make the brief train journey from Heidelberg to Frankfurt: now once more the locale of
the famous Institut für Sozialforschung, which during the Hitler
period emigrated first to Paris and later to New York. Some of its
better-known founders, notably Karl Wittfogel, have settled in the
United States, but the Institut reorganized itself in the 1950s under the direction of Max Horkheimer, and, what is perhaps more
important, it has over the past decade provided a focus for the
activities of its most celebrated and controversial figure, Theodor
W. Adorno: philosopher, sociologist, musical historian, literary
critic, and in all these various capacities the principal gadfly of

the West German Establishment, though himself a pillar of academical learning.[6]

Adorno—like Herbert Marcuse, who has remained in the United States—represents an aspect of the Weimar period's intellectual life which has also found a confused echo in the writings of Bloch: the synthesis of a Hegelianized Marxism with the kind of *Kulturkritik* that was formerly carried on under the liberal-individualist banner. Concern over the fate of the individual in an increasingly organized and centralized society is a theme which recurs in Adorno's writings, though, living as he does in a Western environment, his targets tend to be the manipulators of our new "affluent" society rather than the political functionaries who perform a similar role in the East. This attitude lends a defensive tone to his work, perhaps inevitable in a thinker who regards the transition from the old liberal to the new planned and "managerial" order as potentially a change for the worse, at any rate so far as culture is concerned. What Marcuse (another pessimistic Marxist) calls the "one-dimensional" character of modern existence—that is, the absence of philosophical thinking that transcends the status quo—is also Adorno's chief worry. "Nothing remains of ideology," he says plaintively, "but the recognition of that which is—a model of a behavior which submits to the overwhelming power of the established state of affairs."[7]

There are moments when this uncompromising radical sounds almost like a traditionalist. In fact he is continuing a line of thought which during the Weimar period had already been initiated by the literary critic Walter Benjamin, another "unofficial"

6. A list of Adorno's publications would be lengthy, though unlike Lukács, with whom he has feuded for years, he does not suffer from lack of concision. His *Aspekte der Hegelschen Philosophie* (1957) cannot be recommended to beginners, and the same must be said of his *Einleitung in die Musiksoziologie*, a series of lectures on the theory and practice of contemporary music.

Noten zur Literatur, two volumes of critical essays published in 1958–61, make fewer demands on the reader but are virtually untranslatable, and the same applies to the 1955 essay collection *Prismen: Kulturkritik und Gesellschaft*, which rings the changes on a number of themes familiar to Western readers, but does so in a radicalized Hegelian or neo-Marxist terminology. For Adorno's (and Horkheimer's) postwar attempt to refashion Marxism into an instrument of philosophical criticism of society, see their joint *Dialektik der Aufklärung: Philosophische Fragmente* (Amsterdam, 1947).

7. See K. Lenk, ed., *Ideologie* (Neuwied, 1961), pp. 266 ff.

Marxist writer. Instead of celebrating the *juste milieu* of the
Weimar Republic, these writers diagnosed it as an interval between two catastrophes induced by the secular decay of liberalism. At the same time—and this sets them off both from the
conservatives and from Leninists like Lukács—their attitude toward the "modern movement" was one of critical support, in
so far as it reflected an attempt to get beyond the petrified structures of late-nineteenth-century bourgeois civilization. The
resulting complexities are echoed in an occasionally somewhat
mannered and esoteric language which plainly is not that of East
European cultural populism. In the idiom favored by Soviet critics (even of the less-uncivilized sort) Adorno—though plainly a
Marxist—must be held guilty of "aristocratic contempt for the
people."

It would be tempting to confront Adorno at length with George
Lukács. Fortunately it is possible to resist the temptation, without
for that reason abandoning the subject, for Adorno has undertaken his own confrontation, in a brief but devastating essay on
Lukács (in the second volume of his *Noten zur Literatur*). If the
two men—so alike in some ways, so sharply divided in others, and
not only by geography—are to be compared, perhaps the matter
is best summed up by saying that Adorno's work represents the
kind of sophisticated critique of contemporary society which
Lukács *might* have performed, had he not abandoned analysis for
apologetics. No doubt Lukács sees his activities in a different
light. The fact remains that to a former associate like Adorno he
appears to have committed intellectual suicide. Sentimentalists
who may doubt the literal accuracy of this remark are referred
to Adorno's own statements on the subject, which lose nothing of
their polemical edge for being highly polished and couched in
an idiom remote from Communist vituperation. (They may also
profit from reading what a genuine critic of art like Adorno has
to say about Lukács's dreary platitudes on the subject of "formalism.")

These polemical exchanges on the intellectual Left are necessarily conducted over the heads of the East German cultural functionaries. Since the death of Brecht and the enforced emigration
of Ernst Bloch and Hans Mayer, East Germany has become a

spiritual dust bowl, in which only the most naïve of foreign visitors still manage to find sustenance.

It is a minor paradox among many others that Marxism has remained alive and even experienced something like a spiritual rejuvenation in Western Germany while dying out in the eastern half of the country. That this is not a necessary consequence of living under a Communist dictatorship is evident from the case of Poland. Why the East German regime has failed so completely in holding the loyalty of that part of the left-wing intelligentsia which after 1945 was willing to give it a chance is a question that cannot be gone into here, though it may be suggested that the subsequent debacle was already foreshadowed during the Weimar years, when the Communist Party tried without success to acclimatize Leninism on German soil. The experiment proved disastrous politically and—Lukács's obstinate assertions to the contrary—it has turned out to be no less of a catastrophe in the intellectual domain.

The Concept of Social Class

❊ ❊ ❊

"Britain is notoriously a country in which class counts for much," observed Donald MacRae in his essay collection *Ideology and Society* in 1961. "Some people, very far from being Marxists, would make British class structure identical with British social structure." This identification, he thought, was pardonable, even though mistaken. "The social perception of the British people is very largely a perception of status and of class expressed not merely in income, type of occupation and capital, not merely in ways of consumption, but in the least nuances of inter-personal behaviour, manner, speech, bearing and dress." And because of this obsession with rank and status it was plausible "to mistake class structure for the whole of social structure."

This judgment may stand as an instance of what is undoubtedly the accepted view of the matter, among the learned and the unlearned alike. The learned, of course, have the advantage of being able to state their opinion with a precision denied to their fellow citizens, but the viewpoint they express is deeply ingrained in the national culture. Academic sociologists, no less than the man in the street, are in the habit of equating class with social status, or even with the idiosyncratic perception of rank and manners in literature and daily life. On this assumption, the phenomenon of social mobility—talented individuals moving from an inferior to a superior position—is an important subject of research, while "social distance" (also known as snobbery) becomes a favorite topic of popular literature. There is no theoretical problem to be solved; we all know what "class" signifies, and only a few Marxists are benighted enough to take a different view of the matter.

The Times Literary Supplement, October 8, 1971.

The Marxists, for their part, are handicapped by the awkward fact that Marx never elaborated a systematic theory of social class. While he ignored stratification based on income, education, or occupation, he nowhere defined "class" in an entirely unambiguous manner. Z. A. Jordan, in a recent introduction to some Marxian texts,[1] concludes that a social class in Marx's sense of the term is defined by at least three different characteristics: first, its place in the system of social production and/or its relation to the means of production; second, competition for political power to protect economic interests; and third, class consciousness, that is, a widespread common awareness which members of the class have of their relative standing in society. On the penultimate page of the third volume of *Capital*, the reader is told that "wage-labourers, capitalists and land-owners constitute three big classes of modern society based upon the capitalist mode of production." But this assessment—which would not have surprised Smith or Ricardo—is not followed up by an investigation into what Marx himself describes as "the infinite fragmentation of interest and rank into which the division of social labour splits labourers as well as capitalists, and landlords." The manuscript breaks off precisely at this point, and it has thus been possible for Marxists to hold widely different views on the topic. In particular, it has become a matter for serious debate whether the abolition of private property in the means of production entails the disappearance of social stratification.

So far as the Marx of *Capital* is concerned, one may say that he did not diverge in essentials from his bourgeois predecessors, notably Ricardo, in his analysis of class in modern society. He did not aim at a universal theory of social stratification, but rather at a description related to the functioning of capitalism. Where he differed from the orthodoxy of his age was in the stress he laid upon the historical significance of the whole phenomenon. For the liberals, civilization was synonymous with bourgeois society, just as industrial production was synonymous with capitalism and inconceivable under any other social arrangement. For Marx, bourgeois society was a unique historical constellation dating back to the fourteenth century, in its origins limited to

1. *Karl Marx: Economy, Class, and Social Revolution*, Z. A. Jordan, ed. (London, 1971).

Western Europe, destined to create a world market, and thereafter due to make way for a new and higher stage of societal evolution. This transformation is brought about by class antagonisms,.
but "class" itself is a feature peculiar to modern society. The
point is already made in an early work, *The German Ideology* of
1845–46:

> In the course of historical evolution, and precisely through the in-
> evitable fact that within the division of labour social relationships.
> take on an independent existence, there appears a division within
> the life of each individual, insofar as it is personal and insofar as it
> is determined by some branch of labour and the conditions per-
> taining to it. . . . In the estate (and even more in the tribe) this
> is as yet concealed: for instance, a nobleman always remains a
> nobleman, a commoner always a commoner, apart from his other
> relationships, a quality inseparable from his individuality. The di-
> vision between the personal and the class individual, the accidental
> nature of the conditions of life for the individual, appears only
> with the emergence of the class, which is itself a product of the
> bourgeoisie. This accidental character is only engendered and de-
> veloped by competition and the struggle of individuals among
> themselves. Thus, in imagination, individuals seem freer under the
> dominance of the bourgeoisie than before, because their conditions.
> of life seem accidental; in reality, of course, they are less free, be-
> cause they are more subjected to the violence of things.

Class conflict is an aspect of bourgeois society and destined to
disappear with it. Does this mean that perfect social harmony
will reign thereafter? Not necessarily, but social *evolution* will
no longer be promoted by political *revolution*. The point is made,
with a good deal of emphasis, in Marx's polemic against Proudhon (1847) and driven home in the *Communist Manifesto* of
1848. Whereas in earlier historical epochs "we find almost everywhere a complicated arrangement of society into various orders,.
a manifold gradation of social rank," modern bourgeois society
"has simplified the class antagonisms." Communist society by
definition is going to be classless, albeit in its earlier stage it is
"still stamped with the birth marks of the old society from whose
womb it emerges." This qualification dates from 1875 and may be
regarded as Marx's final word on the subject. Complete freedom
and equality will prevail only "in a higher phase of communist

society, after the enslaving subordination of the individual to the division of labour, and therewith also the antithesis between mental and physical labour, has vanished" (*Critique of the Gotha Programme*).

By this standard, the Soviet Union and its East European satellites are merely "socialist," not "communist." This distinction indeed forms part of the official ideology and is constantly invoked to explain departures from the egalitarian norm. But "revisionist" Marxists have notoriously come to believe that the functional separation of physical from mental toil has given rise to a new social division: between the ruling bureaucracy and the workers it controls. This leads to the larger question whether class analysis is still applicable in a situation where the state has become the instrument of a revolution which reshapes the economy. The late Stanislaw Ossowski, who after 1945 had occasion to watch this process in his native Poland, in 1957 had this to say on the topic:

> In situations where changes of social structure are to a greater or lesser degree governed by the decision of the political authorities, we are a long way from social classes as interpreted by Marx, Ward, Veblen or Weber, from classes conceived of as groups determined by their relations to the means of production or, as others would say, by their relations to the market. We are a long way from classes conceived of as groups arising out of the spontaneous activities of individuals. . . . In situations where the political authorities can overtly and effectively change the class structure; where the privileges that are most essential for social status, including that of a higher share in the national income, are conferred by a decision of the political authorities; where a large part or even the majority of the population is included in a stratification of the type to be found in a bureaucratic hierarchy—the nineteenth-century concept of class becomes more or less an anachronism, and class conflicts give way to other forms of social antagonism.[2]

Thus the Marxian analysis is seen to be historically conditioned by the bourgeois environment, or as Ossowski puts it, "the more closely the social system approximates to the ideal type of a free and competitive capitalist society, the more are classes de-

2. *Class Structure in the Social Consciousness* (London and New York, 1963).

termined by their relation to the means of production, and the more are human relationships determined by ownership of the means of production." State control does away with the capitalist market economy and with the class struggle which arises out of its functioning. It is perhaps unnecessary to remark that this circumstance does not eliminate social conflict between the governing and the governed. The official ideology describes such conflicts as "nonantagonistic"—an awkward circumlocution designed to minimize the significance of events such as the Hungarian uprising of 1956 or the rather less catastrophic upheaval in Poland in December 1970.

It should by now be clear that "class," "status," "rank," and "position" are not interchangeable labels to be pinned on the topic of sociological investigation. It should also be clear that what is sometimes described as the relative "classlessness" of American as distinct from British society is nothing more than a situation in which social status is not to the same degree determined by descent (setting aside the racial dilemma caused by the presence of a large and increasingly vocal black minority). American "classlessness" is part of the middle-class ideology embodied in the characteristic institutions of American society. These institutions were created and maintained for the purpose of making liberal democracy operative in a society based on the market economy and the class structure which is the inevitable accompaniment of such an economy. Even so, the official image of a classless democracy grew up against the background of a caste relationship between white and black, where caste membership and caste-bound social status were and are determined by descent, and where social separation is founded on caste endogamy.

If the racial barrier can be eliminated, American society will greatly benefit; but it will be no nearer the ideological image of "classlessness" which American writers have concocted out of their perception that the United States did not possess "estates" and other relics of European feudalism. The whole topic has been constantly bedeviled by ideological constructs, and this on both sides of the East-West divide. American "classlessness" is as spurious a fabrication as the "nonantagonistic classes" of Stalinism and its East European offshoots. Classes remain in being, even if caste barriers are torn down, as long as property in the means of production is monopolized by a small minority. On the other hand, the substitution of state ownership for private capitalism does not by itself constitute socialism: it rather helps to entrench a new privileged stratum which takes shelter behind the ruling party, itself consubstantial with the state bureaucracy. A society run by state functionaries is classless by definition. This does not make it democratic, and it does not eliminate social conflict.

There remains the question whether light is shed on our topic by the introduction of terms such as "political class" or "governing elite." The elite concept was worked out by Pareto and Mosca as part of their critique of liberal democracy. According to Mosca, all historically known societies are divided into two separate layers: a class that rules and a class that is ruled. Minority rule is made possible by the fact that the governing class is organized, monopolizes political power, and controls the unorganized majority. This looks at first sight like a realistic forecast of what occurred in Italy when liberal democracy broke down in the 1920s, but on Mosca's and Pareto's principles the elite concept applies uniformly to all conceivable forms of government, democracy included. It is therefore useless as a tool of analysis designed to explain the rise of fascism or the persistence of its Stalinist counterpart. If democracy is a sham, we may as well give up the attempt to specify criteria for discriminating between democratic and totalitarian systems.

The last word on this topic belongs to Antonio Gramsci, who in his prison diary noted that "Mosca's political class is nothing but the intellectual section of the ruling group. Mosca's term approximates Pareto's *élite* concept—another attempt to interpret the historical phenomenon of the intelligentsia and its function in political and social life." For all that, the concept of the political elite is not without value. When freed from Pareto's and Mosca's antidemocratic bias and their obsession with the malfunctioning of Italy's parliamentary system, it helps one to grasp the difference between a class in the Marxian sense and its intellectual representatives, who may also be holders of power. In this sense, democracy is compatible with the notion that any political system requires the existence of an educated minority which is able to govern. The whole thesis may not amount to very much, but it states a fact which democrats have been inclined to overlook.

To return to our starting point: Britain is indeed "a country in which class counts for much," the chief reason being that even the most trivial phenomena of social life are commonly discussed in a language unsuited to the topic. If social gradations are invariably ascribed to class differences, the real significance of the term is lost and we are cast into a linguistic labyrinth where rank and status are systematically confused with the key problem of political power and its economic foundation. It is arguable that class is no longer the principal element of social change, the state having taken over large tracts of public life formerly abandoned to the mechanism of class conflict. Whether or not one accepts this, it must be clear that neither liberal nor Marxian literature supplies a general theory of social stratification which attempts to lay down a universally valid scheme of rank or gradation. Class, caste, and status relate to different aspects of the social whole, and so far as class is concerned it seems best to retain its connection with the economic mechanism underlying the market economy of mature capitalism. This leaves one free to consider the infinite gradations of social life without troubling to relate them all to the mainspring of class conflict: the fact that wage earners are "free" only to choose between starvation and the monotony of the factory and the office. It is of course this circumstance which accounts for the general malaise of industrial society—capitalist and (nominally) socialist alike. If these distinctions are kept in mind, the debate between defenders and opponents of the market economy can proceed without terminological confusion.

FROM LENIN TO
MAO TSE-TUNG

What Is Left of Communism?

✿ ✿ ✿

I

HALF A CENTURY after Lenin's seizure of power started the global chain reaction associated with his name, there no longer is a single center to direct what is still conventionally described as the world communist movement. The shock waves released by the original explosion continue to travel, but they follow a course profoundly divergent from that formerly traced out by the Bolshevik Party and the Third International. Communism as a global phenomenon and the U.S.S.R. as the focus of a planned industrial transformation do not inhabit the same universe. Rhetorical assertions to the contrary notwithstanding, their respective lines of development increasingly point away from each other.

At the ideological level, this divergence manifests itself in the steady erosion of Moscow's hold over the loyalty of its nominal followers. Dark planets circling the dying sun of the October Revolution, the communist parties of Europe, Asia, and Latin America revolve in their separate orbits—now drawn together by geography or the pressures of the East-West conflict, now propelled in different directions by the resurgence of nationalism or the impact of the Sino-Soviet split. Deeply riven by the conflicting claims of Moscow and Peking, the communist movement has begun to display unmistakable symptoms of disintegration. Numerical growth is purchased at the cost of doctrinal enfeeblement. "Polycentrism," from being a heresy, shows signs of becoming the norm. Even the first principle of Leninism, the political monopoly of the single-party regime, has ceased to be sacrosanct.

Foreign Affairs, October 1967.

The fiftieth anniversary of the October coup, by an unwelcome coincidence, falls at a time when the celebrants are confronted with the Chinese schism in a new and menacing form—an open confrontation of Asia and Russia. In the struggle to hold the loyalties of their respective followers, Moscow and Peking are increasingly driven back upon barely camouflaged nationalism. The Maoist heresy, from being an obscure quarrel over the interpretation of the *depositum fidei*, has turned into a rebellion sustained by China's ancient claims to hegemony in Central Asia. Longstanding national and cultural animosities, for years submerged by common acceptance of the Leninist creed, are rising to the surface. Even the possibility of armed conflict between the two major centers of what used to be called the Sino-Soviet camp can no longer be wholly excluded.

Concurrently with this disintegration of the Stalinist inheritance—an inheritance made possible by the Eurasian character of the regime established by Lenin's successor—there goes a revival of those aspects of the Marxist-Leninist synthesis which stemmed from European radicalism and from the prerevolutionary Europeanization of Russia itself. As China draws further away from the original sources of the common faith, the guardians of Soviet orthodoxy are obliged in self-defense to lay stress upon those elements of the Leninist heritage that connect it with the unbroken tradition of Marxian socialism. Caught between a Western environment which imperceptibly transforms communists into social-democrats, and an Eastern heresy which eliminates the last surviving remnants of classical Marxism, the Soviet regime has come to wear a defensive look. No longer a lodestar for revolutionaries in Africa or Asia, and not yet acceptable to the democratic labor movements of the West, it is in danger of appearing irrelevant to both.

The October Revolution, in Lenin's interpretation, was to have been the opening phase of a gigantic effort to link the proletarian revolution in the West with the national and anticolonial upheaval in the East. Despite the widely advertised disputes among Lenin's successors, this perspective was shared by Trotskyists, Stalinists, and Bukharinists alike. It underlay both their doctrinal quarrels over the correct line to be pursued abroad, and the actual conduct of Soviet foreign policy in the age of the

Third International and beyond. Its virtual abandonment by Stalin's heirs signifies more than the normal loss of fervor to be expected from the rulers of an increasingly conservative and stratified society; it must be regarded as evidence that the perils inherent in the original Leninist program have finally become apparent to the rulers of the postrevolutionary U.S.S.R. The prime danger is a commitment to world-revolutionary utopianism which rules out any hope of "peaceful coexistence" with the United States, and such a commitment the Soviet leadership at present seems determined to avoid.

II

What then is left of communism? The question is not intended as a pun, although recent events in China have perhaps made a degree of levity permissible. The "cultural revolution," for all its brutalities and the destruction wreaked upon the country's heritage, is too grotesque wholly to escape the penalty of ridicule. Was there ever anything to match this centrally controlled super-purge whose organizers contrived to dupe themselves with the borrowed language of popular insurrection? Anything to excel the spectacle of a mass movement supposedly launched to overcome the resistance of a handful of "plotters in high places"? Could anything have been more anachronistic than the solemn evocation of the Paris Commune—that tragic uprising of a doomed city—by military leaders acting in conjunction with a fanaticized youth movement? And was there not an element of plain buffoonery in the spectacle of millions dutifully echoing whatever slogans were broadcast over the local radio station by assorted "rightists," "leftists," "ultraleftists," "plotters," "militarists," or all of them combined? At the very least, the spectacle served to demonstrate that conditioned reflexes still count for more in China than the "thought of Mao Tse-tung."

For that matter, what was one to make of the spectacle of Mao giving the army its head, thereby contravening the first principle of a political doctrine which asserts the pre-eminence of the party? To say that the dictator was driven to this departure from orthodoxy by the miscarriage of his original plans is to concede that the "cultural revolution" had escaped its originator. From the

three-cornered struggle between the bureaucracy, the juvenile
Red Guards, and the army, the last named was bound to emerge
as the real (if for the moment decently silent) victor. If Mao was
unable to foresee this, what was the worth of his Marxist-Leninist
indoctrination? Had it not occurred to him that the synthesizing
element of this particular triad must either be the party or the
army, and that if the party were wrecked, the final outcome must
bear a military stamp? Of what use years of brooding in the wilderness over the sacred texts if this simple conclusion escaped
him? Among all the Chinese millions dutifully reciting the Maoist
catechism, it would seem that the man least capable of deciphering its meaning was Mao Tse-tung himself.

It may be argued that an intensive militarization of public life
is not in principle incompatible with the maintenance of party
control, especially if the party is determined to pursue a policy
of economic austerity and social egalitarianism. Such a choice
could even be defended on rational grounds quite extraneous to
Mao's own highly idiosyncratic version of "war communism." It
can be held that in a large, poor, and overpopulated country with
China's special problems, a combination of military discipline
and ideological rigor is an effective means (perhaps the only
effective means) of wringing an economic surplus from an unwilling population. If this be granted for argument's sake, one still
has to account for the transformation of a doctrine which originally expressed the spontaneous protest of the proletariat of
early capitalism. The utopian literature of modern communism,
as it arose after the French Revolution, was egalitarian enough,
but the aims it defined had little in common with the revolutionary nationalism of the Maoist regime. Communism in those
days—broadly speaking the half-century ending with the 1848
upheaval and the *Manifesto*—defined the terms in which an
elite of French and British workingmen and their intellectual
leaders envisaged the distant future. That future was seen under
the aspect of a stateless and classless order which would inherit
the economic wealth created by the industrial revolution. It never
occurred to the early pioneers of this faith, or to the authors of
the *Manifesto*, that communism might become the "ideology"
(in the precise sense of "false consciousness") of a movement

seeking to substitute itself for what Marx called the "bourgeois revolution." Yet this is what has been happening in China since 1949, following the precedent set in the U.S.S.R. since 1917.

The paradox is not lessened by the fact that the Chinese have come to stress the purity of their own system as compared to the once-admired Soviet model, which is now rejected as insufficiently egalitarian and tainted by bourgeois corruption. Maoism has shown itself even more terroristic than Stalinism in trying to impose uniformity and to prevent the satisfaction of immediate material wants. This kind of terrorism, if successful (a big "if"), can only serve to channel the economic surplus into those sectors of activity to which the highest political authority has chosen to give priority. There is no secret about these priorities: they are military and technological. That is to say, they are at the furthest possible remove from the satisfaction of ordinary individual and social claims.

Once more it may be said that in a poor country on the threshold of modernization this is inevitable, and that other Asian societies (India, for choice) might count themselves fortunate if they possessed the social discipline required for the aim of guaranteeing all citizens a minimum of essentials. But the more this argument is pressed, the clearer it becomes that what is being asserted is the superior effectiveness of Chinese communism in promoting the aims historically associated with the capitalist mode of production and the social order built upon it: above all, the sacrifice of immediate satisfaction for the sake of building up the wealth-creating apparatus of industrial civilization. Such an achievement, however important, is quite extraneous to the original signification of the term "communism," not to mention the historic traditions of the labor movement. It is the goal of virtually every dictatorship in a backward country, be its ideology communist, fascist, or simply nationalist. The originality of Maoism lies in the methods employed to mobilize the masses in the name of communism for the achievement of aims proper to any national-revolutionary movement: the industrialization of China and the acquisition of military means (including nuclear ones) adequate to the pursuit of great-power politics.

It is irrelevant in this context that these aims are conceived as forming part of the uprising of the world's preindustrial hinterland, and it is useless to inquire how far such motives are intermingled with more traditional ones. The power of an ideology (in the Marxist sense of the term, not in the trivial meaning assigned to it by pragmatism) is measured by the degree to which it raises men above themselves, gives them a sense of purpose, drives them to sacrifice themselves for what they conceive to be the greater good. It is not the least unnerving aspect of the current situation that the moral austerity of Chinese communism has channeled the energies of a great people into a direction potentially dangerous to itself and its neighbors. The whole phenomenon, whatever the short-range determinants of the conflict between Moscow and Peking, is best understood as an upsurge of national sentiment within the limitations imposed by the acceptance of communism. The genuineness of this acceptance is just what renders the conflict so acute, since it is essential for the Chinese to adhere to the Leninist creed and simultaneously to impose their own interpretation upon it.

The problem has been solved, as usual in such cases, by a doctrinal schism. China now has its own version of the faith: much as in an earlier age the imposition of Islam upon Persia gave birth by way of the Shiite heresy to a local variant of the conquering religion. As in all such cases, the resulting pseudomorphosis—the underlying culture reasserting itself in the guise of the new universal faith—must be distinguished from the overt manifestations of the schism, which are largely accidental and secondary. Given the circumstances in which the Chinese Communists won power—namely by gaining the leadership of a national-revolutionary movement whose original inspiration had run dry—an attempt to "Sinify" the Marxist-Leninist inheritance was inevitable. The particular form it has taken is another matter. It is a waste of time to examine Peking's claims to doctrinal orthodoxy. The Chinese are too remote from the origins of European socialism to be taken seriously in the role of exegetes of the classical texts. What matters is that the schism has laid bare the contradictions inherent in Lenin's view of the Russian Revolution as the link between an awakening Asia and a potentially socialist Europe. In so far as Leninism signified such a vision, the Chinese are

Leninists no longer, for they no longer believe that the industrial proletariat of the West has a privileged part to play in what is still called the "world revolution."

III

Marxism-Leninism is in process of disintegration. The vision of a global movement encompassing both advanced and backward countries has been abandoned by Moscow and Peking alike: by Moscow because the growing conservatism of Soviet society is incompatible with such alarming notions; by Peking because there is no longer a revolutionary workers' movement in the West that could be regarded as a reliable ally of a resurgent China. Leninism and Stalinism alike implied a commitment to the goal of a union linking East and West, the Asian peasant and the European or American city-worker. From 1920 onward, when Lenin formulated this concept at the Second Congress of the Third International, the effective political meaning of "communism" hinged upon the belief that the October Revolution had been the first act in this great drama. Leninism, both in its narrower Stalinist and in its more romantic Trotskyist understanding, was the doctrine of a world revolution. Shorn of this perspective, it is no more than the theory of the *Russian* Revolution. Inasmuch as this latter interpretation is now gaining ground among communists in the U.S.S.R. and throughout Eastern Europe, the Chinese have some cause for asserting that the Russians and their allies in the communist movement are no longer serious about the conclusion Lenin set out in his last published piece of writing, when he looked forward to a great confrontation between "the counterrevolutionary imperialist West and the revolutionary and nationalist East": a confrontation in which he expected the U.S.S.R. to side with China and India against Europe and America.[1]

1. Lenin, "Better Fewer, But Better," *Pravda*, March 4, 1923, in *Collected Works*, XXXIII, 487 ff. "In the last analysis, the outcome of the struggle will be determined by the fact that Russia, India, China, etc., account for the overwhelming majority of the population of the globe. . . . In this sense, the complete victory of socialism is fully and absolutely assured" (ibid., p. 500). This Eurasian perspective was already inherently Stalinist,

The tacit abandonment of this line of thought by the Soviet regime does constitute a drastic revision of Leninism (though not of Marxism, since neither Marx nor his European followers had ever dreamed of such a thing). Unfortunately for the Chinese it is not really possible for the remnant of the "revolutionary and nationalist East" to assume the role once held by the U.S.S.R. Without the latter, plus its East European satellites, Maoism is no more than an Asian phenomenon, which is another way of saying that the Leninist strategy of 1920–23 has become inapplicable. If Moscow refuses the global role assigned to it in the original scheme, and contents itself with the part of mediator between West and East (or between the United States and China), there is an end to world-revolutionary strategy. It is useless to affirm that an adequate substitute can be reconstituted on Chinese soil. Anything may be asserted on paper, but in the eyes of Asian revolutionaries "Leninism" signified primarily the willingness of the Russian Communist Party to follow the line laid down by its founder when he explicitly defined world communism in terms of an alliance between the Russian worker and the Asian peasant. To do the Chinese justice, Moscow's departure from this line *does* represent the abandonment of at least one significant aspect of Lenin's heritage.

If the question be raised how Lenin ever came to associate the coming triumph of what he called "socialism" with such a perspective, the answer must be that he was following out the logic of his lifelong adherence to the Populist (or Bakuninist) notion of a "dictatorship of workers and peasants," which in his theoretical scheme was to administer the tasks of the revolution during a lengthy interim period after the fall of the monarchy. As late as 1923 one finds him discussing the immediate prospects of the Soviet regime in these terms: "We . . . lack enough civilization to enable us to pass straight on to socialism, although we do have the political requisites for it. . . . We must strive to build up a state in which the workers retain the leadership of the peasants,

---

in that it identified "the victory of socialism" with the military superiority of an Eastern bloc led by the U.S.S.R. As long as Moscow adhered to such notions, it was possible for the Chinese to tolerate Soviet pre-eminence (not to mention Stalin's personal whims). To that extent the Maoist claim to the succession is well-founded.

in which they retain the confidence of the peasants. . . . If we see to it that the working class retains its leadership over the peasantry, we shall be able . . . to develop electrification . . ." etc.[2]

The naïveté of this trust in the capacity of "the workers" to exercise political leadership requires no comment. What matters is the essential coherence of the Leninist viewpoint: the Russian "worker" was to "build socialism" at home and "retain the confidence of the peasant" while doing it. In practice, the "building of socialism" devolved upon the party, which in turn became the nucleus of a new privileged stratum. For all their blinkered ignorance, the Maoists are shrewd enough to see that the jettisoning of Lenin's global strategy ("East against West") has been brought about by what they have come to describe as the degeneracy of the Soviet regime—notably the formal dismantling of the "proletarian dictatorship." It is irrelevant that the latter was always a fiction, for to a communist what truly matters is that his party should *represent* the masses. What the Chinese cannot forgive is the growing identification of the Soviet regime with the aims of the privileged stratum that has grown out of the postrevolutionary society. It is quite wrong to describe this reaction as "Trotskyist," superficial resemblances notwithstanding. The Maoists are ultra-Stalinists, that is to say, believers in the efficacy of terrorism. What was valuable about Stalin's leadership in their eyes was precisely his readiness to subordinate the material interests of all classes to the aims laid down by political authority. Mao is as certain as Stalin ever was that communism can and must be built by force—even in a country possessing no industry to speak of—and that the new society must remain totally subordinate to the controlling elite until such time as all its citizens have become good communists and lost their appetite for private property. All other notions (including the Trotskyist utopia of a proletarian revolution in the West) are heretical and must be rooted out, for what matters is that the transformation

2. Ibid., p. 501: "In this and in this alone lies our hope. Only when we have done this shall we be able, speaking figuratively, to change horses, to change from the peasant, muzhik, horse of poverty . . . to the horse which the proletariat is seeking and must seek—the horse of largescale machine industry, of electrification, of the Volkhov Power Station, etc."

must be *willed*. Given the necessary willpower, the material problems will take care of themselves.

To say that Lenin opened this Pandora's box when he committed his party to the task of "building socialism" in Russia is not to suggest that he would have welcomed the present consequences. He was after all a Russian Social Democrat by upbringing and, for all his heresies, enough of a Marxist to believe that communism made no sense without a workers' movement. At the same time it is plain enough that between 1917 and 1923 he had traveled a good distance toward the conclusions now reached by his Chinese disciples. None the less, he still retained his faith in the revolutionary potential of Europe. The inherent instability of this Marxist-Leninist synthesis was masked for a while by the existence of the Third International, notably by its involvement in the mythical "German revolution"—an experiment whose outcome was the National Socialist dictatorship, passively supported for twelve years by the bulk of the German working class. Yet if this sobering experience has made Moscow's followers more cautious, it has not shaken their doctrinal commitments to a Leninism which shall at any rate continue to bear the marks of its East European origin. It is indeed not possible for orthodox communists to accept the complete dissociation of Leninism from Marxism—something the Chinese have now brought about by setting the army and a state-controlled youth movement against the urban working class.

"Marxism-Leninism" was always a shotgun marriage, for what was original in Lenin (the notion of a world revolution centering on Russia) was not to be found in Marx. Yet for all its equivocal attempts to combine Marx and Bakunin, the Bolshevism of 1917–23 signified an unwillingness to turn one's back altogether upon the Marxian inheritance. Leninism, it was asserted in those days, was the contemporary form of Marxism, and the October Revolution, by bringing socialism to backward Russia, had bridged the gulf between Europe and Asia. One may suppose that Stalin still believed this. His successors plainly do not, and neither do the Chinese, whatever their propaganda may assert to the contrary. For the Maoists, the tradition of the old revolutionary workers' movement has ceased to possess any relevance. It is no longer a matter of asserting that socialism and communism *can* be built outside Europe; they *must* be built outside Europe, and there must be no illusions about the ability or the willingness of the European or American proletariat to take the lead in the matter, or even to render significant aid to China's struggle. What was once the faith of the European socialist movement has, after a century of eastward migration, become the ideology of an elite in charge of a national revolution in a retarded country.

This new Islam has its Koran, albeit due reverence is paid to the Old Testament, and why not? Pious Muslims respect the memory of Abraham, but their allegiance goes to the Prophet. The Chinese communists are unlikely to relinquish the claim that Mao stands in the direct succession to Marx and Lenin. To do so would be to renounce the universalism which has become their pride and which, to do them justice, sets them off from the parochialism of an earlier generation of nationalists, for whom the indigenous tradition had to suffice. But in the absence of any tradition linking the Chinese Revolution with the Western labor movement, such manifestations of the will to believe must remain ideological. They translate not a shared experience—for what is there to connect the former nationalist agitator from Hunan with the heirs of the Chartists or the followers of Proudhon?—but the determination not to be excluded from what is perceived as a claim to universal import. This transformation of a Western faith into the fighting creed of a movement born and raised under very different stars is precisely what the term "ideology" signifies.

IV

If the disintegration of Marxism-Leninism has the effect of leaving the Kremlin and its adherents in an uncomfortable position midway between East and West, it may be said that Lenin's heirs are thus belatedly paying for their master's originality. One could assemble quite a number of quotations testifying to the fact that in the final year of his political life Lenin had come to realize the perils inherent in what he himself on one occasion likened to the ascent of a high mountain. What this comparison amounted to was an implicit acknowledgment that the October coup had been an adventure into unmapped territory. In his customary fashion Lenin sought assurance by invoking the example of the earlier revolution in France (a bourgeois one). Thus one finds him writing (in February 1922): "Russia's proletariat rose to a gigantic height in its revolution, not only when it is compared with 1789 and 1793, but also when compared with 1871. We must take stock of what we have done . . . as dispassionately . . . as possible." [3]

To anyone familiar with Russian Marxism, what stands out here is the casual linking of the French Revolution (1789 and 1793) and the Paris Commune of 1871—the first a successful, if sanguinary, transformation carried through by Lenin's Jacobin ancestors; the second an abortive proletarian insurrection against the bourgeois republic which had arisen from the subsequent turmoil. It is true that the Parisian Communards of 1871 counted a good many latter-day Jacobins in their own ranks; in particular the Blanquist faction (which more or less ran the Commune) was descended from the radical republicans of the 1840s, though Blanqui himself was fond of describing himself as a "communist." It is also true that Clemenceau, the archetypal bourgeois Radical under the Third Republic, had begun his political life in the 1860s as a follower of Blanqui and in 1871 duly sympathized with the Communards, though he stood aside from the fighting. All this belongs to the inner history of French republicanism—a movement largely inspired by a Robespierrist faith in "temporary" dictatorship.

This tradition is the ultimate source of those passages in the *Communist Manifesto* (1848) and *Class Struggles in France* (1850) in which Marx paid his residual debt to Jacobinism. Marxism, in one of its aspects, has been the link between 1789 and 1917, between the French Revolution and its Russian successor. The reason is quite simply that Marx obtained his political education in the Paris of the 1840s, where the nascent communist sects were led by men like Blanqui who still thought in Jacobin terms. After 1850, Marx (and even more so Engels) abandoned these rather episodic attachments and gradually transformed themselves into democratic socialists. But this transformation became effective only in Germany and England. It was half-heartedly accepted in France after the disaster of the 1871 Paris

3. "Notes of a Publicist," first published in *Pravda*, April 16, 1924, ibid., p. 206.

Commune, and it evoked no genuine echo in Eastern Europe, where Marxism continued to signify the *Communist Manifesto* rather than *Capital*. In a word, the Marx whom the Russians liked was the early Marx—the man of 1848. And they continued to admire Blanqui. The Russian radicals of the 1860s and 1870s, who transmitted the Blanquist faith in revolutionary terrorism to Lenin, were proud to style themselves "Jacobins." So far, so good. After all, even moderate Marxists like Lenin's teacher Plekhanov believed, for sound reason, that Russia would one day re-enact the earlier drama in France.

For all that, Lenin's casual allusion to these French examples slid over what to a Marxist is the central difficulty. The French Revolution, after all, had been led by the bourgeoisie—and been successful for this reason. The Paris Commune of 1871, on the other hand, had been bloodily suppressed after two months, and thus could hardly count as evidence that "proletarian dictatorship" was workable. Lenin's own party had launched a victorious uprising and by 1922, when he penned his "Notes of a Publicist," had been in power for almost five years. Was Bolshevism, then, the legitimate successor of Jacobinism? And if it was, could it also claim the heritage of that luckless rebellion in 1871 which had burst the bounds of bourgeois society?

To ask such questions is, of course, to challenge the whole theoretical construction supporting Lenin's system of beliefs, for had he been less certain about the answer he would not have been the man he was, and neither would the Bolshevik Party have become what he made of it. It was essential to his outlook, and to that of his followers, that he and they should see themselves *both* as "Jacobins" *and* as communists leading a "proletarian revolution" (and therefore also in the tradition of the 1871 Commune). The self-contradictory character of this notion was plain enough to the Mensheviks, for whom Lenin's "Jacobinism" was just what rendered his Marxism suspect. He had after all made it clear, from 1902 and *What Is to Be Done?* onward, that—unlike the mature Marx—he did *not* believe the working class could emancipate itself by its own efforts. That task, in his view, devolved upon "the party." But (as one can see from his 1922 writings) the reality of party control must on no account be allowed to weaken the faith that the October Revolution had been a "proletarian" one. In short, he was determined to have it both ways—not merely as a political leader, but as a theoretician too. When confronted with the resulting contradictions, he fell back upon the notion that history was always producing unforeseen situations. Thus, although by 1922 his regime had come to terms with what he himself called "state capitalism," he was by no means willing to let his critics have the last word on the subject. Replying to one of them, the economist Preobrazhensky (who as it happened was a left-wing Bolshevik), he flatly asserted that some of the traditional Marxian distinctions were no longer applicable:

> Up to now nobody could have written a book about this sort of capitalism, because this is the first time in human history that we see anything like it. . . . Now things are different, and neither Marx nor the Marxists could foresee this . . . for nobody could foresee that the proletariat would achieve power in one of the least developed countries, and would first try to organize large-scale production and distribution for the peasantry and then, finding that it could not cope with the task owing to the low standard of culture, would enlist the services of capitalism. Nobody ever foresaw this; but it is an incontrovertible fact.[4]

The "incontrovertible fact" was that the proletariat had *not* "achieved power," either in October 1917 or at any other time; but had he been able to see that his party "represented" not the proletariat but the ruling stratum of a new society, Lenin could not have made the revolution. Illusions of this sort (as Marx had pointed out in connection with the French Revolution) are a vital factor in promoting those historical changes whose true meaning discloses itself after the event.

The meaning of Lenin's revolution disclosed itself under Stalin. By now it requires a considerable act of faith for anyone to believe that the political dispossession of the working class by Lenin's party was merely a temporary affair, for Soviet society plainly is neither classless nor tending in that direction. So much must be granted to its Chinese critics. What the latter fail to perceive is that this outcome was inevitable and by no means the fault of Stalin's "revisionist" heirs. Indeed the term "revisionism" makes no sense in this context, for what is being revised is merely the

4. Closing speech at the eleventh congress of the RCP, March 28, 1922, ibid., pp. 310–11.

vocabulary. It is true that calling the U.S.S.R. a "state of the whole people" is ludicrous if one affects to retain Marx's view of the state as an instrument of coercion. But if Lenin was prepared to argue that Bolshevik state capitalism was different from ordinary state capitalism, why should not his successors claim that the state they govern is unlike any other state—not oppressive but liberating? If it is a matter of revisionism, Lenin was the greatest revisionist of them all. After all, it was he who stood the social-democratic tradition on its head by seizing power and then claiming to hold it for "the proletariat." And there was Stalin's subsequent decision to "build socialism" in "one country"—a decision already inherent in Lenin's pronouncements, whatever Trotsky might affirm to the contrary.[5]

V

Does it follow from all this that there is no longer something that can be called "world communism"? A movement may be in a state of disintegration and still have considerable staying power. Moreover, the elements that are now being set free may enter new combinations. If Peking has adopted the Leninist part of the Marxist-Leninist synthesis, the West European communist parties show signs of reviving the Marxist inheritance. In doing this they are, after all, simply reverting to a tradition older than the Russian Revolution—a tradition, moreover, which grew on European soil and does not have to be laboriously retranslated into English, German, French, Spanish, or Italian. Even the Russians can at a pinch revive the orthodox Marxism of Plekhanov, though doubtless they will continue to assert that he took the wrong line in 1914–18. A fortiori in Western Europe, where the communist parties are still rooted in the labor movement, it should not be too difficult for them to resurrect those elements of the Marxist tradition which they have in common with the social-

5. There had of course to be a theoretical warrant: this time Marx's letter of November 1877 to the editors of the *Otechestvenniye Zapiski*, setting out his reasons for believing that Russia had a chance to avoid the "fatal vicissitudes of the capitalist regime." As a justification for forced-draft industrialization at any cost, this was rather thin, but it has now become the warrant for what is called "communism" in all preindustrial countries, China among them.

democrats: above all, faith in the ability of the working class to emancipate itself by its own efforts and without the benefit of an omniscient vanguard of "professional revolutionaries." Conceivably the communist parties in these countries could even be brought to accept political democracy and to renounce, once and for all, the dream of one-party dictatorship, for which the preconditions are anyhow becoming increasingly unfavorable.

Something of the sort may indeed already be under way within the two largest and most important West European parties, the Italian and the French. Faced with the choice between permanent isolation and partial attainment of their aims, their leaders appear to have quietly opted for virtual acceptance of political democracy and toleration of other parties. The social revolution is still affirmed, but there is no longer the same insistence that it must of necessity pass through a dictatorial phase. Since this was the line Marx and Engels themselves took after 1871, when the quarrel with Bakunin obliged them to come down firmly on the democratic side, there should be no trouble about finding scriptural warrant for a position that is both Marxist and democratic.

What stands in the way of such a reorientation is not Marx but Lenin (to say nothing of Stalin, the symbol of terrorism). The communists in the West would have to admit that the Bolshevik experience does not after all provide a suitable model for the advanced societies of Western Europe and North America. If they could bring themselves to do this—and in Western Europe the time seems to be almost ripe—their tactical problems would no longer be insoluble, and in due course they might even win the confidence of their fellow citizens. What such a realignment cannot do is to reconstitute the lost unity of the world communist movement. It is bound on the contrary to hasten its demise as a *movement,* though not necessarily as a loose assemblage of like-minded parties. For communism since 1917 has defined itself in terms of fidelity to Lenin and the Bolshevik model. A "return to Marx," whatever its attraction after World War II to the pupils of Antonio Gramsci, has little meaning for communists in Asia, Africa, and Latin America. To them it signifies quite plainly the renunciation of those hopes and illusions that were symbolized by the myth of the October Revolution.

And yet one does not see how the drift away from Marxist-

Leninist orthodoxy can be halted, at any rate outside Eastern Europe, where the problem of gaining power has been solved. Both the rigid ultra-Stalinism of the Chinese and the traditional Marxism of Western Europe represent possible options, whereas the Leninist synthesis of 1917–23 looks more artificial with every year that passes. Too undemocratic for the West, it is still too Marxist for the East. Above all, it is too dependent upon the Marxian notion that there must be *some* concordance between the development of the productive forces and the evolution to a higher type of society, and that communism cannot simply be legislated into existence by an act of will. Lenin, after all, never quite renounced the primary assumption that socialism (let alone communism) presupposes a high degree of industrial development and a concomitant level of civilization. Indeed, he justified the adoption of the New Economic Policy in 1921–22 on the grounds that Russia was too backward for a shortcut to socialism. It has been left for Mao Tse-tung to take the final step of proclaiming communism the means of overcoming China's preindustrial backwardness. In doing so he has finally stood Marx on his head, though he can hardly be aware of it.

What is rather more important is that he has severed the link between his own brand of "communism" and the historic workers' movement from which the communist protest against exploitation and alienation originally arose. For what kept this movement going for a century was the faith that the purgatory of the industrial revolution would one day be succeeded by an age when men would find something better to do than to sacrifice themselves and their offspring for the wealth-creating apparatus of capitalist industry. If the European proletariat responded to Marxian socialism, it did so because Marx had taught the workers that "capital" was stored-up labor—their own sweat and blood which had gone to build up the great pyramid of modern industry. His followers then did not conceive that "communism" would one day come to signify an iron dictatorship dedicated to the goal of extracting the last ounce of surplus labor from the toilers, for the purpose of erecting an even more monstrous structure of totally state-owned and bureaucratically controlled capital. They did not, that is to say, foresee the advent of Stalinism, still less of Maoism, which is the application of Stalinist principles to a country far poorer and more primitive than the Russia of the first five-year plan. Whatever the pragmatic value of this gigantic experiment, it holds no promise for men and women whose ancestors in the last century passed through this particular kind of hell, though to be sure the ideology then was a different one.

Nothing can cure the Chinese of their notion that they are "building communism," though in fact they are laying the foundation of yet another state-capitalist structure. The illusion is as necessary to them as the air they breathe, for it legitimizes the drive to make their country great and self-sufficient. But just because the entire nation has been dedicated by its rulers to this backbreaking enterprise, what is officially described as communism has found expression in a riot of populist and nationalist exaltation. The appeal of Maoism is to *the people of China*—all of them (minus the celebrated "handful of plotters")—and to no one besides. Here, for all the solemn tributes to Stalin's legacy, Mao and his followers have perforce abandoned even the Stalinist form of Leninism which still retained some connection with the idea of a class dictatorship exercised in the name of "the workers." Maoism is a populist ideology which equates all the toilers, and if anything prefers the peasants to the city workers. Its appeal is to "the people," not to the proletariat, and its deepest urge is to restore the primitive community of the folk, as it is supposed to have existed in a golden age before the coming of class society. In short, what we have here is the last of the great national-popular convulsions inaugurated in the France of 1793, revived in the Russia of 1917, grotesquely parodied in the Germany of 1933, and now for a change exported to Asia. Impressive enough in its own way, the phenomenon makes sense only if one dissociates it from the Marxian perspective it has inherited from a European movement of the past century. National socialism does not acquire a different character merely because it chooses to style itself communism. But the revolution is real enough, and its ultimate direction remains to be determined.

Stalinism

✻✻✻

I

THE EMPHASIS PLACED in communist literature upon the union of theory and practice [1] is apt to encourage the notion that an adequate understanding of Soviet policy can be obtained through patient study of what are assumed to be its theoretical foundations. And since the latter include Stalin's writings as well as Lenin's, it has become not unusual to preface the discussion of Soviet aims with an analysis of Stalinist doctrine. Yet Stalin, as his most recent biographer has convincingly shown,[2] owed his steady rise in the party hierarchy to qualities very different from those of his more doctrinaire rivals, so much so that it is difficult at first sight to identify him with anything in the nature of a distinctive political conception. For a long time he appeared only as the pupil of Lenin. Thereafter came a period in which he emerged as a master tactician seeking new and violent means of implementing the revolutionary program, yet careful to eschew any formal departure from Leninist orthodoxy. Finally, as the society established by the "Second Revolution" of 1929–33 consolidated itself during and after the great "purges" of the late 1930s, Stalin lent his authority to a limited revision of Leninist concepts insofar as they interfered with the operation of the new political system, but in a manner calculated to preserve the appearance of a continuing tradition dating back to the October

The Political Quarterly, October 1950.
The Political Quarterly, October 1950.
   1. See Lenin: "Without revolutionary theory there can be no revolutionary movement," *Selected Works* (English ed., 1947), I, 165.
   2. Isaac Deutscher, *Stalin: A Political Biography* (London and New York, 1949).

Revolution and beyond. In matters of doctrine he has thus consistently acted the part of a conservative rather than that of an innovator, and it is arguable that his personal attitude has been an important factor in opening a gap between communist theory and Soviet practice. Conversely, he may be said to have bridged the distance between the inevitable utopianism of the Revolution's early days and the equally inevitable disillusionment and cynicism of its present "realist" phase, wherein the original drive to revolutionize the world has been transformed into imperialism. But viewed in this light Stalinism appears as an "ideology" rather than a "theory" of the Revolution; and it is not immediately apparent why its theoretical pretensions should be treated with any seriousness.

A study of Stalin's writing and speeches discloses little beyond a shrewd tactical day-to-day adaptation of Leninist concepts to a changing set of circumstances diverging ever more widely from the Leninist model of 1917. As a theorist, indeed, he shows a distinct tendency to arrive *post festum*. Even "Socialism in One Country," the slogan for which he is best known, turns out to have been an improvisation which was hastily extemporized during the struggle against Trotsky in 1924. There is no evidence that he formulated it himself or that he realized its full implications. More important, there exists no record of anything said or written by him on the subject of state control and economic planning that goes beyond the barest commonplace. On this subject he was content to repeat what he found in Lenin. Nor is there any sign that he understood the significance of fascism until it was brought home to him by Hitler. On the other hand, he showed considerable skill in estimating the importance of national revolutionary movements in Asia and in working out the techniques for bringing them under communist control. Here he clearly felt in his element, largely because for once he was able to make genuine use of Lenin's theories, instead of having to "interpret" them out of existence. Fascism (about which there was nothing in Lenin) bewildered him, whereas "imperialism" and "proletarian revolution" were fully comprehensive; the more so since he shared Lenin's instinctive identification of imperialism with British and British-type overseas influence. It is scarcely an accident that the only major success scored by a communist movement not directly supported by the Soviet Army was achieved in China.

On the subject of imperialism and its corollary, Soviet-Western antagonism, deviations from orthodoxy have on the whole not been encouraged—an unconscious but effective tribute to the strength of traditional Russian hostility to the West. Important fluctuations have, however, occurred from time to time, though their significance has frequently been overrated. Thus the slogan "Socialism in One Country" was for a time allotted the status of a major "theory," and a good deal was made of some rather brief and sketchy suggestions thrown out by Lenin in 1915 which seemed to imply that the "uneven" development of world capitalism was favorable to the emergence and consolidation of isolated socialist regimes.[3] But when new perspectives of expansion opened in 1939, and especially in 1945, greater stress was once more laid upon Lenin's post-1917 insistence that world capitalism in its present imperialist phase forms a whole, and that the relationship of the Soviet Union to the remainder of the world is bound to be one of unremitting hostility, leading through "a series of the most terrible collisions" to final victory for one or the other side.[4] In particular since the Varga controversy [5] and the subsequent official condemnation of those Soviet economists who, however tentatively, envisaged the possibility of permanently peaceful relations between the "two camps," there has been a return to the more uncompromising postulates of Soviet Marxism and a tendency to stress the "sharpening of contradictions in the imperialist camp." None of this is specifically Stalinist, and a good deal of it, in fact, goes back to the early Leninist period. It is thus not altogether easy to define the precise theoretical content of Soviet Marxism in its present form, itself reflecting the steady development of the Revolution from its early "Jacobin" to its current "Bonapartist" stage. On the theoretical level there would appear at first sight to be little to distinguish it from Leninism save greater rigidity. Mingled with this there has undoubtedly occurred a significant lowering of intellectual standards and

3. See "The United States of Europe Slogan," *Selected Works,* I, 630–32.
4. See "Stalin on Revolution," by "Historicus", *Foreign Affairs,* January 1949, p. 204.
5. See *Soviet Studies,* Nos. 1 and 2 (June, Oct. 1949).

a growing obtrusion of certain cultural features, usually described as "Byzantine" or "Oriental," which lend a special flavor to the atmosphere. The description of these symptoms, however, does not carry one much further. We are still far from having understood the inwardness of Stalinism if we define it merely as Russified Marxism at a second remove from Europe (Leninism being the first). It is indeed undeniable that the adaptation of Marxism to the requirements of the Russian Revolution—begun with Plekhanov's popularization, in the 1890s, of some of the more elementary aspects of Marx's thought, as previously interpreted by Engels for the benefit of the German socialists—has since about 1930 been carried a stage further, beyond the point where Lenin had left it. But while this fact has an important bearing upon the growing inability of Western communists to square their political loyalties with the requirements of critical thinking, it does not really explain what it is that makes Stalinism the particular historical force it has become.

Recent attempts by British and American authors of conservative or liberal views to approach the subject from the angle of textual criticism have not, in my opinion, done a great deal to clarify the issue. Critical studies of this kind, however thorough, are initially handicapped by the mistaken assumption that "Marxist communism" forms an organic whole, rooted in the Marxian texts and gradually unfolding—though no doubt incompletely—to its present material realization in the U.S.S.R. Carefully fostered by the Stalinists, who are alone to benefit from it, this myth acts as a solvent of critical thinking in a number of current efforts to relate communist theory to Soviet practice. Writers who regard "Marxism" as the source of present Soviet reality are inevitably inclined to underrate the extent to which it has been transformed into a mere ideology. They also tend to overlook the ambiguity of such Marxian concepts as "proletarian dictatorship," which probably meant several different things to Marx (including the Paris Commune, which was not a dictatorship in the modern sense at all), but certainly never meant the one-party state. Such ex post facto attempts to draw out the theoretical implications of Marxian concepts by an analysis of current Soviet reality not only are academic but suffer from the graver fault of taking the Soviet myth at its face value. This is particularly true of the recurrent failure to perceive that the "proletarian revolution" which Marx expected to occur in Germany or France in 1848 is a very different thing from the final decay of capitalist society, to which he occasionally gave the same description, and that both differ in essentials from the Russian Revolution. It is, to say the least, surprising that noncommunists should swallow whole the Leninist-Stalinist identification of the October Revolution, however world-shattering its importance, with the "proletarian revolution" against capitalism, which in actual fact is taking place at the present time, in a fairly peaceful and democratic manner, throughout the Western world, without benefit of Soviet assistance. The confusion really goes back to the accidental circumstance that Marx, writing at a time when memories of the French Revolution were still fresh, tended to picture the coming socialist transformation in terms derived from the heroic legends of 1793. When in 1917 it was Lenin's turn to telescope past history and present reality, he did so on a scale which we have come to regard as epochal. Stalin gave the matter a further twist by emphasizing the creative role of the state, in striking contrast to both Lenin and Marx. To ignore these changes is to fall victim to what was at first a genuine illusion and has by now become a systematic misuse of Marxian terminology in the service of a movement which has repudiated the libertarian intentions of its founders. It is doubtful whether much is gained by looking for the (nonexistent) missing link between the *Communist Manifesto* of 1848 and Lenin's and Trotsky's revolutionary ukases seventy years later. The intervening period, after all, saw the real emergence of modern society in the West, including the spread of democracy and the growth of a genuine labor movement, and even the Marx of *Capital* and the First International was not the Marx of 1848, whom the Bolsheviks were glad to resurrect: from being the prophet of communist-led revolution against absolutism he had in the interval become the theorist of the socialist labor movement, which was beginning to develop on democratic lines, as it has steadily done ever since. Lenin's fateful muddling of the issue, due to the immense confusion engendered by the simultaneous breakdown of the three eastern empires in 1917–18, and the perpetuation of his misconception by the Stalinists, are sufficiently misleading by themselves, without the gratis support of Western writers eager to make Marx appear as the progenitor of everything they happen to dislike.

II

It has become a commonplace that the Bolshevik Party, as reorganized by Lenin after the historic split of 1903, differed from most other contemporary socialist parties in being a tightly knit fraternity of "professional revolutionaries" rather than a democratic labor organization: authority resting ultimately with a self-appointed central committee of leaders who represented the outlook of the revolutionary intelligentsia rather than that of the backward and undeveloped working class of Tsarist Russia.[6] Put in this form, however, the statement remains incomplete, for it ignores the fact that virtually all revolutionary movements in Russia were organized in similar fashion, the Bolsheviks merely carrying furthest certain features imposed upon all revolutionaries by the special circumstances under which all parties were forced to operate during the Tsarist regime, at any rate until 1905. Discipline among, for instance, the Mensheviks was looser, but they were no less an organization of Marxist intellectuals with a following among the workers (chiefly the better paid, more highly skilled, and more Europeanized), rather than a labor party in the Western sense. What differentiated Lenin's party from all others was its ready acceptance of the role of "vanguard"; its refusal to apologize for what its socialist opponents regarded as undesirable features, e.g., centralism and other quasi-military forms of organization; and its insistent justification of the "van-

6. See on this point especially Bertram D. Wolfe, *Three Who Made a Revolution* (New York, 1948), pp. 147–69 and passim. There now exists a considerable literature on the subject, much of it accessible in English. It is the more surprising that so many writers should continue to discuss the conflict between present-day social-democracy and communism (i.e., Stalinism) without reference to the organizational issue on which the Bolsheviks first split off from the Western socialist labor movement. Conservative writers can even be found to echo the Stalinist contention that what differentiates communism from democratic socialism is the latter's addiction to "reformism" and "parliamentary tactics." It never seems to occur to them that what really makes democratic socialism a different affair is the fact that it is a *labor* movement.

guard" concept, on the grounds that the working-class movement,
left to itself, was not and never would become socialist. As
Lenin put it in 1902, in a formulation which has become classic:

> The history of all countries shows that the working class,
> exclusively by its own efforts, is able to develop only trade union
> consciousness, i.e. it may itself realize the necessity for combining
> in unions, for fighting the employers, and for striving to compel the
> government to pass necessary labour legislation, etc. The theory of
> socialism, however, grew out of the philosophic, historical and
> economic theories elaborated by the educated representatives of the
> propertied classes, the intellectuals. . . . in Russia, the theoretical
> doctrine of social-democracy arose quite independently of the spon-
> taneous growth of the labour movement; it arose as a natural and
> inevitable outcome of the development of ideas among the revolu-
> tionary socialist intelligentsia.[7]

As a general statement this might, indeed, have been echoed
by the Fabians, and possibly even by Hyndman's social-democrats. But what differentiated Russian from West European conditions in the late nineteenth and early twentieth centuries was
that the "permeation" of the Russian working-class movement by
socialist ideas occurred not through the "conversion" of recognized labor leaders chosen by and answerable to the rank and
file but through the agency of the Marxist "professional revolutionaries," themselves welded together in a totalitarian party
organization. There were no Russian equivalents of Ben Tillett
and Tom Mann, of the elder Liebknecht, or of Bebel. There was
not, among the whole galaxy of Russian revolutionaries, a single
one whom contemporary German, French, British, American or
Australian workers would have regarded as a genuine labor
leader, i.e., a leader answerable to his followers. In the West, the
socialist theoreticians approached the rapidly growing and democratically organized labor movement through its recognized
spokesmen, who were themselves workers or of working-class
origin, and who in any case represented the rank and file by
whom they had been elected and to whom they were account-
able. In Russia, at the critical period, no such autochthonous
working-class leadership existed. Its place was taken by the
"professional revolutionaries," who were no less eager than the

7. *What Is to Be Done?*, in *Selected Works*, I, 170.

Tsarist police to get the nascent movement under their control. Instead of being democratically led by spokesmen of their own choosing, the workers fell under the direction of a political organization which supplied not only the ideas but the institutional framework, and which in time was to establish a cast-iron control over all forms of public life. Thus did the Leninist vanguard prepare the way for the Stalinist bureaucracy.[8]

The manner in which Lenin turned a perfectly reasonable and unexceptionable statement of fact, i.e., the fact that the labor movement normally acquires its socialist consciousness from outside its own ranks, into a justification of practices running counter to the whole socialist tradition establishes him as the true progenitor of Stalinism. If there is a difference it lies in the fact that under Stalin the process of revamping socialist theory in the service of totalitarian practice has lost its unconscious and spontaneous character and become a mass-production industry controlled by the party hierarchy, which has long shed its pristine innocence in theoretical matters and is fully aware of the uses to which carefully selected quotations from approved authors can be put—notably under conditions where criticism is not encouraged, unless it happens to be "Bolshevik self-criticism," i.e., self-flagellation. The difference is not merely one of style. Until the Revolution, and for some years after it, the Communist Party (the appellation "social-democratic" was abandoned, along with a good many other things, in 1918) continued to "represent the masses," if not in actual fact, at least subjectively, in its own mind. The realization that "proletarian dictatorship" and working-class interests could not possibly be made to square in either the short or the long run, that the regime had few supporters outside the ranks of the party, and that most

8. As on other occasions when he departed from Marxism, Lenin in 1902 fortified his conscience with quotations from "orthodox" Western Marxists, in this instance from Kautsky. But although he went to great lengths to make it appear that he was only following the example set by the German and Austrian social-democrats (then regarded by him as model Marxists) he never troubled to deal with the only real issue in the whole controversy: namely, by whom the movement was to be led after it had become permeated with socialist consciousness. To have answered, as the Mensheviks did, that democratically elected working-class leaders should then take over from the "professionals," who would thereafter occupy a back seat as they did in Europe, would have ruined his whole conception.

workers, given the choice, would vote for its socialist rivals developed only gradually. An important milestone was reached at the time of the Kronstadt rising in 1921, when it became clear that the masses in town and country were hostile to the dictatorship, and it is extremely significant that it was this period that saw the rise of Stalin to genuine eminence in the party councils. What gave the Stalinist faction, then and more especially after Lenin's death, its unique hold over the party, and through the party over the state, was its conviction that "Bolshevik leadership" could impose its own solutions from above, aided—after the immediate post-civil-war weariness had worn off—by carefully channeled "mass support" from below. The faction constituted itself in a struggle to obtain control of the "machine," but its program was already that of the Second Revolution, and its ideology was "Robespierrist" rather than "Bonapartist," to employ Trotsky's favorite terminology. It was held together by a conviction that the "correct" solution could be imposed by force; and in this it proved right. The fund of secularized religious energy, which was the original motive force of the revolutionary drive to remake society, had not been exhausted by the civil war; nor was it, as Trotsky thought, the prerogative of the proletariat. Its locus was rather the party itself, which despite its growing bureaucratization remained the principal repository of whatever revolutionary idealism was left after 1921. In this sense it was perfectly correct to regard the NEP period as a tactical retreat. When Stalin during these years reproached his opponents with "lack of faith in the Party," he found a ready response among the communist "cadres," and once the Second Revolution got under way in 1929, the party managed to tap fresh sources of energy among the masses. Combined with brutal and widespread repression, these proved just sufficient to overcome the crisis caused by the initial failure of forced collectivization and the resulting famine, which at one moment came close to bringing the whole edifice down to the ground.

But though the party pulled through, the tremendous strains of these years permanently changed its character. Having been compelled to impose the Second Revolution upon the masses by force, at the cost of human sacrifices unparalleled in history, it could no longer retain its naïve faith in the ideology of the

October Revolution. Stalinism acquired its character during these grim years. It came to rest upon a combination of revolutionary despotism, exaltation of the "toilers" in the abstract, and callous contempt for the individual "toiler" and his rights in actuality. In this manner it expressed both the standpoint of the new bureaucracy and the exhaustion of the party which had carried the Revolution through to its conclusion. By the middle 1930s, the upper strata of the party had finally been amalgamated with the new ruling hierarchy in town and country. In a rigorously stratified society this process spelled the death of primitive Leninism. The "vanguard," having at long last reached its predetermined goal, could no longer view itself in the relatively simple terms elaborated by Lenin. Still less could it afford to proclaim the truth about itself and the society it had fashioned. It was forced to develop a double consciousness: one for the elect and the (more or less innocent) fellow travelers, and another for the masses. Hence the peculiar moral climate of Stalinism, with its promotion of the individual conscience to the position of Public Enemy Number One.

In the dim light of retrospective wisdom, it seems evident that only those in control of the party hierarchy who had genuinely worked themselves free of the primitive Leninist strait jacket, with its tiresome insistence upon at least a semblance of "workers' democracy," had a chance of saving the day, though at the cost of a permanent reign of terror. When Stalin began to assume control, the Leninist phase of the Revolution had pretty well run its course and in the process landed the regime in a cul-de-sac from which only the most violent means could extricate it. Further "advance" along the lines laid down by Lenin in 1921 must have spelled collapse and restoration. This was the background of the intraparty struggle in the course of which the Stalinist faction transformed itself into the nucleus of a new ruling class. The leaders of the October Revolution had been misled by their own ideology. What distinguished the Stalinist faction was not simply its hold over the machine (largely effected through the GPU, self-appointed guardian of the Revolution as well as prime instrument of repression) but its gradual realization that the working class was destined to play a strictly subordinate part in the new society. The party, in this scheme, became an instrument for reconciling the masses to their lot in an increasingly hierarchical society, but it also served as a means for disciplining the managerial caste. Its outlook had to be remodeled accordingly, a process which took years and was not completed until the blood bath of 1936–38 had laid the ghost of primitive Leninism and simultaneously taught all ranks of society a lesson in obedience to their communist masters. For the masters remained communists, even though they exchanged primitive Leninism for a more sophisticated version of the faith. The expansion of the Soviet empire since 1939 has introduced the world to a new type of ruling-class personnel, well able to accommodate its principles to the practice of revolutionary despotism. The party has thus managed to exchange one social milieu (the proletariat) for a totally different one (the bureaucracy) without its identity: proof positive that it had never in fact been a working-class organization to begin with.

III

It has been argued so far that the organizational structure of the Leninist "vanguard" made possible the seizure of power in a backward country by socialist revolutionaries, while their Marxist ideology enabled them to identify their own aims with those of the industrial proletariat. The point is crucial. Left to itself, the Russian working class, as Lenin correctly perceived, was neither more nor less revolutionary than the working class generally tends to be in the early stage of capitalist development. The revolutionary edge was lent to its struggle by the simultaneous efforts of the intelligentsia to throw off the yoke of the semi-absolutist state. The resulting phenomenon of revolutionary professionalism within the ranks of a nominally social-democratic movement was a historical innovation. Lenin's organization was the first of the great modern totalitarian parties, and it assumed this character many years before it acquired a totalitarian program to match. For while the actual seizure of power in 1917 was unforeseen even by the Bolsheviks, the organization of the party was from the first adapted to precisely the sort of circumstances which arose, spontaneously and unforeseen, owing to the impact of World War I upon Tsarist Russia. In this instance, therefore, practice outran theory. The Bolsheviks managed to win and hold power because their organization was more centralist than that of the other socialist parties and, being centralist, it easily merged with the state apparatus.

The totalitarian state party is a twentieth-cenury phenomenon, and the problem of working out a suitable ideology for it, without openly repudiating the democratic traditions inherited by socialism from earlier libertarian movements, was and is the most difficult which the Soviet regime has had to solve. At first the question was simply ignored. The "proletarian dictatorship" established by the October Revolution was supposed to be a provisional affair, which would "wither away" when its task was accomplished. Although the civil war led to growing concentration of authority at the center, the party for a while continued to resist the full implications of this trend. In view of the subsequent personal conflicts among the leadership, it is noteworthy that Trotsky became for a while the leading representative of centralism. But a party centralized by Trotsky, apart from being unacceptable to the other leaders, would probably have fallen short of full-fledged totalitarianism. The issue in any case came to a head after Stalin had won control, by which time the GPU had replaced the Army as the principal pacemaker of centralization. By this time, too, the horrors of the Second Revolution had made it impossible to maintain the fiction that the Soviet state represented "the proletariat organized as the ruling class." A class stripped of the right to organize itself, to fight for better economic conditions, etc., was plainly not the "ruling class." Lastly, the dictatorship showed every sign of becoming permanent, and so did the terror. For all that, the official ideology retained its libertarian overtones, which in the circumstances were bound to appear increasingly unreal. Something had to give way, and not unnaturally it was the ideology of the party—or that part of it which had been formulated in accordance with the democratic traditions of nineteenth-century Europe. (The fact that these traditions were still valid in the West, where democracy was a reality and not a slogan, was not, of course, admitted, and Stalinism to this day resists any suggestion that the remainder of the world is not necessarily bound to become totalitarian.)

Under a despotic regime, every moral problem is also a political one. Morally, the party was bound by Lenin's dictum that the state—every state—is an instrument of oppression. Politically, it followed that if the Soviet state failed to "wither away" despite the success of collectivization, the majority of the people must be in opposition to the regime. The convulsion of the late 1930s was the outcome of the intolerable dilemma in which the party was placed by its failure to harmonize the ferocious conflicts unleashed by the Second Revolution and the reign of terror against the peasantry. At the ideological level at which it entered the collective consciousness of the communist elite, the conflict presented itself as a clash between the old Leninist and the new Stalinist doctrine of the state. At the political level, it took the form of a more or less spontaneous rebellion of the party membership against the dictatorship of the Stalinist faction and the GPU. The "purge" eliminated the political threat by terrorizing the party into absolute obedience to the ruling faction, but it did not solve the moral problem, and therewith the problem of authority. The new regime was still in search of its legitimation. It could no longer appeal to Lenin, because Lenin had laid it down (in *State and Revolution*) that the state is *always and everywhere* an instrument of minority rule in a society torn by social antagonisms. By the late 1930s it had become clear that this subversive doctrine would have to be repudiated, yet to do so was to lift the veil from the most closely guarded of Soviet secrets: the transformation of the Communist Party into an instrument of state control over the people.

It is not surprising that Stalin hesitated until the purges had confirmed his hold over the machine and forced the party to open its doors without reservation to all ranks of the "Soviet intelligentsia," i.e., all grades of the new administrative hierarchy. The 1939 Party Congress, which made the relevant change in the membership rules, significantly became the venue for an unprecedented innovation in doctrine: not only was the state proclaimed the principal instrument of socialization but the Marxian view of its genesis and historical function was repudiated as well. As Stalin put it with his customary bluntness: "Certain of the general propositions in the Marxist doctrine of the state were incompletely worked out and inadequate." As might have been expected, the "inadequate" propositions turned out to be those

which were most likely to cause people to wonder why despite
the "liquidation of class antagonism," the Soviet state showed no
tendency to "wither away." For it appeared that the state was
destined to become more and more important, since "we now
have an entirely new, socialist state, without precedent in history
and differing considerably in form and function from the socialist
state of the first phase," i.e., the "proletarian dictatorship" established in 1917. What was more, this "unprecedented" state
would continue to flourish even under full communism "unless
the capitalist encirclement is liquidated." And it would most
certainly allow the fullest latitude to the "numerous, new, popular, socialist intelligentsia," a term so elastic that the privileged
upper crust might well expect to shelter behind it. In short,
Stalin's authority was employed to legitimize the new hierarchical
society in the eyes of the Communist Party, and through the
party in the consciousness of "the masses." In a sense this had
been his function ever since the first sharp departure from equali-
tarianism was made in 1931, when "payment by results" became
general. Now the process had reached completion.

IV

The history of Stalinism is the history of the Russian state
party. State parties drawn from the left have the advantage of
being able to build upon traditional working-class loyalties,
though the problem of ridding themselves of their democratic
ideology is not an easy one. From the current Soviet viewpoint,
even the communist parties of Eastern Europe are still barnacled
by remnants of their past and in urgent need of transforming
themselves into fully fledged state parties before they can become genuinely trustworthy, i.e., Stalinist. Hence the recurrent
purges and, of course, the impossibility of tolerating any activity
on the part of democratic socialists, however willing to cooperate
with the regime. The state party cannot renounce its monopoly
without losing control altogether. The slightest breath of political
freedom is fatal to its purpose, which is not to represent "interests" but to remold society.

Stalinism thus presents itself either as a disease of the labor
movement or as an alternative to the "normal," i.e., capitalist,

process of modernization hitherto followed by backward countries. Both descriptions are equally valid, depending on whether one adopts a Western or an Eastern standpoint. Regarded from the angle of Western democracy, Stalinism is a menace both to democratic socialism and to Western civilization. Viewed from the angle of Asiatic nationalism, it is a fully valid and remarkably successful, though extremely brutal, alternative to the liberal integration. These contrasting and contradictory aspects make it difficult to adopt a rigidly uniform attitude towards the spread of this "socialist Islam." It is obvious by now that communism in China, for instance, with its puritanical insistence upon the virtues of hard work and civic responsibility, bears a totally different relationship to traditional society and culture than would be the case in a Western country with a democratic tradition. What is genuine progress in Manchuria may spell disintegration or barbarization in Czechoslovakia. The practice of equating both processes can only lead to confusion and is best left to the Stalinist propagandists, who are past masters in the art of yoking incompatibles together. Even Lenin's dictum "In the last analysis the upshot of the struggle will be determined by the fact that Russia, India, China, etc., account for the overwhelming majority of the population of the globe" does not dispense one from the duty of drawing a critical distinction between Asiatic and European communism; and, as the Yugoslav example has shown, even the latter is not a monolithic structure.

It is, moreover, obvious that although Soviet communism seems destined to score its greatest triumphs in Asia, its impact upon the West gives rise to the more significant intellectual and moral problems. Few of us share the optimism of Professor E. H. Carr, and socialists in particular have every reason to beware of the suggestion that some sort of political and cultural rejuvenation is to be expected from the judicious transplantation of Soviet precepts to the West. This is so not only because Soviet culture is comparatively primitive—certainly a great deal more primitive than prerevolutionary Russian culture was in relation to the then-existing civilization of Western Europe—but also because the peculiar nature of Soviet totalitarianism precludes the possibility of either the West learning anything worthwhile from Russia or the Russians profiting from Western example. This again is not simply a matter of cultural isolation, naïve chauvinism, traditional xenophobia, or "police rule." All these factors are present in abundance, as we have learned in recent years, but they are held together and validated by the semireligious element injected into the modern Soviet consciousness by the myth of the October Revolution. The half-conscious manipulation of this myth by the ruling element of the state party gives to present Soviet reality its special ideological flavor (ideology being defined, textbookwise, as "false consciousness," i.e., inability to see through the currently accepted rationalizations to the real situation as it exists "in itself"). The Stalinist stands midway between the primitive Leninist and the average representative of the present-day Soviet managerial class, in whom the original communist urge to change the world has shrunk to a determination to better his own material status. Stalinism, that is to say, is still to some extent rooted in the October Revolution, with its claim to represent a new human and social integration. But it maintains this position only at the cost of increasingly violent attempts to repress the growth of social and cultural relations within the new society. The party's efforts, for instance, to introduce an integrative principle into the various fields of cultural activity, i.e., to interpret them in the light of the ruling ideology—whether it is a question of musical composition or biological science—are typically conducted at such a low level as to blight the work of the specialized agencies of culture.

That this is true not only of art criticism but also of economics has been shown by the Varga discussion, in the course of which the representatives of party orthodoxy, as currently interpreted, went to remarkable lengths to deny inconvenient facts, e.g., the growing importance of public control in the United States and Britain, the vastly increased influence of the labor movement in both countries and throughout the Western world generally, the immensity of the change in the relationship between Britain and India, compared with what it was before the war, etc. It is here that one comes up against a problem in Soviet-Western relations barely glimpsed by those writers who painstakingly assemble evidence to show that Stalin's view of international affairs in the year 1950 is still determined by what Lenin thought in 1916 of the causes of Anglo-German rivalry, in the light of his reading of J. A. Hobson's analysis of British imperialism in 1900. Interesting though these biographical details are—Stalin's personal conservatism in theoretical matters undoubtedly plays a part in stifling such development of thought as may still be possible even within the confines of Soviet Marxism—they acquire genuine significance only against the background of a wider question: to what extent is the state party capable of interpreting world affairs in a matter conducive to the rational pursuit of Soviet foreign and domestic policy? The answer must depend on what one believes to be the truth about the nature of the Soviet-American antagonism. One thing is certain: thirty or even twenty years ago, when "the party" was the agent of a revolutionary transformation along lines laid down in no textbook, Bolshevik or otherwise, its view of the world concerned nobody but itself, whereas today it has become the guardian of a whole new society with interests and tendencies of its own, which may diverge from the Stalinist model once they are given an opportunity to manifest themselves. Behind the party, closely amalgamated with it and wholly dependent upon its monopoly of specialized information-cum-interpretation about the world in general and the non-Soviet world in particular, but yet not entirely identical with it, there stands the Soviet hierarchy—military, bureaucratic, managerial, professional—as it has gradually evolved over the past generation since the "proletarian dictatorship" sent the proletariat packing and imposed its totalitarian rule upon all classes of Russian society. If the natural leaders of this new hierarchy, whose lineaments can today be glimpsed only with difficulty, should ever be taught by experience to distrust the kind of factual information and theoretical interpretation which the party still monopolizes, they may be tempted to dispense with its services—even though it is their only shield against the masses, and even though the Leninist-Stalinist myth is more or less genuinely accepted by most leading representatives of the society which has grown up since 1917.

It is not possible here to follow up more than one line of thought leading to the conclusion that Soviet Marxism is already riddled with "internal contractions" which preclude its further development along the lines imposed by current political orthodoxy. In principle, the existence of such "contradictions" ought to act as a spur, and no doubt would if Stalinism (like certain schools of theology) did not secure itself against such unpleasant surprises by imposing an institutional veto upon internal growth and development. For it is one of the many characteristic oddities of this supremely undialectical brand of "dialectical materialism" that it denies the existence, or even the possibility, of actual contradictions within the body of Soviet society (other than the perennial sham fight against "bourgeois agents," kulaks, spies, Trotskyists, "homeless cosmopolitans," and other scarecrows) and of theoretical contradictions within the corpus of Marxist-Leninist doctrine. And it does this despite an increasingly rigid insistence upon the letter of the Marxist canon, which has thus been rendered totally sterile and inoperative so far as the understanding of political and social reality is concerned: so much so that Mr. Vyshinsky was forced to rely on Professor Blackett when he was at a loss for arguments to defend the Soviet attitude on international control of atomic energy. It is thus difficult to resist the impression that Soviet Marxism has achieved its integrative character at the cost of losing its hold upon an important part of contemporary reality. Its growing rigidity may be interpreted as an attempt to preserve its systematic character under conditions—e.g., the growth of nationalist and Pan-Slav tendencies, feeding upon the military chauvinism unleashed by the war and the Bonapartist transformation of the regime itself—the least favorable to the organic development of socialist forms of consciousness. Ideologically, it is on the defensive. Politically, it is validated by the degree of success achieved in cementing the alliance of the army and the party: twin pillars of the totalitarian state, who must stand or fall together. The amalgamation of these two forces is as much the chief practical problem of the ruling group as the preparation for what it regards as the inevitable trial of strength with "world imperialism" is its principal political preoccupation. The directorate which must succeed Stalin on the day he retires can justify its absolute rule in the eyes of the Soviet hierarchy—including the marshals recently victorious in a war which the Politburo vainly tried to stave off—only by asserting its guardianship of the Leninist-Stalinist "science of revolution." The testing time cannot be far off, for Stalin has passed his seventieth year and his effective leadership must be nearing its term. He has enabled the regime to weather a succession of storms and provided it with a chart by which to set its course after he has stepped down from the bridge. But what if the chart turns out to be faulty?

The Armed Intellectual

❊❊❊

The Prophet Unarmed[1] is the best book Isaac Deutscher has yet written. It is a much better book than his overpraised Stalin biography a decade ago, and it is superior also to the earlier volume in his projected trilogy on Trotsky. This is not to say that it is faultless in matter or tone: the very first sentence of the preface, with its labored evocation of Carlyle's biography of Cromwell, strikes a jarring note. Similar traces of pompousness are not infrequent; Mr. Deutscher has become more urbane, but as a stylist he still tends to solemnity. Yet this second volume on Trotsky establishes him as a historian of the Russian Revolution. The student in search of detail will continue to go to E. H. Carr for an exhaustive study of the intraparty conflicts of the mid-1920s, but he will henceforth have to reckon with Mr. Deutscher. For in this new work Trotsky's fall from power is at last brought into proper focus and related to the crisis of the Soviet regime after Lenin's death. Even those who do not accept Mr. Deutscher's somewhat pedantically Leninist reading of the facts can learn from him, and few will fail to find his account fascinating: if only because it reflects something of the somber drama of those days.

In 1921, with the civil war over, Trotsky was at the height of his power and prestige; in 1929 he was expelled from the U.S.S.R., never to return. What happened in the intervening eight years? The story has been told before—notably by Trotsky himself—and its outline might seem familiar by now. But Mr. Deutscher has

Partisan Review, Winter 1960.

1. *The Prophet Unarmed: Trotsky, 1921–1929* (London and New York, 1959).

had access to the unpublished Trotsky archives at Harvard, and his analysis does add something new. In particular he makes it clear how impossible it was for Trotsky to hold his own in the Politburo and the Central Committee once Lenin's essential support had been withdrawn. He even suggests that Trotsky knew this or at least was subconsciously aware of it. Certainly his tactics became increasingly suicidal as time went on, and by 1927–28—when his followers were being expelled from the party and shipped off to Siberia—he no longer gave the impression of aiming at anything beyond a moral victory in the distant future. Yet unlike some of the earlier oppositionists—notably those who left the party or were driven out after the Kronstadt rising of 1921—he obstinately clung to the notion that the regime was inherently socialist and only needed to be reformed politically. From the viewpoint of those earlier exiles who had already written the entire Bolshevik dictatorship off as the hopelessly corrupt reign of a new exploiting class, the Trotskyist newcomers of 1928 were but a dissident faction of the "Establishment"; and most of them in the end confirmed this analysis by making their peace with Stalin.

The description of this process, whereby the majority of Trotsky's followers were reluctantly brought to accept the "temporary" necessity of Stalin's personal rule, forms the most instructive part of Mr. Deutscher's final chapter. Earlier he devotes a good deal of space to the rather scholastic disputation over the supposed "Thermidorian" or counterrevolutionary menace on which Trotsky and Zinoviev fell back in 1926–27, when they had run out of more convincing and less academic arguments. All the factions operated with historical analogies; and all the leading figures—with the noteworthy exception of Stalin—were genuinely in the grip of fear that they might be re-enacting some disastrous episode from the earlier drama. When the ruling group tried to discredit Trotsky in 1924, they established a precedent by muttering that he might have Bonapartist ambitions (a grotesque suggestion to which Mr. Deutscher unaccountably lends some indirect support by affecting to take it seriously instead of dismissing it as the obvious humbug it was). In 1926 Bukharin—then under suspicion of favoring a "Soviet Thermidor"—reacted with hysterical rage against the accusation. And as late as July 1927, five months before his expulsion, Trotsky was able to shake the morale of the Old Bolsheviks on the Central Control Commission with a lengthy disquisition on the Jacobin disintegration after Robespierre's fall. But the weapon was two-edged: by 1929 some of the exiled Trotskyists had begun to ponder the notion that Stalin might after all incarnate the Robespierrist inheritance, in which case it was *they* who were the potential Thermidorians! This thought alarmed them to such a degree that they promptly made their peace with him! Clearly there were alternative ways of deciphering the riddle of the historical Sphinx. It speaks for Mr. Deutscher's good sense that in the end he discards these analogies—albeit a trifle reluctantly—on the grounds that Jacobinism and Bolshevism were after all separated by an entire epoch. What he does not quite explain is how Trotsky rationalized his decision to oppose a current which on his own reading of the facts was irresistible.

In psychological terms, the answer doubtless is that he was both a revolutionary and a historian. In his chosen political role he had no option but to continue struggling against what, in his intellectual capacity, he regarded as destiny. This obscure rift in his personality debilitated him and sapped even his physical powers. There is evidence that he tended to fall ill at critical moments: always a bad sign. It seems plain that Stalin, by contrast, benefited not merely from his control of the machine—which he owed to Lenin—but from his lack of imagination. *He* never worried about his place in history, until he had won and could have the history books rewritten to suit his purpose. Objectionable though this procedure doubtless is, it was of considerable help to him politically; whereas Trotsky was hampered by trying to fill two roles at once. This is not to suggest that with a different attitude he might have won, but that his failure was not simply predetermined by "objective" circumstances: he contributed his share to the defeat of his faction, and then abused Stalin for carrying out the opposition's program. This was natural behavior, but it disclosed an impractical streak, about which his biographer is not indeed silent but which he does not stress sufficiently.

This reticence is in keeping with Mr. Deutscher's belief—discreetly voiced in his preface—that we are now witnessing the first dawn of a post-Stalinist age, when justice will at last be done, officially and publicly, to Trotsky's true role in the Revolution. This is unlikely for many reasons. The Soviet intelligentsia may indeed gradually become more curious about its past, and if it does it will certainly discover in Trotsky's writings—notably in his nonpolitical essays composed during the mid-1920s—an interesting anticipation of some of its own demands for greater intellectual freedom. But as a political doctrine Trotskyism is as sterile as anarchism. It may linger on in the more remote parts of Latin America, but its contribution to post-Stalinist thinking in Eastern Europe has been small. Trotsky stands for the myth of the October Revolution, and myths, though potent in their own domain, cannot serve as guideposts to action.

In his preface Mr. Deutscher suggests that Stalin's heirs still walk in fear of Trotsky's shade "because they are afraid of coming to grips with the issues with which he, so much ahead of his time, did come to grips." It would be interesting to know what he thinks those issues are. A possible glimpse is afforded by his remark that around 1921 "the proletarian dictatorship was triumphant, but the proletariat had vanished." If after all these years he still believes that Bolshevik rule in some sense represented, or incorporated, the "proletarian dictatorship" proclaimed (but not established) by Lenin and Trotsky in 1917, it seems reasonable to suppose that he regards the present regime as a stage on the road to a genuinely socialist democracy in which the heritage of Trotsky's thought will at last flower, side by side with the material accomplishments of the Stalin epoch; and indeed he more or less says so. Unfortunately there is no evidence that the Soviet Union is turning into a democracy, though it is a fact that the increasingly numerous privileged stratum is beginning to elude the totalitarian strait jacket, while keeping it firmly strapped upon the toiling masses.

It is odd that Mr. Deutscher, who is so conscious of the many analogies between Jacobinism and Bolshevism, cannot quite bring himself to draw the obvious conclusion: namely that there is very little to connect the thoughts and anticipations of those who started the revolution with the new social reality to which it gave rise. After all, the men of 1793 did not have a great deal to teach their respectably bourgeois successors. It is true that the

French Left has retained a sentimental loyalty to the *grands ancêtres*. Perhaps the day will come when there is a monument to Trotsky in Moscow (there is none to Danton in Paris, save for the Rue Danton which is not exactly one of the main thoroughfares). He certainly deserves one, although it was Lenin who made the crucial decisions in 1917–21, and Stalin who a decade later inaugurated the "revolution from above." But more than that, plus of course a notable place in the history books? If Russia ever manages to escape from Stalinist tutelage, the result is likely to be a decided reluctance to worship at the shrine of "permanent revolution." After all, Trotsky's chief contribution to Marxist thinking was the idea that socialist revolutions are possible in backward countries. This has now been proved to the hilt, but experience has likewise shown that it takes a dictatorship to stabilize the new society, and that this society is not classless. In the circumstances it seems a little visionary on Mr. Deutscher's part to suppose that modern socialism can go on nourishing itself from this source.

Nor is it likely that Trotsky's interpretation of what happened to the Revolution after Lenin's death will find greater acceptance as time goes on; for that interpretation was distorted by— partly misunderstood—reminiscences of the French Revolution. Trotsky's thinking revolved around a certain conception of what had taken place in France between 1789 and 1799. Mr. Deutscher, who is still under the spell, faithfully reproduces the illusions of his hero and even hints that future ages will come to recognize Trotsky as the outstanding intellect of the entire historical period which has now come to an end. This is to misconceive the real significance of the Russian Revolution, and in particular to overlook the fact that it can have no lessons for Western countries, while the chief lesson it has for the East may well be that the era of proletarian uprisings is closed.

In a sense these criticisms are unfair. Trotsky now belongs to history, and his importance no longer depends on what one thinks of his own interpretation of the events in which he figured. It is easy to see from Mr. Deutscher's biography what it was that held the loyalty of his followers long after it was plain that the fight was hopeless. Prometheus on his rock is a more attractive

figure than Zeus on his throne, and most people will continue to
prefer the former, though they may submit to the latter. Whence
the virtual certainty that Trotsky, not Stalin, will be the hero of
the future literary epic to take its place beside Buechner's *Danton*. "Was im Lied soll ewig leben, muss im Leben untergehn."

Lives of Lenin

✳ ✳ ✳

1964 PROMISES TO BE a vintage year for biographies of Lenin. It is, after all, exactly four decades since his death in 1924. It also happens to be the year of the formal dissolution of "world Communism" into rival camps. As matters now stand, the proper procedure, for anyone with an urge to be up to date, is to begin with the image of the prophet—shrouded and embalmed in his gloomy mausoleum—and then work backward to 1917, and forward to the present year. In this way one obtains the correct historical perspective and at the same time links the subject with immediate topical concerns, such as the relation of Russia to Asia. We are all getting expert at this kind of thing. Before long anyone equipped with a college degree and a typewriter may feel able to join the fray.

Meanwhile here are these new biographies: all based on wide reading, all addressed to the general public, though remarkably dissimilar in scope and level of comprehension.[1] Robert Payne's *The Life and Death of Lenin* is the easiest to read. It is also the easiest to forget. The particular genre to which it belongs may be said to have been established by the various nonprofessional biographers of Napoleon: notably those among them who insisted that his death on Saint Helena was due not to cancer, nor the climate, but to the machinations of the British, or to poison administered by someone in his entourage. Mr. Payne, a firm adherent to the conspiracy theory of politics, asserts that Lenin was

The New York Review of Books, June 11, 1964.

1. Robert Payne, *The Life and Death of Lenin* (New York and London, 1964); Stefan T. Possony, *Lenin: The Compulsive Revolutionary* (Chicago, 1964); Angelica Balabanoff, *Impressions of Lenin* (Ann Arbor, Mich., 1964); Louis Fischer, *The Life of Lenin* (New York, 1964; London, 1965).

poisoned by Stalin. Perhaps he was. Trotsky thought Stalin might have had a hand in the matter, and it would certainly have been consistent with the rest of his career if in January 1924 he had manipulated the situation around the dying man to his own advantage. But the fact remains that Lenin had suffered repeated strokes, or brain hemorrhages, in the last two years of his life, and during those final months was a very sick man indeed: his last attempt to dictate a letter occurred in March 1923, ten months before his death. So, even if Mr. Payne is right, it does not amount to much.

Apart from this bit of sensationalism, which should help to promote the sale, Mr. Payne's work is standard amateur biography. Being the work of a literary man, it is consistently readable; it is also consistently superficial and cliché-ridden. Lenin, one learns, was a great destroyer in the tradition of the terrorists portrayed in *The Possessed:* indeed the authentic embodiment of the "professional revolutionary" foreshadowed by the sinister Nechaev—Bakunin's luckless emissary to the student youth. The grain of sense in this notion is relentlessly expanded into a forest, and in the end the reader is left with the firm impression that Vladimir Ilyich Ulyanov was a character straight out of Dostoevsky. But of how many others, notably among the Narodniks, might this not have been said? And why did they all fail where Lenin succeeded? It is easy to see why the Mensheviks failed: Russia was no place for Westernizing Social Democrats. Besides, most of their leaders were Jewish intellectuals who shrank from violence. But the major radical party, the Social Revolutionaries? They were an authentically Russian movement, with roots in village life; there were plenty of terrorists among them (Savinkov alone would repay study), and their ideology appealed both to the masses and to the intelligentsia. In fact if they had won (they nearly did) Mr. Payne would have had an easy time proving to his readers' satisfaction that Marxism was unsuited to Russia.

It is perhaps unfair to raise such questions, since they properly belong to the province of historians. But this is just the trouble: books about Lenin ought to be written by historians, not by amateurs with a smattering of Russian. However, there is a public demand for fictionalized biography, and Mr. Payne's friends need not worry—his work is clearly destined to become a best seller. In a later edition he should try to find another title for the chapter on the "sealed train" in which the Bolshevik leader is supposed to have crossed Germany in 1917. There was no sealed train. It was just an ordinary train, no different from any other.

Professor Stefan Possony, who directs a course in political studies at the Hoover Institution attached to Stanford University, does not believe in the sealed train: at least not in the text of *Lenin: The Compulsive Revolutionary*, although he has forgotten to amend the relevant chapter heading. He does believe—let it be said, on good evidence—that in 1917 Lenin accepted money from the Germans. This is now denied by few serious historians, for the German archives have become available and there seems to be little doubt about it. What one makes of the political significance is another matter. Professor Possony makes a great deal of it, while keeping silent on the Western funds which went to the democratic parties. These parties, after the fall of tsarism in February–March 1917, consistently championed war against Germany as part of the general democratic crusade. The Bolsheviks opposed the war. Now did they do this, as Professor Possony hints, because the German government had a secret hold over Lenin, or because they thought (as some Western historians have come to think) that the war was ruinous for Russia? And were their democratic opponents, who went on with the war, merely misguided, or did the Entente governments have a hold over *them*? Professor Possony does not ask these questions, which is a pity, since a lot depends on them.

The whole business of taking money from foreign governments in wartime is wrapped up with the psychology of revolutionaries. There is evidence that in 1905 Lenin accepted either arms or funds from the Japanese, Japan being then at war with Russia. But then so did other revolutionary groups, including the wing of the Polish Socialists led by Pilsudski, later the national hero of Poland and an archfoe of Bolshevism. Even that staunch Monarchist Gapon may have had a finger in this pie. Professor Possony's indignation is, however, reserved for Lenin. Clearly it is all a matter of whose ox is being gored. It would not be in the least surprising if in 1917 both the Bolsheviks and their opponents had accepted foreign subsidies. Whether such conduct should be called praiseworthy is disputable, but there is clearly something a little unbalanced about the moral indignation usually expended on this theme. In any case it seems unlikely that many of today's political émigrés will share Professor Possony's sentiments on the subject. The age of innocence is past for all of us. Surely it is also past for consultants to American government institutions? Taking money from foreign governments to finance one's revolution (or counterrevolution) has become quite respectable. If all countries now or in the past guilty of such behavior were expelled from the United Nations, how many would be left?

Apart from his search for the sources of Bolshevik affluence, Professor Possony is mainly concerned with the complex story of factional intrigue and political controversy among the Russian revolutionary movements. He approaches the matter from what might be called an organizational standpoint. Unlike Mr. Payne he is fully conversant with the issues, but his chief interest lies on the personal side: it is to the unraveling of conspiratorial politics that his effort is directed. As such his work is clearly of value, even though his political judgments are frequently puzzling, not to say eccentric. So far as Bolshevik finances and organizational skulduggery in the lean years between 1905 and 1917 can be disentangled at this late date, Professor Possony is the man to disentangle them. His documentation is impressive. He is expert at learned footnotes and elaborate cross-references: even the story of Lenin and Inessa Armand (with which by now everyone must be familiar from Bertram Wolfe's researches) is told once more in detail, down to the food they consumed during their meetings in Paris. I got a little tired of all this sleuthing, but there is no denying that when it comes to tracking a bank account, or spotting a double agent, there is no one to beat Professor Possony.

His analysis of Russian revolutionary politics is another matter. Though competently handled, it betrays a certain impatience with mere ideas, as distinct from facts. Unfortunately ideas are all-important in the early history of a movement, notably in a society such as that of Tsarist Russia. On this topic Professor Possony does not compare favorably with historians such as Professor Venturi of Turin. I recommend Venturi's great history

of Populism to anyone trying to understand that formative movement, which left so profound an imprint on the mentality of later
revolutionaries, including the Bolsheviks. Possony does make a
brief effort to dissect the student milieu at Samara in the early
1890s, but he does not get very far. He has the usual comment on
the execution of Lenin's elder brother in 1887, but he does not
see how important it is to make plain that Bolshevism really
stemmed from the same basic tradition as did the terrorist
Narodnaya Volya, which finally collapsed in the 1880s. The manner in which Russian Marxism emerged during these years from
its Populist chrysalis has been analyzed by Leopold Haimson in
a brief study that is both scholarly and readable.[2] Earlier, the
reader of Bertram Wolfe's well-known work *Three Who Made a
Revolution* [3] had his attention directed to the theme. Professor
Possony is familiar with the facts, but he does not make much
of them, so busy is he explaining what a disagreeable person
Lenin was.

All this is a pity. One cannot understand Bolshevism unless one
realizes that Lenin's lifelong attachment to Chernyshevsky—the
father of Russian Socialism—is one of the keys to the riddle. One
can see, of course, why this theme is unwelcome to Communists
and anti-Communists alike. For if it is conceded that the founder
of Bolshevism was in the Populist tradition, it is impossible to
avoid the conclusion that the party he founded, for all its Marxist
doctrines, had Russian national roots. This is an admission all
concerned find hard to make. But it has to be made if the subsequent story is to be properly understood.

Angelica Balabanoff, born in the Ukraine in 1878, knew Lenin
intimately for years before the Revolution, and afterward for a
while functioned as secretary to the Communist International,
until its underhand methods got on her nerves. Her memoirs,
Impressions of Lenin, are of interest not only for their lively
sketches of Lenin, Trotsky, Zinoviev, and other personalities of
the heroic period but because they show so clearly what it was
that divided West European Socialists—even the most radical

2. *The Russian Marxists and the Origins of Bolshevism* (Cambridge,
Mass., 1955; London, 1956).
3. New York, 1948.

among them—from the Bolsheviks. Differences over policy might have been resolved. What could not be resolved was the clash between Socialists accustomed to free debate and the conspiratorial atmosphere of Bolshevism, with its reliance on intrigue, corruption, and character assassination. In the end she broke free and went back to her spiritual home in Italy (to be expelled by Mussolini, whom she had known before 1914, when he was still a Socialist).

Though a bit disjointed, her memoirs present an animated portrait of Lenin and a lively account of Moscow in the first few years after the Revolution. One gets a glimpse of Trotsky deploring the crudity of his Bolshevik colleagues and at the same time being subtly corrupted by power. There are excellent pen portraits of minor Comintern personalities. But the little book is dominated by Lenin, and the reader is made to feel that, after all these years, Angelica Balabanoff is still puzzled by her old comrade. What made him so different from the others? Why was he at once so selfless and so ruthless? One fact she brings out very clearly is that Lenin could never have worked with authentic labor leaders in the way European Socialists in the tradition of Marx and Engels did. He could work *through* them, but not *with* them. But then he was not a democrat, and "the Party" to him was something very different from an organization based on free discussion and voting.

Louis Fischer, whose weighty *Life of Lenin* crowns a lifetime of literary achievement largely concerned with the Russian Revolution, is better on the subject of early Bolshevism than Professor Possony, and he has of course a great deal more source material at his disposal than did Mr. Wolfe in 1948. His book is the most substantial of all these biographies. In some ways it is almost too substantial: over seven hundred pages is rather a lot, even for Lenin. Also the author is not always in full control of his material: several lengthy sections—including an account of Chicherin's handling of foreign affairs during the early years of the new regime—seen to have been included for no better reason than that Mr. Fischer happened to be acquainted with the dramatis personae. There are altogether too many of these biographical excursions. Thus the reader once more is told at length about those loquacious secret agents Bruce Lockhart, Jacques Sadoul, and Raymond Robins—especially the latter. The romantic appeal of these cloak-and-dagger stories palls somewhat after the lapse of almost half a century, even though it is useful to be reminded (on George Kennan's authority) that in 1917 Colonel William B. Thompson—officially head of the American Red Cross mission to Russia—drew on his personal account with J. P. Morgan to the extent of one million dollars, for the benefit of those anti-Bolshevik and prowar Social Revolutionaries who supported the Kerensky government. Clearly the Bolsheviks were not alone in regarding foreign money as morally neutral. But there is altogether too much about Robins, Lansing, Wilson, and the Fourteen Points. None of this—as Mr. Kennan has made clear in his authoritative study *Russia Leaves the War* [4]—was of the slightest consequence.

A more serious criticism of Mr. Fischer's work is that it is neither determinedly popular nor genuinely intended for a serious student. It seems to have been written with the intention of popularizing the results of scholarship (including Mr. Fischer's own study of Soviet diplomacy). The upshot is something like William Shirer's bloated history of the Third Reich: a heavy tome which manages to look formidable without disclosing anything not previously known. Of course we can always do with *haute vulgarisation,* but for that Mr. Fischer's style is not quite easy enough. Writing for middlebrows, who need to have the basic facts explained in popular language, imposes severe limitations upon the most expert of writers. One never quite knows whom Mr. Fischer is addressing. On the whole he seems to be aiming at the kind of reader for whom a story has to be broken up into short, disjointed paragraphs if he is not to get discouraged; but in the later part of his work the historian briefly takes over from the popularizer, and the reader is treated to a detailed discussion of the New Economic Policy and the so-called trade-union controversy of 1921–22: these soberly written and documented chapters certainly add to the weight of the work (in every sense) and show that the author has a grasp of the issues and the internal political stresses. The only trouble is that they are not properly integrated into the remainder of the story, and

4. Princeton and London, 1956.

by the time Mr. Fischer gets onto the subject of Lenin's illness he is once more wallowing in purple prose and reminding the reader of his own presence (as a reporter) at the last Comintern congress addressed by Lenin. All this is a pity. Here was Mr. Fischer's opportunity to write a major historical study, and instead he prefers to dwell at length on the scenes of his youthful journalistic triumphs.

For information about the inner history of Bolshevism the reader has to turn to the earlier chapters. The comparison here perhaps is with Mr. Deutscher's biography of Trotsky. Mr. Fischer's account of Lenin's personal and political struggles is less detailed, but it is well documented and at the same time succeeds in holding the reader's attention. It is a tribute to Mr. Fischer's skill in this domain that he manages to be lively without being sensational, and factual without being dull. He is at heart rather fond of his subject, which always helps in a biographer. Others may treat Lenin as a kind of Mohammed who destroyed a Christian civilization: Mr. Fischer sorrows over him and gives due credit to his good intentions, though he regrets his descent into dictatorship and terrorism, which paved the way for Stalin. A circumstance he fails to bring out is that Lenin owed much of his organizational hold to his intellectual capacity, notably as an interpreter of Marxist economic theorizing. This point has escaped those numerous writers who are repelled by his awful style and his philosophical crudities. The fact is that Lenin—unlike the Narodniks, who were always pretty weak in the thinking department—had a first-rate mind, though one has to plod through his bulky works on Russian economics and the agrarian problem to discover this. Most people have not the patience, which is why they are amazed when told that, compared to Lenin, Trotsky, for all his brilliance, was no theorist at all. It is fair to say that Lenin is usually judged by *State and Revolution* —probably the worst thing he ever wrote—and by his pamphlet on *Imperialism,* which is merely a piece of superior journalism. He could do a lot better, and on occasion did, but this is a side of the story that does not appeal to his biographers.

On the issues that divided the Russian Marxists, Mr. Fischer follows the tradition that stresses Lenin's centralized organizational model, with heavy emphasis on his psychological urge for tight control over his allies. This is all very well, but the crux of the matter is that Lenin fused Marxism with Narodism, and this fusion was not just a psychological affair: it involved genuine political and theoretical issues. For Lenin (as he put it on one occasion) the agrarian question was "the national question of . . . development" in Russia. This formulation already anticipated the upheavals of our own age. It pointed toward that confluence of national and social movements which has become the hallmark of revolution in backward countries influenced by Communism. The Mensheviks, with their attention riveted on what Lenin called "the German model," never grasped the point. They realized, though, that Lenin was somehow more "Russian" than they were, and indeed frequently complained about his tendency to translate European Marxism into a peculiarly Russian idiom. Trotsky (before the Revolution) went a step further: in 1911 he casually observed that the whole dispute between Bolsheviks and Mensheviks was "a struggle for influence over the politically immature proletariat"—a struggle conducted by the "Marxist intelligentsia." This really went home, and the diatribe Lenin composed in reply contained some of his bitterest invectives on the subject of Martov's and Trotsky's inability to understand the nature of the coming revolution. Trotsky later repented, but it is plain that Lenin never quite forgave him; neither did the true Leninists.

Of all this the reader will not find much in the books discussed here, which is why it should be stressed that Leninism was more than one man's intervention in Russian history. If Communism is still going strong in backward countries, the reason is that Lenin brought off something like a nuclear explosion in politics. The thunders we hear around us today are the echoes of what at one time seemed to be no more than a modest laboratory experiment conducted by a handful of quarreling emigrants. The key figure in the story was a man who fused Marxist theory with the practice of an authentically Russian revolutionary movement. Therein lies his enduring importance.

From the Finland Station

❊❊❊

LET US TRY a mental experiment. Suppose Lenin had not got to Petrograd in 1917, had arrived too late, or had been jailed by the Provisional Government. Would there have been a Bolshevik seizure of power? It seems most unlikely. Lenin himself in October (old style) insisted that it was now or never: the fleeting chance might not return; the government would somehow extricate itself from the war, satisfy some of the peasants, and disarm the workers; then the opportunity would be gone. Lenin's opponents agreed: this was indeed what they were working for. Most of his colleagues were against an armed rising and followed him with the greatest reluctance. No other leader had either the ability or the will to act in his manner. Trotsky indeed was willing, but he lacked an organization. The others were for a coalition with the Mensheviks and the Populists. None dreamed of dictatorship. In February (March) they had been ready to support liberal democracy and the Provisional Government.

The October Revolution, then, was the work of one man, in the sense that without him it could not, would not, have happened. This was the view of Lenin's opponents at the time. It was the judgment of Trotsky years later. It is reflected in the numberless incidents that crowd the pages of Sukhanov's famous *Diary* (edited by Joel Carmichael some years ago). It appears to be the conclusion to which Mr. Carmichael is brought in his excellent *Short History* now published.[1] Yet it is totally subversive of Leninism as a doctrine. For if the October Revolution depended

The New York Review of Books, December 17, 1964.

1. Joel Carmichael, *A Short History of the Russian Revolution* (New York, 1964).

upon one man, it was fortuitous; and a fortuitous event cannot be in tune with "determined necessity."

Or can it? The Third Reich depended on Hitler, and Hitler ruined Germany; but perhaps it is arguable that Germany's overweening ambition would anyhow have caused trouble sooner or later. But trouble on this scale, leading to national catastrophe, and much else besides? Clearly the element of chance in history can have fateful consequences. Lenin's arrival in Petrograd, in April 1917, fated Russia, in the sense that once he was there and had got control of the Bolshevik Party he was able to exploit a unique opportunity. Whence a historical breakthrough: not just a revolution (there have been many revolutions) but the phenomenon called Communism. For Communism is defined not by anything Marx wrote but by what Lenin did in 1917. Thus the shape of our present world depended on one man.

Or so it seems. In fact, of course, we do not know what would have happened to Russia and the world if Lenin had failed. Yet certain things are tolerably clear. For example, Russia would surely have become a great industrial and military power (it was already a sizable one in 1914). Pretty certainly, too, liberal democracy would have proved a failure in Russia. After all, it failed in Spain twenty years later, and Spain was better prepared. Already in 1917 the battle lines of the future were being drawn. The ruling democrats were beset on their right as well as on their left. Failing the Bolshevik seizure of power, there might—there probably would—have been a brief Anarchist rising, followed by the inevitable military repression and dictatorship. Russia would then have passed under the rule of White generals and landowners. And how long would *that* have lasted? After all, the revolutionary forces were still powerful, and the peasants dissatisfied. Before long a democratic upheaval would have brought the Left to power. But it would not have been a Communist Left —its leaders would have pursued the old Narodnik dream of agrarian socialism. After a while these illusions would have faded (as they are now fading in India), and the Russian bourgeoisie would at last have taken over. And would its leaders have looked and sounded so very different from technocrats like Brezhnev and Kosygin?

Or try another tack. Suppose there had been Fascism—i.e.,

Russian National Socialism. But what was Stalinism if not National Socialism? A Fascist dictatorship would doubtless have crushed the labor movement, dragooned the peasants, set up concentration camps, militarized the country, persecuted national minorities, Jews, and intellectuals. In short, it would have done what Stalin did (though probably less effectively). Would there have been a difference? Industrialization might have been pushed a shade less rapidly, and there would certainly have been no kolkhoz. But heavy industry would surely have been nationalized (much of it was under state control *before* the Revolution), and everything would have been done to turn Russia into a great power. War with Germany would have been more, not less, likely. The annexation of Eastern Europe would have been pursued, as it was under the Tsars. It is true the ideology would have been different: there would have been no Marxism, just plain Russian National Socialism. But it is arguable that this is going to happen anyhow. The Chinese think it has already happened. They may be right.

What I am suggesting, of course, is that in the end Lenin made no difference. Millions of people died, or were killed, for the sake of Communism; but Communism has not been established in the U.S.S.R. What has been established is a great industrial structure (and a somewhat shaky agricultural one). The structure is centrally planned, but then this seems to be an economic necessity, especially in backward countries. If one is so minded, one may call it socialism, though Trotskyists and others insist that the proper term is "state capitalism." (There are objections to this, on Marxist grounds, since "capitalism" without private property and the market hardly makes sense.) Whatever one chooses to call it, the system is such that it can be operated by people who are not Communists and who do not believe in Marx or Lenin. If Russia's rulers turned Fascist tomorrow (Stalin was pretty close to it in 1940, at the time of his alliance with Hitler), they could go on operating the system without changing its essentials. They would indeed have to change the ideology—admittedly not an easy job. On the whole they are better off with Leninism, on condition that they do not take it seriously. For Leninism is not really relevant to Russia any more, and the troubles of the regime really spring from the fact that the political elite has to operate with concepts derived from the traditions of a revolutionary movement which at one stage had genuinely utopian aims in view. The reality of technocratic planning, hierarchical control in industry, and great-power politics abroad undermines the official creed. Yet the creed also serves the regime by providing it with a doctrine, a good conscience, even the semblance of a universal idea. The political elite is *not yet* an ordinary ruling class: sheltering behind slogans it has ceased to believe, despising in private what it professes to hold sacred in public. It will probably get there in the end (and then we shall see the start of true political warfare, perhaps even a two-party system), but for the time being the veil of illusion still holds.

I have wandered some distance from the theme of Mr. Carmichael's admirably compressed work. Yet not, I hope, so far as to lose sight of the two ends of the argument: Lenin's central role in 1917, and the ultimate irrelevance even of Lenin. This last naturally does not appear from Mr. Carmichael's account, since he is concerned with the October coup and what made it possible. Yet the future already cast its shadow in 1917–18: Mr. Carmichael reminds us that, although the Bolsheviks officially introduced workers' control (the workers having anyhow seized the factories), the real agent of economic coordination was the state: in other words, the bureaucracy. Thus the cloven hoof made a very early appearance. True, the Communist leaders at the time still thought of themselves as representatives of the workers and were determined to keep the bureaucracy in its place. But the decisive step had been taken: in the three-cornered struggle between the old capitalist owners, the working class, and the state bureaucracy, the latter had gained the key position. All it needed now was a leader who would identify the state with the party, and himself with both. Then it would become apparent that it was not the workers who had won power.

As with the workers, so with the peasants: they seized the land, won formal ownership of it in 1917, and lost it some years later when Stalin went back on the promises of the October Revolution. Stalin hardly appears in Mr. Carmichael's account (or for that matter in Sukhanov's). Which is as it should be: after all, his role in 1917 was quite secondary. To Sukhanov he seemed no more than a "gray blur"—a remark which cost its author dear at a later stage, when the "gray blur" had come to fill the center of the stage. Among the numerous legends which find no room in Mr. Carmichael's scholarly account (so much more reliable, and so much more readable, than some of the volumes to which we have been lately treated) there is that of Stalin's important role in 1917. But he is perhaps entitled to even more praise for having put Trotsky in his place. For there is a myth which comes close to suggesting that Trotsky might have taken Lenin's place in 1917, had the Bolshevik leader been killed or incapacitated. This is not so, and the reader of Mr. Carmichael's *Short History* will discover the reason. Bolshevism was Lenin's creation from start to finish, and though his colleagues balked at the critical moment, he was able to carry the party machine with him and drive his reluctant associates into what they privately regarded as the crazy gamble of the October rising, a rising predicated on the utopian idea that a worldwide proletarian revolution was only waiting for the signal from Russia. When these phantom armies failed to make an appearance, the Bolsheviks knew in their hearts that they were lost, unless they could turn Russia into an invincible fortress. By 1921 at the latest it was clear that the initial gamble had not come off; but by then it was too late to go back.

Raya Dunayevskaya's lengthy essay *Marxism and Freedom* [2] plays variations on this theme. A former close associate of Trotsky —with whom she broke in 1939 over the Hitler-Stalin pact and other matters—Mrs. Dunayevskaya belongs to the "ultraleft" or libertarian stream of socialist thought. Understandably in the circumstances she treats the Revolution as a tragedy, and Lenin as a genius whose vision ran ahead of its time. Though sentimentally attached to him, and even inclined to overrate his intellectual accomplishments (notably his rather amateurish Hegel commentaries), she has a firm grasp of the essentials so far as the descent from Lenin to Stalin is concerned. Her own utopianism comes out in the chapter devoted to 1921, the NEP, and the failure of the "Workers Opposition." It is true that Lenin in 1921 tried to salvage what was left of party democracy, where Stalin later ruthlessly destroyed it. But to say that the Kronstadt mutiny "compelled sharp measures which are certainly no model for a

2. 2nd ed. (New York, 1964).

workers' state to follow" is to display a rather ingenuous view
of politics. *What* "workers' state"? There never was such a thing.
And conversely, if the Bolshevik regime in 1921 was what she
imagines it to have been, why should it not have suppressed the
rebellion? "The tragedy of the Russian Revolution," in her view,
was that "the masses" were not really drawn into public life in
the way Lenin had envisaged when he wrote *State and Revolution*. But in the absence of democracy, how *could* they have been
so drawn in? Mrs. Dunayevskaya might have learned the reasons of the failure from Rosa Luxemburg, whose general outlook
is somewhat akin to hers. It is not enough to say that "the young
workers' state could not lift itself by its own bootstraps, particularly as it didn't have any boots." When will these utopians
realize that there never was a "workers' state"? Probably never.
If they did they would have to stop being romantic about it.

In the case of Mrs Dunayevskaya and those who think along
similar lines, the matter is complicated by arguments over "state
capitalism." This is now the label fixed by these purists upon all
Communist regimes, including that of Mao Tse-tung. (Oddly,
they combine this approach with naïve adulation of colonial liberation movements.) Stalinism and Maoism are both "state capitalist." Very well, but then why do the Russians and the Chinese
quarrel? Because it is in the nature of the unregenerate to come
to blows? Because they are not *really* Communists? But where
and when shall we see real Communism if it is not embodied in
these self-styled regimes? The answer seems to be: when the
workers and the intellectuals have seized power from the bureaucrats and installed true socialist democracy, on the model of the
Hungarian rebellion in 1956. One would like to see some hint
that, even in this happy event (for which we are all waiting),
the workers will not in fact become a new "ruling class." At most
they will have some of the liberty now denied them. They will
also, one hopes, be able to restrain the planners, with whom the
ultimate control will continue to rest. But more than that? These
neo-Marxists really must get it into their heads that a "workers'
state" is no more possible than a "peasants' state." Even Marx
never went beyond saying that it was the task of the workers to
"liberate the elements of the new society already forming in the

womb of the old." His disciples would do well to ponder this message. It holds no encouragement for utopianism.

Be that as it may. By the time the fiftieth anniversary of the October Revolution comes around, we shall still see the new technocracy installed in the seats of power, disputing border issues with the Chinese, and combining Leninist rhetoric about the class struggle with discreet overtures to whoever sits in the White House. But when, if ever, will these men, who hold power over 220 million Soviet citizens, cut the Gordian knot and proclaim that the goals of the Revolution have been attained? Khrushchev was getting close to it, and this may have been a factor in his political demise. But the problem remains what it was: the new society needs an ideology appropriate to its real (as distinct from its spurious) aims and interests. Lenin left his successors an immense estate, but he also saddled them with the problem of legitimizing themselves in the eyes of their own people and the world. Hitherto they have not solved it. Utopia continues to beckon, and the lesser breeds (most of them colored) are getting obstreperous: they dimly sense that Russia is no longer the revolutionary power it once was—may indeed be on the point of turning conservative. Will the Leninist synthesis of nationalism and socialism hold in the face of this challenge? There have been other revolutions, but none with a universal creed claiming to offer mankind a solution for all its ills. Lenin's heirs are also the prisoners of this claim. To become realists they would have to repudiate it. Perhaps they will. But it is well to remember that nations have committed suicide for less. Spain ruined itself for the sake of the Counter Reformation, Turkey for Islam, Germany for the myth of the Nordic Race. Russia might just conceivably ruin itself for the sake of Communism. One must hope that it will not.

Happy Birthday

❋ ❋ ❋

CAST YOUR MIND BACK half a century, if you can, and try to recapture the mood—a mixture of bewilderment and exaltation—stirred in millions of people all over the world by the news from Petrograd (soon to be called Leningrad) in the late autumn of 1917. Then try to imagine the enthusiasm which the fall of the Bastille in 1789 evoked in an earlier generation of bystanders soon to be appalled by news of the Terror. If you are historically minded, compare the Jacobin record with that of the Bolsheviks. Note the differences: the Jacobins were a club, the Bolsheviks a disciplined and centralized party. Note too the similarities (in outlook and temper, if not in doctrine). Bear in mind that Lenin's predecessors among the Russian radicals of the 1870s were proud to style themselves "Jacobins." Recall that this nomenclature had been rendered plausible by the resemblance which the last of the Romanovs bore to the least fortunate of the Bourbons. The fall of the autocracy in March 1917 (February according to the old Russian calendar) closely paralleled the demise of the *ancien régime* in 1789. But in France it took three years before liberalism and constitutionalism yielded to civil war and dictatorship. In Russia the corresponding historical space was traversed in eight months. Moreover, the Bolsheviks, unlike the Jacobins, retained power (and wrote the history books). There was violence and terror in plenty, and for three dreadful decades the rule of a savage despot; but no restoration.

Or try another approach. Stalin was Lenin's successor, and Lenin prided himself on being a Marxist. But everyone (even in his own party) knew that his Marxism was unorthodox. In the

1920s, when such candor was still barely permitted, a few Soviet historians even possessed the temerity to suggest that Lenin had, as it were, synthesized Marx and Bakunin. Others, especially among the exiled Mensheviks, recalled the links between Lenin's faction and the *Narodovoltsy* of the 1870s and 1880s who preceded Marxism. But then the Marxist did not have an altogether unambiguous record on the issue of dictatorship. Their grand old man, Plekhanov, in 1903 delighted the future Bolsheviks at the famous Second Party Congress by exclaiming "salus revolutionis suprema lex!" Not a very democratic utterance, though perhaps understandable in the circumstances. At any rate Lenin on this occasion was very pleased with Plekhanov and went so far as to call him a "true Jacobin": the highest praise he could think of. In 1917–18 Plekhanov, by now a democrat and even a "social patriot," denounced the Bolshevik seizure of power as madness, and was in turn excommunicated from the newly founded Communist movement.

By then Menshevism had reorganized itself under the leadership of Martov, who until the end of 1920 kept a "loyal opposition" going in Moscow: loyal to the Soviet regime in the civil war, but disloyal from the Bolshevik standpoint, since Martov insisted upon a speedy return to democracy and would have nothing to do with terrorism or the one-party regime. In the end his paper was suppressed and he himself obliged to emigrate. Yet he and Lenin were old and close friends. They had jointly helped to found the illegal Social Democratic movement in 1895, and been arrested and sent to Siberia together. When Lenin lay dying in 1923, his thoughts went back to his old companion, now driven abroad by the Bolshevik regime and slowly succumbing to tuberculosis. "They say that Martov too is dying," he said (according to Krupskaya). Later, already speechless and paralyzed, he would silently point at Martov's writings on his shelves. Meanwhile the Politburo sat for hours debating means of getting money for medical aid through to the mortally stricken Martov in Berlin. ("He won't accept it from you," Ryazanov told Lenin.) This was during the grim winter of 1922–23, when hundreds of thousands in Russia were dying of cold and starvation. Yet when the matter was raised (at Lenin's insistence) in the Politburo, no one objected—not even Stalin.

What held these men together? A common faith? The memory
of past comradeship? The unspoken creed of the radical intelligentsia—that fraternity of chosen spirits which one entered by
way of imprisonment and from which one could exile oneself
only by death or betrayal? But what did "betrayal" *mean* if it did
not signify going over to the obvious enemy, the Tsarist autocracy? After 1917 most of the former Mensheviks were "enemies
of the October Revolution," but how could Martov ever be
thought a "traitor"? (It was different with those right-wing
Mensheviks in Georgia who in 1917 collaborated with Kerensky,
and later with the "Whites" or the Entente.) Martov was a heretic
—and to the end Lenin went on hoping that he would see the
light (after all, Trotsky, another one-time Menshevik, had done
so). But Martov would not oblige, though he stayed on in Moscow all through the civil war, called upon the workers to defend
the Soviet regime against the White armies, and relentlessly expelled any member of his own faction who refused to follow his
line.

Martov was a democrat: he loathed terrorism; he did not
believe the Bolshevik dictatorship was either necessary or legitimate; and he invariably used every opportunity to denounce
Lenin and Trotsky in public, while still urging the workers to
save the remnants of democracy they owed to the revolution. In
June 1918, with the civil war already in full swing, the Bolshevik
majority expelled Martov and his few remaining associates from
the Soviet "parliament": the All-Union Central Executive Committee of Soviets, in theory the highest governing body. A furious
scene followed. In his authoritative and very readable biography
of Martov,[1] Israel Getzler cites a Bolshevik eyewitness:

> Martov, swearing at the "dictators," "Bonapartists," "usurpers," and
> "grabbers," in his sick, tubercular voice, grabbed his coat and tried
> to put it on, but his shaking hands could not get into the sleeves.
> Lenin, white as chalk, stood and looked at Martov. A Left S.R.
> [Social Revolutionaries: then in temporary alliance with the Bolshe-
> viks], pointing his finger at Martov, burst into laughter. Martov
> turned around to him and said: "Young man, you have no reason

1. *Martov: A Political Biography of a Russian Social Democrat* (London
and New York, 1967).

to be happy. Within three months you will follow us." His hands trembling, Martov opened the door and left.

On this occasion at least his prophetic instinct had not deserted him. The Soviet Revolutionaries broke with Lenin a month later (on the issue of armed resistance to the Germans in occupied territory) and for a change employed terrorist tactics against their former Bolshevik allies. Martov would have none of that either. He stood for peace and freedom, and for a civilized sort of democratic socialism. Utopian in the Russia of those days? No doubt, but then whose fault was it that the country had been plunged into civil war? Martov held Lenin responsible. They had been opponents since the fatal split of 1903 which Lenin had forced upon the nascent Social Democratic movement. Now "Bolshevism" (in its origins a purely factional term) assumed a new and sinister significance: Lenin, in Martov's eyes, had become the exponent of a deliberate return to the most primitive aspects of Russia's past system of government:

> War *en permanence* not only feeds Bolshevik terror and the international halo of Bolshevism, but also Bolshevism itself as a monstrous economic system and an equally monstrous system of Asiatic government. Bolshevism is therefore vitally interested that war should be permanent and unconsciously shies away when confronted with the possibility of peace.

That was Martov's considered judgment in 1920, when his former friend and ally Leon Trotsky stood at the head of the Red Army. Since 1903 they had jointly opposed Lenin, until Trotsky went over to him in the summer of 1917. Now Trotsky was co-responsible for the "monstrous system of Asiatic government," but ten years later he himself would be expelled from the party and then driven into exile, there to resume the theme of Martov's furious imprecations against Lenin, the only difference being that in the meantime Lenin's place had been taken by Stalin, for whose savagery no parallel could be found even in the excesses of the Terror during the civil war of 1918–21.

Is there some logic in all this? Prima facie it does not seem surprising that men like Martov and Trotsky should have found it impossible to stay the course. Trotsky was a great deal tougher than Martov (as indeed he proved when he defended the Terror and smashed the Kronstadt rebellion in 1921), but in the end they had something in common: both were Jewish intellectuals, the flower of a generation which had abandoned the ancestral faith, drunk deep from the well of Russian literature, and yet conserved some inherited sensibilities of temper and outlook which caused them to shudder at the barbarities of Stalin.

Mr. Getzler, whose researches into Martov's background are illuminating, makes a good deal of his personal antecedents and his early association with a purely Jewish labor movement in Vilna: the Bund. He also brings out a circumstance usually overlooked by writers unfamiliar with the political landscape of the 1890s: the fact that the Bund, having been founded a few years before the Russian movement (properly so described) got under way, became the training school of a whole generation of early Marxists, most of whom, after the split, chose the Menshevik side.

Martov himself eventually repudiated the idea of a separate Jewish socialist movement; others stuck to it, but continued to cooperate with the Menshevik faction of the Russian party. Does all this mean that the Bolshevik wing was the more "national" of the two? It was certainly closer to the masses of recently uprooted peasants then streaming into the cities. Both Mr. Getzler's biography of Martov and Vera Broido's edition of her mother's autobiography[2] (an abridged Russian version of which was legally printed in Moscow in 1928) make it clear that on the eve of 1914—that is, *before* the outbreak of war—Bolshevism was gaining ground among the workers in Saint Petersburg and Moscow. Indeed it would seem that by 1914 the Mensheviks, representing the "reformist" wing of the Social Democratic movement, were already losing the fight so far as the working masses in the two capital cities and the other industrial centers were concerned. Most of the newly constituted factory proletariat, "romantic, primitive and rebellious," responded favorably to the slogans of the local Bolshevik leadership:

. . . a handful of people literally without names or with names that had an unsavoury ring, a group which belonged rather to the in-

2. Eva L'vovna Broido, *Memoirs of a Revolutionary*, tr. and ed. Vera Broido (London and New York, 1967).

tellectual *Lumpenproletariat* than to the intelligentsia. Having taken the baton into their hands, they turned corporals, carrying the name of one intellectual—Lenin—as their ideological banner. . . . This means that in the Bolshevik section of the proletariat there was a demand for such a baton and for such corporals.

But if this was Martov's judgment in 1914, when Russia was at peace and had just acquired an elected parliament and other quasi-liberal institutions (including a free press), was it really so surprising that he and his colleagues were unable to ride the storm in 1917, when the war-weary cities were hungry, the monarchy had fallen, and ten million peasant-soldiers were clamoring to come home and seize the land from the landlords? Against Martov's complaints about Bolshevik barbarism in 1917, there must be set the verdict of a Western social-democratic author who has never shown the slightest sympathy for the Soviet regime and all its works: "Lenin alone understood the mood of the revolting soldiers and peasants." [3]

The reader in search of a portrayal of the men and women who prepared the ground for the upheaval of 1917 must saturate himself in Mrs. Broido's admirably translated and edited memoirs of her mother, one of the pioneers of that intelligentsia from which the minority faction of Russian Social Democracy was in due course to arise. The failure of Menshevism was the failure of a thin stratum of Europeanized intellectuals (mainly Jews from comfortable "assimilated" families), plus a not much broader layer of Russian workers who were proud of their unions and had acquired the civilized values of European Social Democracy: the famous "labor aristocracy" against which Lenin in 1917 mobilized the masses of the proletariat and the peasantry. There was a fleeting moment in the summer of 1917—before the mountebank Kerensky had plunged the army and the country into disaster by launching a crazy military offensive against Germany—when the democratic parties could have pulled Russia out of the war and satisfied the land hunger of the peasants. Once this opportunity had been missed, the choice lay between Bolshevism and a military dictatorship of the Right. This constellation determined the civil-war years of 1918 to 1921. It also determined Martov's despairing resolve to stay at his post—and

3. W. Klatt, "Fifty Years of Soviet Agriculture," *Survey*, Oct. 1967.

Trotsky's adventurous decision to opt for dictatorship and terrorism. The one man who never doubted or faltered was Lenin.
From start to finish he, and he alone, knew what he wanted and
was ready to pay the price. But then he was the heir of the
Narodnaya Volya and its terrorists as much as he was the disciple
of Plekhanov and the "Emancipation of Labor" group who had
been proud to style themselves Marxists. It was this unique combination which made Bolshevism possible. It has also proved to
be its organic limit.

Not a great deal of light is cast upon this fateful theme by the
late Isaac Deutscher's Cambridge lectures now assembled under
the title *The Unfinished Revolution*.[4] They display the familiar
characteristics of their author: solid learning, an impressive com-
mand of the English language, and an unflagging devotion to the
cult of Lenin. Deutscher's work indeed is proof that one can
swallow Lenin without renouncing the spiritual heritage of Rosa
Luxemburg and Trotsky. This is not really so surprising, for, had
it been otherwise, the Polish Communist party (of which he was
a member until 1932) could not have come into being. The trouble is that if one wants to hold on to this particular tradition, one
has to stay within the conceptual world of Eastern Europe: more
precisely, of Leninist Communism, as it existed until 1936 or
thereabouts. For in those years it was still possible to believe
that the Soviet regime might one day be democratized and
brought back to its primitive origins. These hopes, if not precisely dead, have today acquired a connotation very different
from the one they possessed during the interwar period, when
Jewish intellectuals in Warsaw were busy arguing the respective
merits of Communism, Zionism, or Bundism. There is one country
in the world where a political movement shaped in this image
still has a place: Israel. Paradoxically, considering his dislike of
Zionism and his readiness to echo the conventional Communist
line on the subject, Deutscher had (and still has) a more
numerous following in Israel than in his native Poland, where his
writings are difficult to obtain. For his particular kind of romanticism, a Jewish intelligentsia by itself was not enough: one also

4. *The Unfinished Revolution: Russia, 1917–1967* (London and New
York, 1967).

needed a Jewish proletariat. Once Stalin had liquidated the former, and Hitler the latter, the spiritual world of Isaac Deutscher
had vanished from the map of Eastern Europe. Hence his work,
for all its undoubted literary merits, has become a monument to
a myth.

The myth is that of the revolution which "went wrong." To the
question why it went wrong, his answer is: because there was
no world revolution. Russia remained isolated, and Lenin's successors thus had to make the best of unforeseen circumstances.
Their political and doctrinal conflicts were forced upon them by
the failure of the original movement to spread further west, and
in the end Stalin chose autarchy, with all that it entailed in suffering and horror:

> In the middle 1920's, the fact of Russia's isolation in the world
> struck home with a vengeance, and Stalin and Bukharin came for-
> ward to expound Socialism in One Country. The Bolsheviks had
> to take cognizance of the bitter necessity for Russia to "go it alone"
> for as long as she had to—that was the rational kernel in the new
> doctrine which captivated many good internationalists; and with it
> neither Trotsky nor Zinoviev nor Kamenev had any quarrel.[5]

This places rather too much weight upon the disputes among
Lenin's followers. Their master after all had left them a testament—not the celebrated letter usually mentioned in this context but his final public pronouncement: the essay bearing the
title "Better Fewer, but Better," which appeared in *Pravda* a
few days before the second stroke, which incapacitated him.[6]
In this programmatic piece of writing, Lenin outlined the situation with his customary unflinching logic. On the one hand, the
revolution in the West had been temporarily stalemated. "On
the other hand, precisely as a result of the first imperialist war,
the East has been definitely drawn into the revolutionary movement, has been definitely drawn into the general maelstrom of
the world revolutionary movement." When one took into account
the interimperialist rivalries, the world balance was not unfavorable,

> because in the long run capitalism itself is educating and training
> the vast majority of the population of the globe for the struggle. In

5. Ibid., p. 67.
6. *Collected Works*, XXXIII, 487 ff.

the last analysis, the outcome of the struggle will be determined by the fact that Russia, India, China, etc. account for the overwhelming majority of the population of the globe. . . . In this sense the complete victory of socialism is fully and absolutely assured.

But what was to be done in the meantime? "To ensure our existence until the next military conflict between the counterrevolutionary imperialist West and the revolutionary and nationalist East, between the most civilized countries of the world and the Orientally backward countries—which, however, comprise the majority—this majority must become civilized. We, too, lack enough civilization to enable us to pass straight on to socialism, although we do have the political requisites for it." Follow various practical proposals for making sure that industrialization should get under way. "In this, and in this alone, lies our hope."

Thus Lenin in 1923, on the very last occasion when he was able to communicate his thoughts to the party. The article—one of the most important and influential ever to come from his pen—appeared in *Pravda* on March 4, 1923, exactly thirty years before Stalin's death. During those thirty years, Stalin was carrying out the instructions of his leader and teacher. It really is time, after all the nonsense that has lately been written on this subject, to set the record straight: Stalin was a savage brute and toward the end a half-mad despot. He was also a good Bolshevik—a better one than Trotsky, who never quite got over his understandable longing for a socialist revolution in the West which would restore the universality of the movement (and incidentally make it unnecessary for Russia to raise itself by its own bootstraps). Hence all that desperate scurrying around for a revolution abroad: in Germany, in France, in Spain—in Bulgaria if necessary. Anything to get rid of the awful sense of isolation that gripped the Bolsheviks from the mid-1920s onward. Stalin had the sense to realize that all this frantic stuff was no substitute for a "military-industrial complex" big enough to stand the test of war. As he put it in 1931: "We are fifty or a hundred years behind the advanced countries. We must make good this distance in ten years. Either we do it or they crush us." How right he was! Exactly ten years later, with Hitler's attack in 1941, the test came, and the U.S.S.R. (largely owing to Stalin's own insanities) very nearly failed it.

These reflections are not to be found in Mr. Deutscher's eloquent little tract, but then its author was not a real Bolshevik (any more than his hero, Trotsky, was). Stalin was—with all that it implied. He was prepared to let millions die of starvation and to ship other millions off to labor camps if Plan fulfillment demanded it. In 1931, the very year when he told an assembly of industrial managers they had one decade to get ready, he "collected" and sold abroad five million tons of grain to pay for machine imports. Those five million tons, extracted from a hungry peasantry at the point of the gun, cost the lives of five million people who did not survive the great famine of 1932–33. *That* was what "Socialism in One Country" meant in practice. Necessary? Of course it was, once the Bolsheviks had landed themselves in the sort of mess they were in when Lenin died! Was it worth it? Might it not have been better to let the industrialization of Russia go forward under bourgeois auspices (if the bourgeoisie was capable of it)? The question is meaningless. Once Lenin had taken the plunge in 1917, all the rest followed. The most one can say is that under his leadership the pace in the 1930s would probably have been somewhat less frenzied, and the crowning horror of the great purge in 1936–38 would certainly have been avoided. For the Purge was Stalin's personal contribution, just as the "Final Solution" was Hitler's. In the short, if not in the long run, individuals do make a difference.

Some of these topics, and a large number of others, are analyzed, with great care and scholarly exactitude, in the learned volume put out by the Royal Institute of International Affairs under the title *The Impact of the Russian Revolution 1917–1967.*[7] The contributors cover more ground than can possibly be indicated even in the briefest and most synoptic fashion. It must be sufficient to say that the volume lives up to the expectations aroused by such an assemblage of talent; it should be a godsend to students in search of reliable information about Soviet politics and economics. The same can be said of Julius Braunthal's *History of the International 1864–1914,*[8] the work of a distinguished socialist historian who is himself a veteran of the great age of Austro-Marxism and has been personally acquainted with most

7. London and New York, 1967.
8. London and New York, 1967.

of the leading figures of European Social Democracy over the past half-century. His introductory chapter on the Communist League of 1847 and its antecedents supplies a link between his account of the First and Second Internationals (1864–1914) and the storm that broke over the Socialist movement thereafter; for in it he brings out the underground filiation running from the extreme wing of the French Revolution, via the *Communist Manifesto* of 1848 to the Communism of Lenin's day.

Marx, who in 1848 launched the *Manifesto* upon a far from startled world (the air then was full of revolutionary utterances, though none of them had the sweep of Marx's analysis), lived for another thirty-five years and did most of his real work after he had broken with his old Communist associates. In 1864, while settled comfortably in Hampstead—it is a myth that he always lived in poverty—he sat down and composed the statutes of the First International, an organization so moderate and democratic that the British trade unions for eight years helped to keep it going. What was later called "democratic socialism" received its birth certificate from the author of the *Manifesto* (then at work on *Capital*). Was Marx then an ex-Communist? Had he and Engels by 1864 become Social Democrats? Well, yes and no. They had acquired some faith in the democratic process by way of England (and America). For France and Germany they were less sure that it would work. As to Russia they had no doubt at all: the Russians would have to take up the burden which the French had dropped. This indeed was accepted by all Russian Marxists, including the Mensheviks. Even Martov's writings contain endless references to the French Revolution and its hoped-for and longed-for Russian successor.

But would the coming Russian revolution be a socialist one, or would it limit itself to turning the country into a democracy? This was where the uncertainty began. Even Lenin changed his mind on this crucial issue. As late as 1905 he stood for radical democracy, welcomed the introduction of capitalism ("European, not Asiatic"), and dismissed all talk of a socialist revolution in backward Russia as anarchist nonsense. As late as 1917 his party still clung to this line and, but for his timely arrival in Petrograd, would unquestionably have stuck to it. In that case

Russia in all probability would—after an interval of military rule—have become a democracy in the Western sense of the term. Well, not quite Western perhaps, but near enough. After all, the democratic parties won a huge majority in the only free election Russia has ever had: the one in December 1917. Even though Kerensky had spoiled the chances of democracy in that year, these parties—but for Lenin's fateful intervention—might have got their second wind after the Right had failed. For there would no doubt have been a period of military rule, if only because the Army could not reconcile itself to the threatened advent of democracy. But how long would it have lasted? On balance it seems likely that Russia would in the end have got its "French Revolution" under democratic auspices. The poverty of the peasants would have supplied the necessary driving force. Then Stalinism would not have been the "historical necessity" it did become after Lenin had forclosed all other options.

Be that as it may, the Soviet Union is now the world's second industrial and military power. It has also acquired universal semi-literacy, mass production of shoddy consumer goods, motor cars for the elite, television, and the other appurtenances of the good life. In another ten or fifteen years it may even be ready for the message of behaviorism, or McLuhanism, or some other kind of fashionable foolishness. In all probability these results could have been secured at a less extravagant cost and without an interlude of utopianism finally drowned in the Stalinist blood bath of 1936–38. But that is the way history operates—especially in Russia. Other countries have their own manner of solving, or failing to solve, their problems. For most of them the Bolshevik model is unsuitable. Even Latin America is unlikely to copy it (indeed Castro has virtually said so).

What of the other strand in the socialist tradition—the one that got its theoretical underpinning from the Marx of *Capital* and the First International? The centenary of that highly respectable organization's founding fell in 1964, when—by an agreeable co-incidence—the British Labour Party won an election and Harold Wilson became Prime Minister, thus adding his name to that of a lengthening list of Social Democratic dignitaries in countries such as Holland, Sweden, Denmark, and Norway. Let no one protest that this juxtaposition is unfair. It is undoubtedly striking. From Stalin to Wilson—*du terrible au somnolent*. But if Wilson puts one to sleep, is this not better than being taken out and shot? The British at any rate think so (including, if the truth be told, most members of the British Communist Party).

When all is said and done, the fact remains that Marx *did* lend his authority to the democratic tradition, which is why his grave in Highgate Cemetery is carefully tended by the local council. For Communists, there is the consoling thought that the second congress of the Communist League met in London in November 1847, with Marx in attendance (it was then that he was commissioned to write the *Manifesto*). London can thus lay claim to the rank of a holy city of the faith, and although currently governed by a Conservative municipality, it has manifested its own brand of devotion: a Marx memorial exhibition was opened at the British Museum last September to commemorate the centenary of *Capital,* and at the same time a plaque was solemnly affixed to the house in Dean Street, Soho, where its author lived for seven miserable years from 1849 to 1856. The ceremony was attended by a Conservative municipal councilor (a lady dressed in Tory blue) and was reported at length in all the papers, from the Communist *Morning Star* (circulation 60,000), through *The Times* and the *Guardian,* to the *Daily Mirror* (circulation five million). If this proves nothing else, it shows at least that Marx has become respectable.

Is it frivolous to draw such comparisons? Not if one realizes that Communism in the West is gradually reverting to its Social Democratic origins. The process is furthest advanced, as might be expected, in Scandinavia, where the local Communist parties have now formally renounced the Stalinist inheritance (though not as yet the cult of Lenin). It proceeds a trifle more slowly, but quite steadily, in Britain. It has begun in France and is making rather more rapid headway in Italy. It is still blocked in Spain by the Franco regime, and has recently suffered a setback in Greece. Most remarkable of all, it is under way in Central and Eastern Europe, where the spread of "revisionism" is motivated by the discovery that Bolshevism was, after all, a very Russian affair—not ordained by "historical necessity" but brought about by a unique constellation of circumstances: the fall of tsarism and the failure of the democrats to exploit their opportunity, while a revolutionary leader of ruthless genius and titanic will power—Lenin—dragged his reluctant party into an uprising which but for him would never have taken place. Fifty years later even the Communists are coming to understand the uniqueness of this event, and that is the beginning of wisdom.

The New Elite

❊ ❊ ❊

"We were prepared for a harsh dispute with political dogmatists. What we encountered was a bunch of gangsters." This shattering comment by one of the Czechoslovak leaders on their return from Moscow at the end of August found an echo around the globe while the Soviet tanks were still rolling around Prague. It summed up an experience that has burned itself into the minds of Communists the world over for reasons not immediately perceptible to people who have spent their lives outside the closed universe of Stalinism. The former inhabitants of that demonic realm were sustained, in the midst of indescribable terror and suffering, by a faith which now lies in ruins: the faith that the Russian leadership, whatever its blunders and crimes, was composed of men to whom socialism mattered. The discovery that nothing matters to them save their power and the military security of the U.S.S.R. spells the effective end of Communism as a world movement centered on Moscow. From now on, a Communist is going to be defined as someone who has written the Soviet Union off as a lost cause.

It is easy to say that the "god has failed," experience repeats itself in every generation, and that faith in the Soviet Union has hitherto survived everything: even the Hitler-Stalin pact in 1939, even the Hungarian blood bath in 1956. But on those earlier occasions it was still possible to find excuses (the U.S.S.R. had to protect itself, the counterrevolution had to be crushed). This time there are none. What is more, the leaders of the Soviet state have publicly flaunted their contempt for the opinion of foreign Communist parties, in addition to exhibiting brutality and treach-

The Listener, September 26, 1968.

ery toward their Czechoslovak comrades. It may be said that Stalin would have displayed far greater ruthlessness than Brezhnev & Co. He would have had the entire Czechoslovak leadership shot and might even have deported half the population to Siberia. But this is to miss the point. Stalin perpetrated his abominations in the name of Bolshevism, and he demanded unquestioning loyalty from the Communist International on the grounds that it was the duty of the world proletariat to defend the Workers' State. His successors no longer seem to care whether or not the Communist movement is led from Moscow, or indeed whether it continues to exist at all. What matters to them is control of what Bismarck called the "Bohemian bastion." As long as they have that, they are prepared to let world Communism go hang.

Robert Conquest's exhaustive study of the great purge [1] thus appears at a time when it is peculiarly important to be clear about the significance of Stalinism as a stage in the evolution of Soviet society. He begins by stating that Stalin created a new political order and that the men now in control are in every sense his heirs. Did he also create a new social order? On balance one may suspect that, with or without him, the U.S.S.R. would have become pretty much what it is today, although perhaps minus the total collectivization of agriculture. Mr. Conquest gets around the difficulty by concentrating on the political regime, or as he puts it, "the new state he built on the ruins left in 1938." This is an important topic to which he might perhaps have given more space, at the cost if necessary of eliminating some of the rather convoluted stories told by survivors and defectors about the Byzantine intrigues within the secret-police empire. However, we all have our foibles. Mr. Conquest is clearly fascinated by personal and political machinations such as those surrounding the assassination of Kirov on December 1, 1934: the opening shot (in every sense) of a reign of terror lasting four years. He is not alone in thinking that Stalin masterminded the murder of a potential rival (Khrushchev hinted as much in his "secret speech" of February 1956), and certainly it was the death of Kirov that set the avalanche in motion. It seems probable, though, that if the operation had miscarried (it almost did), Stalin would have

1. *The Great Terror: Stalin's Purge of the Thirties* (London and New York, 1968).

found another way of terrorizing the party into complete, un-thinking obedience to his autocratic rule. He had, after all, al-ready obtained effective control of the hard-core terror apparatus, the NKVD, and once he was prepared to give the signal for the great purge, the residual opposition within the Central Com-mittee could be put out of action by the simple expedient of mass arrest and mass liquidation.

Conquest describes and analyzes the events of 1934–38 in de-tail. His documentation is impressive, and it is unlikely that the specialists will find flaws. What he does not quite convey, to at least one reader, is the ease with which Stalin got rid of political opponents such as Bukharin, who by 1935 had become positively suicidal; not to mention Trotsky, who never had a substantial following and moreover was temperamentally unfitted for politi-cal leadership. The real bother came from Politburo members such as Kirov, Kuibyshev, Ordzhonikidze, and Rudzutak, who had backed Stalin all along until he showed signs of wanting to extend the terror to party members (it was of course all right to terrorize everyone else). Such men had to be got rid of, else Stalin could not have smashed the Old Guard and built a new party in his own image. Mr. Conquest is very good on this aspect of the great purge, which is frequently overlooked. He shows in detail how and why the Stalinist faction, which by 1935 had obtained complete control of the party and the state, was rent by Stalin's determination to assert his unquestioned personal despot-ism. But was it only Stalin's maniacal power drive that supplied the motive force? Was there not also an element of political and institutional rivalry between the secret-police empire (with its control over the slave-labor camps) and the rest of the party machine? One gets the impression that the NKVD followed Stalin through blood and mud because he alone among the party leaders was willing and able to impose the kind of arbitrary and unlimited reign of terror in which these former Chekists had come to believe as a permanent principle of rule. These men were the true core of the Stalinist faction, much as under Hitler it was the SS that really ran the state. In both cases the leader sup-plied the necessary charisma, without which they could not have carried on. But it was *their* empire that was being built—on the ruins of the old political movement that had wafted them into power.

There is at least one aspect of this topic that Mr. Conquest seems imperfectly equipped to analyze in depth: the relationship of state and society. Here and there he does have a shot at it, but since for the most part he relies on Alexander Weissberg and Arthur Koestler—in other words on psychological guesswork about Stalin's personality—the outcome is inevitably a botch. When he permits himself a sociological generalization, he promptly goes wrong. "Contrary to all that Marx had thought," he writes, "we shall find in the Soviet Union of the Stalin epoch a situation in which the economic and social forces were not creating the method of rule. On the contrary, the central factor was ideas in the mind of the ruler impelling him to action very often against the natural trend of such forces." But Hobbes and Hegel were already familiar with this kind of situation, and Marx went beyond them toward an insight deeper than theirs. Witness his brief characterization of the Napoleonic regime (in *The Holy Family*):

> Napoleon was the last fight of revolutionary terrorism against the bourgeois society which had likewise been proclaimed by the revolution. . . . Napoleon indeed already understood the nature of the modern state, its dependence upon the unhampered development of bourgeois society. . . . He was no romantic terrorist. But Napoleon still regarded the state as an end in itself, and civil life as its treasurer and its subject which must not be permitted to have a will of its own. He perfected the Terror by substituting permanent war for permanent revolution. . . . If he despotically suppressed the liberalism of bourgeois society—the political idealism of its daily practice—he showed no more concern for its vital material interests, commerce and industry, if they conflicted with his political interests. His contempt for the industrial *hommes d'affaires* was the counterpart of his contempt for the ideologists.

This was written in 1845. Mr. Conquest is rightly critical of the sociologism of so many Russian Marxists (Trotsky was the worst offender in this respect, but Bukharin was not far behind) which blinded them to the autonomy of the political sphere: the state and its leader. It is quite true that they misunderstood the situation. Trotsky in particular was always going on about the Thermidor: an episode he misinterpreted, never having made a profound study of the French Revolution (or of anything else for that matter). But Mr. Conquest dismisses rather too lightly these "interesting parallels," as he calls them. "Stalin's regime—indeed Lenin's regime—had its own laws of development and potentialities," he writes. Very true, but revolutionary dictatorships do resemble each other at least in this respect: at an early stage the concentrated power of the regime becomes an effective agent in stabilizing a new social order build upon inequality and exploitation. At a later stage the state comes into conflict with the new society whose first spontaneous manifestations it had despotically suppressed in the interest of "order." To that extent the parallel between Bonapartism and Stalinism is more than a literary conceit: it can still tell us something about the probable evolution of the society that after fifty years has now emerged from the crucible of the Revolution.

MARX AND BEYOND

Soviet Marxism: From Theory to Ideology

✴ ✴ ✴ ·

CRITICISM PROCEEDS by way of defining its object and rendering explicit those "internal contradictions" which not only Hegel regarded as being inherent in reality. The critique of Soviet Marxism—viewed as a totality of social relations, and standardized thought about these relations—starts from the recognition that there really is such a thing, i.e., that Soviet reality is to be understood in terms of Leninist-Stalinist doctrine, and vice versa. Such criticism does not, in the manner of a growing army of dilettantes, posit an incomprehensible ideology imposed on an uncomprehending mass of passive human beings; instead it inquires how Soviet society came to assume a shape which turns Marxism from a *theory* of history into the *ideology* of a ruling caste convinced that it has got history under control. From this point onward, the facts to be examined fall into place, and even the weirdest manifestations of official imbecility or hysteria cease to be baffling or mysterious. They fit into the logic of a system equipped with an officially manufactured "false consciousness," a consciousness at odds with observable facts: notably the fact that by its own constantly proclaimed standards the U.S.S.R. is not a socialist society.

A recurrent emphasis upon this tension between appearance and reality is among the merits of Herbert Marcuse's recently published study *Soviet Marxism*.[1] True, the author has been blamed for injecting a certain amount of qualified apologia into

Survey, January–March 1959.
1. *Soviet Marxism: A Critical Analysis* (New York and London, 1958).

his critical analysis of Stalinism. His emphasis upon the theme of coexistence does indeed blend here and there into a discreet advocacy of Soviet views, notably in the political field, where he is clearly an amateur. Fortunately he is much sounder where his own speciality is engaged. It is useful to have it on his authority, as a Marxist in the straight line of descent from Hegel, that

> In the Soviet system, the "general interest" is hypostatised in the state—an entity separate from the individual interests. To the extent that the latter are still unfulfilled and repelled by reality, they strive for ideological expression; and their force is the more explosive to the régime the more the new economic basis is propagandised as insuring the total liberation of man under communism. The fight against ideological transcendence thus becomes a life-and-death struggle for the régime. Within the ideological sphere, the centre of gravity shifts from philosophy to literature and art. The danger zone of *philosophical* transcendence has been brought under control through the absorption of philosophy into the official theory. Metaphysics, traditionally the chief refuge for the still unrealised ideals of human freedom and fulfilment, is declared to be totally superseded by dialectical materialism and by the emergence of a rational society in socialism. Ethical philosophy, transformed into a pragmatic system of rules and standards, has become an integral part of state policy.[2]

The fate of philosophy under such a system can easily be imagined. Before entering upon this subject, let us note the author's view that an implicit commitment to the status quo is the real secret of "socialist realism" (a doctrine to which a notable contribution has been made by George Lukács, current assertions to the contrary notwithstanding). The trouble with this pseudorealism is not its stress on commitment per se, but the fact that (in Mr. Marcuse's words) it "goes beyond the artistic implementation of political norms by accepting the established social reality as the final framework for the artistic content, transcending it neither in style nor in substance." Genuine conflict is ruled out. Yet

> It is precisely the catastrophic element inherent in the conflict between man's essence and his existence that has been the centre toward which art has gravitated since its secession from ritual. The

2. Ibid., pp. 127–28.

artistic images have preserved the determinate negation of the established reality—ultimate freedom. When Soviet aesthetics attacks the notion of the "insurmountable antagonism between essence and existence" as the theoretical principle of "formalism," it thereby attacks the principle of art itself.[3]

It was time this was said by a Marxist, and for the sake of it I for one am prepared to forgive Professor Marcuse some of his less felicitous utterances. The author is equally enlightening (up to a point) on the more technical aspects of Soviet philosophy. Having noted some of the vicissitudes which the dialectic has undergone since it became the instrument of Leninism, he observes:

> While not a single of the basic dialectical concepts has been revised or rejected in Soviet Marxism, the function of the dialectic itself has undergone a significant change: it has been transformed from a mode of critical thought into a universal "world outlook" and universal method with rigidly fixed rules and regulations, and this transformation destroys the dialectic more thoroughly than any revision. The change corresponds to that of Marxism itself from theory to ideology; dialectic is vested with the magical qualities of official thought and communication. As Marxian theory ceases to be the organon of revolutionary consciousness and practice, and enters the superstructure of an established system of domination, the movement of dialectical thought is codified into a philosophical system.[4]

The last sentence establishes Professor Marcuse as the direct inheritor of a tradition inaugurated by the early, pre-Leninist Lukács, and even more so by the German Marxist philosopher Karl Korsch,[5] who (unlike Lukács) went the whole distance in rejecting Leninism (not to mention Stalinism). The awkward part of this argument is that it fails to account for the role which Engels' theories played in the history of the Social Democratic movement. It is all very well for Professor Marcuse to protest against the "Soviet Marxist hypostatisation of dialectic into a scientific world outlook," on the grounds that the division of Marxian theory into dialectical and historical materialism "would

3. Ibid., p. 130.
4. Ibid., p. 137.
5. See the latter's *Marxismus und Philosophie* (Leipzig, 1930), passim.

have been meaningless to Marx, for whom dialectical materialism was synonymous with historical materialism." [6] But after all,
the principal culprit in the matter was Engels, followed at a
brief remove by Karl Kautsky and G. V. Plekhanov, the two leading theorists of Social Democracy during the pre-1914 period.
It was from them that Lenin inherited the notion of a Marxian
Weltanschauung embracing nature and history. It simply will
not do to blame everything on the notorious Russian backwardness in philosophy. What about the backwardness of the labor
movement? Did this movement turn so readily to Engels' interpretation of Marx because it required an integrative ideology to
take the place of lost religious certitudes? And what of Engels
himself, with his marked reliance upon the positivist and sci-
entistic currents of his age? For the existentialist wing of neo-
Marxism, Engels is rapidly becoming the villain of the piece, and
not without cause; but if "dialectical materialism" is to be dis-
carded, it must be done on philosophical grounds and not for
the curious reason that it corresponds to a particular political
situation. Once this is conceded, the case against *diamat* becomes
fairly simple—unless one chooses to assert, with some neo-Thom-
ists, that the "positive" aspects of Leninism can be incorporated
into the traditional Aristotelian-scholastic world view.

Before I turn to this startling assertion, it may be pertinent
to cite the opinion of a writer who shares some of Professor
Marcuse's views on Soviet Marxism but is distinguished by even
greater tolerance for its aims and methods, Rudolf Schlesinger:

> The actual reason for the Marxist, and even the Hegelian, interest
> in dialectics in general (as distinct from a helpful generalisation in
> studying transformations of society) was the quest for a "world-
> outlook," *i.e.*, for a scientific substitute for the religious myths. All
> philosophy has originated from such a quest, whether it was politi-
> cally compromising like the Hegelian . . . or else politically radical
> like the Marxist.[7]

If "all philosophy" has originated from a quest for a nontheological world view, it is difficult to understand why the philosophers have been so slow in coming up with the dialectic. But
the validity of Dr. Schlesinger's assertion is less relevant in our

6. Marcuse, op. cit., pp. 144–45.
7. *Marx: His Time and Ours* (London and New York, 1950), p. 14.

present context than his evident reluctance to abandon diamat
to its neo-Hegelian critics (who have always been numerous but
never politically influential). The truth seems to be that no mass
movement can do without an integrationist ideology. In this
respect the Marxist critics of diamat are somewhat in the position of the modern existentialist theologians: they may have reason, and even Scripture, on their side, but one doubts whether
they are going to make an impact on the hierarchy. Bureaucracies have an infallible instinct for the realities of power and
the emotional requirements of adherents who need more certainty than existentialism can give them. It is the intellectuals
who toy with the concept of absolute freedom; the ordinary
person, not unreasonably, requires a few unchallenged certitudes.

For obvious reasons, none of these problems arises for Professor Gustav Wetter, an Austrian Jesuit and the author of a massive critical history of Soviet philosophy.[8] While fully persuaded
that "in present-day Soviet philosophy there is very little left of
real dialectics, and that it consists rather of a materialistic evo-
lutionism, decked out in dialectical terminology," he sees no
reason to lament this development. If in current Soviet philosophy "the individual categories have again taken on the values
they had in the preidealist scheme of things, which ultimately
goes back to Aristotle," and if in consequence "Soviet philosophy
has come to share a common pattern of concepts with the
Aristotelian and scholastic tradition," that clearly is all to the
good. Not that Professor Wetter rates the chances of ideological
coexistence very high. In the concluding chapter, stress is laid
on "the nature of Communism as a perversion of Christianity and
a counter-church" whose antireligious prepossessions constitute
an unbridgeable obstacle to contact or cooperation. Or again,
"That of all the historical forms of Christianity it should prove
to be Catholicism which exhibits the largest number of formal
similarities with Bolshevism, albeit with the signs reversed, is
perhaps an indication that, on the other side, the opposition between Bolshevism and the Catholic Church is also the most radi-

---

8. Gustav A. Wetter, *Dialectical Materialism: A Historical and Systematic
Survey of Philosophy in the Soviet Union* (London and New York, 1958).

cal of all." [9] But these reflections relate to the phenomenology of
Russian Communism rather than to the theoretical structure of
Soviet Marxism. It is the latter with which the author is profes-
sionally concerned, and here the verdict is in some respects remarkably favorable.

> One of the most surprising things that our exposition of the Soviet
> philosophical system has revealed to us is the existence of a very
> wide-ranging correspondence between certain fundamental cate-
> gories of thought and lines of inquiry in Soviet philosophy on the
> one hand, and those of Scholasticism or even Thomism, on the
> other. We think it no exaggeration to maintain that dialectical ma-
> terialism, in its present-day official Soviet form, bears a far greater
> resemblance to the *forma mentis* of Scholasticism than to that of
> Hegelian dialectics, notwithstanding the presence of certain Hege-
> lian concepts and expressions which are still adhered to, though
> robbed by the "materialist inversion" of their idealistic meaning,
> and accorded an interpretation which is simply that appropriate to
> ordinary commonsense. Indeed, the curse put upon the dialectic by
> its transference to the realm of Nature, like the special meanings
> attached to the Stalinist categories of "possibility" and "actuality,"
> is directly responsible for the fact that in contemporary Soviet
> dialectical materialism we find ourselves dealing with a mode of
> thought that is internally far more akin to the Aristotelian and
> Scholastic doctrines of act and potency than to the true Hegelian
> dialectic.[10]

The clue to this remarkable passage—doubly remarkable in a
lecturer at the Papal Oriental Institute in Rome—lies in the author's undisguised hostility to Hegel and, indeed, to the entire
German Idealist tradition, of which Marxism, in one of its aspects, is the heir. Wetter is at one with his fellow Thomists in
regarding Hegel's philosophy as a dangerous spiritualist fallacy,
and this is why in his eyes "the curse put upon the dialectic by
its transference to the realm of Nature" is really a blessing in
disguise: philosophically it may be nonsense, since a dialectic
embedded in nature is an absurdity, but this is all the more
reason to welcome the trend. What matters is that Soviet philosophy should retain the "realist" theory of knowledge to which Lenin
wrongly gave the label "materialism"; once this is assured, the

9. Ibid., pp. xi, 560.
10. Ibid., pp. 556–57.

Soviet theorists will be driven by the logic of their system toward fuller acceptance of the Aristotelian categories implicit in their epistemology.

It is true that this still leaves untouched the crucial difficulty of Soviet atheism—the real reason, in Wetter's opinion, why Lenin insisted on describing his theory of knowledge as "materialist" instead of contenting himself with the harmless (and philosophically accurate) term "realist." Here no understanding is possible. But meanwhile something is gained by establishing those "formal resemblances" between Leninism and Thomism which are inherent in their joint repudiation of the idealist (in the Kantian-Hegelian sense of the term) approach, and it is precisely to this aim that a large part of Wetter's enormously learned and systematic analysis of Soviet philosophy is explicitly addressed.

This interpretation has not remained unchallenged. Wetter himself is obliged to qualify it, inasmuch as he notes Lenin's enthusiasm for Hegel's dialectic, and the tradition, reaching back to the early nineteenth century, of a pre-Marxist cult of Hegel among Russian intellectuals.[11] Nonetheless his carefully balanced account of the present situation in Soviet philosophy leaves the impression that he is hopeful of a gradual extrusion of the dialectic from the official system. Since this evaluation is backed by a quite extraordinary display of erudition and what looks like comprehensive knowledge of intellectual developments in all fields of Soviet science, it cannot be lightly dismissed. Given the inherent absurdity of diamat as presently taught, it is at least conceivable that the future belongs to a synthesis in which the dialectic (i.e., history) has been finally swallowed up by materialism (i.e., nature).

One may indeed conjecture that most Soviet scientists would welcome such a change. By contrast, it seems improbable that the party authorities will freely consent to a philosophical revolution which would signal their own abdication. The present arrangement, with all its intellectual absurdities, suits them, inas-

11. Ibid., p. 553, where Wetter, likewise notes "a surprising resemblance" between the Leninist concept of *partiinost* and the "basic idea of Slavophile thought, the doctrine of 'total knowledge.'" For the Slavophiles too, cognition was not simply a theoretical affair: it had an existential significance.

much as it validates their authority as the spokesmen of doctrine and therefore the ultimate controllers over all spheres of thought. This control would certainly be endangered if Soviet philosophy came to be taught in an unambiguous form requiring no interpretation by the party authorities. The latter are currently the guardians of an orthodoxy that lays down the lines of future advance, which is why it is possible for them to censor new scientific developments in the name of philosophy while denouncing modern philosophy in the name of science. The resulting ambiguity has its roots in the "dialectical materialism" constructed by Engels,[12] but the determination to employ diamat in the fashion just described springs from nontheoretical considerations. If Soviet Marxism is to maintain its controlling function it cannot renounce the claim to represent a systematic world view superior to that of positive science. As a Thomist, Wetter is well placed to understand why this is so, and indeed he regards the antipositivist attitude of Soviet Marxism, i.e., its commitment to an overarching philosophy, as a sign of spiritual health.[13] It is possible to feel, however, that he overrates the prospects of a Soviet ontology from which the dialectic has been expelled in favor of an all-inclusive realism (in the Aristotelian sense of the term). At any rate the Communist Party would have to become considerably more conservative—though perhaps not quite as conservative as Wetter's own Church—before it gave its sanction to such an innovation; conversely, Soviet society in general would have to become a good deal more liberal, i.e., nontotalitarian, for the

12. The term itself goes back to Plekhanov. It is significant that the "father of Russian Marxism" was the first to systematize that part of the Marxian inheritance which could be turned into a materialist *Weltanschauung*.

13. "In this conception of philosophy, the Soviet philosophers make a definite break with that anti-philosophical attitude which is here and there encountered in Engels" (Wetter, op. cit., pp. 251 ff). "Whereas Engels, having driven philosophy out of Nature and history, had sought to restrict it to the realm of pure thought, 'logic and dialectics,' Soviet philosophy interprets the dialectic in the sense elsewhere conceded to it by Engels, namely as a 'science of the general laws of motion and development of Nature, human society and thought.' The result has been that in this way Nature and history have again been smuggled back into the jurisdiction of philosophy from which Engels wished to exclude them" (ibid., p. 255). Wetter leaves no doubt that he regards this trend toward an all-embracing ontology as one of the most hopeful developments in Soviet thinking.

positive sciences to emancipate themselves from *any* kind of officially controlled philosophy. In principle, of course, both developments are possible, but the former is perhaps somewhat less improbable.

It is not untypical that the whole discussion reached the Anglo-American world with a lag of between five and ten years. In Germany, France, and Italy it has been going on continuously since at least 1948 (incidentally the date of Wetter's Italian-language study on the subject. *Il materialismo dialettico Soviet-ico*). In some respects indeed the current argument represents a revival of an earlier ferment, which was provoked in part by the publication of some of Marx's pre-1848 writings, in the late 1920s and early 1930s. The postwar period has, however, introduced a distinctive new feature, in that neo-Marxism and neo-Hegelianism have formed an uneasy alliance with existentialism. For obvious reasons this tendency has been most marked in France, but Germany and Italy have not remained unaffected. The importance of Antonio Gramsci to Italian Marxists (not only Communists) clearly owes something to this trend. In Germany the chief beneficiaries so far, curiously enough, have been the theologians: the *Marxismusstudien* published under the auspices of a study group set up by the Evangelical Church in West Germany contain some of the most incisive and scholarly work hitherto done on the subject, so that it is no exaggeration to say that German Protestant theologians must now be among the leading Marxologists in Europe.

In Britain and, so far as can be judged from a distance, in the United States, the discussion still follows the lines laid down in the 1930s. The difference is perhaps best summarized by saying that in the English-speaking world, both defenders and critics of Marxism are concerned to eliminate the Hegelian element, while in continental Europe neo-Marxism has become almost identical with neo-Hegelianism. Here the later positivist accretions—largely blamed on Engels—are now seen as the chief impediment to the acceptance of Marxism *as a philosophy.* Soviet Marxism is likewise rejected, on the grounds of its obvious incompatibility with the philosophy of Hegel and the young Marx. In all respects, the writers in question—who are particularly numerous and influential in France—clearly stand at the opposite pole from a Thomist like Wetter, for whom the Hegelian dialectic represents the *damnosa hereditas* of the system.

It is not surprising that Wetter's massive study has suffered attacks from these quarters, the sharpest criticism coming from no less a personage than the Professor of Philosophy at the Philosophico-Theological High School in Regensburg, Jakob Hommes,[14] himself a representative of the Heideggerian wing of Existentialism. The fascinating details of this controversy cannot be reported in this space; suffice it to say that Hommes had the misfortune of running counter to the considered views of his Parisian colleague Merleau-Ponty, whose own book appeared almost simultaneously and did much to undermine Hommes' interpretation of Soviet Marxism as a philosophy embodying the essence of Marx's "Promethean-metaphysical idea of freedom." A reader of both works cannot fail to notice that Merleau-Ponty's more realistic assessment of Soviet Marxism as an ideology has something to do with his superior understanding of Communist Party strategy. He has been almost the first qualified critic in France to state bluntly that, however contradictory and even absurd "dialectical materialism" may be as a philosophy, the Communist Party—whether in Russia or in France—cannot do without it, since it translates into philosophical terms the essential muddle in the heads of its adherents. Hence the futility of all attempts—e.g., that of Sartre—to replace it by an existentialist doctrine of "pure choice." In Sartre's version of world history, from which the Hegelian dialectic has been expelled (though for reasons different from those of his Thomist opponents), the future lies open, and—so far from being "necessary"—is brought into being by the creative act of men who freely determine their own activity and the shape of things to come. Whatever the strictly philosophical merits of this doctrine (which somehow sounds Cartesian rather than Marxist), it clearly does nothing to bolster the faith of the average *militant*, who, if he cannot believe that history is working for him, is liable to lose heart. That Sartre should in all seriousness have tried to press this philosophy on the French Com-

14. See Hommes, *Der Technische Eros* (Freiburg, 1955).

munist Party, as an improvement on Leninism, suggests a certain political innocence for which he has been duly taken to task both by the remaining Stalinist theoreticians in France and by his former friend and colleague Merleau-Ponty.

Although these controversies in France and West Germany occurred for the most part in 1955–56, they are worth recalling for the light they shed on the current situation in Britain and America, where only the dimmest echo of this debate has hitherto penetrated (for the most part in the form of a somewhat scholastic dispute over certain Marxian texts dating back to his early, or Young Hegelian, period). Existentialism has as yet won no real hold over the Anglo-American public; if and when it does, we can expect to hear more about the incompatibility of Soviet Marxism with "genuine" Hegelian Marxism *as a philosophy:* the latter qualification must be stressed because Marxism is more than a philosophy. Indeed it is arguable that to treat it as one is to discount its claim to represent a radical break in history. After all, what was wrong with philosophy, according to Marx, was its contemplative bent: it interpreted the world instead of changing it. Hence to say that Marxism can be regarded as a philosophy is to suggest that it has failed in its attempt to "realize" the values traditionally proclaimed in philosophy, by producing a situation in which the "tension between existence and essence" has disappeared.

Western Marxist Literature 1953–1963

❋❋❋

A BRIEF SURVEY OF LITERATURE on Marxism during the past decade may usefully begin with a side glance at what is sometimes called Marxology. The distinction is not always quite clear-cut, for the discovery of neglected source material may give rise to theoretical reinterpretations. The publication in 1932 of the so-called *Paris Manuscripts* of 1844 is a case in point. It took several decades before translation from German into other languages had familiarized West European and American readers with a hitherto unknown chapter in Marx's intellectual development. A more recent point concerns the publication in 1953 of a one-volume edition of the first draft of *Capital*.[1] This important work has not so far been translated into any other Western language, and only a few specialists have made use of it, notably Professor Karl Wittfogel in his well-known study of Asiatic society.[2] Similarly it is too early to express an opinion about the long-range usefulness of the edition of Marx's and Engels' works now nearing completion in East Germany.[3]

West of what it is now perhaps no longer fashionable to describe as the Iron Curtain, the study of Marxism properly so called may be said to have been institutionalized in at least two important centers: the Amsterdam Internationaal Instituut voor Sociale Geschiedenis and the Istituto Giangiacomo Feltrinelli in Milan. Both have in recent years published original manuscripts, as well as historical and critical studies too numerous to mention.

Survey, January 1964.

1. *Grundrisse der Kritik der politischen Oekonomie 1857–1858* (Berlin, 1953).
2. *Oriental Despotism* (New Haven, 1957).
3. *Karl Marx–Friedrich Engels: Werke* (Berlin, 1959–   ).

Feltrinelli's *Annali* and the Amsterdam *International Review of Social History* are now indispensable to the student of socialist history. Since 1961 their West German pendant, the Archiv für Sozialgeschichte in Hanover, has once more resumed the tradition of German Social Democratic interest in the study of socialist origins in general and Marxism in particular. With the SPD's official dissociation from its own past, this literature has come to wear an academic look, but a certain continuity of thought with the older Social Democratic tradition is maintained in the publications of the Archiv, which for the rest are distinguished by the scholarly tone to be expected from an enterprise of this character.

For a variety of reasons, Germany—to be exact, the Federal Republic—Switzerland, and France are currently the main centers of study devoted to the philosophic side of Marxism. Of these, Germany (with Austria) is making the biggest contribution to the detailed investigation of what is actually going on in Eastern Europe. While Professor G. A. Wetter's work [4] still stands unrivaled as a general introduction to the subject, his colleague Professor J. M. Bochenski has lately placed the German-language public under an obligation by his editorship of a series of studies published under the general title *Sovietica* by the East European Institute of the Catholic University of Freiburg, Switzerland (not to be confused with its nondenominational namesake in West Germany). The resulting confrontation of Leninist ideology with what it is not unfair to describe as Thomist dogmatism lends a special flavor to a debate which would be of interest to philosophers under any circumstances. The works here under review can, however, stand on their own feet and sustain critical reflection quite apart from any theological interest they may have for some readers.

Dr. Bochenski—himself the author of a well-known introduction to dialectical materialism, the first edition of which appeared a decade ago—sets the tone with a summary exposition of the latest authoritative compendium of Soviet philosophy, the *Osnovy Marksistskoi Filosofii*, published in 1958 by the Philosophical Institute of the Soviet Academy of Sciences. His brief analytical exegesis of this massive work sets itself the limited aim of

4. *Dialectical Materialism* (London and New York, 1958).

acquainting the reader with the theoretical skeleton of the Soviet textbook, and achieves its purpose well enough in less than seventy pages of text, rigorously subdivided into numbered sentences or "theses."[5] This quasi-mathematical procedure at least has the advantage of reducing the voluminous literature to the dimensions of a handbook, whose perusal should enable the philosophical layman to discover what the current official line is on such intractable subjects as the nature of causality (No. 6.21—chapter and verse of the Russian original being indicated by decimal points), the relationship of quantity to quality (7.24), or the definition of logic (10.13). If this sounds forbidding, the practical value of such a compilation to the student must nonetheless be considerable. There is also a rather more technical study, Dr. Nikolaus Lobkowicz's critical edition, in the same series, of some recent Soviet writings on questions of formal logic, again a handy volume of some eighty pages, but so densely argued and highly concentrated as to call for considerable mental effort.[6] Here, too, the text is based on translations—in this case of lectures and conference reports published in Moscow, Warsaw, and Prague in 1958–59—and the diligent reader is offered a bonus in the shape of explicit and implicit "contradictions" (in both senses of the term) brought to light by a comparison of the respective contributions made by the Russian, Polish, and Czech participants in the various debates. Not surprisingly, the non-Russian writings are shown to display a level of sophistication considerably superior to the official Soviet contributions (and a cast of mind correspondingly less rigid, and closer to the Western standpoint). Indeed the most notable feature of the 1958 discussion was a marked cleavage between the Russian hosts and their guests from East Europe. The Czech philosopher-physicist Kolman went so far as to criticize an important formulation of the dialectical logic of change in Engels' *Anti-Dühring*—an unprecedented display of independence, though he was careful to buttress his remarks with an orthodox appeal to other classical texts. This procedure may be regarded as typical for those representa-

5. *Die Dogmatischen Grundlagen der Sowjetischen Philosophie* (Dordrecht, Holland, 1959).
6. *Das Widerspruchsprinzip in der Neueren Sowjetischen Philosophie* (Dordrecht, 1960).

tives of East European Marxism (such as Kolman and Schaff) who combine genuine attachment to the Marxist classics with a sophisticated awareness that the world has not stood still since Engels and Lenin tried to harmonize philosophy and science, and who in consequence are anxious to "develop" Soviet Marxism so as to render it more flexible and less sterile. Their somewhat eclectic attitude to modern science clearly has something in common with the corresponding efforts made by Catholic philosophers to renovate Thomist doctrine—which may be the reason why the *Sovietica* editors at Freiburg show a certain tenderness for the evident desire of these Polish and Czech neo-Marxists to bring their Soviet colleagues up to date. Materially, the dispute still hinges on the relative autonomy of formal logic, as distinct from the pseudo-Hegelian "materialist dialectic" sponsored by Lenin. In other words, it concerns the attempt of scientists to evade the close control of the party philosophers; the latter of course have the advantage of combining the guardianship of orthodoxy with close proximity to the seat of political power. In this respect the situation has not altered. The most one can say is that both sides are now working for an accommodation, whereas formerly the party propagandists simply laid down the law and expected the scientists to follow suit.

To cross the Rhine is to re-enter politics. France, like Italy, is a country where Marxism coexists with an intellectually viable Catholicism, as well as with the official liberalism of Western society. All three elements are curiously combined in a recent enterprise of considerable distinction: the Pléiade edition of Marx, edited by Maximilien Rubel, a noted exegete of Central European extraction. With an impressive combination of scholarship and elegance, this edition blandly ranges Marx among the classics of European literature. It also brings together two intellectual traditions hitherto regarded as mutually exclusive, for the preface to Volume I (1963)—containing *inter alia* the whole of the first volume of *Capital*—has been contributed by François Perroux, who may fairly be described as a left-wing Christian Democrat: his employment of the term "socialization" clearly owes something to the 1961 papal encyclical *Mater et Magistra*. The event was duly noted by Jean-Yves Calvez—best known for his massive study *La Pensée de Karl Marx*—in an appreciative review in the daily *Le Monde*. M. Calvez, a critical student of Marx's philosophy, is a prominent Jesuit theologian with a solid knowledge of the German language. M. Rubel for his part can lay claim to being not only an outstanding Marx scholar (and, it should be added, an excellent translator and editor) but an orthodox Marxist, though several light-years removed from what is regarded as orthodoxy in Moscow. *His* Marx is not only the greatest of socialists but an authentic democrat as well, and moreover a philosopher in the central tradition of Western thought since the Renaissance: in his political philosophy indeed a direct descendant of Spinoza. Enshrined in the splendors of the Pléiade edition, these unconventional Social Democratic and Christian Socialist interpretations bring to the surface of French intellectual life a question which has long agitated its depths: what will ultimately become of Marxism in a predominantly Roman Catholic country? Or, to put it differently, how can Catholics with socialist sympathies, such as MM. Calvez and Perroux, employ their recently gained freedom to promote "socialization"? How far indeed can they make use of Marx without falling into heresy?

Perhaps one ought not to expect an unambiguous reply to this delicate question. M. Perroux gets around the difficulty by expressing the hope that it may become possible to work for "une socialisation humaine plénière, c'est-à-dire qui embrasse tous les hommes et soit propice à l'épanouissement de chacun." Meanwhile one notes that he treats the United States and the Soviet Union as polarized, yet parallel, examples of an industrial society wherein the producers are controlled by dominant minorities in actual possession of power—"masters and servants of the machine." These systems have a similar structure, but different aims and are thus rivals for global hegemony. General de Gaulle would doubtless agree; so (from a different viewpoint) might those left-wingers in France whose periodical literature has recently struck a judicious balance between traditional Trotskyist and modish "Chinese" themes: for them too there is no basic difference between Western capitalism and Eastern state-ownership. (Where they depart from the "revisionist" or Christian Socialist analysis is in affirming that the Vatican and the Kremlin

are about to conclude an alliance against the revolutionary proletariat.)

These clearly are political issues not in evidence some years
ago, when virtually every French writer on Marxism introduced
the subject with a lengthy analysis of "human alienation." (In
M. Calvez's work, which inaugurated the fashion, some 560 out
of a total 630 pages were devoted to various aspects of this
theme.) Yet there is a link, for does the alienation of man not
arise from the split of society into a minority of controllers and
a majority of machine-minders? The crucial point here is that
for the modern sociologist this dissociation is inherent not just
in capitalism but in industrial society as such. This is the point
rammed home by M. Perroux, who challenges the Marxists to
show how the power of the technocrats can be overcome. Can the
workers in fact emancipate themselves, if emancipation is taken
to signify the overcoming of those functional (class) differences
which have their roots in the division of labor? The question has
been asked before by liberals such as Raymond Aron, by "New
Left" socialists such as Kostas Axelos, by former Leninists who
are still orthodox Marxists such as Henri Lefebvre. It has now
been given an additional twist by M. Perroux, for whom "the
power of the technicians" negates "the power of the proletariat,"
the "negation of this negation" perhaps taking the form of the
"rise of a new political elite, neither exclusively proletarian nor
exclusively technocratic."

The new element in the French situation since 1945 has been
the assimilation of German philosophy. With Sartre and Merleau-
Ponty, whose "revolutionary humanism" represented the philosophical counterpart of their political fellow-traveling (terminated
in Merleau-Ponty's case some years before his untimely death
in 1961), this was primarily a matter of translating existentialism into political terms. With Jean Hyppolite and Alexandre
Kojève (who stems from an earlier phase), it was a matter
of absorbing the Hegelian tradition. With Raymond Aron and
Georges Gurvitch—whose *Dialectique et Sociologie* performs the
interesting feat of turning positivism into a critical weapon
against both Hegel and Marx—one may say that liberalism and
empiricism have at last recovered some of the intellectual relevance they lost in the 1930s. Among the minor figures, who

strictly speaking represent Marx-scholarship rather than theorizing *about* Marx, one may mention two postwar immigrants from Central Europe: Maximilien Rubel and Lucien Goldmann, the latter a follower of Lukács and the author of, among other things, a collection of essays and polemics (*Recherches dialectiques*) which in some degree revive the tradition of Central European Marxism, both in their lively sense of continuity with the great age of German-Austrian theorizing before 1933 and in their somewhat doctrinaire treatment of literary and metaphysical themes. One consequence of all this passionate involvement is that the French are now familiar with the intellectual background of Marxism and no longer surprised when a scholar like Gurvitch links the critique of Marx to that of Fichte and Hegel. There is indeed something academic about all this learning; but from the confident manner in which it is being handled one gets the impression that the French have now become thoroughly European in their assumptions, and are no longer content to stay at home and rehash their own inherited concepts.

Reason and Revolution

✳ ✳ ✳

THE OWL OF MINERVA starts its flight when the shades of dusk are falling. Hegel's celebrated aphorism has often been invoked to characterize the difference between his own contemplative bent and the activism of his rebellious disciples. Philosophy (it was said) was indeed backward-looking by its very nature. Hegel had been right to emphasize this truth but wrong to suggest that contemplation of the past was the only mode of thought proper to rational comprehension of the world. History, after all, was still going on, and its understanding could not be put off until the time had once more come to sum up the achievements of a bygone epoch. It was possible to theorize about the future as well as about the past. More than that: the future could be shaped by conscious action guided by experience. Hegel had severed theory from practice, thought from action, reason from revolution. The task was to reunite them. "The philosophers have merely interpreted the world in different ways. What matters is to transform it."

Today the Promethean revolt of the Hegelian Left has in its turn become a chapter in the history of that process which Hegel sought to analyze, and which his more radical pupils tried to shape. The world has indeed been transformed, not least by those of Marx's followers who took to heart the eleventh of his *Theses on Feuerbach:* stop interpreting the world and start changing it. But the transformation, although partly conscious and occasionally guided by true insight into the material needs of the human species, has created new and unforeseen problems to which neither classical liberalism nor classical Marxism offers

The New York Review of Books, April 11, 1968.

a solution. Moreover, the ancient fatality has not really been shaken off: what is actually happening (the technological unification of the planet) occurs not under intelligent direction, but blindly, catastrophically, through wars, revolutions, and the turmoil of conflicting passions: national, social, racial. The half-hidden logic of the process has to be inferred from an accumulation of seemingly pointless disasters. Its human agents—not merely individuals but entire nations—are sacrificed to aims they had not consciously willed. The "Cunning of Reason" reasserts itself. Hegel takes his revenge upon the empiricists who consigned his teachings to the dustbin of history. Science is powerless to control the instrumentarium of death it has let loose upon the world. Statecraft sinks to the level of manipulation. Alternatively, it pursues senseless or utopian aims, then stands appalled at the result. None of this would have surprised the thinker for whom world history was a "slaughterhouse."

Nikolaus Lobkowicz has devoted a huge volume [1] (the first part, it appears, of an even larger work) to the study of Marx's Hegelian origins and to the notion of "revolutionary practice" generally. His book would be important for its theme alone. What makes it an intellectual event is the light it sheds (at times a trifle obliquely) upon the radical discontinuity of classical and modern thought. This *History of a Concept from Aristotle to Marx* is also, among other things, a defense of Aristotle *against* Marx (and against Kant, Fichte, and Hegel too). What we have here is a Thomist critique of Marxism—and of German Idealism as well (albeit mainly by implication). Professor Lobkowicz stands in a tradition which is able to look back, across the gulf of nineteen centuries of Church history, to the Greek sources of Christian theology. Specifically, he draws upon the Aristotelian inspiration of Thomism, hence of the major Catholic tradition. For although in the currently fashionable climate of ecumenism he is polite about heretical variants of the faith, the attentive reader is left in no doubt that the great adventure of German Idealism—with its unexpected culmination in Marx—is ultimately traceable to the Reformation. However, the accent falls upon the Luciferian revolt of the Young Hegelians, rather than upon

1. *Theory and Practice: History of a Concept from Aristotle to Marx* (Notre Dame, Ind., 1967).

Hegel's secularized Lutheranism, which even in its speculative guise still trailed transcendental clouds of glory. Lobkowicz sees Kant and Hegel as fellow Christians gone wrong. He even affirms (with good reason) that in reacting against Kant's phenomenalism, which denied the possibility of true insight into supersensible reality, Hegel had executed a half-turn back to Aristotle. The question he poses to himself and to the reader is why this promising approach should in the end have yielded the dragon seed of revolutionary praxis.

The theme is pursued at two levels: the biographical (to which we shall come in a moment) and the logical. To start with the latter, Lobkowicz confronts the awkward circumstance that it was precisely Hegel's all-embracing rationalism which made possible the world-transforming activism of his radical followers. They could do nothing with Kant, for the Kantian distinction between physics and ethics led to the conclusion that moral (and political) decisions could not be reached theoretically: what ought to be cannot be deduced from what is. Hegel did away with this distinction and thereby *opened the road to revolution!* Not that he had the slightest intention of doing anything of the sort: he was an instinctive conservative long before he had become the official apologist of the Prussian State. But his grandiose metaphysical construction had implications of the most world-shaking kind, once its meaning had been grasped. For what was it that he affirmed? Simply that the Kantian *ought* was unnecessary, because the "noumenal" realm, the realm of absolute knowledge, was accessible to Reason after all!

For Kant, "practical" philosophy had been a matter of the individual conscience. Its true ground could not be met anywhere in actual experience and hence took on the character of an "ideal," of something that *ought* to be but *is* not. Hegel demolished this barrier, along with the Kantian thing-in-itself and the cautious agnosticism that flowed from it. Not that Kant lacked self-confidence: his ethics (by implication at least) did away with the idea of a supersensible deity. But the notion that *there is absolutely nothing beyond the reach of human thought* belongs to Hegel. Once this faith had sunk in, it did not take his bolder followers long to conclude that *the material world can be* (and therefore must be) *transformed* so as to turn it into a crea-

tion of the human spirit (itself consubstantial with the divinity).
But how could the link between Reason and Revolution be
forged by men who thought of themselves as interpreters of the
Master? No group of theorists ever detonated a greater explosion
than the Hegelians—the thunder is still rolling around the globe;
by comparison with it, all the noise made by modern technology,
nuclear fission included, is trivial—yet none were less aware of
the practical consequences of what they were doing. Hegel's
mature thought rivaled Aristotle's in its attempt to interpret the
universe as a *mundus intelligibilis,* satisfying both to the minds
and to the hearts of men. What he demanded of his readers (as
Lobkowicz puts it) was "an ascent to the standpoint from which
it becomes obvious that reality is exactly as it ought to be, namely
'rational.'" The real world having thus been transfigured into an
Absolute, how could "theory" turn into "practice"? Lobkowicz
lets the cat out of the bag in a passage which deserves to be
quoted:

> We are using the expression "transfiguration" in order to indicate
> the point at which most of the problems of Hegel's disciples will
> arise: instead of either *predicting* that the world will become per-
> fect through and through, or trying to *transform* the world in order
> to make it perfect, Hegel simply *describes* it as perfect. His dis-
> ciples soon will discover that Hegel overcame the *ought* only at
> the level of speculative thought, leaving reality itself unchanged;
> and the romantic philosophy of *Sollen* will re-emerge, though in a
> quite different form.[2]

The urge to make the real truly rational could be read into
the system because Hegel had affirmed that world history is nothing other than "the gradual emergence and the eventual definite
breakthrough of reason." As if this were not enough, the first
decisive step away from contemplation toward revolution was
taken by a conservative aristocrat, who for good measure was a
Catholic mystic: the Polish nobleman and Hegelian philosopher
August von Cieszkowski.

This is not an altogether new discovery. There is a small literature on Cieszkowski (as the reader of Professor Martin Malia's

2. Ibid., pp. 149–50.

biography of Alexander Herzen can discover for himself in a somewhat different context). Perhaps by way of reaction against the conventional emphasis upon better-known figures, such as Strauss and Feuerbach, Lobkowicz makes a bit too much (it seems to me) of Hegel's Polish pupil. He is, however, quite right in saying that Cieszkowski is rarely mentioned in Anglo-American writing. This is unfortunate, for his *Prolegomena zur Historiosophie* (1838) is an important link between Hegel and Marx (and more particularly between Hegel and Bakunin). There is no evidence that Marx (who in the 1840s was personally acquainted with Cieszkowski and thought him a long-winded bore) ever read the *Prolegomena*. But we know that Moses Hess did, and Hess for three critical years (1842–45) was Marx's teacher. We also know that it was Cieszkowski's book which launched Bakunin on the road to revolutionary anarchism—an outcome that must have appalled the Polish aristocrat. Bakunin was then in Germany studying Hegel's philosophy, and his radical interpretation of Cieszkowski's mystical doctrine that the future can be known was soon to ferment in the heads of Russian students. In far-away Vladimir, the youthful Alexander Herzen— exiled from Moscow for having toyed with the notion of aristocratic conspiracy against the Tsar—read the *Prolegomena* soon after their appearance and drew from them the assurance that mankind's future could be known and shaped.

A faithful Catholic—his *God and the Palingenesis* (1842) was devoted to the defense of orthodox Christianity against its detractors among the left-wing Hegelians—Cieszkowski nonetheless had taken the first halting step from theory to practice, from philosophy as contemplative understanding of the past to philosophy as speculative construction and *practical determination* of the future. For the coming age could be molded (thanks to Hegel) by "posttheoretical practice": that was Cieszkowski's great discovery. Absolute knowledge having been attained, "humanity has become mature enough to make its own determinations perfectly identical with the Divine Plan of Providence." Hegel's universal system was the beginning of the end. "Philosophy has now reached so classical a point that it must transcend itself and yield up the universal empire to another." This "other" could only be "practical, social life." Being and thought "must perish in action, art and philosophy in social life, in order to re-emerge and to unfold in the ultimate form of social existence." For his own part, Cieszkowski remained a philosopher, and a Catholic philosopher at that (even though he toyed with the utopian socialism of Fourier). He had nevertheless set the ava-lanche in motion. Within three years of the *Prolegomena*, the mes-sage of political revolution was sounded by Moses Hess (from whom Marx inherited it) in another important and neglected piece of writing, the *Europäische Triarchie* (1841).

None of this is altogether to Professor Lobkowicz's taste, but he is too good a scholar to obscure the connection between Cieszkowski and Marx. If anything he makes too much of it. For the rest, the Left Hegelians are so unsympathetic to him that he even revives the standard complaint about their overweening self-confidence and the purely destructive character of their writ-ings. As if in the Germany of their day they could have done any-thing but criticize! It is revelatory of his conservative bias that he stays silent on the awkward topic of Lutheranism as a state church, and says as little as possible about Bruno Bauer's influ-ence on Nietzsche. His principal target anyway is Marx, against whom he scores polemical points by the simple expedient of treating him as an errant Hegelian. If he had been no more than that, the world would not have been obliged to take notice of him.

It is, however, the case that Marx can be understood only in relation to Hegel, and it is the great merit of Lobkowicz's work that he emphasizes the central importance of Hegel's philosophy for Marx's thinking. He also brings out the dilemma in which Marx found himself when confronted with the question *why* anyone should proceed from theory to practice. On Hegelian principles (even as reinterpreted by Cieszkowski, Bauer, and Hess) there was no very convincing answer, which is why Marx in the end broke with Bauer and the Left Hegelians generally. Yet he never quite came to terms with an ambiguity in his thinking which had probably been implanted by the early influ-ence of Hegel's great predecessor Fichte. The eleventh of the *Theses on Feuerbach* simply does not make sense on any interpre-tation other than the "idealist" one that "the world" must be "changed" because it is not as it ought to be: which was just what Hegel had stigmatized as nonsense.

As a Thomist, and therefore a believer in the existence of an objective and intelligible moral order, Lobkowicz is well placed to measure the depth of the spiritual crisis into which post-Reformation Germany was plunged after Kant had extruded the last shadowy remnant of the older medieval world picture. He sees clearly enough what is usually concealed from philosophers unfamiliar with intellectual history and groping helplessly among the disembodied categories of Hegelian logic—that Hegel and his successors were wrestling with a set of problems which were ultimately "existential," to employ the fashionable term. He also sees that Hegel's grandiose system, though conceived as an attempt to restore a pre-Kantian sense of the objectivity and universality of truth, was vitiated by the hidden subjectivism of the idealist approach which assumes the ontological primacy of an Absolute called mind or spirit. What he does not quite seem to grasp is that Marx's "materialism" was in its own way a return to a less exalted and more commonsensible view of the world.

It is true that his first volume terminates in 1845, when Marx was still struggling with the unsolved problem of relating German idealist "theory" to French materialist "practice." But even then it was already obvious that the author of the *Holy Family* had at any rate abandoned one cardinal assumption of German Idealism: the unspoken conviction that within the subject-object dialectic the last word must always lie with the thinking subject. The Aristotelian in Lobkowicz might have given Marx more credit for having (at great cost) freed himself from this idealist hypostatization of the mind into the role of creator of its own universe.

Here and there the critical reader of Lobkowicz's work encounters traces of a more conventional kind of misunderstanding, e.g., the suggestion that Marx positively welcomed pauperization as a necessary precondition of revolution, or that he "never made the slightest effort to help the proletariat" since on Hegelian principles he viewed such activities as useless (p. 371). No one familiar with socialist history, and specifically with the history of the First International, could for a moment entertain such a singular misconception, but then Lobkowicz is outside the socialist tradition. He is also insufficiently attentive to the change that came over Marx once he had made his escape from the Hegelian Olympus and established contact with ordinary political reality in France. However, this is an important and immensely learned work which compresses a mountain of erudition into a few hundred pages. As an analysis of the fate which overtook speculative metaphysics on the road from Aquinas to Kant and Hegel, it also possesses the singular merit of being truly original.

Z. A. Jordan has set himself a narrower theme, but within its context he too may be said to have broken new ground. *The Evolution of Dialectical Materialism*[3] can be treated as a companion volume to Gustav A. Wetter's study of Soviet philosophy[4] inasmuch as he too devotes a good deal of space to Lenin (and, rather surprisingly, Stalin). But the emphasis is differently placed. Wetter paid little attention to Hegel and hardly noticed the differences between Marx and Engels. Professor Jordan (already known as the author of an authoritative account of philosophy in Poland) has tackled the subject from the other end, and provided a much-needed historical and critical study of both Marxism and Marxism-Leninism, in their respective philosophical aspects. Anyone who takes the trouble to read him will at any rate have gained a clearer mental picture of how the peculiar construct known as "dialectical materialism" came into being.

That the "historical materialism" of Marx and the "dialectical materialism" of Engels represent different *aspects* of what is conventionally known as "Marxism" would not nowadays be denied even by orthodox Marxist-Leninists. They would simply maintain that Engels systematized the philosophical hints thrown out by Marx. What Marx himself thought of Engels' philosophical writings (so far as he was aware of them) remains uncertain and is in any case a matter for his biographers rather than for historians of philosophy. I should myself be inclined to argue that Professor Jordan overstresses the incompatibilty of Marx's naturalism (an inheritance from the French materialists of the eighteenth century, principally Holbach and Diderot) with the speculative or "metaphysical" materialism of the later Engels. It

3. New York, 1967.
4. *Dialectical Materialism* (London and New York, 1958).

is true that their starting points were different, that Marx was more profoundly affected by French thinking, and that Engels never shook off the abiding influence of German Romantic *Naturphilosophie*. Yet Jordan himself notes that, while Marx modified the Hegelian approach, he did not altogether abandon it. It is indeed difficult to see how he could have done so without falling into positivism—something he never did, albeit at times sorely tempted (though not by Comte, of whom he notoriously held a poor opinion).

In his discussion of "dialectical materialism" as a philosophy of nature, Jordan is on firm ground in treating Engels as the sole originator of this extraordinary successor to Hegel's (and Schelling's) *Naturphilosophie*. He is perhaps a trifle unfair in failing to credit Engels with a quite justifiable desire to get rid of the Hegelian spiritualism. But since Engels' own adoption of an ontological Absolute called "matter" was still within the tradition of *Naturphilosophie* in the Romantic manner, one may agree that "dialectical materialism" (for all that Engels intended nothing of the kind) was fated to become a metaphysical system: a theory of the universe purporting to state a general "law of motion" applicable to natural and historical processes alike.

For reasons having to do with the secularization of religion and the spiritual crisis through which the Russian intelligentsia was then passing, this was just what the Russian Marxists needed to underpin the revolutionary activism they had inherited from their Populist predecessors: Herzen, Bakunin, and Chernyshevsky. Hence the enthusiasm with which Plekhanov and Lenin welcomed Engels' philosophical writings, which to West European Marxists have proved a standing embarrassment. Indeed it was Plekhanov who coined the term "dialectical materialism" and Lenin who imposed the doctrine on his followers and ultimately on the Soviet intelligentsia. (To make matters worse, Lenin read Hegel *after* he had committed himself to "materialism," and then filled some notebooks with jottings about Hegel's logic whose publication in 1929 stupefied the more "materialist" of his own followers.)

These topics, as well as the resulting ideological contortions during the Stalin era, provide the principal theme of Jordan's extremely detailed and searching account of the subject. He is less convincing when he moves from dialectical to historical materialism. Not that he is unsympathetic to the Marxian approach: on the contrary, he has the deepest admiration for Marx. He just wishes he had been less of a Hegelian, and does his best to make him sound like Comte. He even asserts in one place (p. 132) that "for Saint-Simon, Comte and Marx alike, society is the true reality, and the individual the abstraction." This happens not to be so, although it is true that Marx's French followers have always had trouble telling his sociology apart from that of Durkheim (now that structuralism is all the rage in Paris, this particular misconception can also appeal to anthropology for support).

One can see why a distinguished scholar like Jordan, currently settled in England but still writing from within the tradition of pre-1939 radical empiricism in Poland, would like to salvage Marx the historian-sociologist while consigning Engels, Lenin, and the Soviet Marxists to the perdition reserved in Positivist doctrine for Hegel and his progeny. But even Jordan's learning —his erudition is staggering and makes most other writers on the subject look like beginners—cannot quite conceal what must, I suppose, be called a methodological fault in his treatment: he separates Marx the philosopher from Marx the sociologist. One may, if one likes, regret that Marx never quite emancipated himself from Hegel (personally I do not regret it in the least), but if one asserts that he did, one fails to see in what respect he was not an empiricist. In particular, one fails to realize that, even at his most empirical and scientific, Marx did not divorce factual from value judgments in the manner of Weber and his school. Take a remark like the following, which occurs quite casually in the context of a passage about ground rent:

> Even a whole society, a nation, or even all simultaneously existing societies taken together, are not the owners of the globe. They are only its possessors, its usufructuaries, and like *boni patres familias,* they must hand it down to succeeding generations in an improved condition.[5]

The man who wrote these words was a philosopher, and no amount of exegesis is ever going to turn him into anything else.

5. *Capital,* III, 757.

He may have been inconsistent in pulling normative principles out of the hat when it suited him, but that is what he did, just as Montesquieu, Hume, Smith, and Kant had done before him. The value system of the Enlightenment was part of his mental baggage. He carried it about with him, and never dreamed of challenging it. Nor is there any good reason why he should have.

Shlomo Avineri, who teaches at Jerusalem University, has written several learned monographs on Hegel's and Marx's political philosophy. He has now expanded the subject into a book, *The Social and Political Thought of Karl Marx*,[6] which deserves commendation, if only because it is brief, lucid, scholarly, and infused with an undoctrinaire democratic socialism reminiscent of the earlier (and less embattled) Sidney Hook. Some of the territory he covers—e.g., the theory-practice problem, and Cieszkowski's role in anticipating the revolutionary activism of the Left Hegelians—is discussed at greater length by Lobkowicz. Elsewhere he breaks new ground, notably in going back to those of Marx's early writings which antedated his acquaintance with the French socialists and communists. One of these, the *Critique of Hegel's Philosophy of Right* (1842–43), has hitherto escaped attention, and Professor Avineri does well to emphasize its relevance for Marx's later political views. It marked a transition in his thought, in that he then took the first step toward what later became the "materialist conception of history."

This (as Avineri points out) had nothing to do with "materialism" in the metaphysical sense. What it signified was quite simply that Marx—then the editor of a bourgeois-liberal journal in Cologne and in sharp conflict with Prussian censorship—had begun to see through the conservative implications of Hegel's thinking. In particular, he had begun to treat *society* as being logically and historically anterior to the *state*. In other words, he applied to Hegel the critical canon of Anglo-French political and economic theorizing. One may also say that he confronted the philosopher of the Prussian State with the theorists of Western European liberalism. This is an aspect of Marx which seems to have escaped Lobkowicz, perhaps because he has not much use for liberalism and thus fails to realize that in the 1840s Prussia was

6. London and New York, 1968.

already beginning to look somewhat grotesque to anyone in Paris, London, or Amsterdam. Avineri does well to bring it out, just as he is right to emphasize that political democracy remained a problem for Marx and his followers: their brief and qualified defense of the Paris Commune was by no means the end of the matter.

The central section of the book, and its most original contribution to the swelling literature on the subject, analyzes the link between Marx's anthropology and his economics: specifically between the 1844 *Manuscripts* and *Capital*. These chapters provide a useful antidote to the standard view of Marx as a great economist in the Ricardian tradition who unfortunately bewildered his readers with a farfetched Hegelian terminology: the sort of misinterpretation one finds in Schumpeter. There is just enough truth in it to make it important to see where it misses the point, and the reader who looks for light on this topic can now go to Avineri. The link between the critique of classical German philosophy and the critique of liberal British economics may have been a bit tenuous here and there, but it was no figment of anyone's imagination. These topics were related in *fact* before Marx took the trouble to relate them *in logic*. Why and how he did this is the subject of Avineri's best chapters. They should satisfy even those of his readers who cannot quite follow him in all his political conclusions, e.g., in what appears to me to be his underestimation of the Jacobin-Blanquist streak in Marx's early thinking.

There remains a general consideration, which perhaps has more to do with Hegel than with Marx. All three authors here discussed—professional philosophers of widely differing views and standpoints—share the assumption that if we want to understand Marx or Hegel we had best begin by asking how they relate to Aristotle. Lobkowicz and Avineri do this explicitly, Jordan by implication. They are likewise agreed in treating Hegel's "historiosophy" as a form of secularized theology, and Marxism as a reaction to it. Lastly, they make it clear that the tension between the theological inheritance of the Judaeo-Christian world and the rationalism of the Enlightenment had already come to a critical point in Hegel before it exploded in Marx. It is of course Marx rather than Hegel who has provided the driving force for the practical revolutionizing of those areas of the world where other forms of Westernization (those stemming from the American and French Revolution, for example) have for some reason fallen short of their goal. But it is still Hegel's historiosophy which lies at the back of the whole phenomenon, by now about to merge with a worldwide political upheaval.

Thereby hangs, if not a moral, at least a paradox, for Hegel had seen himself as the end of an epoch, and his followers viewed him as the last great thinker in the tradition of Aristotle: that is to say, the last great *European* thinker. They also believed (with what justification need not concern us) that there had never been any philosophy worth mentioning other than that of the Greeks and their successors. In an age when the mental rubbish of Calcutta and Benares flows into the gutters of Europe and America, a thinker who held that no worthwhile idea had ever come out of Asia seems an unlikely candidate for hero-worship in Peking or Hanoi. Yet it is Hegel who reigns in those distant capitals (albeit in the interpretation given to his philosophy by Marx). There is food for thought here—especially at a time when it is fashionable in advanced circles to denigrate the Western inheritance. From Aristotle to Marx, this inheritance is at work when Asians brood over the future of their civilization. It provides the conceptual tools for their critique of the West. It even has the power to set armies on the march. Zen and Yoga may appeal to dropouts in New York, London, and Paris. Those who carry on the fight (whichever side they are engaged on) draw their sustenance from other sources.

Sartre, Marxism, and History

❋❋❋

I

In postwar France the philosophers were resolved not to interpret the world but to change it. For a few years it looked as though the forces let loose at the liberation might transform society and bridge the gap between the intellectual elite and the masses. But history refused to be rewritten, the revolution did not take place, and the philosophers returned to their studies. Sartre is the inheritor of this failure. The formal peculiarities of his work are not accidental. They are imposed upon him by his commitment to a goal which he shares with the Communists but interprets in a spirit incompatible with their rigid doctrine. To understand his position in present-day France one must relate his attempt to forge a new intellectual synthesis to the antecedent loss of his earlier political hopes. It is not the first example of an aborted revolution having produced, as a side effect, a philosophical sanctuary wherein the unrealized aims of men are preserved against the day when thought and action shall once more be made to coincide.

The *Critique de la raison dialectique* is Sartre's most ambitious work to date. Moreover, unlike *L'Etre et le néant,* whose appearance in 1943 inevitably partook of the nature of a clandestine operation, it is among the best-advertised philosophical productions to have seen the light in recent years. In de Gaulle's France, Sartre is very much a public figure—the unofficial philosopher of the non-Communist Left—and his pronouncements are treated with respectful attention by a public not averse in its

History and Theory, III, No. 2 (1963).

own fashion to a modest degree of hero worship. These external circumstances are interiorized (to employ a favorite Sartrean concept) in the structure and tonality of his work, whose goal is nothing less than the completion of Marxist thought: itself deemed by the author to be unsurpassable in the present epoch of history. The first volume of the *Critique*—a massive tome, the principal part of which bears the subtitle *Théorie des ensembles pratiques*—outlines the general scheme. We are promised a successor which will, one may suppose, spell out some of the detailed implications of Sartre's theory of history. But even at the current preparatory stage it is evident that this is to be the fulfillment of a program sketched out more briefly in earlier days, when Sartre was still the exponent of German philosophy on French soil. By its very title the *Critique* reveals both its inspiration and the ambition to pass beyond Kant and his successors. At the same time the original commitment to practice (*engagement*) remains in force. Sartre's magnum opus is no mere investigation of other men's ideas, let alone a sketch for a new and improved academic philosophy. As a thinker he is concerned with changing the world: in this respect at least he remains a Marxist. Yet his Marxism is not that of the Communists, not even that of a former Communist like Henri Lefebvre, whose polite but implacable criticism of Sartre[1] has drawn the line between traditional Marxism and Sartre's own highly individual synthesis of Hegel, Marx, and Heidegger. It is not the least intriguing aspect of this situation that Lefebvre—though pardonably a less original and fertile mind—is quite obviously superior to Sartre in his understanding of Marx. Indeed his criticism, for all its urbanity, has the remorseless tone one associates with painfully acquired professionalism. It is as though a veteran practitioner were patiently explaining to a gifted novice what all these technical terms are about. Yet Sartre can claim to have spent many years in the arduous task of penetrating the mysteries of Hegelian and Marxian dialectics. If he can still be faulted by a writer inferior to him in general ability, the cause must lie in some radical incongruity of his subject matter with the cast of mind he brings to it. In fact, as we shall see, the original tension between Marxism and

1. "Critique de la critique non-critique," *Nouvelle Revue Marxiste*, July 1961.

Existentialism, which lies at the root of Sartre's political and literary activity over the past two decades, has not been resolved, though in his latest work he has made a truly monumental effort to effect a synthesis of these two modes of thought. But before considering the implications of this failure—perhaps the most interesting in contemporary French literature, and certainly the one most pregnant with consequences of a political order—we must take the plunge into Sartre's philosophy as spelled out in his earlier writings, and then inquire how far he has remained true to his original standpoint.[2]

II

To be aware is to be aware of something, and at a second remove to be aware of myself as a reflecting being. I am conscious of an object, and of other objects forming a world, but I am not conscious of my own consciousness, as though I could watch myself from an imagined outside. Yet I know that I exist, and this awareness sets me off from objects which are "simply there." In transcending my contingent existence I remain a being which is incomplete and, because it is incomplete, strives after union with that which is given in thought. This union is unattainable for man, but the urge to attain it determines man's being. Consciousness separates me from that which merely subsists, and propels me toward that which is imagined. This propulsion is freedom, which is not *a* human property but *the* human property, or rather the particular mode of human existence in the world. In consciousness I am aware of myself as a being whose aim is to overcome the contingency of mere existence. But the aim is unattainable, for the mind is eternally separated from that with which it is trying to unite. Having thus chased the dialectic of

2. For details concerning Sartre's "deviations" from Marxian orthodoxy the reader must be referred to Lefebvre's essay. In what follows his critical points are taken for granted. They are valid against Sartre, whether or not one accepts Lefebvre's own standpoint (which is not that of the present writer). Their validity is quite simply due to the fact that Sartre has evolved an all-embracing system of his own whose internal logic is at variance with the Marxism he professes. For a rather more rigidly Leninist criticism of Sartre than that offered by Lefebvre, see Jacques Houbart, *Un Père dénaturé* (Paris, 1964), where Sartre's philosophy is described, unkindly but not inaccurately, as "une idéologie parasitaire" (p. 141).

en-soi, and *pour-soi,* being and consciousness, through seven hundred pages in *L'Etre et le néant,* Sartre concludes that the urge to become *causa sui* is doomed to failure. "L'homme est une passion inutile."

In the *Critique,* Sartre returns to the charge, though this time from a different standpoint. *L'Etre et le néant* was fundamentally a treatise on individual existence, and only at a second remove concerned with human society. The *Critique* is meant to bridge the gap (and to meet the charge that Existentialism is simply a variant of individualism). At the same time Sartre intends to show that his philosophical approach is superior to what he describes as "contemporary Marxism," although "I consider Marxism the ultimate philosophy of our age." Present-day Marxism, in Sartre's view, has shed its philosophical dimension and moreover has become the tool of short-range political purposes. It has thus lost the capacity (if it ever possessed it) to grasp the complex mediations which link the individual to the social whole. These mediations relate back to the dialectic of being and consciousness which Sartre had described in *L'Etre et le néant.* Thus, although he has now become critical of Existentialism and even describes it as a parasite on the major philosophies, Sartre still believes that the analysis of Being he undertook in his earlier work is a step towards his mature synthesis. His theory of society is intended as an advance beyond Marxism. Formally, however, the *Critique* presents itself as an attempt to outline the logic of a Marxist anthropology. The "profound significance of History and of dialectical rationality" is to disclose itself through an analysis of human nature, but of human nature correctly understood, that is, in its concrete historical setting. Such an analysis will both illuminate history and "reconquer man inside Marxism" through a proper understanding of the Marxian notion of praxis.

The manner in which Sartre goes about his task has exposed him to the charge of not really understanding the dialectic, while on the other hand his obsessive concern with the totality of history has laid him open to the damaging suggestion that his thinking has been shaped by recent political experiences. Yet even at the peak of his frenetic fellow-traveling, Sartre was never a theoretical Leninist; and today, when he has recovered his poise, he remains estranged from the conventional rationalism which for over a century has shaped the outlook of the Left in France.

The fact is that all these correlations do not really help one to grasp the peculiarity of Sartre's position in a France which has not undergone a Communist revolution, and consequently has not adopted Marxism as its official philosophy. In a country which in some respects remained both bourgeois and Cartesian, he—at bottom a Cartesian of bourgeois origin—has to struggle hard against the traditional pull which tends to reintegrate every thinker of the "Left" within the confines of traditional bourgeois radicalism. Hence his determination not to be mistaken for just another rationalist. Hence too his emphasis on German thinkers —from Hegel to Heidegger—and his unflagging (and occasionally ludicrous) attempts to impose himself upon the Communists as one who understands their aims better than they do themselves. To the intellectuals, Marxism is a philosophy, and since Sartre treats it as such, he is apparently closer to the "real" Marx than the Party theorists, who are obliged to operate at a level not too remote from the understanding of their followers. At the same time they are in no position to retort that Marxism is not really a philosophy at all, but rather a radical critique of philosophy, since this would mean going back on the whole bizarre systematization undertaken (in France as elsewhere) by the Communists in response to the petrifaction of Marxism in the Soviet Union.[3]

But enough of Sartre's role as the philosopher of a nonexistent revolutionary movement. What is he actually saying that has not been said before by either Marxists or Existentialists? Here one must differentiate between the opening section of the *Critique*,

3. Since the above was written, there has been a change in this respect, a change associated with name of Louis Althusser. Here at last there is a professional philosopher who is also a prominent Party member without being committed to the official eclecticism. For Althusser, a complete Marxist philosophy remains an unfulfilled desideratum. (See his *Pour Marx* [Paris, 1960], passim.) Only the cornerstone of the building has been laid: the structure remains to be erected (ibid., p. 21). For all its apparent modesty, this approach discloses a resolute determination to build a total system. Is it an accident that Althusser (like Antonio Gramsci a generation earlier) operates within a Catholic culture, as the theorist of a movement which for its adherents has become a substitute for the Church? At any rate the effective completion of his project points in the direction of an all-encompassing synthesis. Impressive in its way, there is nonetheless something scholastic about it. One wonders what Marx would have thought of it.

subtitled *Question de méthode,* and the much bulkier part titled *Théorie des ensembles pratiques.* The introductory section— hardly more than a lengthy essay, and published as such origi- nally in *Temps Modernes* in the autumn of 1957—contains both Sartre's critique of traditional Marxism and his reaffirmation of the general position set out in *L'Etre et le néant.* As such it out- lines an aim and indicates the methodological principles to be followed in the main work. The latter—the real *Critique,* for which *Question de méthode* serves merely as an appetizer—is a very different matter indeed. Here Sartre expounds, at tremendous length and with a formidable display of logical ingenuity, his conception of how society operates, once individual pratice has been effectively socialized into group behavior. Here then is the test of the method. Does it in fact contribute something new? In order to simplify matters I shall treat the opening essay as the key to Sartre's performance, and the bulk of the *Critique* as the more or less successful application of his peculiar methodological principle. By way of anticipation it may be observed that the relative dimensions of these two sections are inversely propor- tionate to their real value: most of the genuinely novel and fruit- ful ideas are to be found in the introduction, while the enor- mously inflated second part revolves around the exposition of a few not very startling notions about the socialization of human behavior. This may be an illustration of the familiar rule that criticism is easier than construction, or it may be due to Sartre's greater expertise in philosophy and literature compared with the subjects he tackles in the main work. Whatever the reason, it imparts an extra grimness to the *Critique* and renders its study far from pleasurable. This, however, is unimportant. Hegel's *Phenomenology* was not easy reading either, and Sartre's evi- dent conviction that the time has come for a successor to that seminal work deserves careful consideration. The execution of so ambitious a project would clearly be worth a great effort; the question is whether he has brought it off.

III

The argument of the introductory section (*Question de méth- ode*) is fairly straightforward, though the reasoning behind it is complex. Sartre begins by reasserting the Hegelian principle that History discloses the Truth about Man and his place in the world. This disclosure he describes as Reason: once more a concept derived from Hegel, but a given polemical edge by Sartre's stress on the contrast between his own philosophical anthropology and that of positivism, with its casual acceptance of many truths and many histories. What Sartre calls the "totalizing" character of his enterprise amounts to saying that he aims at the intellectual perception of the world insofar as it can be understood. This understanding is historical (because Reality is Process) and dialectical (because there is interaction between Being and Consciousness). "No one, not even the empiricists, has ever described as Reason the simple arrangement—whatever it may be—of our thoughts. 'Rationalism' requires that this arrangement should reproduce or constitute the order of being. Hence Reason is a certain relationship of consciousness and being." [4] If this relationship is a "twofold movement within consciousness and being," such a *relation mouvante* can legitimately be termed Reason. The question then arises whether the *Raison positiviste des Sciences naturelles* is that which we actually encounter in anthropology or whether a true understanding of man does not imply a different kind of Reason. Sartre's reply to this preliminary question is affirmative: the understanding which permits us to grasp the process of history is the dialectical Reason of Hegel and Marx.

So far we seem to be on familiar ground, but Sartre's invocation of Hegel and his employment of concepts previously elaborated in *L'Etre et le néant* already point in the direction of his subsequent repudiation of "orthodox Marxism," as formulated not by Marx himself but by Engels, Plekhanov, and Lenin. The dialectic of being and consciousness is the common property of Hegel, Marx, and the Existentialists, but it does not fit the categories of "dialectical materialism" as understood since Engels. In consequence Sartre feels obliged to expel Engels from the Marxist pantheon, but while this purge makes his task easier, it also sharpens the contrast between his existentialized Marxism and that of the orthodox and semiorthodox, including Lukács. In fact Sartre has several brushes with Lukács, whom in one place he rebukes, with good reason, for having presented a caricature of

4. *Critique de la raison dialectique*, p. 10.

Existentialism during the early postwar discussion.[5] Behind these disputations lies the fact that Sartre—like the early Lukács of *History and Class Consciousness* (1923), but unlike the later Lukács, for all his much publicized heresies—has no use for the simple-minded epistemological realism of Engels and Lenin. In intellectual terms this is a considerable gain, but it makes it difficult for him to stake out a claim for the Marxist succession. In fact he is obliged to state that "Marxism has come to a stop" (*s'est arrêté*), and this not only for external reasons but because the central truth revealed to the Existentialists was never, after the death of Marx, adequately perceived by his followers. This truth is the absolutely irreducible character of the historical event, taken in its concreteness. Instead of trying to grasp the individual manifold as it presents itself in history, Marx's followers have typically tried to subsume its manifestations under a few general concepts which were invested with a spurious supersensible reality. Thus we now have, on the one hand, the conservative sterility of academic positivism and, on the other, the frozen apparatus of orthodox Marxism. "In the face of this twofold ignorance, Existentialism was able to revive and maintain itself because it reaffirmed the reality of man, as Kierkegaard affirmed his own reality against Hegel." [6] But Existentialism is merely a signpost. The true task of dialectical Reason consists in bringing the whole of history within the compass of understanding, and to this end the Marxian categories are indispensable. Moreover, the Marxian union of theory and practice remains "une évidence indépassable" until there is genuine freedom *for all* beyond the mere production of material life. When this stage has been reached, Marxism will disappear. "A philosophy of liberty will take its place. But we possess no means, no intellectual instrument, no concrete experience, which permits us to conceive either that liberty or that philosophy." [7]

The problem which Marxism, in its contemporary guise, has failed to solve, or even to take seriously, is that of mediation. It

5. Ibid., pp. 24, 34. The reference is to Lukács's polemical work *Existentialisme ou Marxisme* (Paris, 1948; second ed., 1961).
6. Ibid., p. 28.
7. Ibid., p. 32.

treats personalities and events abstractly because it subordinates them to a preconceived schematization. Thus, in studying the history of the French Revolution, the Marxist historians—Sartre makes a point of citing the Trotskyist sympathizer Daniel Guérin, but his criticism applies to French Marxists in general—lose sight of the particularity of events, and even misinterpret their meaning, because they start from fixed premises which have acquired the force of dogma: for example, that the struggle between Girondists and Montagnards represented a class conflict, whereas in actual fact it was an upheaval within a fairly homogeneous stratum of politicians and intellectuals.[8] Most Marxists likewise presume to know what is basic and what is merely accidental, so that for example they dismiss Napoleon's career as a mere episode, though they might have learned from Marx's own analysis of the 1848 revolution and its aftermath, the Bonapartist coup d'état, that history is always the history of *this* particular event and *those* particular actors, whose appearance at *this* particular moment must be understood in all its concreteness.[9]

Plainly, Sartre's criticism of the usual run-of-the-mill Marxist historiography is sound. It is less clear what he proposes to put in its place. The general principle, namely that the sense of an epoch is to be understood through an imaginative grasp of its central events and personalities in all their concreteness, is unobjectionable; but it remains a mere aspiration as long as we are not given some instances of how it is to be done. A related difficulty arises from Sartre's insistence that the imaginative understanding of the single event is the *raison d'être* of Existentialism. This leaves it uncertain whether his own kind of analysis is

8. Ibid., pp 33 ff. Reflections on the French Revolution recur at length throughout Parts I and II, sometimes where they are least expected. By contrast, there are only the briefest references to Russian events since 1917. This may be due to Sartre's greater familiarity with French history, but it also seems to reflect an underlying awareness that it is easier for Marxists to make sense of Jacobinism than of Bolshevism. At any rate Sartre has nothing very illuminating to say about either Lenin or Stalin, whereas he is extremely knowledgeable and informative about Robespierre. In the same way, his literary analyses are concerned with Flaubert and Valéry, not with Tolstoy and Gorky, let alone "Socialist Realism," which he treats with contemptuous silence.

9. Ibid., pp. 56 ff.

to be included within the Marxist canon or merged with it to form a higher synthesis. On balance Sartre seems to favor the latter procedure, but his remarks are open to varying interpretations. The point where he comes closest to a confrontation with Marx himself and not merely with his bumbling acolytes is marked by an interesting reflection on the materialist conception of history: [10] if men are molded by anterior circumstances, how can they develop the spontaneity required to inaugurate a radical break with the past? In reply, Sartre introduces a familiar solution: if history is not simply a *vis a tergo,* it is because consciousness represents the element of freedom which enables the participants to educate themselves through what Marx called "praxis." The contradiction is lived by the whole society, but in particular by the exploited class, which is at once the passive object of external determinations and the active agent of a transformation which will make Man the master of his fate. Men anticipate the future by shaping their circumstances in accordance with their desires. The element of freedom is embedded in the time sequence, inasmuch as men relate themselves consciously to their future as well as to their past. "The dialectic as a movement of reality collapses if time is not dialectical, that is, if one refuses a certain action of the future as such." [11] This line of thought permits Sartre to integrate his version of the dialectic with his analysis of consciousness, for the notion that "man defines himself by his project" acquires a practical content if it can be shown that the historical process is kept going by a dialectic of ends and means which is both *imposed* (by material pressure) and *willed* (by the human agents of what from one particular angle looks like necessity). And this in fact is what Sartre proposes to demonstrate.[12]

Before trying to decide how far his own project has in fact been executed, let us note in passing that Sartre treats Marxism as a system of thought which can be brought up to date by grafting a different philosophy—Existentialism—upon the main

10. Ibid., pp. 60 ff.
11. Ibid., pp. 63–64n.
12. Ibid., p. 95: "Donc l'homme se définit par son projet. Cet être matériel dépasse perpétuellement la condition qui lui est faite; il dévoile et détermine sa situation en la transcendant pour s'objectiver, par le travail, l'action ou le geste."

stem. This seems reasonable enough until one recalls that the youthful Marx saw in the revolutionary "union of theory and practice" the means of *overcoming* philosophy, while the mature Marx got rid of the dualism of thought and reality by investing his faith in *science* (though he left it to Engels to complete the circle with the construction of a materialist ontology which reads the dialectic back into nature). In contrast, the *Critique of Dialectical Reason* is intended as the legitimate successor of the *Critique of Pure Reason*, not because Sartre means to remain in the Kantian tradition but because Kant's (and Descartes's) manner of posing the problem is also his own. Like them he is out to elaborate a unified world view by way of deduction from a few self-evident propositions. The main difference is that instead of asking, "How is experience possible?" or "How are synthetic judgments possible?" he asks, "How is history possible?" "How is the dialectic possible?" And since this problem is tied up for him with the question of man's nature, the answer quite naturally leads back to the traditional themes of ontology: existence, essence, freedom, immortality. While this metaphysical concern represents Sartre's claim to being taken seriously as a philosopher, it evidently constitutes an additional hazard to his search for an empirical basis on which to rest his thinking. For if the foundations are laid by philosophical reflection on the nature of man, the subsequent empirical investigations into the actual workings of society must be largely predetermined. There is of course no way of approaching the subject in abstraction from some kind of philosophy, but Sartre goes very far in prejudging the outcome of his findings. In fact his empirical excursions largely boil down to a kind of self-questioning about the reliability of the principles from which he proceeds.

The truth is, however, that Sartre has no choice. For it is one of his root assumptions that the inherent problems of dialectical reasoning are ultimately ontological. He makes this clear in a passage toward the beginning of Part II [13] where he refers briefly to "the fundamental difficulty of dialectical materialism" as being due to the fact that Marx, by inverting Hegel's philosophy, "laid bare the true contradictions of realism." Hegel's sys-

13. Ibid., pp. 120–27.

tem was self-consistent because, granted its metaphysical starting point, the unhampered process of reasoning could only
result in the discovery of the essential reasonableness of the
world, thus enabling the mind to identify itself with its object,
whereas Marx established once and for all that there is no such
circularity and that reality remains irreducible to speculative
thinking. Yet Marx wanted to retain the dialectic, and Sartre is
obliged to note that this raises a difficulty, especially if Engels'
solution of a "materialist dialectic" embracing the physical universe is rejected. For if Hegel's idealist system is untenable, and
if there is no materialist dialectic in the sense postulated by Engels (and by the "orthodox Marxists" who followed his lead),
how can we be sure that the logical concepts in our heads correspond to something in the structure of reality? One cannot
elude this question by taking refuge in the scientific study of real
or supposed interconnections in nature, for this is to sink to the
level of empiricism. Alternatively, for a materialism which treats
the world as "given," history becomes a special case of natural
evolution. But Sartre is persuaded that the meaning of history
can never be approached by this route. It must be discovered in
the historical process itself, through an investigation of man's
activity, his praxis. The Marxian antinomies of being and consciousness, which came to light when the Hegelian synthesis collapsed, must be overcome through an effort to lay bare the ontological structure of historical reality. The elucidation of this
structure will demonstrate that Man does not simply submit to
the dialectic but that he *makes* it.[14] This demonstration is the
subject of what Sartre calls his theory of the *ensembles pratiques*.

IV

With the foregoing in mind, we seem to have secured a vantage
point from which to proceed straight to the goal of rendering
plain the dialectical character of human action. Nothing of the
kind. Instead of plunging into history we are made to embark
upon an enormous and very wearisome detour into anthropology, in which the few stable landmarks are submerged under an
endless and largely irrelevant conceptualization of a few sup-

14. Ibid., p. 131.

posedly typical human activities and character traits. Instead of
the promised land we are offered the purgatory of Sartre's logical treadmill.

The trouble begins with his notion of the *"pratico-inerte,"* by
which he designates the unrelated practice of human beings
caught up in the immediacy of their daily toil. This is done
through a process to whose analysis Sartre devotes over two hundred pages of hairsplitting ingenuity. The "inert practicality" of
society—that is, its failure to comprehend itself *as* society—is
traced back to its anthropological ground in the blind activity of
isolated beings, each of whom takes himself as the sole center of
reference. The only bond that unites them is *need* in an environment of *scarcity,* the latter designating at once a social milieu
and a time sequence from the primitive tribe to present-day society. Within this universe of toil, scarcity, material pressure,
and constant danger of famine, the primitive individuals originally come together for purposes of food gathering, production,
and other economic activities which gradually form a bond between them. One might suppose that they do this by cooperat-
ing, but in the nightmare universe of which Sartre is the creator
and which he controls and operates, cooperation plays a very
minor role. Men are from the start pitted against each other, in
such a fashion as to make violence and mutual slaughter not
simply a daily occurrence—that would scarcely be news to anthropologists—but *the* constitutive element of their lives and
consequently of their "natures." Everyone sees in his fellow man
the Other who threatens to deprive him of his own meager food
supply. This constant exercise of distrust, enmity, and violence
is rooted in the "world of scarcity." In Sartre's opinion, Marx
and Engels did not give sufficient attention to "scarcity as the
negative unity (imposed) by matter via labor and the conflicts
of men." "The historical process is not to be understood without a permanent element of negativity, at once exterior and interior to man, namely the perpetual possibility *within his own
existence* of being the one who causes the Others to die, or
whom the Others cause to die, in other words scarcity." Sartre
rejects the theological notion of a fixed and permanent human
nature, but insists that, although violence is not to be regarded
as an inborn trait, "it is the constant inhumanity of human con-

duct as interiorized scarcity, in brief, that which causes everyone to see everyone else as Other and as the principle of Evil." [15] This relationship governs not merely primitive society, but the whole of history down to our days. It is therefore not the case that class society represents the disturbance of an original primitive concord, as Engels tries to make out in his *Origin of the Family,* and as the Marxists have continued to maintain. On the contrary, enmity to one's fellow man has always been the unwritten law of human history. The argument must be cited at some length:

> This means that scarcity, as the negation within man of man by matter, is an intelligible dialectical principle. It is not my purpose here to give an interpretation of prehistory or to revert to the notion of classes and to show, after so many others, how they came to be founded. . . . I only want to show that the disintegration of the agricultural commune (where it has existed) and the appearance of classes (even admitting with Engels that they arise from a differentiation of functions), whatever may be the actual conditions, is intelligible only within the original negation. Materially in effect, if the laborers produce *a little more* than is strictly necessary for the society, and if they are administered by a group freed from productive labor which . . . can divide the surplus among itself, one does not see why the situation . . . should change; it seems to me on the contrary that we seize the mechanism of transformation and its intelligibility if we admit . . . that the differentiation occurs in a society whose members produce always *a little less* than is necessary for the whole, so that the constitution of an unproductive group has for its condition the undernourishment of all, and that one of its functions is to select those who are to be eliminated. . . . It is within a humanity of which even today millions literally die of starvation that History has developed through the differentiation of functions and sub-groups. . . . Inversely, the unproductive groups, always in danger of being liquidated because they are the absolutely Other (those who live upon the labor of others), internalize this ambivalent otherness and comport themselves vis-à-vis the individuals either as though they were Other than man (but positively, like gods), or as though they were the only men in the midst of another species (reduced to subhumanity). As for the group which is sacrificed, one can truly speak of struggle in characterizing its relations with the Others.

15. Ibid., p. 221.

. . . We shall see later how these . . . attitudes transform themselves. . . . What mattered was to show the first conditioning of men by internalized matter. . . . It is this which even today furnishes an intelligible foundation to that accursed aspect of human history where man at every instance sees his action stolen from him and totally deformed by the milieu in which he inscribes it. It is this tension which . . . by the possibility for everyone to see his closest friend coming toward him like a strange and ferocious beast, lends to every praxis, at the most elementary level, a perpetual statute of extreme urgency and turns it . . . into an act of hostility against other individuals or groups. . . . One must look for the negation *at the start*. And we have stated [*nous venons de constater*] that under the regime of scarcity the negation of man by man was taken up and internalized by praxis, the negation of man by matter insofar as [matter represents] the organization of his being outside him in Nature." [16]

Thus human nature is shown to have been conditioned by a state of affairs which bears a marked resemblance to a concentration camp. And let it not be objected that Sartre at first refused to believe the evidence when around 1948 it began to be rumored that Stalin's *univers concentrationnaire* was based on the twin principles of forced labor and no food for those who fell short of the target. Philosophers are entitled to take some time before they assimilate the common stock of factual information at the disposal of their fellow men. At most one might observe that Sartre has fallen from one extreme into the other and projected his discoveries backwards into prehistory. But readers of his novels and plays will realize that this too would not be quite fair. The author of *La Nausée* and *Huis clos* has always taken a dim view of the capacity of human beings to overcome their ingrained destructiveness. And who shall blame him? Are we not all the beneficiaries of an experience which has made Freud's disillusioned view of humanity seem mere common sense? If there is ground for skepticism it concerns not so much Sartre's anthropology as the use he makes of it in linking individual praxis with the collective *pratico-inerte*. The starting point of his analysis is the assertion that man from the outset sees his fellow man as the Other, to be exploited or liquidated,

16. Ibid., pp. 221–23; trans. from the original.

and that it is this "negativity" which has kept history going. This may be a useful antidote to idyllic notions, but Sartre relies rather too much on the category of Otherness (*altérité*). He attempts, for example, to deduce the nature of political authority from it. I have not so far quoted the key sentences from the lengthy passage already referred to:

Thus we grasp immediately that the groups concerned with administration, management, and direction are at once *the same* as those whom they administer (insofar as the latter accept them) and *other than they*. For they are at once those charged with determining *the Others* within the group, that is to say, with choosing the victims of the next redistribution [of the exiguous food supply], and those who are themselves *the Others*, in the sense that they are totally superfluous [*excédentaires*], consume without producing, and constitute for everyone a pure menace. In the milieu of scarcity, the differentiation of function (however it may have come about, for Engels takes a very simplistic view of it) implies *necessarily* the constitution of an excessive (but accepted) group, and the constitution through the latter, via the complicity of many Others, of a group of undernourished producers.[17]

It is probably no accident that Sartre wrote this during the years of the Algerian conflict, to which he and other Frenchmen gave much anguished thought and which clearly inspired his lengthy analyses of colonialism in the later sections of the *Critique*. As a description of a certain type of primitive exploitation it may pass muster. As a theory of the state—even an imperial slave state such as the Roman Empire—it is inadequate. But Sartre is not content to put his blood-chilling picture forward as an account of certain historically conditioned relationships. He will have it that it discloses a universal typology of human behavior, which at one and the same time illustrates the dialectic of history and the psychology of the individual "in the milieu of scarcity." In fact his whole theory hinges on this conjunction of *altérité* and *aliénation:* it is only because everyone sees in his neighbor primarily the Other that history has developed as it has.

Compared with this framework, the concrete examples Sartre

17. Ibid., p. 222.

brings forward to illustrate what he calls the *pratico-inerte*—that is, the blind operation of social forces uncontrolled by critical insight into the outcome of their activities—are not very startling; nor do they throw a great deal of light on his favorite category, Otherness (*altérité*), unless its meaning is stretched to include the failure to perceive what one's actions mean to others. This may be simply a consequence of not knowing what other people are doing, which is scarcely blameworthy, though it is likely to have disagreeable consequences. Sartre cites two familiar instances which historians and economists had noticed before: the progressive deforestation of China through the uncoordinated activities of millions of peasants over thousands of years; and the self-defeating attempts of European governments in the sixteenth and seventeenth centuries to import gold from America without causing a price rise. The case of deforestation had already occurred to Engels (though with reference not to China but to the Mediterranean lands); the other example was cited by Marx (and before him by Adam Smith) without reference to philosophy. There is of course no reason why Sartre should not illustrate the concept of "inert practicality" by seizing upon these well-known instances of human imbecility, but by themselves they do not establish his claim to have evolved a new method of investigation, though he is doubtless right in complaining that "the simpletons of Marxism have calmly suppressed the moment of individual praxis as an original experience of the dialectic, or in other words, as the dialectic which realizes itself in practical experience. They failed to see that one must conserve the basic reality of this moment or suppress the truth of alienation." [18]

Perhaps the whole matter comes down to the point that Sartre is concerned primarily with the descriptive analysis of individual and collective patterns of behavior. He certainly shows a tendency to confuse such description with the discovery of a dynamic principle that "totalizes" uncoordinated behavior into "wholes." Hence Book II (pp. 381–755) is given over in its entirety to an intricate analysis of group and class structures as social wholes whose functioning is supposed to lay bare the peculiar mechanism whereby history comes into operation (this

18. Ibid., p. 373.

part of the work bears the title *Du groupe à l'histoire*). It is here that the category of "totalization" finally comes into its own. Previously one had only caught glimpses of it. On page 18 of the opening section, Hegel's thought was described as "the most ample philosophic totalization" yet achieved, which seemed to suggest that the totalizing faculty is located in the consciousness of the philosopher. But that would be Hegelianism pure and simple. Sartre (in this respect following Marx) believes that the meaning of the historical process can be grasped from the inside, as it were, only by those who are actively engaged in promoting its forward movement. At the same time he is clearly fascinated by the Hegelian notion of a dialectical process which "comes to itself" in the consciousness of the beholder. Thus on page 154 he speaks of a constitutive dialectic that "grasps itself . . . via the individual praxis," which rather sounds as though the dialectic were an independent motive force; and in Book II he expounds at length a methodological principle best described by saying that he identifies "totality" with structure. Although he makes the point that the "ontological structure of the group" (p. 438) is constituted by human praxis (instead of being "organic" as with the Romantics), the praxis that constitutes the group is precisely the "inert practicality" of Book I, which in its turn exemplified no more than a certain community of destiny imposed by uncomprehended material necessity. Sartre's humans do not cooperate: they are thrown together, or, as he puts it, "serialized," by danger, by hunger, by external pressure, by group hostility, by machinery, or simply by having to wait for the bus. Insofar as they rise above this primitive level (that of the *"groupe de survivance"*) to form a more active and conscious unit, they define themselves once more by the presence of an external enemy, while in relation to longer stretches of time Sartre seems to believe that the archetypal group is the sworn confederacy.

It would be wrong to give the impression that Sartre's approach is wholly abstract. Where he has at his disposal historical or sociological material that happens to fit his preconceptions —such as studies of the French Revolution or of modern syndicalism—his analyses are often instructive and even brilliant. Unfortunately such excursions into genuine history are rare. For the most part the reader has to make do with the rotation of Sartre's logical steam engine.

Sartre in fact is at his best when he deals not with history but with individuals, and this is perhaps the central weakness of his ambitious synthesis. The point has been made by his critics that for all his employment of the terms "dialectic" and "totality," he remains schematic in his description of how the "dialectical totality" articulates itself into its components. This, however, is not due to any weakness in his analysis of human motivation: he has the dramatist's eye for "character" and for the dense opacity of individual behavior. The trouble seems rather to stem from his obsessive concern with "structures" inside which the individuals are encased like flies in amber. This is related to what appears to be an ingrained peculiarity of his mode of viewing the world. As a former Cartesian who by an effort of will has turned himself into a thinker of the modern post-Hegelian kind, Sartre remains haunted by the Cartesian problem of relating the outside world to the solitary individual, while at the same time his intellectual conscience tells him that he ought to be thinking about the ongoing historical process. The result, as often as not, is an uncertain compromise between ontology and empiricism. It may seem a trifle harsh to say, as Lefebvre does, that "precisely because he pursues speculatively the search for the foundation, he does not attain anything fundamental," but one sees what his critic has in mind. Notwithstanding some brilliant excursions into applied sociology, Sartre on the whole remains "abstract" in that he rarely succeeds in grasping the historical moment in its uniqueness. "Matter" and "consciousness," when brought face to face, turn out to be linked only by the tenuous bond of his own speculative construction; the transition from one stage to the next is managed only with the greatest difficulty, whereas hundreds of pages are devoted to the analysis of static relationships; and finally the dialectic, from being an intelligible principle of historical existence, becomes an independent motive force. None of this is surprising to the student of his earlier work, or indeed of the literary and philosophical tradition in which he grew up. Sartre would not be the important figure he is were he not profoundly steeped in the French philosophical tradition. It is his indebtedness to the cast of thought established by his ancestors which causes his peculiar synthesis of Marxism and Existentialism to have so strange a flavor of Port-Royal about it.

V

An adequate critique of the *Critique* would take up too much space, but something must be said about Sartre's theory of the state. This topic, which occurs towards the end of this work (pp. 586 ff.), is rooted in his concept of "the whole," and at the same time it concerns politics properly so called. It can therefore be treated as the link between his anthropology and his political commitments.

To start from the nonmetaphysical end, Sartre's political philosophy is substantially that of Hobbes, though his language is that of Heidegger. The essence of the state is sovereignty; the latter is defined as the particular way in which institutions emerge by taking up into themselves the "reified" life of their members. As the "inert persistence of a reified organization" in the midst of a social grouping, the institution establishes itself "as the elementary and abstract permanence of the social past *as Being. . . .*" The institution in turn, "as the exteriority of inertia," gives rise to *authority* as power over the subordinate functions which keep the system in balance. The root of authority is the position of the mediator between conflicting individuals and subgroups, and we have seen that for Sartre social life is a *bellum omnium contra omnes* which can be held in check only by the constant exercise of a factor whose extreme manifestation is terrorism. "Thus the *chief* is produced at the same time as the group itself, and produces the group which produces him, so much so that in this elementary moment of experience the chief can be anyone. Or if one prefers it, the quasi sovereignty of each is one of the constitutive bonds of the group." [19] Authority is an institutionalization of the personal power which arises spontaneously from the fact that conflicts must be settled by "regulators" who lend themselves to this role. Demagogues, terrorists, organizers, and military chiefs all have their root in the primitive nexus which is "the diffused power of life and death over the

19. Ibid., p. 586.

traitor, or if one prefers it, the fraternity-terror, as the basic determinant of sociality. This permanent and living structure of coercion is a necessary determinant of sovereignty as authority." The mediator (*"tiers régulateur"*) originally embodies and concentrates "the internal violence of the group as the power to impose his regulation," [20] and this is the source of all later sovereignty. Authority is constituted power to impose the death sentence. It never loses its original character, however much it may be mediated and watered down by subsequent social developments. At a higher level the atomized ("serialized") community discovers its spurious unity in the chief or ruler it has projected from its inert midst, and the ruler then enters into a dialectical relationship with the other social institutions, while appearing (or pretending) to be their original fountainhead. The ultimate source of sovereignty is thus not a social contract but quite simply the praxis whereby an individual organizes and reorganizes his personal field of reference with a view to goals of his own choosing. Man is, so to speak, sovereign by nature, and historical sovereignty is the extension of this primary relationship to other persons whose activities are unified, the only limit being the sovereignty of rivals. At the historical level the ruler mediates between institutions which have themselves arisen from the reification of relationships among men rendered passive. "And this institution need not in the least be accompanied by a group consensus, since on the contrary it establishes itself on the impotence of its members." [21] If the *ultima ratio* of the state is violence, this is because the ruler draws his authority from this source. "Produit par la terreur, le souverain doit devenir l'agent responsable de la terreur." [22]

All this is rather Hobbesian, and in retrospect one sees why Sartre had little difficulty in accommodating himself to Stalinism, as long as he felt reasonably certain that the ultimate aims of the regime were more or less his own. Even in the *Critique*, although he now dismisses "proletarian dictatorship" as a mystification and remarks quite accurately that "the real dictatorship was that of a group which reproduced itself and exercised its

20. Ibid., p. 587.
21. Ibid., p. 595.
22. Ibid., p. 600.

power in the name of a delegation which the proletariat had not given to it," [23] he insists that this was inevitable and "from the viewpoint of the masses neither legitimate nor illegitimate. . . . Historical experience has undeniably revealed that the first moment of socialist society in process of construction could only be . . . the indissoluble aggregation of the bureaucracy, the Terror, and the cult of personality." [24] In short, Sartre's attitude to the Russian Revolution and Stalin is more or less that of Hegel to the French Revolution and Napoleon. In both cases, too, the philosopher who sums up the sense of the epoch is obliged to acknowledge that Minerva's owl had to wait until it got dark enough to fly out. The chief hope he offers for the future is that this inability to get beyond the terroristic relationship of the "regulator" to the group is not necessarily final. Other forms of reciprocity may become possible, and already one can perceive—that is to say, Sartre can perceive, now that Stalin's successors have spelled it out for him—that "the sovereign must gradually abandon the monopoly of the group." For a change we have Montesquieu instead of Hobbes: enlightened despotism is expected to reform itself, peacefully and from above. But not, it seems, to the extent of bringing about the "withering away of the state." This may be a realistic perspective, but it rules out the centerpiece of the original vision, for if the state remains in being *after* the Revolution, genuine freedom is as far off as ever.

Like the French Army advancing to Waterloo, "without fear and without hope," Sartre thus approaches the future with a strong dose of stoicism. To some extent his political philosophy represents a tacit acknowledgment that the particular type of human self-estrangement embodied in the relationship of domination and subjection can at most change its form. The reverse side of this coin is his tendency to take for granted the permanence of alienation, in particular the disjunction of particular wills and the "general will" which has been one of the perennial themes of political thought. Sartre is in a dilemma here, for which of course he is not personally responsible: history has not borne out the hope that this cleavage can be overcome. To a

23. Ibid., p. 629.
24. Ibid., p. 630.

Marxist this might suggest the probability that the proletariat may fail to accomplish what was supposed to be its historic mission. In that case, alienation will persist and so will philosophy: either as a repository of unfulfilled human aspirations (its traditional role), or as an assemblage of scientific techniques enabling the new ruling elites to manipulate the societies they control. There are some signs that Sartre is not altogether blind to this prospect. It might, however, have been better if he had spelled it out, instead of leaving the reader in an uncertain twilight of doubt concerning Leviathan's future.

As matters stand, Sartre's philosophy of history presents itself as a speculative system which transforms the concepts of Marxian analysis—history, praxis, class conflict—into ontological notions and then sets up a dialectic between them. At the same time he clearly regards his own theorizing as a guide to action— as though it were not in the nature of philosophy to come *after* the event! This contradiction is something Sartre refuses to acknowledge. He therefore remains at the Hegelian level, though his purpose is to complete the critique of Hegel. This is perhaps only another way of saying that he may have misconceived his current role, for in actual fact the revolution to which he still looks forward is already completed and lies in the past. Moreover, it is just this which makes it possible for him to take a synoptic view of it. Subjectively, however, Sartre's commitment to the idea of "changing the world" is unquestionable, as is his belief that the last battle has not yet been fought.

This commitment comes out in his concern with history as "totalization," and here he is able to play off the Hegelian theme to some effect. Traditional philosophy assumed that the totality of the world is an ordered Whole whose essence can be grasped by the intellect. Now to say that "the Whole" is intelligible is tantamount to saying that it has an identifiable structure.[25] It also presupposes, if not an "absolute moment" in time, at any rate a critical moment. Time need not stand still to oblige the philosopher, but there have to be privileged moments when

25. Leo Strauss, *Natural Right and History* (Chicago, 1953), pp. 22 ff. But the Whole need not be "unchangeable" in order to be intelligible, nor does the historical approach necessarily do away with the category of totality.

the process discloses its meaning. In their different ways both Hegel and Marx thought they had lived through and perceived such a moment. This sets the dialectic off from historical relativism with which it is sometimes confused: a thinker who believes he knows what Man is and what History does, has no need to concern himself with the argument that all our knowledge is subject to the flux of time and circumstance. If there are moments when history discloses its own secret, we are relieved of the pseudo problems with which positivists and skeptical relativists occupy their leisure hours.

This vantage point enables Sartre to escape from the dilemma posed by critics of "historicism." The problem is usually seen to reside in the need for the "historicist" to abandon the search for objective truth and agree to relativize his own judgment, if he wants to be consistent within the terms of his own approach. The contradiction into which it is held he is bound to slide, if he refuses to be thus consistent, may be put as follows: Philosophy is thinking about Man and his position in the world, but Man is a historical being, and his situation is constantly changing. Hence the only kind of thinking which can interpret his role is historical thinking. This, however, is itself subject to change and cannot rise above the horizon of its particular epoch. Yet truth must be timeless. Thus in order to overcome skepticism, the historicist has to exempt historical thought from its own verdict and render its discoveries absolute. But this is inconsistent and leads to an obvious contradiction, for if thought can attain something that manifests itself unaltered through all historical changes, then clearly the Being of the world does not articulate itself completely into transitory events and ideologies. Thus the attainment of timeless truths through philosophy is shown to be possible, but only by relinquishing the historical approach from which the whole train of thought began. Therefore historicism is either absurd or self-contradictory. Now for Sartre this is precisely where Existentialism comes into its own, yet he would reject the assertion that ontology and historicism are incompatible. On the contrary, it is the very essence of his position that the permanent element is not something transhistorical (and therefore timeless and metaphysical) but the historical process itself, that is, the process of Man's self-creation. What Man experiences in history (and at a remove in thinking about it) is simply his own being as it comes back to him mediated by the time sequence. The thinking that reveals the logic of history at the same time makes transparent the onto-logical structure of human existence. The two come together in the act whereby Man creates himself and his world. History is *causa sui*. There is nothing "behind it," neither God nor Na-ture. Sartre expressly refuses to ground historical materialism in dialectical materialisms. There is no dialectic of nature to render plausible the human story as a special case within the universal process. The *pour-soi* has no need of a metaphysic to sustain itself in its flight from the frozen past of the *en-soi*. All it needs is the awareness that it has made the world of history and can never cease to project itself forward in an endless quest for a union that cannot be attained.

This position appears to be unassailable in logic, but I think it must be added that Sartre skates on ice that cannot sustain any-one who stays in the same place for very long. The whole dizzy-ing operation ultimately depends on the notion that conscious-ness is "choice of being," and that the entire diversity of existence springs in the last resort from the act of awareness itself, understood as the primary separation of thought from be-ing. Compared with *L'Etre et le néant* the principal difference appears to be that, while in that work Sartre presented human existence as a foredoomed attempt to realize the union of being and consciousness (*en-soi-pour-soi*), he has now adopted the Marxist position that the project is executed in and through his-tory. Unattainable in philosophy (because the world of the indi-vidual is ultimately contingent and "absurd," that is, not re-quired by reason), the overcoming of the split is realized in practice through the activity of Man who strives to bring exist-ence into conformity with his own essence. Possibly Sartre would add that even in the life of the species the discrepancy can never be wholly bridged. However that may be, he has at any rate closed the gap in his own thinking about history by incorporating man's praxis in the dialectic of being and con-sciousness. If human nature can be shown to be of such a kind that it *necessarily* sets the historical process in motion, the di-chotomy of philosophy and science has been overcome and the world has ceased to be mysterious.

Is this the answer to the question how history can be conceived as a whole without entailing either skepticism or dogmatism about timeless values? At any rate it is the most breathtaking attempt yet made to escape from the dilemma. But at this point a consideration of Sartre's work must resign itself to the limitations of an essay and yield the ghost. I merely note in conclusion an argument brought forward years ago by critics of *L'Etre et le néant:* the principle which furnishes the ontological description from within—pure consciousness and awareness of consciousness—could never have produced the reflective report on the process from without. From the opposite standpoint, Sartre's Marxist critics have denounced the attempt to subordinate human praxis to ontology. Conceivably Sartre has overreached himself and fallen between the positions he seeks to transcend. It is nonetheless apparent that his tour de force has created a new situation for the philosophy of history: things are never going to be quite the same again. For whatever he may have failed to do, Sartre has demonstrated that if "historicism" is pushed to its furthest limit, it becomes a self-consistent position and thus has to be taken seriously.

What Is History?

❊ ❊ ❊

WHAT IS HISTORY ABOUT? What, to be more specific, is the so-called philosophy of history about? We know who invented the term: it was Voltaire who in 1765 wrote a pseudonymous tract on the subject (characteristically, to amuse a lady friend). But Voltaire, as was his habit, popularized a notion already developed by a more original thinker—in this case Turgot, who in 1750, at the ripe age of twenty-three, had addressed the Sorbonne on a topic then quite new and startling: "The Progressions of the Human Mind." The title was preserved by Condorcet for his famous essay of 1794, composed in the shadow of the guillotine, the *Sketch of a Historical Survey of the Progressions of the Human Mind*. Thus the concept of a philosophical history, or philosophical treatment of history, made its appearance on the eve of the Revolution and took final form while the great event was in progress. After Turgot and Condorcet had left the scene, it was taken up and converted into a rudimentary sociology by Saint-Simon, Fourier, and Comte—the second generation of the "prophets of Paris" discussed by Frank Manuel [1]—while across the Rhine, in the footsteps of Kant and Herder, Hegel set about to underpin the new doctrine with a metaphysic of his own, later to be "stood on its feet" by Marx.

But we still need to be told what exactly the term "philosophy of history" was meant to convey. Voltaire, Condorcet, and the other pioneers clearly supposed that they were describing mankind's emergence from barbarism to civilization. Their successors

The New York Review of Books, December 15, 1966.

1. *The Prophets of Paris: Turgot, Condorcet, Saint-Simon, Fourier, Comte* (New York, 1965).

became progressively more modest. As time went on, they narrowed their field of vision from the whole of human history to that of Western Europe, then to the history of particular institutions, and finally to their own age. Then it occurred to someone that the business of the historian was itself an interesting subject, worthy of sustained thought. "Philosophy of history" thus came to mean "reflection upon the writing of history" rather than concern with the historical process (if there was one). By now the circle is closed: historians are so busy writing about historiography that they scarcely have time left to consider what actually happened. As for the philosophers, their task has been redefined for them: it is no longer to write about the meaning of history but to ascertain what historians have thought of it. "Philosophy of history today is about historical knowledge, not about history itself," as one writer has put it.

This seems worth pondering. It is true, of course, that other branches of specialized investigation too can be viewed under a double aspect: that of their ostensible theme, and that of the mental discipline to which the study of the subject gives rise. "Chemistry," to take an example, is the name given to the theory and practice of chemists, and it is also the description of a certain field of natural phenomena. "History" then, we may say, is about the *res gestae*—the fall of Rome, the Crusades, the French Revolution, and so on—and it is likewise the label applied to the collective endeavor of certain specialists, the historians. There appears to be no problem here, but hold on: the subject matter of history, we are told, exists as such only because the historians have sorted it out for us. But for the collective enterprise of "history" (the discipline), there would be no history known to us: we would never have heard of the French Revolution. For that matter, the participants themselves would have been unable to set to work but for their possession of certain historical concepts which enabled them to distinguish one category of events from another. The Republic, for example, was proclaimed in Paris in 1792 because educated Frenchmen had heard of the Roman Republic. Moreover, what was involved in this appropriation of the past was not mere reminiscence but philosophical interpretation as well. The Republicans thought of themselves as reincarnated Romans because they had imbibed a certain idealized conception of antiquity from their reading of Polybius or Tacitus. These ancient authors indeed lacked the modern notion of progress; they believed that history moved in cycles. But in other respects they furnished their descendants the intellectual tools wherewith to draft political constitutions and laws. Thus the historian not only mediates the past: he also helps to shape the present and the future. What really happened in Rome was perhaps less important—or so it appears—then what the ancient writers have told us about it, for it is from them, rather than from the remote circumstances themselves, that we draw those edifying conclusions which (if we are wise) will determine our own political conduct. It would seem then that history is not only made for historians; it is actually made by them. That at any rate is what the philosophers of history would like to believe, though not all of them have managed to persuade themselves of the importance of their role.

It has taken time for this new consensus to establish itself. The first steps were halting. As Professor Manuel notes in *Shapes of Philosophical History*,[2] "The rediscovery of the classical corpus during the Renaissance was accompanied by a revival of pagan cyclical conceptions of philosophical history." Now this way of looking at things, aside from being heretical, had the additional disadvantage of leading to pessimistic conclusions about the role of policy makers and their learned advisers: If history moved in cycles, the results were foreordained. Hence no Renaissance philosopher could flatter himself with the notion that his own work might inaugurate an epoch-making rupture with the past and the dawn of a new aeon. These writers also had to circumvent the hostility of the Church, which insisted on the unique importance of events such as the rise of Christianity —or the so-called conversion of Constantine (better described perhaps as the incorporation of the Church within the Roman Empire). As late as the eighteenth century, Vico—writing in Naples under the eyes of the Inquisition—thought it prudent to exempt sacred history (that of the Jews and Christians) from his law of cyclical recurrence. The new method had to insert itself gradually into the interstices of the older theological faith,

2. Stanford, Calif., 1965.

"slowly carving out for itself a separate field, secular history, in which the circular views could be applied with relative impunity without disturbing the Judeo-Christian axis of world history," as Professor Manuel puts it. Thus the emancipation from theology was effected by means of the Graeco-Roman myth of eternal recurrence—at any rate in so far as it became permissible to treat the varying fortunes of states and empires as instances of a "law" not ordained by providence. The evident paradox here lies in the fact that these writers had to revert to a pre-Christian viewpoint before their eighteenth-century successors could formulate the distinctively post-Christian approach which had shed the cyclical superstition along with the theological blinkers.

Vico, still rather medieval in his assumptions, forms the link between one age and the next. His *Szienza Nuova* (the final version of which appeared in 1744, a few months after his death) retains the ancient distinction between sacred and profane history which to his French contemporaries—Montesquieu or Voltaire —had become meaningless. But then Naples was a backwater and Vico read neither French nor English. His rediscovery by the German pre-Hegelians, and by Hegel himself in the next generation, was mediated by their common obsession with the history of Rome: the only period that Vico had studied thoroughly. That at any rate appears to be Professor Arnaldo Momigliano's view.[3] I am not quite sure whether Professor Manuel would agree with him, although he notes Vico's dependence on the ancients and his archaic cast of mind. At any rate there can be no doubt that for the Renaissance humanist, down to Vico, who is perhaps the last major representative of the type, Rome was both the source and the guarantor of the cyclical world view, "the exemplar nation of the ancient world" (to quote Professor Manuel once more):

> for Machiavelli, Raleigh, Bodin, Le Roy, as it would still be for Montesquieu and Toynbee. Here they all found the perfect historical cycle, an empire with a dated foundation, an apex, a long continuum, and a known demise. If Rome fell, what nation, however glorious it might appear, could expect to live forever?

3. *Studies in Historiography* (London and New York, 1966).

This theme could indeed be given a theological twist, as may be seen from Toynbee's latter-day treatment of the subject (the "real" history of the world is one of successive religious revelations), but in its origins it responded to the newly felt desire for a "secular" treatment of so-called profane history: nonbiblical history, that is.

I pause here to remark that writers whose instinctive sympathies are with cyclism have some trouble deciding whether or not it is to the credit of the Jewish-Christian tradition that it introduced the notion of a possible escape from the cycle. The difficulty is enhanced for authors who are both Christians and conservatives. To most of them, the Jewish-Christian vision of history constitutes a source of embarrassment. Professor Karl Löwith is a case in point, as readers of his *Meaning in History* [4] must have noticed. Like other writers of this school (Robert Tucker comes to mind) Löwith is torn between two conflicting impulses: that of crediting the Jewish-Christian spirit with a unique insight into the human condition and a corresponding regret that all those subversive prophets of revolt, from Voltaire and Condorcet to Comte and Marx, should have drawn their inspiration from a secularized form of theology. Professor Manuel, being a moderate liberal, is less perturbed by such thoughts, but he too experiences a slight twinge of unease, as may be seen from his introductory chapter on the conflict between Stoic cyclism and the early Church. He even hints at a tenuous connection between Augustine and Auguste Comte. The reverse side of the medal—the filiation from Polybius to Machiavelli and then to Nietzsche and Spengler—offers fewer difficulties, since no one has ever doubted that Nietzsche revived a Hellenic and Stoic conception.

Where does Marx stand in the matter? In spite of his Hegelian leanings and Hegel's own syncretism of the Hellenic and the Christian heritage, there can be no doubt about the answer: he represents a revival of the Hebraic strain within the European tradition (but also of the Promethean theme, which he shared with Goethe and the Romantics). This is an awkward topic, but

4. Chicago, 1949.

Professor Manuel does not flinch from it, though he duly stresses that Marx owed more to the French than to the Germans. The latter, including Hegel, were caught up in the Lutheran disjunction of Spirit (internal) and the world (external), while the French—notwithstanding their Catholic upbringing—had got beyond these dichotomies. "While the French wrote a secular history of man's expanding capacities and his outward achievements, the Germans composed a history of introverted man, a Protestant world history," as he puts it. Marx learned a great deal from Hegel, but for his revolutionary materialism he had to go (quite literally) to Paris: in the 1840s that was the only place where one could encounter authentic revolutionaries and where socialism was allied to materialism. Elsewhere, notably in England, socialist writers tended to find fault with the new economics on the grounds that it was subversive of Christian ethics. In France this type of argument attracted only critics who idealized the past, and they were mostly Catholics who on principle detested both rationalism and the Revolution. Writers like Comte, who combined rationalism with sympathy for Catholicism, and enthusiasm for science with dislike of individualism, were rare. In the main, the new socialist school, though critical of bourgeois liberalism and individualism, stuck to the notion that the Revolution had inaugurated a new epoch whose culmination would witness the fulfillment of the radical program. As for the Communists (then mostly working-class followers of Babeuf, who in 1797 had paid for his conspiratorial fantasies on the scaffold), their doctrine in the 1840s could be succinctly summed up in the phrase that the bourgeoisie had confiscated the Revolution for its own benefit.

The gradual emergence of French socialism from the tradition formed by the intellectual ancestors of the Revolution provides the main theme of Professor Manuel's learned study of the Parisian "prophets." One can only hope that students will make use of this admirably concise and lucid introduction to the subject. It is indeed specially designed for them: unlike *Shapes of Philosophical History*, whose somewhat world-weary tone (and lack of notes) suggests a different destination—that of becoming the successor to Carl Becker's well-known tract on the Heavenly City of rationalism.[5] Becker is now rather dated, and the best advice one can give to readers in search of a critical study of the Enlightenment is to start with *The Prophets of Paris* and then go on to Professor Manuel's lectures on "philosophical history." In the earlier work they will find, among other things, a lively account of the Saint-Simonian school, a splendid portrait of that crotchety old inventor of "utopian" socialism, Fourier, and a brief but incisive discussion of Comte. Utopianism is also the theme of a weighty volume of essays edited by Professor Manuel, with contributions from Lewis Mumford, Northrop Frye, Crane Brinton, Bertrand de Jouvenel, Mircea Eliade, and other scholars.[6] Individually these essays, or most of them, are impressive, but having completed the journey, I, at least, found myself somewhat at a loss for a guiding thread through the labyrinth of a tradition originating (if Eliade can be trusted) in the hermetism and solar symbolism of the Renaissance.

That the single-handed approach still has its advantages may be seen from Bruce Mazlish's *The Riddle of History,*[7] whose subtitle is *The Great Speculators from Vico to Freud.* It goes without saying that the determination to cover so much ground all at once has to be paid for by rather heavy reliance on secondary sources. But granted this necessity, one can see that there is some advantage in bringing a single viewpoint to bear instead of calling up a small army of authors, however distinguished. At any rate I fancy that *The Riddle of History* will be of more use to students than *Utopias and Utopian Thought.* They will find in it what they need first of all: concise summaries of biographical data, plus brief discussions of Vico, Voltaire, Condorcet, Kant, Hegel, Comte, Marx, Spengler, Toynbee, and Freud, all in one volume of less than five hundred pages. This may suitably be termed a *tour de force.* There are not many writers who have the courage to undertake this kind of compression, and if Mr. Mazlish has done nothing else, he has shown that the job

---

5. *The Heavenly City of the Eighteenth-Century Philosophers* (New Haven and London, 1932).
6. *Utopias and Utopian Thought* (Boston, 1966).
7. New York, 1966.

can in fact be performed without sacrificing either scholarly standards or the interest of the reader.

This said, I am obliged to add that Mr. Mazlish does not convince me. That is to say, he does not persuade me that there is a definable theme running through the doctrines he has chosen to dissect, though in a very general sense it can be held that most of them exemplify a certain commitment to the overriding aim of the Enlightenment: that of elaborating a nontheological view of history. So much indeed is common ground among the authors he has selected for critical study (with the notable exception of Toynbee). In other respects it seems to me that he has unduly flattened the radical contrast between the true heirs of rationalism (down to Kant) and the Hegelians or pre-Hegelians (e.g., Herder, who is not discussed at all). And what is Freud doing in this *galère*? His philosophical views, insofar as he had any, were in part derived from Schopenhauer; for the rest they reflected his naïve commitment to Victorian liberalism and positivism. Neither is very relevant to the understanding of the historical process, yet Mr. Mazlish introduces Freud as "the last of the great classical philosophers of history," apparently on the strength of his speculative essays on anthropology. This seems to me mere eccentricity. The fact that Freud has become an American culture hero does not entitle him to a place in a portrait gallery of the great philosophers of history. And there are other aberrations, notably a perverse effort to find a place for Hegel in the Cartesian tradition and an irrelevant attempt to psychoanalyze Marx, in the hope of getting at the blind spot which prevented him from perceiving the true beauty of nineteenth-century bourgeois society. There is something rather endearing about this notion that a man who revolted against Victorian capitalism, or against the Prussia of Frederick William IV, must have had something wrong with him—dislike of his father perhaps? Unluckily for this type of investigation, Marx was notably fond of his father and had an uncommonly happy married life, a circumstance which leaves Mr. Mazlish in a state of acute bewilderment. It never seems to occur to him that an elemental loathing of bourgeois society might be regarded as a sign of spiritual health rather than as a symptom of mental disorder.

When he gets away from his worry about Marx's unconscious

(curiously, he does not attempt to analyze the more conservative writers in his selection and he has missed a splendid opportunity by excluding Rousseau, whose weird habits would surely have confirmed all his dark suspicions about the mental makeup of revolutionaries), Mr. Mazlish is a better guide. He has certainly digested a vast heap of material and made sure of his references, so that even where one disagrees with him, at least one knows exactly what he is getting at. Where the subject lends itself to treatment in the light of contemporary sources, e.g., in relation to Spengler and Toynbee, he makes some effective critical points, apart from giving the student a useful guide to the doctrines under discussion. He is rather good, for example, on Toynbee's Alexandrianism. I confess I had not expected an American critic to see through Toynbee's identification of the British Empire with the Roman. This is really the key to his vast panoramic travesty of world history, but when one lives in London (as I do), one tends to regard this sort of thing as a family secret.

Professor J. L. Talmon, needless to say, has a different perspective altogether. *The Unique and the Universal* [8] relates in the main to a single theme, that of nationalism; and the author's position at the University of Jerusalem makes it inevitable that he should approach the subject with the recent Jewish catastrophe very much in mind. However, these essays (which include an eloquent tribute to the late Lewis Namier) are by no means to be regarded as an emanation of a specifically Zionist consciousness. They relate to their author's antecedent studies of the French Revolution and the rise of democracy in Western Europe. Professor Talmon's theme is the significance of history, not simply of Jewish history, though only one chapter (that on Herder) is explicitly devoted to the "philosophy of history." It will come as no surprise to readers of the author's earlier studies to find him in these collected essays resolutely attached to the neoconservative philosophy of his teacher Lewis Namier (born Bernstein-Namierowsky). There is a difference, though: Namier, a British citizen by adoption, was a Tory in politics as well as philosophy, while Professor Talmon is committed to the State of Israel and is thus a democrat, if no longer a socialist.

8. London, 1965; New York, 1966.

This introduces a certain awkwardness, for while it is (or at any rate was) fairly easy to be a Tory if one had access to the British Establishment, it is less easy for an Israeli scholar to maintain an ideological position historically associated with the long reign of the aristocracy. However, both Namier and Dr. Talmon had a predecessor in Disraeli, and in a manner of speaking they can both claim to have inherited his somewhat romanticized view of European history.

What then—to revert to the question from which this discussion started out—is the philosophy of history designed to accomplish that cannot be done by ordinary historiography? And what sort of place does it occupy in the intellectual consciousness of the present age? Instead of reverting once more to the various doctrines already mentioned in passing, I am going to suggest one or two fairly brief and dogmatic answers to these two related questions. In the first place, it seems obvious that the historical consciousness, as it begins to unfold from the eighteenth century onwards, is indeed a revolutionary innovation. Whatever its own historical roots, it represents a radically new way of seeing the world: neither cyclical (that is, tied to the familiar model of the natural cosmos) nor dependent on the Jewish-Christian mythology, though in its origins it still combines elements of both the Greek and the biblical approach. This last is hardly surprising. It would indeed have been odd if the new world view had emerged ready-made and free from all traces of its own birth. Such miracles do not occur in nature, let alone in history.

Secondly, it must be evident that "philosophy of history"—meaning the attempt to see world history as a whole instead of subdivided into fragments—does not necessarily imply what is called "historicism," that is, the belief that the outcome of the process can be predetermined either in thought or in action. Such notions may indeed be derived from philosophy (and have been derived by theologians, as well as by adherents of the cyclical myth), but so may their opposite: the conviction that history is open-ended and undetermined. Critics of "historicism" overshoot the mark when they read fatalist implications into the attempt to grasp what evolutionists used to call the "law of development" of history. For granted the ability to discern such a law, it might simply tell us that there is a single world-historical continuum underlying the histories of the various cultures known to us; and it is in no way evident that this unitary view implies either fatalistic acceptance of a supposed cycle of growth and decay, or belief in the imminent advent of a golden age. The true fathers of the "philosophy of history," the rationalists of the eighteenth century, simply wished to affirm that world history is a totality held together in the last resort by the fact that it is the history of *man*. This assertion is in principle compatible with both science and theology; it is quite unmetaphysical and commonsensible; and there is a further important point in its favor: it happens to be true. This being so, it is not easy to see why it should evoke so much distrust.

The explanation may be that too much was originally expected from the discovery that mankind had a history which could be understood. In the ideology of early liberalism, and then of nineteenth-century Anglo-French positivism and progressivism, the concept of a unitary world history was employed to underpin what liberals called "civilization." This had the inevitable effect of antagonizing the less civilized nations: first the Germans, then the Russians, and latterly the Chinese. Since for various reasons they either disliked the fruits of progress or felt they had been excluded from them, these nations conceived it their business to denounce the Anglo-French version of historical philosophy as a myth and then to construct countermyths, either cyclical (Nietzsche-Spengler) or revolutionary (Marx-Lenin). The joke here is that Marx was himself a Western progressivist (though not a liberal in the political sense), so that the eastward spread of his doctrines, however barbarized in the process, was bound in the end to promote the Westernization not only of Russia, but also of the Celestial Empire of China. Although this cannot at the moment be said in China without grave risks to one's health, it is a truth which in the course of time may come to dawn even upon the captive audience of Chairman Mao. Since the globe is round, one does not see how the Chinese can escape the consequences flowing from the technical unification of the world, and one of these consequences (as the Vatican has lately begun to realize) is that all doctrines of human evolution have to be cast in universal terms, i.e., in terms appropriate to mankind as a whole and not just to one privileged section of it. In that sense, if in no other, the rationalist enterprise originally involved in the philosophy of history may now safely be said to have attained its goal.

A Polish Revisionist

❋ ❋ ❋

WHEN IN 1960 a collection of essays entitled *Der Mensch ohne Alternative* was published by Piper in Munich, the West German public for the first time made the acquaintance of an author already known to his fellow citizens in Poland as one of the spokesmen of the anti-Stalinist revolt in literature and philosophy. Their original appearance in various Polish journals between 1955 and 1957 was an aspect of what was then known as the "thaw." Since those hopeful days Poland's Communist Party has reverted to a species of neo-Stalinism, and Professor Leszek Kolakowski himself is understood to have been granted an extended leave of absence in Canada: therein at least relatively privileged by comparison with other "revisionists" who had the additional misfortune of being unable to shake off their Jewish ancestry. For in today's "People's Poland" nationalism has become the strongest of emotions even within the ranks of the party, and the systematic exploitation of such sentiments has hit the few surviving members of the Jewish minority a good deal harder than a native-born rebel whose first important publication bore the title *Essays on Catholic Philosophy*.[1] If Professor Kolakowski can today be described as an empiricist in philosophy and a liberal socialist in politics, this unusual combination (for a Pole) testifies to the circumstance that in Eastern Europe it still takes uncommon courage and originality to arrive at conclusions long taken for granted in less troubled lands.

Marxism and Beyond[2] is substantially a revised edition of the

Journal of the History of Philosophy, VII, No. 4 (October 1969).

1. Warsaw, 1955.
2. *Marxism and Beyond: On Historical Understanding and Individual Responsibility*, trans. Jane Zielonko Peel, introduction by Leopold Labedz (London, 1969).

1960 German-language collection, although one would not infer as much from the editorial preface. The principal addition—an extended version of a paper read by the author at the University of Tübingen in December 1958—is of considerable interest but does not constitute a departure from the line of thought inaugurated in the earlier essays. Entitled "Karl Marx and the Classical Definition of Truth," it dissociates Marx's historical materialism from the ontological materialism of Engels and his successors, in the manner currently accepted among Central European and Western neo-Marxists. "Nascent Marxism formulated a germinal project for a theory of cognition that in the course of the development of the current of thinking that identifies itself as Marxist was replaced by the radically different concepts of Engels and especially of Lenin." From the Soviet standpoint this conclusion of course spells heresy, although Engels (but not Lenin) has meanwhile been disavowed by Louis Althusser and his pupils in France, who have nonetheless remained Communists. It is noteworthy that Althusser and Kolakowski also concur in the importance they allot to Spinoza, and in attempting to minimize—if not to exclude altogether—the Hegelian inheritance. When it is added that the principal exponent of philosophical revisionism within the French party, Roger Garaudy, has retained the Hegelian approach rejected by the politically more rigid but philosophically more flexible Althusser, one may gauge the complexity of a debate in which none of the disputants can any longer be regarded as wholly orthodox from the official viewpoint.

In Kolakowski's case there is the additional problem of "situating" him in relation to the prewar tradition of Polish philosophy, as represented by the Catholic Aristotelians on the one hand and the liberal empiricists on the other. Born in 1927, he graduated at Lodz in 1950 and became an assistant to Professor Tadeusz Kotarbinski before attaching himself to Professor Adam Schaff. In the early 1950s the leading spokesman of orthodox Marxism-Leninism, subsequently a revisionist with humanist-existentialist leanings, Schaff is currently out of favor, on racial and political grounds alike, as one of those "repentant Stalinists" of Jewish origin whose subsequent conversion to a form of neo-liberalism rendered them doubly suspect to the reigning nationalist faction. While these complexities are peculiar to the Polish situation, Kolakowski's standpoint—a compound of scientific empiricism and socialist humanism—is a familiar enough phenomenon. The question that inevitably presents itself is whether it constitutes a new formulation of the original Marxian position or a transvaluation of Marx's own beliefs and values, let alone those of later Marxists. It is plain enough that Kolakowski regards himself not merely as a socialist but quite specifically as a follower of Marx. It is equally plain that his revision of what used to be known as "dialectical materialism" has led him to conclusions substantially in agreement with those of neo-Marxist heretics like Ernst Bloch and the Austrian Ernst Fischer, for whom "scientific" certainty about the onward march of history has been replaced by irrational "hope" for a better future. An attitude of this kind can only be grounded in an existentialist anthropology, and such a position was in fact proposed by Kolakowski in an essay published in 1967. "Authentic irreligiosity always arises from an awareness of needs to which religious symbols are an answer. . . ." This is the Marxism of the 1844 *Paris Manuscripts* and the 1845 *Theses on Feuerbach*. It is in principle quite compatible with Spinoza, for whom Kolakowski shows considerable affection, and it represents a distinguished tradition familiar to Western humanists, irrespective of whether or not they accept the formulation given to it by Sartre. What is by no means clear is whether an ethical commitment of this kind is deducible from the theoretical postulates to which Kolakowski subscribes in his capacity as a logician. These postulates are empirical, and it is arguable that a practical morality deprived of its theoretical anchorage is bound to become arbitrary—a matter of pure choice.

Politically and psychologically, this orientation is best understood as a reaction against the outlook of the Stalinist faction, which held complete control until the 1956 shake-up brought Gomulka to power and allowed Kolakowski to publish his first critical essays. Stalinism in practice was wholly cynical—a circumstance deeply embarrassing to idealist Communists who took their creed seriously. At the same time Soviet orthodoxy was sustained by a dogmatic body of beliefs, or quasi beliefs, about the world in general and the political order in particular. In re-

volting against this peculiar compound of dogmatism in theory
and Machiavellianism in practice, Kolakowski developed his own
characteristic mode of thought, which rested upon the twin pillars of scientific empiricism and ethical rigorism. While this circumstance accounts for his current unpopularity in neo-Stalinist
Poland, the question has nonetheless to be asked whether a positivist interpretation of what he takes to be scientific method is
really compatible with his primary aim: that of presenting an
updated version of the Marxian notion of praxis. The latter originally implied a certain interaction between (critical) theory and
(revolutionary) action. It is possible to hold that the historical
moment for this kind of fusion has passed. (This appears to be
the reluctant conclusion drawn by Horkheimer, Adorno, and
other survivors of the school of thought at one time assembled
around the Frankfurt *Zeitschrift für Sozialforschung.*) Alternatively one may argue with Professor Herbert Marcuse that the
"unity of theory and practice" can still be reconstituted—in the
"third world" of impoverished preindustrial societies with their
hungry peasant masses, in which case one is employing Marxist
terminology to underpin the politics of anarchism. Kolakowski's
approach is a different one, in some ways reminiscent of the revisionist Marxism in vogue within the pre-1914 Socialist movement. As a theorist he holds that sociological statements derive
their validity from the analytic-empirical method developed by
the natural sciences, while in his capacity as a moralist he opts
for a kind of permanent protest against the world as it is. The
concluding passage of the programmatic essay titled "The Priest
and the Jester" runs as follows:

> We declare ourselves in favor of the jester's philosophy, and thus
> vigilant against any absolute . . . we opt for a vision of the world
> that offers us the burden of reconciling in our social behavior those
> opposites that are the most difficult to combine: goodness without
> universal toleration, courage without fanaticism, intelligence with-
> out discouragement, and hope without blindness. All other fruits of
> philosophical thinking are unimportant.

While this proclamation of faith on the part of a Polish Communist may gladden the hearts of Western liberals anxious to
promote cultural exchanges and other forms of East-West coexis-

tence, I feel duty bound to observe that there is nothing specifically Marxist about it. It is splendid news that the humanist credo has penetrated to the lands behind the Iron Curtain, but do we really need to be confronted once more with an irrational option of this kind? The failure of contemporary philosophy to bridge the seemingly impassable gulf between a positivist methodology and an existentialist decisionism is just what renders our intellectual situation so precarious. One may "opt" for a humane and rational attitude if one so chooses, but this does not preclude other options, most of them disastrous. What one asks of a radical philosopher is not an existential act of decision-making in the Sartrean manner but an analysis that enables one to ground practice in theory; instead of which the reader is presented in this volume with an irrational choice in favor of rationality. Leopold Labedz, in his editorial preface, places Kolakowski "in the line of Stoic philosophers" such as Seneca. He fails to mention the circumstances of Seneca's death.

In a later essay not included in this volume [3] Kolakowski does confront the real issue. After dealing critically with Dilthey's historicism on the one hand, positivist scientism and pragmatism on the other, he undertakes a defense of materialism which substantially amounts to identifying it with a humanist standpoint freed from the precritical dogmatism of "Democrit or Holbach," and capable of absorbing the legacy of "Kant, Hegel, Marx, Hume or Husserl." The general conclusion amounts to reinstating the reasoning faculty as specifically human and at the same time "not simply an additional instrument for the satisfaction of animal needs, in the pragmatist and generally biologizing interpretation." So far from being merely instrumental, Reason constitutes "a denial of animality; the conflict between the two fundamental aspects of human existence expressed in the opposition of science and metaphysics cannot be eliminated without abolishing man's being as such." Written and published before the author's expulsion from the party and from his native country, this statement represents what may fairly be described as a return to the central tradition of Western philosophy.

3. "Ist der verstehende Materialismus möglich?" in *Georg Lukács: Festschrift zum 80. Geburtstag* (Luchterhand, Neuwied and Berlin, 1965).

THOUGHTS
AMONG
THE
RUINS

Socialism and the Jews

❊ ❊ ❊

THE FOLLOWING ESSAY was occasioned by a revival of interest in the topic of socialist anti-Semitism, or, to put the matter in a different context, by a rereading of scholarly studies dealing with the role assigned in socialist theory to the problem of nationality in general and the Jewish problem in particular. Some of these writings have clearly been inspired by the rise of fascism in Europe, the aftermath of the "final solution," the revival of traditional Russian anti-Semitism in the U.S.S.R., and the Arab-Jewish hostilities consequent upon the establishment of Israel in 1948. Others have concerned themselves primarily with the religious sources of anti-Semitism and the Jewish reaction thereto.

The most recent and most distinguished of these studies—here accorded special mention because it falls outside the theme of the present essay—is Professor Georges Friedmann's *The End of the Jewish People*.[1*] This book presents a critical but friendly analysis of Israel and Zionism by an eminent sociologist who may fairly be described as a representative of the great tradition of French liberal humanism. For reasons that will appear later, he can also be classified as belonging to a tradition associated with Jean Jaurès, which became dominant in the French socialist movement around the turn of the century in response to the political and intellectual upheavals touched off by the Dreyfus Affair. Professor Friedmann's work is, however, marginal to the theme of the present essay which focuses upon earlier phases of the complex process whereby European socialism in general, and French socialism in particular, shed its anti-Semitic aspects.

Dissent, Summer 1968.
* Notes to this essay begin on p. 447.

This rather obscure chapter of European history has been investigated by such distinguished historians as Léon Poliakov, and especially by Edmund Silberner, whose studies are extensively cited in the following pages. Where possible I have gone back to the sources, but for material on the early French socialists I am primarily indebted to Silberner. Other authors will be cited in passing, e.g., J. L. Talmon, who has given special attention to the Jewish component in the Saint-Simonian movement. For Marx there exists a mass of secondary literature (much of it in German and untranslated), and the same applies to Moses Hess and Ferdinand Lassalle.

Readers steeped in this literature will be aware of the problem of rendering the topic comprehensible to those not familiar with the Central European background. The difficulty is somewhat eased in the case of Bakunin, although socialists and anarchists alike have been markedly reluctant to dwell on the theme of his anti-Semitism. Similar considerations apply to Proudhon and his spiritual progeny in France and Belgium, down to and including Georges Sorel. A brief consideration of this latter topic concludes the essay and brings it back to its starting point. It will then, I hope, have become apparent that the anti-Jewish current in the European labor movement, before and after World War I, was rooted in a complex of attitudes going back to the French Revolution and its impact upon traditional society.

If it be asked why France has been singled out in this study, the answer is: because it was the cradle of the socialist movement, German socialism having been founded in the Rhineland around 1840 by Moses Hess and others, a generation after it had come to birth in its French homeland. For different reasons no consideration is given to Anglo-American developments during or after this period. Eastern Europe appears only distantly on the horizon, principally in the person of Bakunin and his progeny, among whom the Narodnaya Volya distinguished itself in 1881 with an appeal for a pogrom against "the Tsar, the nobles, and the Jews," thereby inaugurating a tradition which is not yet exhausted. The Central and East European catastrophe of 1933–45 forms the unspoken background of this study. It is not as such part of my theme, which revolves around an earlier epoch.

My purpose has been to retrace the broad outlines of the story and to throw out a few general suggestions concerning the dialectic of anticapitalism and anti-Semitism. It will then, I think become apparent that what occurred between, roughly speaking, 1800 and 1950 was a debate over a problem that has not yet lost its topical interest. This may seem a rather bloodless way of summing up a controversy whose frequently appalling violence already foreshadowed the catastrophes with which we have become familiar. But it must be borne in mind that every study of ideas —or, if one prefers it, of the interaction between ideology and politics—suffers from the same weakness: it can never be more than a pale shadow of the actual historical record. Still, within its limitations, such an account may be useful if it establishes a perspective from which the events can be seen to have possessed a logic of their own. That this logic did not manifest itself to the participants but has to be discovered by the historian does not mean that it was not present from the start.

I

It needs to be said at the outset that the phenomenon of socialist anti-Semitism was in its origins the poisoned root of a tree planted —alongside the more familiar tree of liberty—in the decade following the French Revolution. The anticapitalist and the anti-Jewish themes were intertwined, and it took considerable time and trouble before they could be disentangled. The confusion was not accidental, although some of the arguments supporting it were. Moreover, the philo-Semitic current which briefly prevailed after 1789, and then surfaced once more among the Saint-Simonian sect of the early socialist movement, was itself a factor in provoking the hostility of rival groups, since it appeared to go with a marked indifference to certain traditional values. The philo-Semites, in fact, were suspected of being liberals even when they described themselves as socialists.

Since the dispute turned largely upon the newly prominent role of industrialists and financiers, it was inevitable that socialist dislike of bourgeois liberalism should fasten upon the Jews as the real or supposed beneficiaries of a political upheaval which had unshackled the market economy. Anyone with eyes in his head could see that the new doctrines of economic liberalism favored the rich rather than the poor. This is the root core of anticapitalism in a writer like Charles Fourier. It does not account for his detestation of the few Jews he met (and the many whom he never encountered), but then Fourier had numerous private crotchets which rendered him an oddity even in the eyes of his followers. What matters in our context is that—unlike his fantastic cosmology, which was quietly abandoned by his disciples—his anti-Semitism took hold among them.

This was not a trifling matter, for Charles Fourier was one of the two founders of the socialist tradition in France, Henri de Saint-Simon being the other. The two men had no use for each other, and the rivalry of their respective followers carried over into a cleavage between supporters and opponents of Jewish emancipation. It is quite wrong to suppose that all "progressives" were united on this issue, with only the "reactionaries" hostile to the granting of equal rights to the Jews. Fourier did reproduce a few standard conservative arguments, but he added others of his own invention. The more offensive of them will be mentioned in due course, but first some consideration must be given to an issue commonly neglected in writings on the subject: namely the logical status of *moral* principles in a debate supposedly concerned with political and economic factors.[2]

At the root of the Enlightenment—which triumphed in 1789 and to which the Jews in France, and subsequently in Germany and elsewhere in Europe, owed their emancipation—there lay an attitude toward morality which was quite new and, for its time and place, remarkably shocking. It could be summed up by saying that moral behavior is individual behavior. Individuals, being endowed (by Nature or by their Creator) with free will, are capable of behaving either morally or immorally toward each other depending on whether or not they possess the strength of will required for the observance of certain ethical precepts: e.g., the duty to speak the truth or to respect the rights of others. Ethics has to do with the way in which individuals make use of this freedom. The free man is morally sovereign, obeys no external authority, and follows the commands of his conscience. Institutional morality merely sets limits to the manner in which people conduct their lives; it therefore permits any way of life not visibly harmful to others. For the rest, it leaves the individual

SOCIALISM AND THE JEWS   417

free to pursue his private interest as he sees it. Since all reasonable people desire peace and freedom, it follows that they will so
conduct themselves as not to encroach upon each other. Metaphysical beliefs are irrelevant, hence any discrimination against
religious minorities is irrational, unjustified, and contrary to the
doctrine of equality under the law. The grant of equal rights to
Jews—or other religious nonconformists, or atheists for that matter—followed as a direct consequence of this kind of reasoning.[3]
   Now the point here is that the same attitude underlay the
elimination of traditional social privileges. Liberalism—whether
of the Voltairean French or the utilitarian English variety—did
not, of course, do away with social inequality. What it did was to
remove *caste* barriers: thereby incidentally sharpening economic
conflicts, since "free enterprise" meant free competition in the
marketplace. On both counts liberalism represented a radical
break with the past of a traditional (and overwhelmingly agrarian) order. It also happened to suit the emerging bourgeoisie, of
which the Jewish community was an important component.
   All this, from the liberal viewpoint, was natural and desirable
—so much so that, for quite a long time, the more doctrinaire
liberals could see in the arguments of their critics only a species
of perversity. There was, however, a respectable alternative to
the prevailing individualist creed: an alternative, moreover,
which could draw upon the authority of Rousseau. Put briefly, it
amounted to saying that man is "by nature" a social being and
that in consequence an ethically meaningful existence can be
lived only in a certain kind of community: one in which men
cooperate rather than compete. Expressed at its simplest, this was
the root of the socialist case against liberal individualism during
the opening decades of the nineteenth century. And because the
Revolution had let loose, at one and the same time, an overdue
liberation from outworn constraints and an unprecedented orgy
of the crudest kind of individualism, it was inevitable that part
of the emotional reaction against these phenomena should be
directed against the Jews—an unpopular community which
seemed to have derived an altogether disproportionate advantage
from the collapse of the *ancien régime*.
   The anti-Semitism of Fourier, upon which historians of the
socialist movement have frequently remarked, becomes com-

prehensible against this background. Setting aside Fourier's personal eccentricities, it amounted to saying that the Jews were among the chief beneficiaries of a way of life which was subversive of communitarian values. Fourier (who had narrowly escaped the firing squad in 1793, when an anti-Jacobin insurrection in Lyons was suppressed) was hostile to the Revolution in general. But the specific form of his hostility differed from the attitude of the conservatives in that he had no desire to revert to the *ancien régime* or to medieval authoritarianism. He wanted to go forward, not backward; this orientation turned him into one of the founders of socialism. But it did not make him more tolerant of the liberals, or of his rivals, the Saint-Simonians, who combined socialism with philo-Semitism.

Fourier had come to see Jewish emancipation as an aspect of modern society to which he was hostile: the unleashing of individualism. It is irrelevant that he also dragged up some of the standard abuse of the Jews as "parasites, merchants, usurers, etc.," whose emancipation was among "the most shameful" of all "the recent vices" of contemporary society.[4] It is equally irrelevant that in one of his last writings, *La fausse industrie* (1835–36), he abandoned anti-Semitism in favor of Zionism. The Jews (he now said) should be helped to escape from their persecutors in Europe by returning to Palestine "and once more become a recognized nation, with their own king, their own flag, their own consuls, and their own money." He even thought some Jewish millionaire (it was the age of the Rothschilds) might lend his aid to the project, and at the same time help the socialist cause along by financing Fourier's own communitarian projects: an "experimental phalange" (the name he gave to his proposed collective settlements) in Palestine would soon spread its fame, and that of its spiritual father, all over the globe. This was Fourier in one of his more amiable moods and toward the end of his career, when some of the rancor against Jews and Jacobins had gone out of him. His followers, or at any rate the more active among them, soon reverted to his earlier manner.[5]

Before turning to this murky subject, it is worth casting a glance in the opposite direction: at the record of the rival Saint-Simonians. The circumstance has often been noted that the followers of Saint-Simon comprised a fair proportion of youthful Jewish intellectuals, for whom the new socialist faith became a vehicle of spiritual emancipation from religious orthodoxy. What is perhaps more remarkable is the philo-Semitism of the school as such: beginning with its aristocratic founder, whose "testament" concluded on a note of religious exaltation explicitly modeled upon Jewish messianism:

> The people of God, that people which received revelations before the coming of Christ, that people which is the most universally spread over the surface of the earth, has always perceived that the Christian doctrine founded by the Fathers of the Church was incomplete. It has always proclaimed that a grand epoch will come, to which has been given the name of Messiah's Kingdom; an epoch in which religious doctrine shall be presented in all the generality of which it is susceptible; that it will regulate alike the action of the temporal and of the spiritual power; and that then all the human race will have but one religion and one organization.
>
> The imagination of the poets has placed the golden age at the cradle of the human race, among the ignorance and brutality of early times; it is rather the iron age which should be relegated to those days. The golden age of mankind is not behind us; it is before us; it is [to be found] in the perfection of the social order. Our fathers have not seen it, our children will arrive there one day; it is for us to pave the way.[6]

This stirring theme was echoed countless times in the Saint-Simonian literature of the late 1820s and early 1830s (most of it produced by non-Jews). The sect indeed went considerably beyond its founder in propagating a synthesis of Judaism and Christianity in a coming "religion of mankind." Its official writings—notably the essay collection *La religion saint-simonienne*—present variations on this topic. They range from the rationalism of Jules Lechevalier ("What is the mission of Saint-Simonism? To reconcile Judaism and Christianity"[7]) to the romantic visions of Prosper Enfantin and the mystical exaltation of Emile Barrault. In the quasi-religious system of early Saint-Simonism, the emancipation of the Jews figured—along with the liberation of women and of the proletariat—among the preconditions of human emancipation in general.[8] The school was unique in bridging both the religious cleavage and the incipient conflict between liberals and socialists. Some of its founders even terminated their career as pioneers of industrialism. But that was in the prosaic 1860s, when the former visionary Enfantin had become a railway director and the economist Michel Chevalier an adviser to Napoleon III. The fact remains that the school made its principal impact upon public opinion at a time when its doctrine was both socialist and tinged with mystical exaltation. At one point Enfantin and Barrault even prophesied a coming reconciliation of the Orient and the Occident, to be mediated by a female Messiah of Jewish origin.[9]

The contrast with Fourier's violent anti-Semitism is startling. It becomes somewhat less surprising when one reflects that both parties to the dispute were reacting in suitably extravagant terms to the greatest politico-ideological upheaval France and Europe had experienced for centuries: the destruction of theocratic monarchy as a system of government, and along with it the downfall of the Catholic Church. To the participants, whichever side they took, this gigantic cataclysm was a great deal more important than the economic changes preceding and following the Revolution. The emancipation of the Jews had occurred on the ruins of a structure which had stood ever since the Papacy and the Frankish monarchy made their pact in the eighth century.[10]

To a liberal grand seigneur like Saint-Simon, brought up on Voltairean anticlericalism, this was simply the belated triumph of Reason. It looked very different to the Catholic, royalist, and bourgeois (or antibourgeois) novelist Honoré de Balzac in the following generation. Fourier occupies an intermediate position. As a rationalist, he disliked the Church. As a representative of the solid provincial middle class (and one who had been personally ruined by the Revolution), he detested the liberal bourgeoisie which had done well out of the upheaval. In particular he detested the Jews. If he called them "the leprosy and the ruin of the body politic" and condemned the decision to grant them French citizenship,[11] he was giving expression to resentments which could be translated into either reactionary or radical-populist terms depending on circumstances and on the orientation of the individuals concerned. His followers in the next generation denounced Jewish financiers with the same fervor with which the Saint-Simonians extolled their civilizing mission: the difference being that anti-Semitism struck a more responsive chord among a people still deeply affected by the Medieval tradition which pictured the Jew in the role of usurer. Philo-Semitism could never be popular, though in time it won converts among the educated. Anti-Semitism could and did become an element of the primitive system of ideas in which the anticapitalist reaction of the 1830s and 1840s at first presented itself. That it had in this guise the sanction of Fourier must be counted among the accidental but important circumstances attending the birth of the socialist movement in France.[12]

II

The anti-Jewish element in the French socialist movement during the three decades following Fourier and Saint-Simon—from the 1840s to the Paris Commune of 1871—is primarily associated with three names: Alphonse Toussenel, Pierre Leroux, and Pierre Joseph Proudhon. Proudhon's relations with Bakunin and with Marx introduce a theme which forms a separate subject. However, before briefly crossing the Rhine (and then recrossing it, for the purpose of taking a look at Proudhon's disciples and their behavior during the Dreyfus Affair at the end of the century), we must give some attention to the socialism of the 1840s. This—be it noted in passing—was the decade during which Marx composed his early political writings, under the impression of what he had seen and heard in Paris and Brussels.

It is no coincidence that these years witnessed a remarkable outburst of anti-Semitism in France, some of which spilled over into the socialist literature of the period; neither is it irrelevant that these sentiments were activated by the prominence of Jewish financiers among the oligarchy in control of the Orleanist regime of 1830–48. The fateful association of Jews with banking—a heritage from an earlier epoch—encouraged a socialist variant of a litany doubly effective in a predominantly Catholic country. That French banking was largely in the hands of Protestants (of French, Swiss, or German origin) did not bother these writers. Protestantism was respectable and influential; Judaism was not. As usual in such cases, the campaigners chose the easiest target they could find: not the *haute bourgeoisie protestante*, which carried real weight in the country (in the person of Guizot it virtually ran the government under Louis Philippe), but the Rothschilds and their associates.

Alphonse Toussenel, who had joined the Fourierists in 1833 and from 1839 to 1843 helped to edit one of their journals, was hardly the most important member of the school after Fourier's death in 1837. That role, by general consent, devolved upon Victor Considérant, who was no anti-Semite. But Toussenel was not unimportant. The first edition of his pamphlet *Les Juifs rois de l'époque* (1845) was favorably reviewed in the Fourierist journals *La Phalange* and *La Démocratie pacifique*.

Nonetheless, there must have been dissensions, for in the following year Toussenel broke with the Fourierists, and the second edition of his book(1847) opened with a personal attack on Considérant, who had refused to sanction a consistently anti-Jewish orientation.[13] Considérant, by now the official head of the school, retorted in the pages of *La Démocratie pacifique* with an expression of relief at this parting of the ways. Even so, his repudiation of anti-Semitism was somewhat halting. It was primarily motivated by what he described as Toussenel's misguided attribution of "inborn and irremediable" faults to particular peoples or races. That Considérant was far from sharing the mystical philo-Semitism of the Saint-Simonians is evident enough from his remark that Jewish messianism implied nothing more exalted than "the triumph of this people and its rule over all the peoples of the world." [14]

Toussenel, for his part, became the pioneer of a literature which linked the medieval image of the Jew as usurer to the populism of a society suddenly plunged into the maelstrom of early capitalism. The Jews, he says, are "the kings of the epoch." They represent "industrial feudalism," newly personified by "the cosmopolitan Jew. . . . Europe is entailed to the domination of Israel. This universal domination, of which so many conquerors have dreamed, the Jews have in their hands." [15] The Saint-Simonians had praised the Jews for being in the van of progress. Toussenel condemned them for personifying the element of finance capital, which, like other Frenchmen of his age, he identified with capitalism in general.

The argument was echoed by Proudhon in his *Confessions d'un révolutionnaire* (1849), in which Toussenel gets favorable mention; and by Marx in his *Class Struggles in France* (1850), where Toussenel is listed among the pamphleteers inveighing against the financial oligarchy prominent under the Orleanist regime.[16] Marx, needless to say, treated the issue as secondary: it was, he thought, part of a subordinate quarrel between the financial plutocracy and the industrial bourgeoisie. For the rest he saw quite clearly that writers like Toussenel, who imaged themselves to be fighting capitalism, were in fact promoting it. The Jewish issue struck him as farcical. Presumably for this reason he saw no harm in giving it some encouragement.

Toussenel may be described as an anti-Semite who also happened to be a socialist. The case of Pierre Leroux is rather more complex. Originally a Saint-Simonian who had quarreled with Enfantin and left the sect, he turned the liberal journal *Le Globe* around 1830 into a socialist propaganda organ. From 1836 onward, he published an eight-volume *Encyclopédie nouvelle* largely devoted to the propagation of socialist ideas. From 1845 to 1848 he edited the *Revue sociale*. He was elected to the National Assembly after the Revolution of 1848, and went into exile when Louis Napoleon established his dictatorship in 1851. Returning to France in 1859, he started a new career—as a student of Judaism and of the Hebrew language, publishing translations of and commentaries on Job (1866) and Isaiah (1869). During these years he was supported by wealthy Saint-Simonists, including the banker Isaac Péreire, a notable competitor of the Rothschilds. Leroux died in April 1871, during the brief reign of the Paris Commune, and was given a solemn burial by the Communards, presumably in recognition of his long years of service to the socialist cause.[17]

Leroux forms part of the tradition of Christian socialism. During the 1840s he was active—in collaboration with the novelist and feminist George Sand whose acquaintance he had made through Sainte-Beuve—in propagating a highly personal doctrine of reformist and pacifist socialism. A one-time Saint-Simonian, he retained the friendship of Jewish members of the sect, who in his last years helped him when he was in the direst straits. And yet he had his share in making a certain form of anti-Semitism respectable. The lengthy essay on the Jewish question which he published in January 1846 in the *Revue Sociale* bore the same title as Toussenel's scurrilous pamphlet: *Les Juifs, rois de l'époque.*

Leroux was convinced, like Toussenel though for different reasons, that the Jews as a group were somehow identified with the phenomenon of capitalism. He thus shared the Fourierist obsession with the Jews as the incarnation of the spirit of Mammon. They were, he thought, doubly blameworthy, for they had once received a unique revelation of the unity of God and mankind. Thus it was all the more deplorable that they had given themselves up to materialism, which was indeed a very widespread evil but had struck the deepest roots among them. It was particularly noxious because of the social evils consequent upon the abandonment of Christian religious principles. What was blameworthy was not the Jewish people (Leroux was no racialist) but its spirit, "a spirit of greed and cupidity." In principle Judaism asserted the unity and universality of mankind, but in practice the Jews lived by the exploitation of others. Historically they had always been a nation of traders, even in biblical times, and in the modern age they had become the very incarnation of the commercial spirit. They were (according to Leroux) the inventors of the banking system, which they used as a means of revenging themselves upon the Christians, whose ancestors had ill-treated them for so many centuries. In short, they were a menace and a factor of disintegration. Notwithstanding all these alarming circumstances, Leroux did not despair altogether: as a good Christian he hoped for the conversion of the Jews, just as he awaited the coming of a Christian socialism. For the rest he rejected anti-Semitism insofar as it was a racial doctrine: the Semites (he observed in a polemic with Ernest Renan) were by no means inferior to other races.[18]

The third member of our trinity, P. J. Proudhon, is too well known to need an introduction, nor is it necessary to go into details of his stormy career as a theorist of early socialism and the ancestor of at any rate one branch of the Anarcho-Syndicalist movement. His celebrated quarrel with Marx in 1846–47 is not very relevant here either, save insofar as it gave him an opportunity to vent in private some rather surprising sentiments on the subject of Judaism: sentiments by no means congruent with the currently fashionable image of Proudhon as an amiable, if slightly eccentric, theorist of the early labor movement, confronted with a disputatious and dictatorial rival in the person of Marx. It is common knowledge that Marx (in his *Poverty of Philosophy*, originally published in French under the title *Misère de la Philosophie: Réponse à la Philosophie de la Misère de M. Proudhon*) had taken issue at some length with Proudhon's economic theories. Proudhon never made a public reply, though he duly annotated his copy of Marx's work with critical marginalia. He did, however, in December 1847, commit to his private notebook a lengthy programmatic observation, the full text of which was only published in 1961. Here are some samples:

Jews—Write an article against this race which poisons everything, by meddling everywhere without ever joining itself to another people.—Demand their expulsion from France, with the exception of individuals married to Frenchwomen.—Abolish the synagogues; don't admit them to any kind of employment; pursue finally the abolition of this cult.

It is not for nothing that the Christians called them deicides. The Jew is the enemy of the human race. One must send this race back to Asia or exterminate it.

H. Heine, A. Weil, and others are nothing but secret spies; Rothschild, Crémieux, Marx, Fould malignant beings, bilious, envious, acrid, etc., etc., who hate us.

By fire or fusion, or by expulsion, the Jew must disappear. . . . Tolerate the aged who no longer give birth to offspring.

Work to be done.—What the peoples of the middle ages hated by instinct, I hate upon reflection, and irrevocably.[19]

These edifying sentiments were for private consumption only. In public Proudhon contented himself with the stock arguments already put into circulation by Toussenel and others. It was in his posthumously published writings that he really let himself go:

The Jew is by temperament an antiproducer, neither a farmer, nor an industrialist, nor even a true merchant. He is an intermediary, always fraudulent and parasitic, who operates in trade as in philosophy, by means of falsification, counterfeiting [and] horse-trading. He knows but the rise and fall of prices, the risks of transportation, the incertitudes of crops, the hazards of demand and supply. His policy in economics has always been entirely negative, entirely usurious. It is the evil principle, Satan, Ahriman incarnated in the race of Shem, which has already been twice exterminated by the Greeks and by the Romans, the first time at Tyre, the second time at Carthage.

This is the Proudhon of *Césarisme et Christianisme*, published posthumously in 1883, eighteen years after his death in 1865. During his lifetime he observed a certain degree of circumspection, but his sentiments on the subject were never in doubt, and he left a rich legacy which gave rise to a fresh crop of hate literature.

Four years after the master's death, in 1869, his pupil George Duchêne set the tone for the next generation:

> Citizens when you hear it said that in a notoriously barbarous country [Russia] the population treats the Jews roughly, do not believe one treacherous word. What you have is simply a case of honest people chasing rascals, usurers, exploiters of labor; religion has nothing to do with this act of high justice.[20]

As we shall see later on, utterances of this kind formed a link between the Proudhonist tradition and that founded by Bakunin. Here it may be noted that Proudhon differentiated himself from those writers of his time who believed in the possibility of a change for the better. The Jews, he thought, were hopelessly corrupt. They were—like the Poles, Greeks, Armenians, and other "vagabonds"—incapable of founding a state.[21] They were a race of sterile intermediaries, productive of nothing original, whether in commerce or in philosophy.[22] Nor had they really invented monotheism: the Hebrew language possessed no abstract concepts and thus could not have given expression to metaphysical ideas. "Monotheism is a creation of the Indo-Germanic spirit, and could not have arisen from any other source."[23] Proudhon is quite certain about this, just as he knows that Italy and Poland have no hope of recovering their national independence, that Negroes are inferior to whites and that in the American Civil War right is on the side of the South, or that woman is "a sort of mean term between man and the rest of the animal creation." [24] On balance, Marx's characterization of Proudhon as a confused petit bourgeois seems to err on the side of charity. What he really represented was a fusion of backwoods barbarism with the mental chaos typical of the autodidact.

It is this streak of primitive barbarism—in the literal sense of hostility to civilization as such: civility being an urban accomplishment—that connects Proudhon with Bakunin and his progeny. In its origins this sentiment was understandable. Proudhon had the countryman's instinctive dislike and distrust for that side of modern civilization which rests upon the subjugation of nature. He was not far wrong when he described the split between urban and rural life as a source of social malady, or when he asserted that in a fundamental sense industrial civilization was being created at the expense of the real producers, the peasants and workmen. This is the side of his teaching that connects him with Marx and the socialist tradition generally. What allied him with Bakunin, and in the end facilitated the division of his spiritual kingdom between Marxists and Bakuninists (for his followers in the 1870s split up between those two) was the strain of primitivism in his mental makeup.

His anti-Semitism was part of this inheritance. How close Bakunin was to him in this respect may be inferred from those passages in which the founder of Russian anarchism described the Jews as "an exploiting sect, a bloodsucking people, a unique devouring parasite, tightly and intimately organized . . . cutting across all the differences in political opinion"—adding for good measure that Marx and the Rothschilds were sure to hold each other in high esteem! [25] This was something very different from Marx's private jokes about Lassalle, or even his public sneers about Jewish financiers. It illuminated a spiritual underworld which was to erupt in the following generation among Proudhon's and Bakunin's followers: paradoxically with the result that the French socialist and syndicalist movement, having at long last glimpsed Caliban in the mirror, made a successful effort to get rid of him.

III

The three decades following the death of Proudhon in 1865 witnessed a major reorientation within the French workers' movement, which in the long run also affected its attitude to the Jewish problem. The most shattering event of the period, the short-lived Paris Commune of 1871, falls outside our theme save insofar as it helped to speed the collapse of Proudhonism and divided Proudhon's spiritual legacy among the conflicting schools of Anarchism and Marxism. The subsequent rise of an Anarcho-Syndicalist movement—in part influenced by Marxist ideas but also embodying something of the Proudhonist inheritance— is more germane to our theme, since the orientation this movement inherited from Proudhon was a factor in determining its initial attitude during the Dreyfus Affair. Some account must also be taken, however, of the two other major currents within the French socialist movement before and after the cataclysm of 1871: the reformist trend associated with Louis Blanc and the "Jacobin" tradition, as exemplified by Auguste Blanqui.

Louis Blanc, a spiritual descendant of Considérant and Leroux, was an amiable Christian socialist, and his followers in the 1880s helped to promote reformist and "solidarist" ideas within the reigning bourgeois parties, notably the Radicals. Blanqui, a militant atheist, had always seen Catholicism as a much greater problem than Judaism; the latter he disliked chiefly because it had given rise to the Christian religion. His unpublished notes on the subject include the customary unflattering references to Jewish "swindlers" and "Shylocks," but this was a common habit in his age and did not make him an anti-Semite in the doctrinaire sense. His followers were another matter, notably Gustave Tridon, whose pamphlet *Du Molochisme Juif* (published posthumously in 1884, but for the most part written while he was serving a prison sentence in 1866–68) played variations on all the specifically anti-Jewish themes of the age: not excluding the menace which the Semites presented to the "Indo-Aryan race." [26]

While Blanquism gradually faded out in the 1880s and 1890s, its more rational adherents amalgamating with the Marxist group founded in 1880 by Jules Guesde and Paul Lafargue, the

Proudhonist inheritance was taken up by Benoit Malon, whose *Revue socialiste* from 1885 onward became the principal vehicle of reformist or "possibilist" socialism. At first sight it is not obvious why this should have induced its editor to take an anti-Semitic line, but Malon—an autodidact who had learned to read at the late age of twenty—had been brought up on Proudhon and inherited the spirit of his master.[27] Malon also had reasons of his own for disliking the Marxists, who were then just beginning to make an impact upon the French labor movement. Like Proudhon and Bakunin, he was not enamored of "German Socialists," especially if they also happened to be Jews.

This is usually overlooked by writers who have become enthralled with the theme of Marx's juvenilia, notably his essay on the Jewish question: quite forgetting that his contemporaries saw him as a German Jew and were not unaware that his German and Austrian followers included a sizable number of Jewish intellectuals. In the France of the 1880s—a country barely recovered from the disastrous war with Germany in 1870–71—being a Marxist was no passport to popularity even among Socialists. Marxism was associated with Germany—and with a German Jew at that. It was only toward the end of the century that this theme vanished from Socialist literature. In the meantime writers like Malon did what they could to keep it alive.

In our context it is noteworthy that Malon thought well of Regnard's *Aryens et Sémites*, that "scholarly and superb study" which breathed a spirit of genuine "Aryanism."[28] This was rather more than Marx's French followers were prepared to swallow, for although Guesde and Lafargue permitted themselves occasional diatribes against Jewish financiers, they represented the nascent Marxist orthodoxy which refused to have truck with racism. Malon for his part was on cordial terms with Edouard Drumont, whose celebrated pamphlet *La France juive* (1886) popularized the theme that France was being ruined by Jewish financiers who were corrupting the body politic. It was the time of the Panama scandal and the ensuing nationalist wave associated with General Boulanger: a movement soon joined by some of the more chauvinist Blanquists. Thus when Malon introduced Drumont to Parisian workingmen, he followed a consistent line, just as he did in throwing his *Revue socialiste* open to the notorious anti-Semite Auguste Chirac, who had revived Toussenel's old battle cry.[29]

It is true that in the 1890s a reaction set in: possibly because Socialist opinion had become alarmed by the antirepublican tendencies of the Boulangist movement, which climaxed (and collapsed) in 1889, the centenary of the Revolution. Thus when Regnard published *Aryens et Sémites* in book form in 1890, he was mildly censured by a reviewer in Malon's journal. In the same year Malon's old friend Gustave Rouanet publicly went back on his previous anti-Jewish utterances. By then, however, a good deal of damage had been done, as the public reaction to the Dreyfus Affair later in the decade was to show.

While all this was going on, a countermovement was slowly taking shape which in the end was destined to prevail. The difficulty in describing it is that it came from quite distinct and uncoordinated parts of the political and intellectual spectrum. Respectable bourgeois liberalism (frequently represented by Protestants belonging to the haute bourgeoisie) had always been immune to the noisier and more vulgar forms of anti-Semitism. Democratic radicalism, of the variety represented by Georges Clemenceau, was opposed to racism, though not immune to propaganda directed against high finance. The Radicals (as any candid history of the Dreyfus Affair shows plainly enough) took their time before they entered the arena, and then they speedily converted the struggle for justice into a partisan campaign against clericalism and the military. Catholic opinion, with the exception of a handful of Christian Socialists (eventually to find an eloquent champion in Charles Péguy), was traditionally unfriendly to the Jews on every possible count: political, social, religious. The monarchist Right was hostile for nationalist reasons and because the Jews were associated with the Republic.

Socialist opinion was split. It is significant that the dividing line within and between the various groups (there was no unified Socialist party before 1905) corresponded in the main to the division between those who clung to tradition, and the innovators of the 1880s and 1890s, whether Marxists, Syndicalists, or democratic Socialists of the Jaurèsian persuasion. Anti-Semitism thus became an issue in the quarrel between the "ancients"

and the "moderns": between those who represented the tradition of a purely "French" Socialism (whether Blanquist or Proudhonist) and a new generation brought up on the internationalist
creed.[30]

In the circumstances it is noteworthy that when in 1898 the
Socialists finally decided to take a stand on the issue of "revision"
(of the original sentence imposed upon Dreyfus), they were
able, after some initial confusion, to find common ground, but
only to the extent of declaring that the Jewish aspect of the
Affaire was irrelevant. What was at stake was justice (according
to Jaurès), or bourgeois legality (according to Guesde). The
issue between the two factions had nothing to do with Dreyfus. It was fought out over the question whether the moral
health of the Republic was a matter of concern to the labor
movement. The Jaurèsists, as descendants of the Jacobin tradition, asserted that no democrat could stand aside on the issue.
The Guesdists (with individual exceptions) adopted what they
considered a Marxist position and what was in fact a sectarian
one: namely that while Dreyfus was probably innocent and racial
anti-Semitism was rubbish, the whole matter was of no concern
to the proletariat.

It is noteworthy that Paul Lafargue dissented from this line:
doubly noteworthy because, being married to Laura Marx, he
incarnated in his person the Marxist tradition, so far as it was
then understood in France. Lafargue had always stood out
against anti-Semitism, and he deplored the policy of abstention
practiced by his associates during the Dreyfus Affair. It was, he
said, "inexcusable and inexplicable" that the Parti Ouvrier Français should have tried to wash its hands of the matter. Guesde's
attitude was sectarian and had condemned the party to irrelevance "in a question concerning militarism, military tribunals,
bourgeois legality, patriotism, anti-Semitism, etc." But this was
a minority viewpoint. The bulk of the party followed Guesde
in adopting a neutral stand, while its parliamentary representatives divided up individually between "revisionists," neutralists,
and "patriots," i.e., supporters of the governmental line that Dreyfus was a traitor. The "patriots" had to change their tune when
the official case began to disintegrate, but there was always the
"class standpoint": the whole *Affaire* was of no concern to the

workers. Let intellectuals like Jaurès—with his following of
university professors, schoolteachers, and students—fight for "abstract justice": the workers had more important matters to think
about. Although decked out with Marxist slogans, this was really
no more than a revival of the traditional disdain for anything
not directly concerned with the "class struggle" in its narrow-
est sense. No wonder Lafargue thought his colleagues had taken
leave of their senses.[31]

If one disregards internal splits and tactical changes—not
to mention the confusion caused by the gradual collapse of the
official case against the accused—it is evident enough in retrospect that the *Affaire* made a deeper impact upon the intelligentsia than upon the working class. In itself this is understandable and no discredit to the workers, many of whom barely
grasped what was at stake, while others probably thought that
it was something for the bourgeois to fight out among themselves. It is hardly surprising that those Socialists who dissented
from this attitude were themselves intellectuals, or that Jaurès
acquired a larger following among schoolteachers and students
than among manual workers. All this was normal and to be expected. What needs some explanation is that an entire section of
the labor movement, led by the Anarchists and the Anarcho-Syndicalists, at the start of the *Affaire* affected indifference to the
issue, or even adopted a frankly anti-Semitic tone.[32]

After what has been said about the Proudhonist heritage, this
in itself should occasion no surprise, but two points are noteworthy. In the first place, Proudhon's lifelong obsession with
the idea of "justice"—however absurd it might appear to the
Guesdists—formed a counterweight to the anti-Jewish mania
he had transmitted to his followers. Unless they were prepared
to go the whole distance with the racialists, they could not, on
their own principles, reject the demand that justice should be
done to an individual unfairly charged with an act he had not
committed. To that extent the Proudhonist tradition (ultimately
an outcrop of the medieval attachment to Natural Law doctrine)
provided a foundation for the "revisionists."

A similar consideration applies to the Jacobinism of Jaurès and
Clemenceau, though in their case it was concern for the spiritual
health of the Republic that drove them into battle. But "the

Republic" meant a great deal more to them than a particular form of government. It stood for principles which had been compromised by the travesty of justice enacted by the original court martial. Lastly, there were the "revisionists of the Right," led by professional army officers like Picquart—a Catholic, a conservative, and a nationalist—who quite simply felt that the honor of the army had been besmirched by the behavior of their superiors in the military hierarchy. In their case, too, the appeal was to normative principles, not to political considerations.

It was precisely for this reason that to many Socialists the invocation of "class solidarity" rang hollow. Lafargue sensed this but was unable to assert himself effectively, thereby laying bare a flaw in the Marxist position: there was no way of formulating a standpoint on the issue except in terms of simple, ordinary, human solidarity. But this—while acceptable to the Anarchists, as well as to Jaurès, or to Christians like Péguy—was not specifically Marxist. It was indeed compatible with Marxism, but it did not necessarily *follow* from anything Marx had said. To put it differently, there might be a socialist ethic, but there was no Marxist ethic, unless the Marxists were prepared to claim the inheritance of traditional humanism. But in that case what became of the "class standpoint"? So far as the Jews belonged to any stratum of French society, it was primarily the middle or lower-middle class. To that extent the Jewish problem was of no particular concern to the labor movement. The way out of the dilemma was that adopted by the Anarchists in 1898–1900, when (after some soul-searching) they sided with the Dreyfusards in the name of liberty, while refusing to pay special attention to the Jewish issue. But "abstract liberty," like "abstract justice," was not a Marxist slogan. The crisis thus disclosed what some contemporary writers had already begun to sense: that orthodox Marxism (as then understood) had nothing to say about ethics; it was a theory of the revolution, but not a philosophy of politics.

But the *Affaire* also disclosed something else: that in an emergency most Frenchmen would stand together on the principles proclaimed in 1789 and 1793. If the nationalist anti-Semites of the extreme Right challenged the statement that a Jew could be a French citizen in the full sense of the term, then they would have the bulk of the nation against them—precisely because "the nation" had been created by men who believed that all Frenchmen were or could become equal citizens. Not that France was without its share of racists—they were present even on the Left. But *in principle* it was not possible for adherents of the Republic to deny that citizenship was open to all.

This kind of universalism was lacking in Germany, where there was not even a suitable concept to designate a "citizen." The term *Bürger* had altogether different connotations. It signified a *Stand* (estate) or rather the tax-paying subject of an authoritarian state whose government would presumably protect the citizens' rights but did not regard them as the ultimate source of its own authority. The distinction between "citizen" and "burgher" (which made it possible for French Socialists to address each other as *citoyen* while abusing the *bourgeois*) did not exist in Germany. Likewise, the nation was conceived not in politico-moral but in racial terms. One was a German if one belonged to the *Volk*. If one did not—and the Jews plainly did not, even if they took the extreme step of having themselves baptized—one was indeed a *Staatsbürger*, with all the usual political and civil rights, but not (to the nationalists) a *German*. This was the rock against which German liberalism beat in vain. The best it could offer the Jews was the hope that by assimilating German culture they would be recognized as members of the German *Kulturgemeinschaft:* a feeble solution which went to pieces after 1918. For that matter Germany is still a country where the basic distinction between "people" and "nation" is not understood. *That* problem at least the French had solved—thanks to the Revolution.[33]

IV

It cannot be the purpose of this essay to go into detail about socialist attitudes on the Jewish problem before and after 1914, but something must be said about that strain in the tradition which ultimately contributed to the Fascist movement: the school of thought associated with the name of Georges Sorel. A brief consideration of this topic brings one down to the crisis of

1914–18, the Russian Revolution, and the rise of reactionary countercurrents.

This was the moment when liberalism began to disintegrate as the cohesive doctrine of European society. In retrospect one sees why Jewish emancipation—one of the principal achievements of the Enlightenment—should at such a time have been not merely called into question but actually reversed in practice. That some writers who formed part of the general tradition of socialism should have made their contribution to this peculiar achievement need not surprise us if we remember that the antiliberal strain had from the beginning involved a certain ambiguity about the principles of 1789: they were treated with reservations whose meaning disclosed itself when it was no longer "bourgeois democracy" but democracy as such that came under fire after 1914.

But first a word about Anarcho-Syndicalism, and here it is important to distinguish what this concept signified to its originators from the meaning it later assumed for literary bystanders like Sorel. Syndicalism had emerged from a fusion of the Proudhonist tradition with the reviving French workers' movement of the 1880s. This movement, which had arisen on the ruins of the Paris Commune (and freed itself from at least some of the illusions that helped to promote this historic disaster), was necessarily eclectic in its outlook. In contrast to its sectarian predecessors of the 1860s, it did not worship blindly at the shrine of some doctrinaire: a change which led Marx to observe in 1880 that France was at last beginning to get a real labor movement.[34] The disputes, splits, and reunions which make up much of the story of the next two decades were tiresome enough. But at least they involved real issues, were conducted in public, and were decided in a democratic manner: by counting heads at delegates' conferences attended by genuine representatives of an authentic labor movement, not by secret conclaves of self-appointed liberators of mankind.

It was this change of atmosphere—an aspect of the democratization of French public life under the Third Republic—that made it possible for democratic Socialism to develop. In this respect the Guesdist Parti Ouvrier Français was just as democratic as its various "reformist" rivals. The same applies to the

Syndicalist movement, although its aims were more revolutionary, Syndicalism having turned its back on parliamentary democracy as being a bourgeois institution. The founders of the
movement were indeed closer to the industrial proletariat than
were most Socialists, and their demand for what today would
be called "workers' control" anticipated a key issue of the
future. But if they counterposed working-class autonomy to
bourgeois democracy, and the unions (*syndicats*) to the political
party, they did not for this reason revive that part of Proudhon's
legacy which was pre-Marxist and indeed preindustrial. Insofar
as they had a theory of bourgeois society, it was that of Marx—
as they were quite willing to recognize.[35]

When therefore Georges Sorel—after a brief career as an ex-
positor of Marx's doctrine between 1893 and 1898—came forward around 1900 as an exponent of Syndicalism, he was invent-
ing nothing new but rather latching on to a movement founded
years before by men who, unlike himself, were genuine representatives of the working class. And when from 1905 onward he
began to give a nationalist and anti-Semitic coloration to his
utterances, he was simply reverting to the shadier aspects of
the Proudhonist tradition, though without the excuse available to
Proudhon. For by the beginning of the twentieth century it was
no longer plausible to make an issue of "Jewish bankers." *That*
stage had been passed, and "Jewish finance" was no longer a
topic for writers with any pretension to being taken seriously.
Talk about the Rothschilds still went down well with petit-bour-
geois audiences, especially in the provinces, for Jewish financiers
had taken their share of speculative gains, from the first railway
boom of the 1840s to the Panama scandal of the 1880s. But
French industry did not depend on Jewish merchant-bankers
and the French labor movement confronted quite different problems.

Sorel, who (unlike Proudhon) had read and assimilated Marx,
knew all this well enough. It did not prevent him from prefacing
a collection of writings in 1905 with an introduction in which
Jaurès was accused of having betrayed the Syndicalist utopia for
the sake of his friendship with what Sorel, in a typically disagreeable phrase, called the *"Dreyfusards de la Bourse."* [36]
Jaurès had in 1904 founded the Socialist daily *l'Humanité* with

the help of Jewish sympathizers (including the well-known sociologists Lévy-Brühl and Marcel Mauss) who had been impressed by his courageous, unpopular stand during the Dreyfus upheaval. This was enough for Sorel (who years before had already complained about Saint-Simonian tendencies among the parliamentary Socialists) to employ the standard vocabulary of anti-Semitism.

In the current literary fashion one might speculate about the personal motivations which impelled a respectable middle-aged, middle-class, retired engineer—with the *Légion d'honneur* in his buttonhole, money in the public funds, and an ex-servant girl to look after him (his relatives saw to it that he did not marry her, though she served him faithfully until her death)—to take up first socialism, then nationalism, and finally anti-Semitism. Nothing could be sillier or a more complete waste of time. Sorel came out of a well-established tradition: particularly well-established in the solid provincial middle class from which he stemmed. If he was better educated than Proudhon, he still shared his predecessor's desire to find a formula which would do justice to France's national (and religious) heritage while accommodating the new working-class movement.

When Sorel at the age of forty-five took up the study of this movement, he did so in the spirit of a learned bystander—a "metaphysician of socialism," as Jaurès called him. He did not change his way of life and never suffered even the most trifling inconvenience for his inflammatory writings. In short, while preaching violence, he remained a typical bourgeois. It is hardly surprising that the actual labor leaders of his day regarded him with a good deal of skepticism. Pelloutier, the founder of the movement, had been of middle-class origin too, but he was a martyr who literally killed himself in the service of the cause. No one ever expected Sorel to make the smallest sacrifice for the sake of anything or anybody; nor did he, for all his endless talk of Nietzschean heroism.

A comparatively recent American study of Sorel, in which the Jewish issue comes in for brief mention, sees an extenuating circumstance in his private friendship with Jewish intellectuals and in his evident absorption in the philosophy of Henri Bergson. The author concludes that, taking Sorel's work as a whole,

"anti-Semitism remains a private, minor motif, existing in large
measure apart from the foundations of his philosophy or sociology." [37] This is hardly borne out by the same writer's citations
from Sorel's polemical tracts during and after the Dreyfus upheaval, from which it emerges quite plainly that his feelings
about Jewish emancipation were, to put it mildly, very mixed
even at a time when he still considered himself a democrat and
had not yet formed a tactical alliance with Charles Maurras and
the Action Française.

Sorel was particularly alarmed by the separation of Church
and State in 1905: perhaps the most important consequence of
the Radicals' recent triumph. (This, incidentally, was a surgical
operation which in the long run facilitated the emergence of a
Christian Democratic movement.) As Sorel saw it, French nationalism was in danger of being severed from its medieval
roots—though he was himself an atheist and did not believe a
word of the Christian story. What he liked about French Catholicism was the legend of Jeanne d'Arc and its mythical folklore: It
was this side of the national tradition that stood in danger, for
Jewish rationalism was the mortal enemy of myth. The Jews,
with the help of neo-Jacobins like Clemenceau and Jaurès, had
won a victory over the Church, hence over the mystical side of
French patriotism. But France could not live without myths—
the truth would kill her, for truth was the enemy of life! [38]

This was also the opinion of Maurras, a conservative Royalist
for whom Catholicism was a necessary fiction: not literally true,
but vital for the continued existence of Latin civilization and
therefore to be defended against Jews, Protestants, and foreigners. It was on this basis that Sorel and Maurras—the former
Anarchist and the consistent Monarchist—were able, on the eve
of 1914, to enter into a spiritual alliance against liberalism, democracy, and the Jews.

Sorel also discovered, as part of this conversion to irrationalism, that the proletariat needed a "myth." And since the Marxist
"myth" seemed to have lost its power (this was before the October Revolution, which turned Sorel into an enthusiastic, if naïve
and uncomprehending, admirer of Lenin), he was ready to oblige
with a confection of his own: the idea of the general strike. This,
as it happened, was the real faith of the Syndicalist movement

before 1914. It was no one's invention but something that had grown spontaneously out of the collective imagination of an elite of French workers. As conceived by the founders of the movement, it possessed a rational core that embodied the authentic strivings of a real labor movement. For Sorel it was a heroic prefiguration of the revolutionary dawn: not to be taken literally but to be treated as an imaginative metaphor prophetic of a coming social transformation. In short, the truth did not matter; nor would it ever matter to Sorel's progeny. His heir was to emerge on Italian soil (for Sorel had a following there too), and it was not the saint of Communism, Antonio Gramsci, but his murderer, Mussolini.

Sorel is in a fundamental sense one of those writers who were responsible for the temporary triumph of Fascism in Italy and for its virulence in France during the 1930s and 1940s. The meeting ground between his disciples and the more radical adherents of Maurras in the Paris of the years 1908–14 was furnished by a study group known to the initiated as the Cercle Proudhon. It was here that nationalist writers and pupils of Sorel elaborated the key elements of what in later years became the French, Italian, Spanish, and Latin American variants of Fascism.[39]

The Cercle issued its own *Cahiers,* the first of which stated the basic principle of the creed as follows:

> Democracy is the greatest error of the past century. . . . in economics and politics [it] permitted the establishment of the capitalist regime which destroys in the State that which democratic ideas dissolve in the spirit: namely the nation, the family, morals, by substituting the law of gold for the laws of blood.

Democracy, of course, was a Jewish invention, or at any rate the Jews profited from it, since it enabled them to go about their nefarious business unhindered. Sorel was far from being innocent of this ideological concoction and its murderous consequences: he was directly responsible for it inasmuch as it was his patronage that made possible the fusion of nationalism with the ancient doctrines of Proudhon. Sorel's favorite pupil, Edouard Berth, subsequently claimed with good reason that *le fascisme avant la lettre* had come to birth in the Cercle Proudhon.[40] This did not prevent Sorel from hailing the advent of Bolshevism in 1917, for he saw it as a triumph over what he hated most—liberal democracy.

Sorel, like many others, interpreted Lenin's successful coup as a spontaneous uprising which would establish a "government of producers." [41] This in itself was simply orthodox Syndicalism and was then generally accepted in France and Italy by the men and women who were soon to found the Communist parties in these two countries. But what of the Jewish element in the Russian upheaval, which by all accounts had been considerable? Sorel had an answer to this too: the constructive side of the October Revolution (he said) was the achievement of Lenin, a true Russian; its unfortunate terrorist aspects were due to the Jews.[42]

The link between Sorel's irrationalism and his anti-Semitism was furnished by his dislike of positive science: a typical *fin-de-siècle* attitude, much in vogue among Parisian intellectuals after 1900 as a result of Bergson's teachings. As bad luck would have it, Bergson was a Jew, but Sorel was able to accommodate this exception to the general rule, as were other anti-Semites of the philosophical kind: notably the Jewish writer Bernard Lazare, who before his conversion to Zionism proposed a metaphysical distinction between "Jews" (bad) and "Israelites" (good).[43] This was just the kind of nonsense that appealed to Sorel. Practically it made no difference to the more vulgar anti-Semites, since their objection was to East European Jewish immigrants (mostly proletarians), while Sorel and his circle disliked the Parisian Jewish bourgeoisie: people like Léon Blum or Marcel Proust. One could be a Jew-hater for different reasons: either because the Jews represented liberal rationalism, or because they had helped to pioneer capitalism, or because they were the carriers of that new abomination, international socialism.

In practical terms the whole issue was trivial, since around 1900 there were fewer than 100,000 Jews in France: about half of them in Paris and of these about half were recent immigrants from Russia and Poland. The fact that most of these newcomers were workers and came from countries where a Jewish labor movement had begun to form, naturally caused a reappraisal of the Jewish problem among French Socialists, some of whom began to sympathize with Zionism, while others maintained that the problem had to be solved by the countries concerned. In either case, the traditional image of the Jew as exploiter had been dented, although the more consistent anti-Semites had an answer to that: the Jews were a menace whatever their social origin or political creed.

To say that Sorel's writings around 1914 lent support to this theme is merely to state the obvious. None of this is to suggest that the Jewish problem was of major importance to him. Quite clearly it was not, any more than it was to his pupil Mussolini, until the latter for tactical reasons adopted racial anti-Semitism on the German pattern in 1938. (And even then the execution of the new policies ran into considerable opposition among leading Fascists and was passively sabotaged by the Italian bureaucracy during the war years.) Sorel thought of the Jewish question as an aspect of what he regarded as the decomposition of traditional European culture under the combined impact of capitalism, liberalism, and secular rationalism. If individual Jews like Bergson broke away from the pattern, he was ready enough to praise them. What appealed to him in Bergson's philosophy was the antimechanist orientation and the critique of scientific positivism.

It can also be argued that Sorel was guided by a sound instinct when he asserted that a socialist morality must be "an ethic of producers," in the sense of being a morality appropriate to cooperative enterprises carried on by autonomous groups of people who run their own affairs. Only there was nothing original in all this: it was simply the faith of Pelloutier and the other founders of Syndicalism. The injection of anti-Semitism into this doctrine had nothing to do with it, but was an outcrop of Sorel's personal adherence to the more reactionary aspects of the Proudhonist tradition.

In justice to Sorel it should be noted that he did not explicitly urge the adoption of doctrines known to be false. Thus when he called the "general strike" a necessary myth, he meant that it was something in which the labor movement had to believe if it wanted to transcend bourgeois society. Myths were essential because they helped to shape the future, which was always open and undetermined. As for "violence," it was simply a fact of life and had to be accepted as such. It did not necessarily imply bloodshed, but rather the uncompromising assertion of one's will to alter the existing state of affairs. Violence was something from which no really serious political movement would shrink. But how did one distinguish one kind of violence from another? Sorel was never able to specify a criterion that would have enabled his followers to make a sensible discrimination between necessary and unnecessary violence, or between the rational application of force and the self-destructive glorification of bloodshed. It was just this ambiguity that made it possible for some of them to switch from Syndicalism to extreme nationalism: both movements were antidemocratic, hence welcome. The later career of Mussolini—and of the Spanish Falangists who helped to precipitate the civil war in 1936—is an object lesson in what happens to a movement that turns itself over to thinkers of this type.

For the political implications of the doctrine, in the form Sorel gave it from 1907 onward, are evident. If political life was regulated by myths (a notion for which Sorel found support in the writings of Gustave Le Bon), the next step was to inquire whether myths could or could not be manipulated. To this question there were two possible answers: one, that it was possible but undesirable, because truth and decency forbade it (the traditional democratic position); two, that it was dangerous but permissible in the interest of leading the movement in a direction perceived by the elite (or the leader), though not by the masses. The instructive thing about Sorel is that while in his early writings he adopted the classical rationalist position (the truth shall make you free), he later became the prisoner of his own irrationalism: if the crowd could be moved by myths (whether religious or political), then it was the responsibility of the leader so to act as to bring the goal nearer, even if he himself had seen through the mythical character of his own slogans.

We all know what became of those who followed this line. What matters in our context is the link between Sorel's irrationalism and his growing antipathy to the Jews: they would not go for myths (this was before he had come across Zionism, which anyhow he did not take seriously), and those Jewish intellectuals who were beginning to influence the French Socialist movement were (with individual exceptions) either Marxists or adherents of traditional Cartesian rationalism. In either case they had no use for Sorel, nor he for them.[44]

V

If in the light of what has here been said one were asked to describe the situation in France since 1945, one might venture something like the following: whereas until that date there existed a specifically socialist variant of anti-Semitism, both within the French labor movement and on its intellectual fringe, this is today no longer the case.

The reasons can be summarized under various heads:

—the experience of the German occupation, which drove Frenchmen of all political beliefs (and some who had none) into the Resistance movement;

—the moral shock delivered to the conscience of most Frenchmen—not least the respectable section of the Right, typified by the Gaullists—by Hitler's "final solution";

—the corresponding, though less violent and dramatic, reaction of Communists and other left-wingers to the anti-Semitic aspects of Stalin's reign during the dictator's last mad years;

—the revelation that the Jews—or some Jews—were after all capable of founding a state, and even of defending themselves unaided or practically unaided;

—lastly, the discovery by Frenchmen of the Right and Left that the longed-for fusion of patriotism with socialism had actually been effected in, of all places, Israel.

Sentiments of this kind—along with occasional echoes of the ancient complaint about "Jewish bankers"—even affected the outlook of the Communist *militants,* as anyone who followed the internal strains within the French CP during the 1967 Arab-Israeli war could not help noticing.

All this is clearly of importance. It is arguable, however, that while the situation has changed, certain underlying problems have not been touched upon. Conceivably some of them are of a kind that defies anything in the nature of a solution. It may well be that the "Jewish problem" as such is inherently insoluble, at any rate within a culture that is still nominally Christian. Yet something can perhaps be said about the specific theme of this study—the relationship of socialism to the process of Jewish emancipation. It is after all arguable that anti-Semitism (or anti-Judaism) will continue to persist within Western culture and that it must necessarily represent a problem for Socialists. That a particular form of Socialist anti-Semitism arose in nineteenth-century Europe may have been due to transitory factors which are no longer operative. On the other hand, it may also reflect a problem permanent enough to warrant some consideration.

Mention has already been made of the paradox which the "principles of 1789" constituted for Frenchmen who in the generation following the Revolution discovered that their ancestors had emancipated not merely the *citoyen* but the *bourgeois*. The awkwardness of this discovery was tempered for a while by the hope that bourgeois society would somehow transform itself peacefully into something else, or that the old agrarian and communitarian values could still be preserved. When these expectations had to be abandoned, it became popular, even among Socialists, to blame the Jews. Toward the end of the century these resentments found expression in more or less rational doctrines, which have been described in outline. The crisis having passed, there is a natural temptation to conclude that there is no more to be said. Even so, it may still be pertinent to ask what made Jewish emancipation an important issue for men like Proudhon and Sorel. When we have answered this question, we shall also have cast some light on a problem in modern society for which the Jews are in no way responsible but which their collective existence has somehow thrown into sharper relief.

The dissociation of personal freedom from communal values is surely a basic feature of the kind of society in which we live. One may also call it the liberation of the individual from constraints not specifically laid down by law. This is an arrangement which liberals have always regarded as an important achievement of Western society, and which even Communists (at any rate in some parts of Eastern Europe) are now beginning to treat as desirable. Unluckily, it is this very dissociation that is at the root of a great deal of the unease caused by the apparent lack of any kind of generally accepted social morality. And by a further stroke of bad luck, the problem has somehow become entangled with the topic of Jewish emancipation.

To say this is not in any way to suggest that the first generation of newly emancipated Jews or their successors were responsible for what was in effect a crisis of modern society. It was neither their merit nor their fault that they were among the beneficiaries of an upheaval which *inter alia* resulted in an enormous enlargement of personal freedom (including the abolition of actual serfdom or slavery). Nor were they to blame because, in a predominantly Catholic and agrarian society such as nineteenth-century France, they rivaled the far more influential Protestant minority in spearheading a new type of economic development. The fact remains that their individualism enabled them to get to the top faster than other groups of society. Moreover, liberalism brought out some of their less lovable traits and gave them public sanction.

To grasp what is at stake it is necessary to stand back a little from the surface configuration of modern society and ask oneself what exactly it is that its citizens take for granted. It will then appear that what they take for granted is something very odd indeed: namely, that there ought to be some kind of social morality—whether of a religious or a secular kind—but that it should not interfere with the personal freedom of the individual. For the citizen of modern society conceives of himself as an autonomous person owing no obligations to others or to the community, save for duties that are either contractual or specifically laid down by law. The assumptions underlying this state of affairs have entered the common language, so that it is no longer regarded as sensible to inquire whether what people "ought" to do as individuals may not be prescribed for them by what they are in fact doing as members of a particular community. Yet any glance at a traditional culture shows that such a state of affairs is most unusual. In medieval society, to take an example, people knew for certain how X or Y ought to behave because it was known what sort of position—that of nobleman, clergyman, peasant, etc.—he occupied. Moral duties did not have to be discussed in abstraction from social roles. How individuals behaved (or were supposed to behave) followed ineluctably from who or what they were. *Is* and *ought* had not yet been sundered.

It is the peculiar distinction, but also the peculiar curse, of modern society that these certainties no longer obtain. A person's moral obligation can no longer be defined in terms of his or her social role—in any event, not over an entire range of activities where certainty had previously been possible because ethical rules applied both to individual and to communal existence. Instead, what we have is an atomization of society into self-propelled individuals held together by legal or contractual ties. What lies beyond these arrangements is an area of free choice where each individual is on his own. Choice here is "free" not in some metaphysical sense but in the concrete sense that it is a matter of private judgment. It is for myself to decide how far I am prepared to exert myself on behalf of my neighbor, beyond the constraint inherent in the prohibition against setting fire to his house. In principle his problems do not concern me. What I do about them is "my own affair" and in no way dependent on communal standards or shared values. This is what we call freedom. In a traditional society—and the early French socialists had come out of a traditional society which was being disrupted by the market economy—it would have been regarded as madness.

We have become so accustomed to this state of affairs that few people even think it odd, although it is in fact very odd indeed and quite without precedent. It is one aspect of what liberals call "civilization" and what socialists have agreed to term "bourgeois society." It also describes a way of looking at the world which the early socialists quite particularly disliked about the Jews.

Liberal individualism was indeed not specifically Jewish, but it could be represented as being in some way favorable to the Jews, especially in a country like France where the Reformation had failed and where the prevalent mores were still more or less medieval. That capitalism and individualism were both immoral—or rather, that capitalism was immoral insofar as it implied the new individualist ethic—was something a great many Frenchmen in the nineteenth century were very willing to believe. The liberal bourgeoisie, of course, did not believe it. Precisely for this reason the individualist ethic lacked a mass following in France, whereas it had no difficulty in acquiring such a following in Protestant England or America. The French bourgeoisie read Voltaire, but the masses instinctively felt with Rousseau. For the essence of Rousseau's teaching lay in a conception of morality as something both public and private, anchored in a particular way of life: one in which people cooperated instead of competing with each other. To the extent that they took this notion as their conscious or unconscious starting point, virtually all nineteenth-century socialists based themselves on Rousseau. By the same token they were not disposed to think highly of people for whom private property and free enterprise established the external framework of moral discourse. A community that was no more than a collection of private individuals did not appeal to them.

When the war of 1914-18 inaugurated the crisis of liberal civilization, the Jews were among the first and worst sufferers. It was part of the achievement of liberalism that it had for so long protected an unpopular minority from the accumulated resentments surrounding it. The experience of the 1940s showed what could happen when these restraints went by the board: notably in Central and Eastern Europe, where the position of the Jews had always been weaker than in the more civilized West.

Since 1945 a reaction has set in—so much so that it has become difficult to understand the intellectual climate of an age in which anti-Semitism constituted an actual menace to democracy, and even extended into the Socialist movement of the most highly civilized and sophisticated country in Western Europe. Although this particular situation is unlikely to recur (if only because history never repeats itself), the problems from which it arose still await a solution.

NOTES

A brief list of secondary sources may be useful to the reader. Most of them (though not all) will inevitably reappear in the individual notes that follow. The exclusion of some well-known recent writings (e.g., Professor Norman Cohn's account of the origins of the *Protocols of the Elders of Zion*) reflects nothing more sinister than a desire to concentrate on the purpose of this essay, which is to summarize one particular chapter in the interaction between the socialist movement and the drive for Jewish emancipation.

Bloom, Solomon F. *The World of Nations: A Study of the National Implications in the Work of Karl Marx.* New York, 1941.
———. "Karl Marx and the Jews," *Jewish Social Studies,* IV, No. 1 (1942).

Jackson, J. Hampden. *Marx, Proudhon, and European Socialism*. London, 1958, 1964. Paperback, New York, 1962.

Joll, James. *The Anarchists*. Boston, 1964.

Maitron, Jean. *Histoire du mouvement anarchiste en France (1880–1914)*, 2nd ed. Paris, 1955.

Ramm, Thilo. *Die Grossen Sozialisten als Rechts und Sozialphilosophen*. Stuttgart, 1955.

Rosdolsky, Roman. "La Neue Rheinische Zeitung et les Juifs," *Cahiers de l'Institut de Science Economique Appliquée; Etudes de Marxologie* No. 7 (Paris, August 1963).

Silberner, Edmund. "The Anti-Semitic Tradition in Modern Socialism." Inaugural Lecture, delivered at the Hebrew University, January 4, 1953. Jerusalem, 1953.

―――. "Anti-Jewish Trends in French Revolutionary Syndicalism," *Jewish Social Studies*, XV, No. 3–4 (1953).

―――. "French Socialism and the Jewish Question 1865–1914," *Historia Judaica*, XVI (April 1954).

―――. "Ferdinand Lassalle: From Maccabeism to Jewish Anti-Semitism," *Hebrew Union College Annual*, XXIV (1952–53).

―――. *Sozialisten zur Judenfrage*. Berlin, 1962.

Talmon, J. L. *Political Messianism: The Romantic Phase*. New York, 1961.

Willard, Claude. *Les Guesdistes: Le mouvement socialiste en France (1893–1905)*. Paris, 1965.

It need hardly be said that this short list is intended merely as a guide to the literature, and that in what follows no attempt has been made to break new ground in any particular area investigated by the specialists.

1. First published in France, 1966. English-language edition, New York, 1967.

I

2. Although Silberner discusses this topic, it seems to me a decided weakness that he remains consistently at the historical level, while ignoring the philosophical dimension. It is of course extremely important to know what was actually being said at the time by writers either friendly or hostile to Jewish emancipation, and in the case of Fourier there is perhaps some excuse for treating his anti-Jewish outbursts as personal deviations from the "progressive" norm. But this will not do with later writers who did not suffer from Fourier's psychological quirks and who had no particular reason for identifying the Jews collectively with habits of lying and stealing. Even if Fourier was in some respects a crank, most of his followers were not. They must have had *some* reason for echoing their master's sentiments, even if in the course of time they abandoned his more extravagant notions: e.g., that the Hebrews were hopelessly debased as a people, or that they "have achieved nothing in art and science, and . . . are distinguished only by a record of crime and brutality which at every page of their loathsome annals makes you sick!" (Fourier, *Oeuvres complètes*, 2nd ed. [Paris, 1846–48], I, 61; cited by Silberner in "The Anti-Semitic Tradition in Modern Socialism," p. 1.)

3. For the philosophical implications of the clash between the ancient Aristotelian-Thomist and the new liberal-individualist view of society, see Alasdair MacIntyre, *A Short History of Ethics* (New York, 1966). This is

by far the most illuminating treatment of the subject known to me. Among other things, it clears up a number of widely current misconceptions concerning the role of Hegelian and Marxian thinking in the evolution of socialist ethics.

4. Silberner, op. cit., p. 2. See also the same author's "Charles Fourier on the Jewish Question," *Jewish Social Studies*, VIII (1946), 245–66. Although a rationalist himself, Fourier in these passages clearly reflects traditional Catholic attitudes widespread even among people who on grounds of principle favored Jewish emancipation as being the best means of integrating the Jews within the general French community (and incidentally improving their moral character). What made Fourier an anti-Semite was that he denied the likelihood of such a change for the better.

5. Silberner, *Sozialisten zur Judenfrage*, pp. 22–23. Fourier seems to have anticipated Disraeli and Moses Hess, though it does not follow that he had any influence on them. The idea had been in the air since Napoleon's Egyptian expedition of 1798–99, when the future Emperor affected an interest in, of all things, the Muslim religion. If Islam, why not Judaism? The Saint-Simonians expected a revelation from the East, to be mediated by a Jewish woman Messiah. Fourier's project of 1835–36 was more practical:

Palestine, with its neighboring regions—Damascus, Palmyra, etc.—will become a valuable country when the deserts between Lebanon and Sinai have been irrigated and re-forested by industrial armies, and when the Jordan and the Dead Sea have obtained a navigable access to the Red Sea, the gulf of Etzion-Geber, or Solomon's port of Ophir.

With the help of some Jewish millionaire the kingdom of "Judea or Lebanon" could be re-established and turned over to the Jews, currently exposed to persecution in Germany, Poland, and other parts of Europe. See Fourier, *La fausse industrie* (Paris, 1835–36), I, 224; II, 783–84.

6. Henri de Saint-Simon, *Le nouveau christianisme* (1825); cf. *New Christianity* (London, 1834), cited in Talmon, *Political Messianism*, p. 70. See also Talmon's discussion of Jewish participation in the Saint-Simonian movement, pp. 77 ff. Silberner deals rather briefly with this subject (*Sozialisten zur Judenfrage*, pp. 12 ff.). Considering the tremendous impact of Saint-Simonian propaganda upon public opinion in the 1830s, it is arguable that he underrates its importance.

7. Lechevalier, *Exposition du système social* (Paris, 1832), p. 73.

8. See Eugène Rodrigues, in *La religion saint-simonienne* (2nd ed., Brussels, 1831). Rodrigues, like Gustave d'Eichthal, belonged to the group of youthful Jewish intellectuals who joined the sect around 1825 or a little later. But they never set the tone: it was the gentile leaders of the school, principally Enfantin and Saint-Amand Bazard, who laid down the basic principles of Saint-Simonism, including the doctrine that Jewish monotheism foreshadowed the coming unity and solidarity of mankind. See Bazard's formulation of the official *Doctrine saint-simonienne* (1829), reprinted in Saint-Simon, *Oeuvres* (Paris, 1865–78), XLII, 145.

9. Talmon, op. cit., pp. 122–24. It is notorious that Enfantin and Barrault in the 1830s led an expedition to the Orient, and that its eventual outcome was not the discovery of the *femme-Messie* but the construction of the Suez Canal. Such ironic transformations were the stuff of history in the age of Romanticism. What needs to be retained is that, in the eyes of the Saint-Simonians, the historic role of the Jewish people was not yet exhausted.

450 THOUGHTS AMONG THE RUINS

10. Walter Ullman, *A History of Political Thought: The Middle Ages* (London, 1965), pp. 58 ff. and passim.

11. Silberner, *The Anti-Semitic Tradition*, p. 2. Cf. *Publication des manuscrits de Charles Fourier* (Paris, 1851–58), III, 35.

12. This is not to say that the subject was of overwhelming importance to Fourier: he had a great many other and more pressing things on his mind. All the same, it seems a trifle odd to dismiss the topic with the remark that he "tried to bribe the Rothschilds with the Kingdom of Jerusalem if they would finance his projects" (Frank E. Manuel, *The Prophets of Paris* [New York, 1962], p. 204). It is more to the point that, as the same author observes, "an authentic and complete history of Fourierism and its influence would have to cover much territory, settlements ranging from the prairies of mid-nineteenth-century America to the *kibbutzim* of modern Israel" (ibid., p. 209). For it is one of the ironies of history that Israel was in the end the only country where a large-scale and successful experiment along Fourierist lines was undertaken: by Jewish immigrants from Eastern Europe brought up on the socialist tradition which Charles Fourier had helped to found.

II

13. A. Toussenel, *Les Juifs, rois de l'époque: histoire de la féodalité financière* (Paris, 1845, 1847). Considérant's rejoinder to the polemical preface of the second edition appeared in the journal *La Démocratie pacifique* on January 31, 1847. For details see Silberner, *Sozialisten zur Judenfrage*, pp. 32–34. Toussenel had *inter alia* poured abuse upon the Protestants, a circumstance unlikely to endear him to the numerous Fourierist sympathizers in the United States. This may have been among the reasons why some of his former colleagues were glad to be rid of him.

14. Victor Considérant, *La Destinée sociale*, 2nd ed. (Paris, 1849), II, 43.

15. Silberner, *The Anti-Semitic Tradition*, p. 2, citing Toussenel, op. cit., pp. 73–74.

16. For the original text see Marx-Engels, *Werke* (Berlin, 1960), VII, 15. Marx cites the correct title of Toussenel's pamphlet, whereas the two-volume English-language selection published in Moscow in 1958 (Marx-Engels *Selected Works*, I, 143) gives the title as "Usurers Kings of the Epoch." In the same passage, "Das Frankreich der Börsenjuden" is translated as "the France of the Bourse jobbers." A tactful concession to the spirit of the post-Stalin era?

17. Silberner, *Sozialisten zur Judenfrage*, pp. 44 ff; see also the same author's "Pierre Leroux's Ideas on the Jewish People," *Jewish Social Studies* VIII (1946), IX (1947), XII (1950). For the general background see H. J. Hunt, *Le Socialisme et le romantisme en France* (Oxford, 1935). Leroux's editorship of the *Revue encyclopédique* from 1831 to 1835 forms an interesting chapter in the history of French literary criticism, but the subject cannot be pursued here. In 1841–42 he edited the *Revue indépendante* together with his friend and disciple George Sand, who shared his ideas and projected them in her novels.

18. Silberner, *Sozialisten zur Judenfrage*, pp. 46–51. Leroux's publication of a dramatized version of Job in 1866 initiated a controversy with Renan, who in a study of the Semitic languages had assigned to the Semites an inferior rank among the races of mankind. The topic afforded Leroux an

opportunity to emphasize his disagreement with Renan's thesis that the Semites were in every respect inferior to the Indo-Europeans. It is not irrelevant that Renan, who expressed such views in the 1860s, was a doctrinaire rationalist and politically a moderate liberal.

19. *Carnets de P.-J. Proudhon. Texte inédit et intégral*, ed. Pierre Haubtmann (Paris, 1960–61), II, 337–38. For the prehistory of this incident see also Haubtmann, *Marx et Proudhon* (Paris, 1947). Georges Gurvitch, in his otherwise very scholarly and balanced *Proudhon: Sa vie, son oeuvre* (Paris, 1965), cites a few polemical shafts directed against Marx by Proudhon in his marginalia to Marx's book but is silent on the topic of Proudhon's maniacal Jew-hatred. It is true that Proudhon was in the habit of fulminating in similar fashion against other opponents, and against entire peoples as well. Thus in the same passage, after the Hitlerian outburst just quoted, one may read the grotesque sentence: "La haine du juif, comme de l'Anglais, doit être un article de notre foi politique" (The hatred of the Jew, as that of the Englishman, must be an article of our political faith). Proudhon could also cite the authority of Voltaire for the notion that the Jews should be sent back to Palestine. Thus in the summer of 1847 one finds him writing, "Je hais cette nation [juive]. Il faut accomplir le voeu de Voltaire, la renvoyer à Jerusalem" (*Carnets*, II, 150). But Voltaire's proposal (like most of his utterances) was no more than a jest, and it proceeded from a spirit of frivolity quite foreign to the mentality of Proudhon. Whatever Proudhon wrote or said, he was always in deadly earnest. See Daniel Halévy, *La vie de Proudhon 1809–1847* (Paris, 1948), *passim*.

20. Duchêne, *L'Empire industriel* (Paris, 1869), p. 196; cited by Silberner, "The Anti-Semitic Tradition," p. 5. Duchêne was perhaps not in every respect representative of the Proudhonist movement, but his pamphlet followed a line of reasoning suggested by Proudhon in his writings of the 1850s, notably his *Philosophie du progrès* (1853) and his *Manuel du Spéculateur à la Bourse* (1857). One of Proudhon's pet hates under the regime of Napoleon III (1852–70) was what he called the *Empire industriel*: in other words, the association of the Imperial regime with the growth of industrial capitalism; and he hated it all the more bitterly because it was being promoted by former Saint-Simonians. To him these men were "initiators of the new feudalism," and he did not think any the better of them because some (though by no means the most important) were Jews.

21. Proudhon, *France et Rhin*, p. 260. See also *Carnets*, I, 133: "Les juifs n'iront jamait à Jerusalem."

22. *Césarisme et christianisme*, I, p. 139.

23. Proudhon, *De la justice dans la révolution et dans l'église* (Paris, 1858), I, 445. This is one of the links between the older religious form of Jew-hatred and the new racialism which replaced it from the 1850s onward. Proudhon, the confused autodidact, adhered to both doctrines simultaneously. In *Jésus et les origines du christianisme* (published posthumously in 1896) the Jews are blamed for having rejected the religious reformation associated with Jesus (in whose divine mission Proudhon, being an atheist, did not believe). But this failure is attributed to their generic incapacity for sound morality and political common sense: had they been more sensible, they would have followed Jesus and thus promoted the peaceful reformation of their own community and of the Roman Empire instead of clinging to their supposed uniqueness (ibid., p. 122). On the other hand, Proudhon

THOUGHTS AMONG THE RUINS

gives them no credit for the Jewish ancestry of Jesus and his disciples. On his assumptions it was indeed scarcely conceivable that Jesus should have been a Jew.

24. "L'être complet . . . c'est le mâle. La femme est un diminutiv d'homme . . . une sorte de moyen terme entre lui et le reste du règne animal" (*De la justice*, IV, 134–35). Elsewhere he established the mathematical rule that the *valeur totale* of men to women was in the proportion of 27 to 8, woman being immoral by nature. "Par sa nature, la femme est dans un état de démoralisation constante." It is true that he might have cited the Church Fathers in support of this thesis. In reading Proudhon one must always bear in mind that, for all his fiery atheism, he was basically the product of a Catholic peasant culture.

25. *Archives Bakounine* (Leiden, 1963), I, part 2, pp. 124–26. See also A. Lehning, Introduction to *Michel Bakounine et les conflits dans l'Internationale, 1872*. For Bakunin's general anti-Semitism see Silberner, *Sozialisten zur Judenfrage*, ch. 18. Bakunin never tired in his denunciation of Hess, Marx, and other "Jewish leaders" of the German labor movement. Writing to Albert Richard in 1870, before his dispute with Marx had broken into the open, he observed that the leading German socialists were largely Jews, "that is, exploiters and bourgeois." All his enemies belonged to the accursed race. "All these mountebanks are Jews: Marx, Hess, Borkheim, Liebknecht [sic!], Jacoby, Weiss, Utin, and many others, they are all Jews. By tradition and instinct they belong to this restless, intriguing and exploitative bourgeois nationality" (see Bakunin, "Lettres à un Français" [1870], in *Oeuvres*, IV, 69). In the passage already cited (dating from the end of 1871 or the beginning of 1872) in which it is asserted that Marx and the Rothschilds are linked by secret sympathies, Bakunin continues:

> This may seem strange. What can there be in common between communism and high finance? Oh, the communism of Marx wants a mighty centralization by the State, and where this exists there must nowadays inevitably be a central State bank, and where such a bank exists, the parasitical Jewish nation, which speculates on the labor of the people, will always find a means to sustain itself. ["Rapports personnels avec Marx," in *Oeuvres*, III, 208–209.]

In the light of such utterances, the notorious appeal of the Narodnaya Volya on September 1, 1881, for a pogrom against the "Jewish Tsar," the Jews, and the nobles, is hardly surprising. It is true that this particular line of conduct eventually went out of fashion among the Russian Populists, but that was *after* Marxism had won a foothold among them. In 1881 the Executive Committee of the Narodnaya Volya still took its line from Bakunin's spiritual heirs, though even then some of its members objected.

III

26. For Blanqui see Alan B. Spitzer, *The Revolutionary Theories of Louis Auguste Blanqui* (New York, 1957), pp. 80 ff.; R. F. Byrnes, *Anti-Semitism in Modern France* (New Brunswick, N.J., 1950), I, 156–58 and passim. In his writings, Blanqui adopts the then customary identification of French capitalism with high finance, and of the latter with Jewish bankers, but he does not make much of it, apart from some standard abuse of the Rothschilds. What he thought of the Jews in general may be inferred from an unpublished reference to them as "the type, the ideal and the incarna-

tion of swindling, usury and rapacity. They are the horror of the nations because of their pitiless cupidity, as they had once been because of their enmity and war to the death against the human race" (Blanqui mss., 9587, p. 305; cited by Spitzer, op. cit., pp. 81–82). This is clearly an echo of Tacitus' characterization of the Jews as *odium generis humani*.

Blanqui's anti-Semitism was of the eighteenth-century variety. Tridon, who came later, had already soaked up the new racialism. *Du Molochisme juif* (Paris, 1884) is full of rant about the Semites as the "evil genius of the world. All their gifts are pestilence. . . . To fight the Semitic spirit and ideas is the aim of the Indo-Aryan race" (op cit., p. 5). The same theme was sounded by another Blanquist, Albert Regnard, a publicist briefly prominent in the 1871 upheaval when he helped to run the Commune's police. His article series "Aryens et Sémites," first published in the *Revue socialiste* in 1887–89 and later expanded into a book, rang the changes upon the topic of Aryan superiority to the Semites, as did his later writings. Capitalism, according to him, was largely a Jewish invention, whereas socialism was "a Franco-German creation, *i.e.*, Aryan in the fullest sense of the term" (op. cit., p. 517, quoted by Silberner, "French Socialism and the Jewish Question.") But then what of Marx? This indeed became an insoluble problem for those Blanquists who were racists; in the end they drew the logical conclusion by quitting a movement which had become, at any rate nominally, Marxist.

27. For Malon's writings, see Silberner, "French Socialism and the Jewish Question," pp. 8 ff. Most of his citations are culled from Malon's essay "La Question juive," *Revue socialiste*, III (1886), and later articles in the same periodical, which was then engaged in a running fight with the Marxists.

28. Malon, in *Revue socialiste*, XI (1890), 349.

29. Chirac, *Les Rois de la République* (Paris, 1888). The Jews were of course ruining France—that went without saying. But they were also working with the Russian nihilists and other conspiratorial sects. Indeed, Jewish "international finance" was behind the attempts on the Tsar's life (Chirac, in *Revue socialiste*, IV [1886], 975). There is hardly a theme of modern anti-Semitism not already sounded by this pamphleteer of the 1880s.

30. This topic is neglected by Silberner, although he notes, reasonably enough, that the Marxist Parti Ouvrier Français of Guesde and Lafargue took the lead in warning the workers to pay no attention to the anti-Semites. Guesde indeed went so far as to tell them that the trade name of the firm exploiting them was "not Moses and Co. but Christ and Co." ("La Question Juive," *Le Socialiste*, June 26, 1892). This was hardly the most tactful way of weaning the workers from religious fanaticism, but then tact was never Guesde's long suit. His subsequent attitude to the Dreyfus Affair was cast in a rigidly doctrinaire mold: it was a subordinate quarrel between two bourgeois clans in which the proletariat had no interest. However sterile (he later modified this stand), this sectarianism at least had the effect of focusing the attention of his supporters on what mattered most to them: the class struggle. Inversely, Jaurès—who now and then fell into the ancient habit of denouncing Jewish rapacity as a particularly disagreeable form of capitalist profit-mongering—took his stand on principle too: the difference being that what mattered to him was *justice*.

31. Claude Willard, *Les Guesdistes* (Paris, 1965), pp. 410 ff. The issue was complicated by the conflict between the Guesdist group and the followers of Jaurès, who stood further to the right and on occasion co-

operated with the bourgeois Radicals led by Clemenceau. It is noteworthy that the Guesdist POF did participate in the general left-wing campaign against militarism, clericalism, and anti-Semitism. The Guesdist election manifesto of April 1898 (when the *Affaire* was nearing its first great climax) made considerable play with the theme that the ruling classes were undermining democratic legality; it also asserted that the working class must defend the Republic, "this instrument of your emancipation." Three months later, following another batch of official charges against Dreyfus (the last), the Guesdist parliamentarians refused to sponsor a "revision" of the original trial, while a formal declaration by the party's national council sounded the sectarian note: what mattered was the social revolution, not an alleged injustice committed against an individual. It was this declaration that evoked Lafargue's protest, as well as an outcry among Socialist student groups favorable to "revision"; see Willard, op. cit., pp. 414–15. The legal case against Dreyfus began to collapse in August 1898 with the confession and suicide of Colonel Henry, but this did not affect the substance of the dispute between the Guesdists and their Jaurèsist opponents. To the end, the argument turned upon the issue of "abstract justice" versus the "class standpoint." The Guesdist party congress in September of that year sought a compromise by passing a unanimous resolution against nationalism and anti-Semitism, while refusing to pronounce judgment on the "individual case" of Captain Dreyfus. This at any rate committed the POF to a line consonant with the tradition of "republicanism," although it did not satisfy the "revisionists," for whom a matter of principle was at stake.

32. See Maitron, *Histoire du mouvement anarchiste en France*, pp. 311 ff. This is the standard work on the subject, written by a scholar of distinction who himself represents what is left of the tradition of "libertarian socialism." It is the more significant that his chapter on the crisis of the 1890s ("Les Anarchistes et l'Affaire Dreyfus") makes no attempt to gloss over the embarrassing aspects of the subject. Pure Anarchism (as distinct from Anarcho-Syndicalism, which was at least semi-Marxist) was then a dying movement and no longer possessed an important following among the industrial working class, but it still had a hold upon some elements of the intelligentsia and the proletariat. Its journals—notably *Le Père Peinard, Le Libertaire,* and *Les Temps Nouveaux*—at first either affected to ignore the *Affaire,* or else blew the anti-Semitic trumpet. For a revelatory specimen, see the following (unfortunately not translatable) passage from an article by the veteran Anarchist Emile Pouget in *La Sociale,* No. 72 (Sept. 20–27, 1896):

. . . le youpin Dreyfus est un galonnard, patriote jusqu'au bout des orteils, qui, gratte-papier au ministère de la guerre, maquignonnait les secrets de polichinelle qu'on garde précieusement dans cette sale boîte. . . . Son commerce malpropre prospérait, lorsque, il y a deux ans, on découvrit le pot-au-roses. . . . [Maitron, op cit., pp. 312–14.]

In fairness it should be added that in 1898 a campaign in favor of Dreyfus began in the most important of the Anarchist journals, S. Faure's *Libertaire.* A prisoner in chains on Devil's Island appealed to the Anarchist temperament, which had after all consistently championed the cause of prison inmates. From 1899 onward most Anarchists (including Pouget) became active in the "revisionist" campaign, although an Anarchist congress in 1900 still heard some warnings against unthinking philo-Semitism: the proper line for the libertarian movement (it was said) lay in ignoring racial and religious considerations altogether. At any rate one can say that by 1900 the poisonous legacy of the past had been shaken off.

33. For the nineteenth-century German background to the Emancipation see Nicholas Lobkowicz, "Marx's Attitude Toward Religion," in *Marx and the Western World*, ed. Lobkowicz (Notre Dame, Ind., 1967), pp. 303 ff. This is not the place to engage in the tangled issue of Marx's paradoxical and rather self-contradictory utterances on the Jewish question. From a theoretical viewpoint his personal psychology—which was quite simply that of an emancipated German Jew of his generation—is considerably less important than his failure to work out a satisfactory doctrine of citizenship. For this he had to thank his Hegelian inheritance, plus the fact that his personal commitment was to a kind of secular messianism which made sense only on assumptions he never spelled out, save here and there in his early writings; and his French followers around 1900 knew nothing of the *Paris Manuscripts*. On Marx's attitude to Jewish emancipation see Silberner, "Was Marx an Anti-Semite?" *Historia Judaica*, XI (1949); Solomon F. Bloom, "Karl Marx and the Jews"; Nathan Rotenstreich, "For and Against Emancipation: The Bruno Bauer Controversy" (*Yearbook IV* [1959] of the Leo Baeck Institute, London). There is no evidence that Marx's essay of 1844 on the Jewish question played any part in disposing the French socialists to reconsider the topic. When Drumont on one occasion referred to it in print, Jaurès (in the *Petite République* of December 13, 1898) retorted that Drumont had misunderstood Marx, although he added that the Jews, "accustomed by centuries of persecution to practice solidarity," had indeed developed an excessive fondness for the precious metals and for capital accumulation in general. In the context of the debate then raging, this line of reasoning was not discordant with Jaurès's frequently expressed admiration for "the Jewish race" (a term then in general use), and especially for such of its representatives as Maimonides, Spinoza, and Marx.

IV

34. Marx to F. A. Sorge, November 5, 1880. See *Selected Correspondence* (Moscow, 1956), p. 404. The first French "Marxists" of the 1880s were largely innocent of any real understanding of Marx's theories, a circumstance which did not bother him, since—unlike some of his later followers— he was convinced that an adequate grasp of the subject would eventually evolve from the maturation of the movement.

35. For this subject see among others Edouard Dolléans, *Histoire du mouvement ouvrier 1871–1936* (Paris, 1946), especially pp. 33 ff.; Maitron, pp. 249 ff. and passim; Pierre Monatte, *Trois scissions syndicales* (Paris, 1958), passim. This is not the place to go into the history of Syndicalism. Let it simply be said that the movement's real founders—Fernand Pelloutier, Victor Griffuelhes, and the others who came together in the 1880s and 1890s—deserved a better fate than that of being treated as precursors of Sorel. Their veritable legacy is to be found in the writings of Antonio Gramsci, who helped to organize the works-council movement in Northern Italy in 1919–20, before he was deflected into the leadership of the newly founded Italian Communist party. Syndicalism from the start rested upon the idea of autonomous producers running their own affairs without interference from anybody (not even from a revolutionary party). Whether this

is feasible is another matter: at any rate, it is what the movement was about.

36. Sorel, Preface of 1905 to *Matériaux d'une théorie du prolétariat* (Paris, 1919). Silberner, in "Anti-Jewish Trends in French Revolutionary Syndicalism" (*Jewish Social Studies*, XV, No. 3-4 [1953]), dates the change in Sorel's attitude from 1912, when he published an apology of the anti-Semitic writer Urbain Gohier, who had recently broken with the Socialist movement. But the Preface of 1905 already prefigured the subsequent drift of his thought in a direction later exploited by Mussolini's followers (though not by the German "National Socialists," for whom Sorel was not racialist enough).

37. Irving Louis Horowitz, *Radicalism and the Revolt Against Reason* (London and New York, 1961), p. 41.

38. Horowitz notes that Sorel began to formulate his viewpoint on this topic in the *Cahiers de la Quinzaine* from 1901 onward. This is a useful corrective to Silberner's account of the subject, which emphasizes the nationalist and anti-Semitic agitation in France between 1910 and 1914. In April 1911 two prominent Syndicalist agitators, Pataud and Janvion, sponsored a mass meeting in Paris which was advertised in advance as "a great anti-Jewish and anti-Masonic" demonstration. An audience of some two thousand people—including numerous *Camelots du Roi*, i.e., followers of Maurras and the Action Française—heard anti-Semitic tirades which reminded a Russian visitor present of the pogromists in his native country. The lead taken by prominent Syndicalists on this occasion drew violent protests from Jean Longuet (Marx's grandson) in the Socialist *l'Humanité*, and from Gustave Hervé and Sébastien Faure in the Anarchist *Guerre Sociale*. The culprits were, however, quite unrepentant. What is more, their assertion that socialist internationalism benefited only the "kikes" (*youtres*) at the expense of honest Frenchmen clearly struck a popular chord: otherwise they would not have continued their agitation in the Anarchist *Terre libre*, which ran a simultaneous campaign against capitalism, philo-Semitism, Jewish immigrant workers, and "the Judaized gang of Jaurès." This was the popular, or populist, side of a movement to which Sorel shortly afterwards became a convert: on January 1, 1912, when he published a lengthy and violent anti-Semitic tirade in support of Gohier's demand that the French learn to defend their traditions against the Jewish invasion (Sorel, "Urbain Gohier," *Indépendance*, January 1, 1912, p. 320; see also his article "Quelques prétentions juives," *Indépendance*, III [1912], where the Jews are collectively accused of subverting Christian civilization, undermining decent moral standards, and encouraging the spread of pornographic literature).

39. Ernst Nolte, in *Three Faces of Fascism* (New York, 1966), p. 71, gives a brief account of this fusion of nationalism with pseudosocialism. He also suggests that "the precipitating factor was the collaboration on the newspaper *Action Française* of the highly gifted son of the working class, George Valois." Maurras himself had no use for national socialism. He was a traditional conservative, and at bottom a paternalist in the fashion common among upholders of the Monarchy and the Church since the early nineteenth century. But if Maurras was to find disciples in Franco and Salazar, Sorel can claim Mussolini—the ex-socialist turned nationalist. As for Valois (whose real name was Alfred Georges Gressent), his doctrine has been called "a strange mixture of Nietzsche, Maurras, Sorel, and Chris-

tianity," though the Christian content is barely visible. He appears to have started a fascist group called Le Faisceau in 1925, deliberately modeled upon Mussolini's regime. In later years he became reconciled to democracy. Nolte, op. cit., p. 473.

40. Ibid., p. 71. It is not quite clear why Nolte regards this claim as unfounded. After all, the first step is the one that counts, and the decisive step in the intellectual prehistory of Fascism was taken by the Cercle Proudhon: appropriately named after Marx's old enemy.

41. Sorel, *Matériaux d'une théorie* (postscriptum of 1918 to the unpublished Preface of 1914). Here the October Revolution is welcomed for having revealed to the proletariat that its mission cannot be accomplished otherwise than by doing away with "formal democracy" and establishing a *gouvernement de producteurs*. The rational core of this idea later entered into the doctrines of Italian Communism. Its irrational glorification of violence and terror was duly inherited by Stalinists and Fascists alike, and to this day forms a common bond between them.

42. Gaëtan Pirou, *Georges Sorel* (Paris, 1927), p. 50. See also the fourth edition of Sorel's *Réflexions sur la violence* (Paris, 1919), p. 450, where he dwells on this theme. The *Réflexions*—originally published in 1907—made Sorel famous. In retrospect the book appears as a bridge from his earlier pseudo-Marxism to his subsequent conversion to Bergson-cum-Nietzsche. Sorel fancied himself a philosopher. It would have pained him had he known in 1918 that Lenin held a poor opinion of his essays on the philosophy of science, in which he had tried his hand at metaphysics in the Bergsonian manner. (See Lenin, *Materialism and Empiriocriticism*, in *Collected Works*, XIV, 292.)

43. For Lazare and the beginnings of pro-Zionism among French Socialists see Silberner, "French Socialism and the Jewish Question," pp. 27 ff. Before 1914 this was hardly an issue. After 1917 Léon Blum and others became active in pro-Palestine committees, though they dissented from the Zionist position that Palestine could offer a solution to the Jewish problem. Lazare was unusual in that, having become a Jewish nationalist under the impact of the Dreyfus Affair, he attended Zionist congresses and maintained that "there is a Jewish nation" and that it must have its own territory so as to accomplish its collective regeneration. This regeneration would have to be social as well as national, for Lazare had no use for the Jewish bourgeoisie. Neither did those East European Jewish Socialists who pioneered the Palestinian land settlements after 1906. By an agreeable paradox, most of them were admirers of Fourier and Proudhon.

44. For the French development during the 1930s see Georges Lefranc, *Le Mouvement Socialiste sous la Troisième République* (Paris, 1963); especially pp. 286 ff., on the internal crisis of the Socialist party which in the end led to the departure of the so-called neo-Socialists in 1933. The reason why some of them eventually turned to Fascism cannot be discussed here, and the same applies to the parallel development in Belgium. See Peter Dodge, *Beyond Marx: The Faith and Works of Hendrik de Man* (The Hague, 1966), passim, for a rather apologetic treatment of this important topic.

Simone Weil

❋ ❋ ❋

I

IN HIS PREFACE to a volume of essays by contributors repesenta-
tive of the Christian-extentialist school in postwar France,[1]
Etienne Gilson refers to Gabriel Marcel as a descendant of
"cette lignée de penseurs français dont la spéculation philoso-
phique n'a d'autre source que leur expérience intérieure et ne
dure qu'en s'y référant continuellement." With even greater justice might this description be applied to a writer whose posthumously published essays, notebooks, and letters have since
1948 caused a stir among French intellectuals, especially of the
younger generation, comparable in some ways to the delayed
impact of Kierkegaard upon many among Germany's student
youth after 1918. If the short life and the fragmentary work of
Simone Weil bear the stamp of uniqueness, the reason lies not
so much in the originality of her mind as in the consistency with
which she fused experience, thought, and action into one single
indivisible whole.

It is in a sense misleading to call her a writer. In her own lifetime she published almost nothing, and the four volumes bearing
her name which have appeared since 1948 were edited by friends
from manuscripts, some of which are no more than rough drafts;
two entire volumes have been filled with excerpts from her notebooks, many of them mere jottings. Simone Weil was neither a
prolific nor a systematic writer. The lengthy programmatic essay

Cambridge Journal, March 1951.
    1. *Extentialisme Chrétien: Gabriel Marcel* (Paris, 1947).

entitled *L'Enracinement,* which was compiled shortly before her death in 1943, stands by itself as her only sustained and comprehensive effort toward systematic statement. Dealing with a wealth of subjects ranging from religion to politics, it constitutes one of the few genuinely impressive attempts yet made to put the philosophy of "Christian democracy" into writing. Some fairly lengthy fragments of what might have become an equally important essay on morals were among the manuscripts deposited with a Dominican priest, Père Perrin, when Simone Weil left France for America in 1942, and these together with a number of letters have been published under the title *Attente de Dieu.* For the rest there are her notebooks, or rather the selection edited by Gustave Thibon, himself a writer of some distinction, with a good deal of help from others, including Gabriel Marcel. Fragmentary as they are, these writings nonetheless form a whole and represent a distinctive point of view, of which the least that can be said is that nothing remotely like it has made its appearance elsewhere. Many of the subjects touched upon in the notebooks are indeed common to the whole group of writers to whom the more or less ill-fitting existentialist label has been attached. Equally it is arguable that the criticism of society put forward in *L'Enracinement* is so plainly in the Proudhonist tradition as to place Simone Weil within a recognizable stream of French thought. The ascription of originality to her work must not, therefore, be misunderstood to suggest that it occupies a kind of vacuum. What it does imply is that Simone Weil is not simply to be classed with any group of contemporary writers, however deeply she may have been influenced at various times by the rationalism of Alain, the socialism of Proudhon and Marx, or the theology and sociology of the Catholic Church. She is original even in her politics, for as will be seen she repudiates both the *ancien régime and* the Revolution, thus giving offense to conservatives and radicals alike. She is also a trenchant critic of the Church and a moralist on a high plane of speculative thinking—but of this less will be said, for I propose to deal only with those aspects of her thought which have a direct bearing upon contemporary problems. Almost everything she has written, however, is worth reading, and although translations will probably begin to appear before long, the extremely personal character of her work, and the peculiar note struck by her style, make it doubly advisable to consult the originals.[2]

II

The life of Simone Weil exemplifies a principle sometimes neglected by the less intelligent camp followers of modern psychology, namely the importance of differentiating between the purely private and the metapersonal aspects of struggle and disharmony in the history of an individual. There is a good deal in the available accounts of her life that suggests a remarkably close intertwining of the neurotic and the genuinely spiritual. The distinction is of course orthodox from the psychoanalytical viewpoint as well as from any other, but how many psychologists are capable of making it in practice? In the case of Simone Weil there is also this to be considered: what we know of her comes mainly from Perrin and Thibon, both orthodox Catholics who nonetheless came to regard her as the bearer of an authentic message, a genuine mystic, and something very near a saint. Simone Weil was born of Jewish parents, went through the usual course of rationalist and anticlerical education, became a socialist, joined the revolutionary side in Spain, refused even after her conversion to Christianity to enter the Catholic Church, and maintained to the end a highly unorthodox mystical theology of her own. Yet her literary remains have been published by the Dominican Perrin and the Catholic conservative Thibon, in each case with prefatory remarks disclosing not merely personal admiration but a profound sense of spiritual kinship. Alain, her first teacher and perhaps, despite all, the most lasting intellectual influence in her life, "garda profondément le souvenir de

2. The following have been published: *La Pesanteur et la Grâce,* with an introduction by Gustave Thibon (Paris, 1948); *L'Enracinement: Prélude à une Déclaration des Devoirs envers l'Etre Humain* (Paris, 1949); *Attente de Dieu,* with an introduction by Père Perrin, O.P. (Paris, 1950); *La Connaissance Surnaturelle* (Paris, 1950). Previously, the New York review *Politics* had published the following essays in English translation: "Reflections on War," Feb. 1945; "The Iliad or the Poem of Force," Nov. 1945; "Words and War," March 1946; "Factory Work," Dec. 1946. Two essays thus far not translated into English—"L'Agonie d'une Civilisation" and "L'Inspiration Occitanienne," both in *Cahiers du Sud,* Aug. 1942—furnish a useful introduction to the study of her major writings.

cette étonnante intelligence et il ne voulait pas croire qu'elle fût morte. 'Ce n'est pas vrai, répétait-il, n'est-ce-pas qu'elle reviendra?' " [3] Lastly, we know that her parents remained intensely loyal to her, and she to them, although she had repudiated the spiritual heritage of Judaism along with traditional upbringing, bourgeois conventions, and all the prevailing orthodoxies of her day—social, political, and religious. Something about her personality must have suggested to all who came in contact with her that she was not to be measured by ordinary standards.

There is, however, a difficulty to be overcome. The importance of psychological stresses in furthering or retarding her spiritual growth cannot be overlooked. From the accounts of her childhood it is evident that at an early age she began to manifest an unusual capacity for identifying herself with the sufferings of others. It is equally evident that the form this tendency took in her was not the common one of self-pity but the exceptional one of self-mortification, mounting to self-sacrifice. The psychologists must be left to deal as best they can with this aspect of the matter. The biographical facts can at any rate be stated with fair accuracy, since Perrin has told us a good deal about them, chiefly on the strength of what he learned from her parents. She was five years old in 1914 when the sight of wounded soldiers made her refuse to touch sugar and insist that it should be given away. At about the same time she took to going barefoot, from sympathy with some pauper children— but also, Perrin notes, to tease her parents. Later we find her described as shy, precociously intelligent—and lonely. Nothing very remarkable appears to have occurred at the lycée, where she came under the influence first of Le Senne and then of Alain, or during the three years (1928–31) she spent at the Ecole Normale, save that her classmates seem to have been less fond of her than her teachers.[4] But from the moment when she took up teaching at Le Puy in 1931, the pattern of her life began to declare itself. She was then twenty-two, rather unprepossessing in

3. Perrin, op. cit., p. 19.
4. The evidence for this has not been published. It reduces itself to a vague characterization of Simone (and her more intimate friends) as "arrogant," presumably because she did not join in the usual social activities. A more important piece of unpublished evidence concerning her later life will be considered presently.

appearance, ironically indifferent toward her official superiors and persons in authority generally, and very much a representative of the left-wing intelligentsia in her views and general bearing—save in one important particular: she tended to translate her opinions into immediate personal practice. Thus when it was laid down that the unemployed at Le Puy must break stones to qualify for financial relief, she not only took part in a protest demonstration but actually joined in manual work thought suitable only for navvies. She also reverted to her childhood practice of rationing herself to essentials and turned over the balance of her income to those who needed it more urgently. After three years of this, her colleagues and superiors must have felt some relief when in 1934 they saw her depart for Paris— to work in the Renault factory as a machine-tender, on the principle apparently that socialist intellectuals ought to know what they are talking about. She cannot have been altogether comfortable to live with.

Up to this point the story might still be regarded as not untypical of her generation. In Paris, however, she suffered a breakdown which became important for her subsequent development: she could not endure life at Renault and found herself compelled to terminate the experiment after less than a year. Extracts from the journal she kept at that time have appeared under the title *Journal d'Usine*. They contain much that is orthodox socialist criticism of the inhumanity of factory life, but they also reveal a degree of nervous sensitivity to the sheer physical strain of mechanical work which would in any case have made longer continuance impossible for her. She had always suffered from violent headaches which at times incapacitated her, and her death from tuberculosis at the age of thirty-four suggests that a metal factory was at no time a suitable environment. But over and above these physical factors a sense of horror at the conditions of industrial life seems to have been implanted in her by the experience she underwent at Renault. It deepened her awareness of social reality and enabled her to fill a whole chapter of *L'Enracinement* with detailed suggestions for improving not merely the conditions of work but the methods of technical and vocational training in modern industry. But it also seems to have produced something like a nervous breakdown and a profound depression of spirit. At any rate when Perrin made her acquaintance in 1941 she told him that the experience had marked her for life. "J'ai reçu là pour toujours la marque de l'esclavage, comme la marque au fer rouge que les Romains mettaient au front de leurs esclaves les plus méprisées. Depuis, je me suit toujours regardée comme une esclave." [5] It is plain from what she told Perrin, and from her remarks on the general subject of industrialism in *L'Enracinement,* that the mental anguish she suffered was in some sense a reflection of what she felt to be the miserable and "uprooted" condition of her workmates, but the fact that she broke down suggests that a personal element entered into the matter. This is even more obvious of her next experience: when the civil war began in Spain in 1936 she promptly put her philosophy into practice by joining up in a noncombatant capacity; but an accident which no psychologist would allow to pass without comment—she somehow managed to spill boiling oil over her feet—soon caused her to be invalided out. It is probably not without significance that about the same time her political views underwent a change. At any rate she returned from Spain thoroughly disillusioned, and her criticism of society from that time onward assumed a conservative and traditionalist coloring, without ceasing to be socialist in character. She was on the way toward the mature view formulated in *L'Enracinement.*

It was then that she started on the last and decisive phase of her spiritual journey. At Easter time 1937 she was at Solesmes, listening to the Gregorian chant and feeling increasingly drawn to the Catholic Church, yet not joining it. About this time she made the acquaintance of a young English Catholic through whom she became aware of the metaphysical poets, particularly Herbert. When she met Perrin four years later, she laid stress on this chance encounter and on the time spent at Solesmes in helping to bring about her conversion. Then or later she went through the mystical experience which is alluded to in her notes and in a letter to Perrin.[6] From this time onward she regarded herself as a Christian, but did not join the Church and maintained her reservations on certain aspects of Catholic doctrine, as well as

5. Perrin, op. cit., p. 20.
6. Ibid., p. 21.

her unreserved condemnation of historical Christianity as manifested in the life of the Church, against all the arguments brought forward by her Catholic friends. Her final refusal to undergo baptism seems, however, to have been motivated by a personal reason which is the subject of one of her last letters to Perrin before leaving France in May 1942. Here she lays stress upon an inner sense of reluctance to hasten a process which must be consummated in its own good time—an argument he naturally could not altogether accept, since it savored of spiritual arrogance and private judgment. On the subject of her attitude toward the Church it is perhaps best to let Perrin speak: "Elle ne dit pas aimer l'Eglise, mais en même temps elle était prête à mourir pour elle, tant elle en comprenait l'importance; elle se sentait dans une situation inextricable, mentant en restant hors de cette Eglise et mentant en frappant à porte sans avoir résolu les difficultés qui encombraient sa route."

What the "difficulties" were will appear in due course. Here it must be sufficient to remark that Perrin has published in full the writings placed in his keeping when she left Marseilles for America, notwithstanding the painful hesitations he had to overcome. His introduction is an extremely interesting and in its way a moving document. It bears witness to the powerful impression Simone Weil had made upon him, although he remarks not unfairly that in some respects her mind had not completely matured. She was notably prone to extreme judgments in instances where her animosity had been aroused, e.g., in everything that concerned Roman history and what she regarded as the enduring influence of Rome upon Europe and the Catholic Church. Similarly he found himself at times placed in the paradoxical position of having to defend the Jewish heritage against her impassioned strictures.

We have another account of her during this period, when she was staying in southern France as a refugee, the Weil family having left Paris in 1941 to escape from the Germans. This is contained in Thibon's preface to the volume edited by him (*La Pesanteur et la Grâce*) from manuscripts, mainly in note form, dealing with questions of faith. The first encounter between these two kindred spirits was anything but promising. She had been

recommended to him by Perrin, who had then met her only once
or twice, as "une jeune fille israélite, agrégée de philosophie et
militante d'extrême gauche, qui, exclue de l'Université par les
nouvelles lois, désirerait travailler quelque temps à la campagne"
—a somewhat misleading description, which did not predispose
Thibon in her favor. An orthodox Catholic, a conservative, a
farmer and a self-taught man of letters who had already published writings critical of the whole trend of modern culture, he
felt some qualms at the thought of making her welcome. What
followed is best described in his own language:

> Nos premiers contacts furent cordiaux, mais pénibles. Sur le plan
> concret, nous n'étions d'accord à peu près sur rien. Elle discutait à
> l'infini, d'une voix inflexible et monotone, et je sortais littéralement
> usé de ces entretiens sans issue. Je m'armai alors, pour la supporter,
> de patience et de courtoisie. Et puis, grâce au privilège de la vie
> commune, je constatai peu à peu que ce côté impossible de son
> caractère, loin d'être l'expression de sa nature profonde, ne tra-
> duisait guère que son moi extérieur et social. . . . contrairement à
> la plupart des hommes, elle gagnait infiniment à être connue dans
> une atmosphère d'intimité; elle extériorisait, avec une spontanéité
> redoutable, le côté déplaisant de sa nature, mais il lui fallait beau-
> coup de temps, d'affection et de pudeur vaincue pour manifester ce
> qu'elle avait de meilleur. . . . je n'ai jamais rencontré, dans un être
> humain, une telle familiarité avec les mystères religieux; jamais le
> mot de *surnaturel* ne m'est apparu plus gonflé de réalité qu'a son
> contact.

It was typical of her that after staying with Thibon for a while
she suddenly decided that she was too comfortable and moved
to a semiderelict annex. She naturally insisted upon doing all the
most backbreaking kinds of farm work, gave up half her rations
to political prisoners in town, and systematically drove herself to
the point of exhaustion. Yet she found time and energy to spend
hours every day after work helping Thibon with his Greek (they
read Plato together and he found her an excellent teacher). For
the rest he was pleasantly surprised to discover that when the
mask had fallen she was good company, gay and animated, and
not in the least put out by her new surroundings. When she returned to Marseilles in the autumn to resume her endless dis-

cussions with Perrin, he seems to have felt the loss severely. After her departure from France in the following spring they remained in contact until the occupation of southern France by the Germans in November 1942 put an end to the correspondence. In 1944, still hoping to see her again, he received the news that she had died of tuberculosis in a hospital in Kent the year before.

It must be borne in mind that when Perrin and Thibon came into contact with her in 1941, Simone Weil was only two years from her end. Her view of life had settled during the four preceding years, concerning which we are left somewhat in the dark by her biographers, but the most important of her writings were composed during the final phase. After Perrin had moved to Montpellier in March 1942, they met less frequently, and from the time when she sailed with her parents for the United States two months later, we are left without a satisfactory substitute biographer. Her spiritual record can in part be deciphered from the notebooks published under the title *La Connaissance Surnaturelle*, which date from this period but are largely composed of disconnected fragments. *L'Enracinement*, part of which was written in London, where she arrived on November 10, 1942, will presently be considered in some detail. It is, in my opinion, one of the more important contributions to the postwar discussion in France, but from the biographical viewpoint it has less significance than her religious and metaphysical writings, with which I do not propose to deal.

Of her life in London during these final months little is known, save that she worked in the Gaullist organization, applied unsuccessfully for permission to be parachuted into occupied France, and spent much time with a small group of personal friends. Her health, which had always been bad, soon gave rise to anxiety, not least because she insisted on reducing her diet to the starvation level then reigning in France. Tuberculosis set in, which she did little to check. There is plainly an element of self-destruction, whether conscious or unconscious, in the circumstances surrounding her death. Did she believe, as has been suggested, that when a certain stage of mystical illumination has been attained the coming of death ought not to be resisted? Her friends at any rate were in no doubt that the regime of self-mortification which she imposed upon herself was a factor in hastening the end. On August 24, 1943, she died at Ashford hospital in Kent.[7]

III

A candid attempt to assess the significance of Simone Weil's thought must start from the admission that her work is too fragmentary to bear the weight of specialist criticism. It belongs to the class of utterances which draw their effect from the production of a kind of shock upon the reader. This is true even of *L'Enracinement*, her most considerable piece of work and the only one that approaches systematic form. Although largely concerned with the causes of the French collapse in 1940, it is an essay on morals—even on metaphysics—as much as an attempt at analysis. Historical and psychological insights, often of astonishing force and brilliance, are scattered throughout its 250 pages, but the emphasis is upon the functioning of society. Simone Weil is a moralist in the classic French tradition, the last of a great line which begins at the opening of the modern era and has ever since produced an unbroken succession of writers concerned with the whole duty of man toward eternity and his fellow beings. Her tone, moreover, is almost as polemical as that of Péguy (whom she resembles in more than one respect), and her emphasis, where she deals with public matters, is commonly upon the moral and intellectual degradation of the elite which led France to destruction in 1940. It will scarcely be supposed that the literary product of this relentless quest for the sources of material disaster and spiritual corruption is of the kind which is commonly preferred in Britain—a careful weighing of arguments and a tolerant attempt to be fair to all concerned. It must also be conceded to the critics, who have already made their voice heard, that there are occasions when she comes close to absurdity, e.g., in proposing that newspapers (as distinct from

7. "Elle est morte Cathare," one who knew her is reported to have said of her last phase. Since this statement has never before appeared in print, it may be as well to append a reservation. Those who believe, or perhaps only repeat the rumor, that she held "Manichean" views and was in touch with others of like mind have yet to offer evidence. It is, however, incontestable that her writings are shot through with sympathetic references to the Albigensians (cf. *L'Enracinement*, pp. 95 ff.).

periodicals) should be forbidden to put forward any kind of editorial opinion, lest the reading public continue to be benumbed by paid propagandists, or in suggesting that special tribunals should watch over the factual truth of everything asserted in print. It may or may not be desirable that some means should be found to bring gross errors to the notice of the public. But when the argument is pushed to the point of suggesting that anyone should have the right to arraign, for example, M. Maritain for having overlooked the existence of those Greek thinkers who, unlike Aristotle, condemned the institution of slavery—it becomes plain that what is proposed is not merely objectionable but impossible. Or to take another instance, the suggestion that political parties in their present form should not be tolerated is frankly utopian and fundamentally undemocratic as well, even when backed by the unimpeachable argument that all modern mass organizations are potentially totalitarian. The tendency of these and similar arguments, scattered throughout the first part of *L'Enracinement,* is towards a sort of idealized "Christian corporatism," of which it is sufficient to say that whatever the intentions of its more democratic proponents, its practical application so far has resulted either in the grotesqueries of the Dollfuss-Schuschnigg regime or in frankly provisional and makeshift institutions such as those of Portugal under Salazar. Neither, incidentally, is mentioned by Simone Weil, and the whole direction of her thought is toward something far more closely in tune with the historic traditions of French socialism, notably as represented by Proudhon and the "Fédérés" of 1871. It is, however, not without significance that although passionately attached to the cause of Free France she seems to have contemplated the disappearance of the Third Republic with a good deal of equanimity. Vichy, she thought, was merely profiting from the hopeless corruption of the Republican regime, an opinion which undoubtedly was shared by many Resistance leaders at the time but which led them to underestimate the fundamental attachment of the French people to the self-governing institutions, however moth-eaten and discredited, of which in 1940 they suddenly found themselves derprived. In her conviction that the prewar regime must on no account be permitted to re-establish itself after Vichy's sham-corporate experiments had been swept away, she doubtless reflected the prevailing mood of the Resistance movement, or at any rate of its intellectuals. *L'Enracinement* is very much a document of this period of soul-searching, out of which have come so many things, some hopeful, others sterile, which have helped to make the Fourth Republic different from its predecessor. But it is only on the left wing of the MRP, among the more radical representatives of "Christian Democracy" and "Christian Socialism," that her pronouncements are likely to find a ready echo. And these friendly critics will inevitably be the first to note that the all-important question of forging a political instrument for carrying out the proposed institutional changes is hardly considered at all. Simone Weil is indeed weakest on the point on which the practitioners of politics are strongest: she obstinately refuses to face the problem of power. She takes it for granted that some authority or other exists and can be relied upon to decree fundamental changes for which majority consent may not be available. The confusion is not improved by demanding that the central government should abdicate its function as far as possible in favor of local, regional, and professional associations. For, since the workers' movement is explicitly described as unable to effect the necessary changes, the political parties are to be dissolved, and the state itself is to surrender the excessive power it has acquired, no adequate authority is left. We are, it seems, back with the utopians, and it is impossible not to remember that Proudhon, who anticipated much of Simone Weil's political and social program, left his followers face to face with problems they had never thought of solving and thus helped to bring on the colossal disaster of the Commune. Even Marx's subsequent suggestion that the program of the Communards, if given a chance, would have regenerated French society and introduced genuine self-government in the place of centralized bureaucracy cannot alter the fact that the catastrophe was chiefly due to the inability of the Fédérés to make use of such authority as they possessed.

L'Enracinement is, however, more than a sketch of a Christian-socialist utopia, with industry decentralized, factories transformed into model institutions, village life ennobled, prostitution abolished, and education directed toward nonutilitarian ends. It contains all this and a good deal besides, e.g., a brilliant thumbnail sketch of French history and a passionate onslaught on the nationalism of Maurras. But its primary significance is moral. If it fails as a statement of aims, it succeeds as a indictment of the status quo and of the intellectuals among its defenders. The indictment, moreover, is delivered not in abstract terms but in the form of a challenge to established values. It is, after all, a fact that France broke down in 1940, and to say that the disaster occurred because "patriotism is not enough" and Frenchmen had nothing else to fall back upon is to question some very deep-rooted national traditions. Again, a writer of the Resistance movement who does not hesitate to assert that France was the aggressor in 1870, that the defeat of 1940 was deserved, and that the cult of Jeanne d'Arc between the wars was a species of na-tionalist idolatry designed to take the place of the forgotten Christian religion is not an everyday phenomenon. Nor is it cus-tomary for French writers to denounce the imposition of French culture upon Provençals, Bretons, Flemings, Arabs, Negroes, and Malays as spiritual murder. If Simone Weil had written nothing but the pages in *L'Enracinement* which describe the extension of French sovereignty to the provinces south of the Loire, a slight tremor must have been caused in the realm of French letters on this account alone. The following passage, far from being un-usual, is typical of her style of writing:

> On peut trouver dans l'histoire des faits d'une atrocité aussi grande, mais non plus grande, sauf peut-être quelques rares exceptions, que la conquête par les Français des territoires situés au sud de la Loire, au debut du XIIIe siècle. Ces territoires où existait un niveau de vie élevé de culture, de tolérance, de liberté, de vie spirituelle, étaient animés d'un patriotisme intense pour ce qu'ils nommaient leur "lan-gage"; mot par lequel ils désignaient la patrie. Les Français étaient pour eux des étrangers et des barbares, comme pour nous les Allemands [written in 1943]. Pour imprimer immédiatement la terreur, les Français commencèrent par exterminer la ville entière de Béziers, et ils obtinrent l'effet cherché. Une fois le pays conquis, ils y installèrent l'Inquisition. Un trouble sourd continua à couver parmi ces populations, et les poussa plus tard à embrasser avec ardeur le Protestantisme, dont d'Aubigny dit, malgré les différences si considérables de doctrine, qu'il procède directement des Albigeois. On peut voir combien était forte dans ces pays la haine du pouvoir central, par la ferveur religieuse témoignée à Toulouse aux restes du Duc de Montmorency, décapité pour rebellion contre Richelieu. La

même protestation latente les jeta avec enthousiasme dans la Révolution française. Plus tard ils devinrent radicaux-socialistes, laïques, anticléricaux; sous la IIIᵉ République ils ne haïssaient plus le pouvoir central; ils s'en étaient dans une large mesure emparés et l'exploitaient.

On peut remarquer qu'à chaque fois leur protestation a pris un caractère de déracinement plus intense et un niveau de spiritualité et de pensée plus bas. On peut remarquer aussi que depuis qu'ils ont été conquis, ces pays ont apporté à la culture française une contribution assez faible, alors qu'auparavant ils étaient tellement brillants. Le pensée française doit d'avantage aux Albigeois et au troubadours du XIIᵉ siécle, qui n'étaient pas français, qu'à tout ce que ces territoires ont produit au cours des siècles suivants.[8]

Remarks such as these help to explain why both the Right and the Left have found it difficult to discover a suitable label for Simone Weil. She has a disconcerting habit of cutting across familiar lines of approach, as when she enlivens an exposition of the socialist faith by rounding upon the Marxists, or as in the above passage where the indictment of the Monarchy and the Church reaches a climax in the casual tossing of a hand grenade at the Republicans and the anticlericals. In this, as well as in her social and moral judgments, she comes closest to Péguy, to whom she has inevitably been compared. But Péguy was more orthodox in religion and a nationalist, though of the anti-Maurrassian stripe, in politics. Worst of all from Simone Weil's point of view, he thought highly of the institutions and traditions of classical Rome, for which she entertained an aversion equalled only by her dislike of the Old Testament. It is thus extremely difficult to "place" her—and that is just why her writings have had such an impact upon young people impatient of the stale dispute between clericals and anticlericals which has now been going on for more than a century and eager likewise to break away from the traditional political feuds. There is a puritanical rigor about her judgments which sets her apart from other postwar writers. After pondering her impassioned indictment of the *ancien régime,* of Richelieu and Bossuet and Louis XIV, and then coming upon her half contemptuous, half pitying attitude toward the Enlightenment and the Revolution, one begins to wonder what French in-

8. *L'Enracinement,* pp. 95–96.

tellectual life would have been like if the Reformation had not
been aborted. To be an unorthodox Christian in a country neatly
split between Catholics and anticlericals, a Proudhonist socialist
in a century of mass organization, a moralist contemptuous of
Latinity, and a mystic more attached to Plato and the Upanishads
than to the Bible requires at the very least an unusual capacity
for going one's own way.

IV

If the foregoing remarks have made it appear that *L'Enracinement* is primarily a tract for the times, that impression must now
be corrected. A considerable part of it, and nearly everything else
that Simone Weil set down in writing, belongs either to the
realm of moral theology—if so antiquated a term can be used to
describe the kind of utterance that expresses the existentialist
consciousness—or alternatively to that of religious introspection.
To the theologian, the mystic, the psychologist, and the student
of the varieties of religious experience, her writings offer a fascinating field of study. Their attention will probably be caught
in the first place by the reflections set down in the group of
manuscripts published under the title *Attente de Dieu* and by the
letters to Perrin (also included in this volume) which define her
attitude toward the Catholic Church. They are likely, even if
they cannot accept her positive beliefs, to be struck by the uncommon beauty and penetration of essays such as the one entitled "Réflexions sur le bon usage des études scolaires en vue de
l'amour de Dieu." And they may find much to interest them in
her other writings, although Alain has professed some disappointment with *La Pesanteur et la Grâce,* the selection made by Thibon. But for the purpose of this study her metaphysics can be
considered only insofar as they bear directly upon her doctrine
of personal and collective responsibility. *L'Enracinement* is significant just because it does attempt to link personal morality and
public affairs. The attempt is made within the framework of
Christian metaphysics, and the Christianity is not that of any
existing church, while the metaphysics are borrowed from Plato
and the neo-Platonists. But in the present context this is im-
material. It now remains to inquire wherein consists the link

between what Simone Weil held to be true of the world and
what she regarded as desirable and possible of fulfillment in the
life of the individual and society. It should then be possible to
indicate whether her thinking forms part of a continuing tradition—as in accordance with her own principles it should: for
Simone Weil is very much a traditionalist and in her writings
outdoes Burke in her attachment to the past and her insistence
upon the importance of the partnership between the living and
the dead. Society itself is declared to draw its *raison d'être* from
the fact that it functions as "l'unique organe de transmission par
l'intermédiaire duquel les morts puissent parler au vivants."
Where in this continuing chain can one place the work of Simone
Weil? [9]

The intellectual life of France since the war is often mislead-
ingly described in terms of a three-cornered dispute, with the
small group of existentialist writers attempting to hold a position
midway between the Christian and Communist camps. Existentialism is thus pictured as a fad specially invented for the benefit
of unattached intellectuals. This legend has had support from
Catholics and Communists alike, since both are anxious to claim
for themselves a monopoly of everything not indubitably belonging to the enemy. In actual fact there has been little if any crossing of swords between orthodox Catholics and orthodox Communists, if only because Rome and Moscow do not favor such
encounters. Marx's writings do, however, contain much that critics
of society cannot find elsewhere. Hence it is not surprising that
argument has raged in the main between unorthodox Marxists

9. Since no attempt is made in the following to comment critically upon
her metaphysics, it may be well to draw attention to an article by Leslie
Fiedler in *Commentary* (Jan. 1951) which contains *inter alia* a sort of
riposte to Simone Weil's assault upon traditional Judaism. That Jewish mystical theology was a closed book to her does not indeed require much evidence. Her relationship to traditional Christianity is perhaps sufficiently
indicated by the fact that she regarded the Iliad, rather than the Old Testament, as its spiritual source. In her eyes, the Catholic Church—aside from
being a mass organization and tainted with all the imperfections of one—
suffered quite simply from being altogether too "Jewish." Her theology, in
short, is of the Gnostic variety and forms a complete counterpart to her
personal asceticism and her cult of *Innerlichkeit*, to use the untranslatable
German expression. It is at the farthest possible remove from traditional
Judaism, but also, it must be supposed, from any conceivable Christian
"theology of the Bible," in the spirit of modern neo-Protestantism.

on the one hand and unorthodox Christains on the other, while the Communist and Catholic organizations have contributed little beyond stereotyped apologetics of no great interest or novelty. The battle, in short, is between the Christian existentialists and those who derive from Marx. The "atheist humanism" of Jean-Paul Sartre and Simone de Beauvoir is plainly Marxism was an admixture of Kierkegaard, just as the Christian existentialism of Gabriel Marcel and Emmanuel Mounier is Kierkegaard with a dash of Marx. The same is true of their followers. To show this in detail would be tedious. It is plain from all their writings, and whoever doubts it need only study *Le Temps Modernes, Esprit, La Table Ronde,* and the other periodicals in which the debate is carried on. This is not to deny that there are still plenty of orthodox Catholics; the point is that the arguments with which they meet their humanist opponents are designed to show that Christian truths can be presented in existentialist terms. When Simone Weil denounces Pascal's apologetics as dishonest because "il a entrepris une recherche intellectuelle en décidant à l'avance où elle devait le mener" or when she pours contempt upon Bergson's pragmatic arguments in defense of religion,[10] she is, whether she knows it or not, echoing Kierkegaard's strictures upon the theologians of his time. There are, as we have seen, other elements in her thought, but it is evident that on this point at any rate she does stand within a tradition.

It is perhaps needless to add that the current alignment itself reflects the fact that Marx and Kierkegaard reacted against Hegel at about the same time and in similar ways, though for different reasons and with different results, and that their respective revolts were directed against related aspects of the culture of their time; so that it is not really surprising to find the contemporary debate largely dominated by their followers, notably in France and Germany, where bourgeois society and bourgeois Christianity have both been more severely shaken than elsewhere, and where for various reasons there has always been a greater readiness to discuss current problems in terms of fundamentals. But the point to be made about Simone Weil is that she does exhibit a novel and possibly significant trait. Hitherto no real en-

10. *l'Enracinement,* pp. 212, 213.

counter between the two sides—to say nothing of the orthodox from whom they have both split off—has been possible, because there has been no common ground between the disciples of Marx, with their hopes placed upon the regeneration of society, and the followers of the Danish theologian, with their insistence upon the supreme importance of the individual. Now Simone Weil, despite the immaturity of much of her thought and the fragmentary character of her work, does represent a step in the direction of establishing common ground. Her rejection of the Communist apocalyptic places her firmly on the Christian side of the dispute, but there is less in her of that insistence upon the regeneration of the individual as the first step to a regenerated society which renders almost all theological writing on the subject so unutterably boring to the humanist.

It will have become plain that to class Simone Weil is not a simple matter. An attempt will probably be made, notwithstanding her unorthodoxies, to claim her for the Catholic Church. This seems unlikely to succeed, though the Jeunesse Ouvrière Catholique in France may take her up unless dissuaded by their elders. The Socialists, being committed to anticlericalism and no longer much interested in the "federalism" of Proudhon, can do nothing with her. At a different level she may serve as a catalyst of tendencies cutting across traditional lines of thought. In the end she is likely to become, like Péguy, one of those lonely figures belonging to no party yet claimed by all.

There is another sense in which she occupies a curiously isolated position. French thinking has in modern times grown increasingly wary of the unhistorical cast of mind so often displayed by its representatives in the past—the attitude castigated as "utopianism" by Marx and denounced before his time by conservative critics of the Revolution. The *philosophes* were notably utopian in their belief that the right order of society could be established by an act of will, and the early socialists—down to and in part including Proudhon—inherited this conviction. Utopianism rests upon idealism, since it implies that the right relationship between human beings in society already exists as a pattern laid up in heaven. For the utopian, all that is needed to bring it down to earth is the right kind of insight, allied to the will. The Revolution was just such an attempt; so, under different circumstances, was the Commune of 1871, which showed that the revolutionary dream was still strong among the workers. It was only after its failure that they were converted to Marxism, which located the fulfillment of the dream at the end of the historical rainbow—or, in more elevated language, put prophetic eschatology in the place of utopian idealism. The contrast must not be pushed too far. In the last resort, Utopia and the classless society turn out to be remarkably alike—not surprisingly, since both derive from the historical *polis,* as seen in the transfiguring light of Jewish-Christian eschatology with its un-Hellenic emphasis upon equality between men and women, free men and slaves, etc. Yet there remains a difference in emphasis. Modern thinking, whether conservative or revolutionary, tends to be historical and to place its hopes within the context of a pattern unfolding in time according to a rhythm of its own. On the whole, French thought since the Revolution has increasingly conformed to this tendency. It would be misleading to suggest that Simone Weil represents an exception or that the utopian strain in her thinking has altogether ousted the eschatological. But it is not without significance that, living in an epoch which had all but made a fetish of history, she seems to have deliberately righted the balance in favor of Utopia. *L'Enracinement* begins and ends with an invocation not of historical fact but of immutable truth. For this reason alone its author is not likely to be soon forgotten or replaced in the consciousness of her compatriots.

Adam's Tree

✳ ✳ ✳

GRAHAM GREENE'S NEW NOVEL *The End of the Affair* [1] seems certain to puzzle, and perhaps to shock, a good many people, and it is important to try to understand why this should be so. From the technical viewpoint it is a very accomplished piece of work, the kind of thing no one else could have written. The construction is extremely skillful, and the narrative is carried along by a style of writing which readers of Mr. Greene's work have come to admire while taking it for granted. The action, moreover, is laid in suburbia, a locale peculiarly adapted to his gift of sardonic description, and identification with the characters is made easier by the introduction of a narrator who also happens to be the central figure. The effect usually produced by the first person singular is heightened in this case by the translucent disguise adopted by the author; for his hero, Maurice Bendrix, is himself a professional novelist, and the harsh, bitter, disillusioned style of writing he affects is already familiar to readers of Mr. Greene's previous works of fiction. Thus the mask is very nearly off, and the contours it discloses have the disturbing quality one usually associates with autobiography. But there are better reasons why this book should provoke reflection among people who take Mr. Greene seriously as a writer.

The central theme, as in *The Heart of the Matter*, is adultery, with all the sordid details relentlessly sketched in. This time, however, it is the woman who is married and who, being a Catholic—to the extent, at any rate, of wanting to become one—is troubled by remorse. So far we seem to be on familiar ground, but whereas

The Twentieth Century, October 1951.
    1. London and New York, 1951.

in *The Heart of the Matter* the moral conflict took place within
the sinner's mind, we are now presented with a duel between
two human beings, a man and a woman, who stand for opposing
principles. Sarah Miles remains to the end a somewhat shadowy
figure, a fact not unrelated to her creator's understanding of theology, but she is clearly intended to stand for qualities opposed
to her lover's destructive selfishness, jealousy, and bitterness. Nor
is her role limited by her earthly span, for after death she gives
evidence of what can only be described as supernatural power.
Her miraculous interventions do not, it is true, exceed the bounds
of what on different assumptions could be described as natural
phenomena—a child suddenly relieved of pain, a disfiguring mark
removed from a man's face—and since they benefit neither her
husband nor her lover (the only miracle worth performing, that
of curing her antagonist of his corrosive self-hatred, is clearly
beyond her capacity) it seems strange at first that Mr. Greene
should have braved skepticism and ridicule by introducing this
implausible device—as it must appear to non-Catholics. The answer to the riddle leads straight to the heart of his predicament,
for it appears that Sarah (who betrays her husband more than
once, refers to herself as "a bitch and a fake," and after her
death is described as "a whore" by her former lover) is not merely
something like a saint but the only embodiment of the divine that
Greene's hero can recognize as such without hatred. This strange
circumstance is the fixed point round which the figures revolve.

   The End of the Affair is, among other things, a novel of postwar suburban Britain, an analysis of a love triangle, and an
exhibition of some very good serio-comic writing. It is also a
detective story. Mr. Greene cannot do without a search for something hidden, but this time his detective is a humorous figure,
and the scales are unfairly weighted against him from the start.
For the Third Man—both Sarah's husband and her former lover
are sure there is a Third Man, and they conspire to track him
down—is God. When Sarah Miles walks away from an assigna-
tion with Maurice Bendrix, a year and a half after their affair has
really come to an end, the trail conscientiously pursued by the
detective leads to a (Roman Catholic) church; and the mysterious Richard Smythe, whom she visits on occasions, turns out
to be not another lover but a rationalist propagandist whom she

consults after religious remorse and the yearning for some kind
of faith (perhaps implanted, we are told, by a baptism undergone
in early childhood, which had been kept secret from her and of
which she was unaware) have begun to undermine her earlier
indifference. And although Smythe—he of the strawberry mark,
the beautiful hands, and the faintly clerical manner—falls in
love with her, it is unrequited love of a Platonic kind, for which
he is duly rewarded after her death by the disappearance of his
disfiguring mark and the even more sudden and surprising
crumpling of his atheist certainty. Yet the staggering naïveté
of this solution is immediately countered by its effect upon the
narrator. For it is after hearing of Smythe's semiconversion that
Maurice rings the book's curtain down upon his final and
effective repudiation of Sarah's God:

> I sat on my bed and I said to God: You've taken her, but You
> haven't got me yet. I know Your cunning. It's You who take us up
> to a high place and offer us the whole universe. You're a devil, God,
> tempting us to leap. But I don't want Your peace and I don't want
> Your love. I wanted something very simple and very easy: I wanted
> Sarah for a life-time and You took her away. With Your great
> schemes You ruin our happiness like a harvester ruins a mouse's
> nest. I hate You, God, I hate You as though You existed.

Maurice Bendrix is an important figure, doubly important because he escapes from Mr. Greene's control and, shedding his
villainous guise, becomes recognizably human; so much so that
in the end he seems to carry a disproportionate load of suffering.
This development rather cuts across the novel's carefully arranged
plot, for a great deal depends upon the contrast between Maurice's
and Sarah's respective accounts of their love affair. Mr. Greene
makes extensive use of the flashback and also introduces a diary
—Sarah's. We are to hear the story told twice: first by the bitter,
cynical, jealousy-twisted man, then by the woman who loved him
and whose love he did not recognize for what it was. But the
contrast is lost. We begin by being informed that Maurice has
come to hate Sarah and her dim, innocuous cuckold of a husband,
though there is no very apparent reason for his hatred. But that,
it seems, is just the point: hatred—bitter, jealous, unmotivated—
is the dominant trait of his character. There is a strong diabolical
flavor about the Maurice of Book One, and it is only to be ex-

pected that he should find his match in a woman whose love can
work miracles (though rather trivial ones) even after her death.
But somewhere along this arduous trail Mr. Greene's original
plan has got mislaid, and having lost his road map he wanders
into what is, for a Catholic, very strange territory indeed. For the
Maurice of Book Five is no longer a sneering devil but a very
human, very unhappy, and very clear-sighted fellow sufferer.
By the time he turns away wearily from the desolation left by
Sarah's death and tramps the rainy Common, side by side with
poor, dim, resigned Henry Miles—two broken men brought together by common misfortune—the original scheme has worn
paper-thin. We are left with human misery—stark, unadorned,
unconsolable. Maurice does not even rail at God any longer. He
simply asks for a little peace:

> I wrote at the start that this was a record of hate, and walking
> there beside Henry towards the evening glass of beer, I found the
> one prayer that seemed to serve the winter mood: O God, You've
> done enough, You've robbed me of enough, I'm too tired and old
> to learn to love, leave me alone for ever.

This unexpected ending—the words just quoted are the concluding sentence of the book—suggests that the Maurice of Book
One was never more than two-dimensional. It was difficult to
believe in him, and now we know the reason: one of his most
important aspects—the aspect called Sarah—was kept out of
sight. For Sarah, when at long last her diary is opened to view,
turns out to be simply Maurice in his religious mood. She is
meant to be his opponent—just as he is meant to sit for a portrait,
if not of the Prince of Darkness in person, at least of one of his
minions—but the contrast breaks down at the crucial point. For
when Sarah tries to put her faith, or lack of faith, into words, she
can find no language substantially different from his. Like Maurice, she is tortured, not consoled, by religion. Like him she rails
and pleads alternately, is obsessed by gruesome fantasies and
images, lacerates herself, yearns for delivery from the flesh, and
in the end destroys herself physically—as he destroys himself
spiritually—by letting her illness take its course from what looks
like carelessness but is clearly disgust with life. Maurice and
Sarah belong together not merely because they are physically

dependent upon each other—when she leaves him during an air raid, having been awakened by fear of death to a sense of guilt, she promptly loses interest in life and contracts the illness which finally kills her—but because they share the puritanical hatred of the body which causes them to oscillate between sexual abandon and religious remorse. They are spiritual twins, condemned to love and destroy one another. Of the two, however, Maurice is more central to the underlying conflict. Thus it is he who writes the story, while Sarah, in her diary, supplies the counterpoint. But he is so much the stronger figure that Sarah's diary talks his language. Maurice "hates" God, and Sarah writes, "I could hate that figure on the Cross with its claim to my gratitude." Sarah accepts separation and death, while Maurice blames her and curses God for his fate, but it remains impossible to think of either without the other. We begin by seeing her through his eyes, and when at last he is alone we still cannot see her any other way.

Though one hesitates to tread on ground hallowed to the believer, it is impossible to ignore the significance of Sarah's posthumous role in Maurice's life. When after her death he first calls her a whore, and then very nearly prays to her, we are permitted to glimpse the reverse side of his (and her) extreme horror of the Cross: she is needed as an intercessor because Christ has become a terrifying figure and the Cross a burden too heavy to be borne. This theme, already present in *The Heart of the Matter*, has now gained overwhelming importance. Throughout the book there are—side by side with absurdly trivial "materialist" arguments against religion—genuine outbursts of fear and hatred whenever the narrator encounters the Cross. There are important religious and historical reasons why this should be so, and it must be regarded as significant that Mr. Greene, who cannot be unaware of them, deliberately ignores them in favor of absurdities supposed to represent the "atheist" position. Thus Henry Miles is given a chance to display his pompous fatuity by explaining to his wife that loyalty to Catholicism, in men of great intelligence like Pascal or Newman, may be due to "a glandular deficiency." And although the shadowy Smythe is briefly allowed to remark that "man creates God in his own image," this dangerous topic is quickly dropped. At the theoretical level, the only choice permitted to the characters lies between a self-torturing faith and an asinine belief in the healing properties of biochemistry. The real problem is shirked. All the more remarkable that these confines are burst in the great crucial passage in which Maurice couples acceptance of God's existence with rejection of His law. "With Your great schemes You ruin our happiness." The Cross has become too heavy. Or, if one happens to be a Christian, one might say the original significance of the gospel has been finally lost sight of.

Even Sarah has moments when she almost hates the figure on the Cross. Thus she discloses her spiritual affinity to Maurice. He, of course, hates all the time, just as he remains unable to shake off the burden of guilt imposed by sexual remorse. The typical hero of Mr. Greene's later novels has ceased to love (or never acquired the capacity) and become conscious of fear, remorse, and hatred of religion. Maurice only learns to love Sarah when it is too late, after her death. In life she is no more to him than a mistress whom he tortures with his senseless jealousy. Adultery is central to the action of these novels because it serves to overlay and explain the absence of love and the consequent disgust with passion. Remorse is introduced via the moral law, but it is already there from the beginning, in the characters. And every time the sense of guilt raises its head, resentment against the faith which imposes it follows in its wake. Mr. Greene has laid hold on a most important discovery, though it has been made before him:

> We thinke that Paradise and Calvarie,
> Christs Crosse, and Adams tree, stood in one place;
> Looke Lord, and finde both Adams met in me;
> As the first Adams sweat surrounds my face,
> May the last Adams blood my soule embrace.

(Donne, "Hymn to God, My God, in my sicknesse")

The Cross, for Mr. Greene's heroes—though this term is misleading—is alternately the refuge of the sinner and the symbol of man's martyrdom. For it is "Adam's tree." It is not fortuitous that the action of his latest work turns upon loveless passion. He cannot imagine love without guilt and self-destruction.

Grand Old Man

✤ ✤ ✤

WHEN THOMAS MANN died in Switzerland in 1955, there was a widespread feeling in Germany that his voluntary self-exile from his native land after the war implied some sort of judgment on his countrymen. It is probable that Mann himself had by then come to regard himself primarily as a European writer, temporarily obliged, like others, to seek refuge in America, and now once more restored to his natural environment. This kind of attitude was not uncommon among representative Germans before the age of Bismarck, and in harking back to it Mann may have intended to signify something beyond a purely personal choice. If so, it is remarkable that a similar decision was taken at about the same time by Karl Jaspers, Heidelberg's loss in this case being Basel's gain. Postwar Germany is not rich in outstanding figures, and the parallel was noted. It may not be accidental that Mann and Jaspers concurred in their admiration of Nietzsche, another German who preferred Switzerland to his own country. It is rare for a Frenchman to exile himself, common enough for a German. Perhaps this helps to account for the strength of European sentiment among postwar German intellectuals.

The selection of writings in Mann's *Last Essays* [1] reinforces the impression that his evolution from "Germanism" to "Europeanism" was a steady process which by the time of his death had carried him far beyond his youthful starting point. Of the four essays in this volume, three—those on Goethe, Nietzsche, and Chekhov—carry implications which, consciously or not, reach beyond the realm of German literature; while the subject of the

1. New York and London, 1959.

fourth is Schiller, the poet of Germany's brief honeymoon with liberalism. Schiller is such an erratic writer that it is difficult for even Thomas Mann to make his rather naïve idealism plausible to us; but though essentially a work of piety, Mann's lengthy tribute to his memory is deserved and may have some pedagogical value for German readers, even if one cannot seriously expect German literature to go on nourishing itself from this source. At the other end of the scale, there is a brief but sympathetic presentation of Chekhov which happily stresses the point that classical Russian literature was not the unrelieved nightmare many West Europeans saw in it; again not perhaps a theme which needs to be expounded outside Germany, but useful as a corrective to the portentous, doom-laden lucubrations of the neoromantic school.

The two important essays are those on Goethe and Nietzsche. With the former, Mann had established a somewhat peculiar relationship of self-identification which seemed a trifle solemn even to sympathetic critics, able and willing to note the irony never far from the surface of Mann's writings. Goethe served Mann as a standard by which to judge not merely his own work and that of his contemporaries, but European civilization itself. "The union of urbanity and daemonic force" extolled in Mann's essay is the theme of the Faust legend, to which Goethe devoted his major dramatic work and Mann his most ambitious (though not, in the estimation of some critics, his most successful) novel. The other side of this particular coin is brought out when Mann affirms that

> in Goethe the folk-oriented Teutonic temper and the European-oriented Mediterranean temper came together in a completely un-forced and perfect synthesis, in a union essentially the same as his personal fusion of genius with rationalism, of mystery with clarity, of the cry *de profundis* with the polished phrase, of the poet with the man of letters, of lyricism with psychology.

Leaving aside the slightly old-fashioned rhapsodical tone of these and similar utterances—Mann is not, strictly speaking, a literary critic in the technical sense—all this is true, though it could be put more simply. The author has merely forgotten to add that the Goethean synthesis proved ineffective in the long run. It was repudiated even by those Germans who did not go all the way back to the Teutoburg forest.

Some of the causes of this collapse are rather gingerly touched upon in the essay on Nietzsche, toward whom Mann's attitude is necessarily ambivalent; he does not quite know whether to regard him as a splendid rebel against mediocrity and conventionality or as a dangerous madman whose appearance heralded the coming of Fascism; and in the end gets out of the difficulty with a judicious distribution of praise for his genius and blame for his immoral utterances, which leaves the subject more or less where other critics had left it—in limbo. This is humanly understandable, for Nietzsche had his most potent liberating effect on the generation to which the youthful Mann belonged; the catastrophe came later. But it does not advance us much. Nietzsche was a compound of contradictory attitudes—at moments he sounds like a disciple of Feuerbach, at others like a precursor of the Third Reich, and most of the time like nothing on earth—and the interesting question is why the effect he had on the Germans was so disastrous; there were other ways of interpreting him. Theologians have not been slow to note that certain elements of his thought are already traceable in Goethe, though discreetly encased in the marmoreal style with which the Olympian court poet at Weimar repelled all efforts to penetrate his reserve. The road from self-worship to inhumanity is perhaps shorter than the age of Goethe supposed it to be. Not surprisingly, neither Thomas Mann nor Karl Jaspers, who shares his infatuation with Nietzsche, has had much to say on this topic.

Across the Channel

***

IRIS MURDOCH'S *Sartre*,[1] the latest in the series Studies in Modern European Literature and Thought, tackles a subject of unusual complexity: Sartre is both a philosopher and an author of what are commonly described as works of imagination, though the *roman à thèse* (and the drama constructed on the same model) do not quite fit this label. Perhaps one should say that both as a playwright and as a novelist he has tried to project the existentialist world view, while as a thinker he has rationalized the moral attitude which lies behind it. This explains his vogue, and also the suspicion with which he is regarded by professional philosophers. His work, to be judged fairly, must be treated as a whole, which is to say that his interpreters must combine the functions of the logician and the literary critic. This is difficult, and British writers on the subject have hitherto failed. Miss Murdoch succeeds.

Her brief study—only eighty pages—of Sartre's status as a writer and thinker is a small masterpiece of compression and lucidity, but above all it is proof that philosophical argument can be technical without being lifeless; this is a notable achievement, considering the current state of academic philosophy in Britain and the widening gap between its practitioners and their European colleagues. There is in fact a twofold problem involved in analyzing Sartre for a British audience: his place in the philosophical tradition and his significance as an intellectual representative of modern Europe. "He is a thinker," says Miss Murdoch, "who stands full in the way of three post-Hegelian

The Twentieth Century, January 1954.

1. *Sartre: Romantic Rationalist* (London and New Haven, 1953).

movements of thought: the Marxist, the existentialist, and the phenomenological." All three, one might add, arose in Central Europe and have only with difficulty been acclimatized in the West.

The process has evidently gone further in France than in Britain, where even professional philosophers have given little attention to Husserl's critique of Descartes and Kant, while Marxism exists only in a caricatured form, as an offshoot of Soviet "philosophy." This has caused some misjudgments. As an interpreter of German philosophical and psychological thinking to his own countrymen Sartre has played a part insufficiently recognized by critics who overrate his originality while underestimating his considerable significance as a representative of modern postnationalist European culture. There is a trace of insularity even in Miss Murdoch's suggestion that "recent continental philosophers have been discovering, with immense fuss, what the English empiricists have known since Hume, whom Husserl himself claimed as an ancestor." Husserl regarded Hume as a fashionable drawing-room philosopher who had had one good idea in his youth on which he dined out for the rest of his life. But no matter. The starting point of this analysis is right: Sartre is in a tradition, or rather he stands at the meeting point of several traditions; for while Hegelianism is the offspring of the German Enlightenment (which was restricted to the Protestant part of Germany), Husserl goes back, via Brentano, to the Scholastics and ultimately to Plato. Phenomenology has affinities with Thomism, and several of Husserl's pupils not surprisingly became Catholic converts. All of which helps to explain why France, with its Catholic tradition and its recent preoccupation with Communism, has become fertile ground for a philosophy which seeks to combine all these warring tendencies.

This complex background is admirably illuminated by Miss Murdoch, though I cannot always follow her individual judgments and lack her sympathy with (and, it must be confessed, her detailed knowledge of) Sartre's literary work. Incidentally, it is a pity that she has not extended her very acute and intricate analysis of the novels to the plays, especially *Huis Clos* and *Les Mains Sales*. Her analysis serves as a bridge to a detailed examination of Sartre's use of language and his theory of literature.

Language, of course, is of overriding importance to modern philosophers—possibly because a scapegoat is needed for the solipsistic self-isolation in which so many of them find themselves. Miss Murdoch is extremely good on this subject, though herself not free from *Angst* induced by uncertainty over communication between writer and reader. This is a very modern problem. One cannot recall any important thinker in the past who suffered from this particular worry. The "sickness of language" is much on Miss Murdoch's mind:

> The more one looks at the phenomenon, the more one has that feeling of a discovery which is made in all spheres simultaneously; the sort of feeling which tempts people to invoke the useless notion of the *Zeitgeist*. One suddenly begins to connect *The Concept of Mind* with the marble sugar lumps of surrealism (attacks on the notion of essence) and Hegel's *Logic* with *Finnegans Wake* (attempts to preserve the universe concretely and nondiscursively as one huge pulsating interpenetrating particular).

This is perhaps treating Joyce, and especially that huge practical joke *Finnegans Wake*, a shade too solemnly.

Every critic must be permitted some idiosyncrasies different from those of his subject. To me it seems that Miss Murdoch has made a little too much of Sartre as a thinker in his own right, and not enough of his admirable talent for translating German metaphysics into French. In the process something has been gained, while not a little has been lost. She notes of Sartre's use of Freudian terminology that "as a psychoanalyst he remains impenitently Cartesian"—which is as much as to say that he has missed the essential point about psychoanalysis. It might be added that his employment of Marxian concepts is equally Procrustean and, to use a well-known term, nondialectical: in the light of Hegel's dialectic of the absolute and the relative, Sartre's complacent relativism—with nothing to relate, since the absolute has simply been dropped—seems curiously naïve and hardly above the level of ordinary skepticism. He is in fact basically an old-fashioned rationalist, though immensely sophisticated in his near-assimilation of all those concepts—ontological, dialectical, and psychological—which Central European thinkers have gradually elaborated during the past century: ever since, that is to say, the Hegelian synthesis fell under attack from various quarters. It is perhaps a sign of the gradual Europeanization of Britain that this set of problems is increasingly being experienced as something internal to the British situation as well. If this process goes on, British philosophers may, for all one knows, begin to write novels and in other ways try to emerge from their positivist strait jacket. Miss Murdoch has illuminated part of the road for them by her ingenious analysis of the links connecting Sartre's use of language with his metaphysics.

Anglo-American

❄ ❄ ❄·

WHEN HEMINGWAY, in *Across the River*, launched his celebrated assault on the British lines, he probably did not suspect that the stylistic instrument forged by him with so much labor over the years would one day recoil with damaging effect upon the troops crouching behind his own national parapet. The occurrence of this recoil in Graham Greene's new novel *The Quiet American* [1] has hitherto escaped attention, possibly because our literary Geiger counters have been too busy registering the political shock waves sent out by Mr. Greene's fictional explosion. The reviewers have fastened on his overt dislike of the United States, and quite overlooked the extent to which he is indebted to contemporary American writing for the creation of his central character, the Yankee-baiting Fowler. Since this line of approach has hitherto been neglected, it may be worth pursuing a little further.

An attentive reader of Mr. Greene's Indochinese reportage pieces could have predicted the tone and temper of his next major fictional effort. Reporting was bound to come into it, to the extent that the Indochinese landscape was relevant to the action. The political approach would be dictated by the author's sympathy for the French, his awareness of the hopelessness of their fight, his mingled liking and disdain for the people of Indochina, and his bitter admiration of the nationalist-Communist Vietminh. The unexpected element in the novel is the strength and consistency of Mr. Greene's dislike of the Americans, a sentiment ranging from disapproval of their policies, suspicion of their motives, and contempt for their methods, to a sour refusal to

The Twentieth Century, January 1956.
    1. London, 1955; New York, 1956.

ANGLO-AMERICAN 491

see anything of value in their way of life. There is a Kiplingesque
strain in his contemptuous dismissal of their professed beliefs,
just as there is an Orwellian note in his dour suspicion of their
aims (Orwell, one recalls, admired Kipling's realism). *But,* and
this is the point which seems to have escaped the reviewers, Mr.
Greene's hero, Thomas Fowler (it is impossible to accept Evelyn
Waugh's embarrassed and unconvincing attempt to dissociate
the protagonist from his creator), exists only by virtue of his
descent from a long line of "tough" characters in modern American fiction. Except for his London address, and the somewhat surprising information that he is due to become foreign editor on an
important British daily (which can it be?), Fowler could have
walked straight out of the fictional Los Angeles of James M. Cain
and Raymond Chandler; indeed, there are moments when one
half expects him to drop the mask and admit that he is really
Philip Marlowe, Mr. Chandler's private eye, sleuthing around in
Indochina improbably disguised as a British correspondent. Put
Fowler down in Hollywood, and you have the ideal part for
Humphrey Bogart, down to the cynical wisecracks about women
and the verbal fencing with the police.

The final joke then is on Mr. Greene, for if the Americanization
of the English novel has reached the point where even a Yankee-
hating character like Fowler can only be presented in terms of
the hard-boiled school of American fiction, the literary war has
really been won by the Americans, however much this result
may be concealed by Greene-Fowler's sarcastic comments on
their manners, morals, and ideals. An elaboration of this point
would require a fairly lengthy and tedious analysis of the book's
style, and particularly of Fowler's internal monologue, with its
recurrent lapses into tough-guy imagery, to say nothing of his
frequent descent into Chandleresque realism. ("I went into the
passage. There was a door opposite marked Men. I went in and
locked the door and sitting with my head against the cold wall,
I cried. I hadn't cried until now. Even their lavatories were air-
conditioned, and presently the temperate tempered air dried my
tears as it dries the spit in your mouth and the seed in your
body.") The only point worth making in this context is that
Greene has added nothing to the kind of mental introspection
with which the American novel has made us familiar ever since

Hemingway's protagonist in *The Sun Also Rises* glared at his image in the mirror and cursed his bad luck. They are all alike, these heroes of our time: tough, cynical, self-reliant, brutal, and not averse to illegality, or even murder, if it can be managed without too much danger. Fowler's pseudopolitical motivation for letting the Vietminh "take care" of the American intruder, Alden Pyle, who has stolen his girl and generally messed up his life, is as factitious and unconvincing as the humanitarian indignation he is supposed to feel over Pyle's callousness in supplying explosives to some murderous faction in Indochina's complex civil war. His final behavior shows that his act was motivated by jealousy and dislike—there were other ways of discouraging Pyle from playing with explosives, but there was no other way of getting rid of him as a successful competitor for the girl's favor.

It is not strange that some people have read a deep political meaning into Fowler's decision to help the Vietminh liquidate Pyle, but they are doing Greene an injustice: in terms of his brilliantly constructed thriller there is no other way out of the difficulty created by the juxtaposition of two such characters. There are echoes of Malraux in the internal monologue with which Fowler tries to justify his action, and in his verbal duel with the philosophical police officer (another stock character of modern detective fiction, though this time French, not American); but in the context of a squalid murder perpetrated for personal ends they do not sound very convincing. Greene is at his best as a writer when he anglicizes the stylistic instruments of the California school. Whether this achievement is worth the expenditure of quite so much political pathos is another question.